PERGAMON GENERAL PSYCHOLOGY SERIES

Editors: Arnold P. Goldstein, *Syracuse University*
Leonard Krasner, *SUNY, Stony Brook*

BEHAVIORAL INTERVENTION
in
HUMAN PROBLEMS
PGPS-10

BEHAVIORAL INTERVENTION
in
HUMAN PROBLEMS

EDITOR

HENRY C. RICKARD
University of Alabama

PERGAMON PRESS INC.

New York   ·   Toronto   ·   Oxford   ·   Sydney   ·   Braunschweig

PERGAMON PRESS INC.
Maxwell House, Fairview Park, Elmsford, N.Y. 10523

PERGAMON OF CANADA LTD.
207 Queen's Quay West, Toronto 117, Ontario

PERGAMON PRESS LTD.
Headington Hill Hall, Oxford

PERGAMON PRESS (AUST.) PTY. LTD.
Rushcutters Bay, Sydney, N.S.W.

VIEWEG & SOHN GmbH
Burgplatz 1, Braunschweig

Printed in the United States of America
08 016327 0

For my parents

Contents

Acknowledgements

The author acknowledges indebtedness to the many individuals who made this volume possible: in particular the chapter contributors who performed the difficult task of describing in print evolving, live-action programs; the colleagues and students whose comments helped conceptualize the direction of the volume; and the graduate students who later reviewed parts of the manuscript, especially Carl Clements who read and commented helpfully upon all of the chapters. The title of the volume was graciously contributed by William Rhodes. Sandy King spent many productive hours proofreading and typing. Thanks are due Leonard Ullmann who read an earlier draft of the manuscript and made valuable suggestions which were subsequently incorporated. A special note of thanks is expressed to Norman Ellis who encouraged the development of the book and frequently served as an informal advisor. Finally, the author wishes to express appreciation to his wife, Barbara, for her encouragement and understanding throughout the compilation of the volume.

The Authors

John M. Atthowe, Jr., *Ph.D.,* Professor of Psychology, Department of Psychology, University of Montana.

Daniel G. Brown, *Ph.D.,* Mental Health Consultant in Psychology, National Institute of Mental Health, Regional Office IV, Atlanta, Georgia.

Carl B. Clements, *B.S.,* Psychology Department, University of Alabama.

Harold L. Cohen, *B.A.,* Principal Investigator and Executive Director of the Institute for Behavioral Research Inc.

Aubrey C. Daniels, *Ph.D.,* Chief Psychologist, Georgia Regional Hospital, Atlanta, Georgia.

Michael Dinoff, *Ph.D.,* Associate Professor and Director of the Psychological Clinic, University of Alabama.

Don F. Driggs, *Ph.D.,* Associate Professor, Director Human Development Clinic, School Psychology Training Program, Department of Psychology, Florida State University.

James Filipczak, *M.S.,* Principal Investigator and Associate Educational Director for the Institute for Behavioral Research Inc.

J. Douglas Grant, *M.A.,* President, Social Action Research Center, Oakland, California.

Joan Grant, *Ph.D.*

John Hamilton, *Ph.D.,* Unit Director, Gracewood State School and Hospital, Gracewood, Georgia.

Norris G. Haring, *Ed.D.,* Professor and Director, Experimental Education Unit, University of Washington. Lecturer in Pediatrics.

Wallace A. Kennedy, *Ph.D.,* Professor and Director of Graduate Affairs, Psychology Department, Florida State University.

Leonard Krasner, *Ph.D.,* Professor and Director of Clinical Training, Department of Psychology, State University of New York, Stony Brook, N.Y.

Wilbert W. Lewis, *Ed. D.,* Director. Re-ED Institute. Tennessee Re-Education Program. Nashville, Tennessee.

Charles H. Madsen, Jr., *Ph.D.,* Assistant Professor, School Psychology Training Program, Department of Psychology, Florida State University.

Clifford K. Madsen, *Ph.D.,* Associate Professor of Music Education, School of Music, Florida State University.

John M. McKee, *Ph.D.,* Director, Rehabilitation Research Foundation, Draper Correctional Center, Elmore, Alabama.

D. A. R. Peyman, *Ph.D.,* Director of Psychology Department, Alabama State Hospitals; Professor, University of Alabama.

Henry C. Rickard, *Ph.D.,* Professor and Coordinator of Clinical Training, Department of Psychology, University of Alabama.

Saleem A. Shah, *Ph.D.,* Chief, Center for Studies of Crime and Delinquency, Department of Health Education and Welfare, National Institute of Mental Health.

Douglas R. Slavin, *Ph.D.,* Assistant Director, Department of Psychology, Georgia Mental Health Institute.

Earl S. Taulbee, *Ph.D.,* Chief, Psychology Service, Veterans Administration Center, Bay Pines, Florida.

H. Wilkes Wright, *Ph.D.,* Coordinator of Counseling Psychology and Assistant Chief, Psychology Service, Veterans Administration Center, Bay Pines, Florida.

SECTION I

Overview

CHAPTER 1

Introduction

Henry C. Rickard

The social conscience of modern man is attuned to whatever innovation offers promise in the long, discouraging encounter with mental illness. For example, the medical discovery that the syphilis spirochete was primarily responsible for the poor judgment, grandiose delusions, and labile responses in the patient suffering from general paresis fostered the attitude that an organic basis existed for all mental illness. Enthusiastic research efforts followed, but the failure to establish clear genetic, structural, or constitutional bases for *most* individuals classified under the rubric, mental illness, soon led to disenchantment with the organic hypothesis and the pursuit of other explanations.

An additional example of a promising innovation was Freud's psychoanalytic theory and the practice of psychoanalysis. The influence of Freud's formulations was profound; they were viewed by many as a "break-through" — a theory which when properly developed and applied would do much to alleviate mental disturbances. Disciples apparently believe that the psychoanalytic method has lived up to the enthusiasm of its early adherents; other practitioners have become increasingly disillusioned by the failure of psychoanalysis to cope with the needs of the many, or even to convincingly demonstrate effectiveness with a favored population of reasonably well-functioning neurotics (Eysenck, 1952).

In the wake of Freud's pioneer efforts, numerous schools of psychotherapy evolved; some followed the steps of the master with only modest deviation while others developed new techniques based on new theoretical views, e.g., nondirective psychotherapy. Different as the schools of interview therapy might be, in theory if not in practice, a number of critical deficiencies were common to them all:

1. The strength of interview therapy lies to a large extent in the ill-defined patient-therapist relationship. Since relationships grow slowly, a severe restriction is placed upon the number of clients who can be seen in the lifetime of a hard-working therapist.

2. Interview therapy demands that communication, primarily verbal, be established between the client and therapist. Small children, severe retardates, recalcitrant juveniles, and seriously disturbed psychotics are examples of vast populations notorious for poor communication skills.

3. The interview therapist must undergo expensive professional training. Much of his skill is frankly artistic and difficult to teach, even in the master-apprentice relationship. The subtleties of psychotherapy cannot be easily encompassed in a curriculum and thus readily passed on to a psychological technician. The present extremely expensive, time-consuming approach to training interview psychotherapists is inadequate to meet existing and projected needs.

4. The interview therapies, in general, are difficult to evaluate. This criticism applies in varying degrees to all psychotherapeutic techniques, but the interview therapies are especially vulnerable. Interview therapies fail to specify goals except at quite molar levels: improved self-concept, fewer inhibitions, less repression: etc. Most of the goals of interview therapy are intrapsychic ones occurring within the context of the psychotherapeutic relationship.

Behavior Modification

The current behavior modification or behavior therapy movement may be considered a further example of an innovative intervention, one which is now receiving a great deal of attention (Critical Comment 1)[1]. A precise definition of what constitutes behavior therapy remains to be formulated, although characteristics of behavior therapy have been identified by contrasting behavior therapy with the practice of psychoanalytic therapy. The behavior therapist views symptoms as behavior and is not concerned with "core" problems. Since insight is not held to be necessary for behavior change, insight is typically not a goal in behavior therapy. Transference is considered unnecessary; in fact, behavior therapy studies have tended to demonstrate that therapeutic results are frequently independent of relationship or transference phenomenon (e.g., Barker, 1969). The concept of behavior regression is foreign to the behavior therapist since regression implies the taking away of defenses without efforts to substitute new adaptive behaviors. Ullmann and Krasner (1965) stress that the

---

[1]Six critical comments have been interspersed throughout this introductory chapter to discuss in more detail some of the important practical and theoretical issues in behavior modification.

therapist who takes away a behavior, through whatever techniques, and does not make available an alternative adaptive response, is doing only half his job.

Hallmarks of Behavior Modification

Perhaps, it is most reasonable to talk in terms of certain identifying "hallmarks" of behavior modification. First of all, the emphasis is upon observable behavior rather than intrapsychic events. Behavior itself is considered worthy of modification. This is in marked contrast to the belief of many interview therapists that observable behavior is unimportant, and that only underlying feelings and attitudes are of real significance. Traditional psychotherapy would hold that if underlying attitudes and dynamics can be altered, overt behavior will take care of itself. The behavior modification viewpoint suggests that the converse is the more likely case; the focus is upon direct alteration of overt behaviors. A second major consideration in the framework of behavior modification is that specific behavior patterns once identified, may be modified by specific operations which can be clearly stated. A third important assumption must be that these changed behaviors will affect the client's adjustment; the removal of socially maladaptive behavior or the acquisition of positive social responses will lead to reinforcing feedback from the client's interpersonal environment. From the traditional therapeutic stance, the modification of overt, observable behavior without an attack upon underlying dynamics would be considered a waste of time or worse, since the modification of observable undesirable behaviors might lead to the substitution of other, perhaps more undesirable symptoms (Critical Comment 2).

The behavior therapist wishes to be both systematic and flexible. He plans ahead, organizes, and attempts to specify his treatment plan as precisely as possible. The behavior therapist wishes to base his techniques on laboratory findings and the experimental method, although attempts to bring rigor to clinical problems and to draw parallels between behavior modification studies and laboratory based principles of learning have not gone uncriticized (Critical Comment 3). Kalish (1965) compares behavior therapy to laboratory experimentation on the grounds that both allow a problem under study to dictate the conditions of the experiment. Such a conceptualization is in contrast to more conventional psychotherapeutic practices in which there is little variation in the therapy setting; interview therapy usually takes place in a vis-à-vis office situation, and the assumption is made that the therapeutic task will be accomplished predominantly through the medium of verbal behavior.

Case Studies

An avalanche of experiments in the manipulation of undesirable behavior has appeared in the literature during the last decade. These experiments could best be described as case studies since most of them lack the rigor and control characteristically found in basic laboratory experiments. Ullmann and Krasner (1965) recognize the shortcomings of the case study approach but stress the hypothesis generation aspects involved. The case study approach has been applied to a wide array of symptoms; some grasp of current interest may be gained by reviewing Orlando's compilation of references in behavior modification which lists 866 studies (Barnard & Orlando, 1967).

A hypothetical case study is presented graphically in Figure 1.[2] Note that the figure itself gives no indication of the subject population studied. The data plotted in Figure 1 could reflect bar presses by a rat in a Skinner box or the frequency of socialization responses emitted by

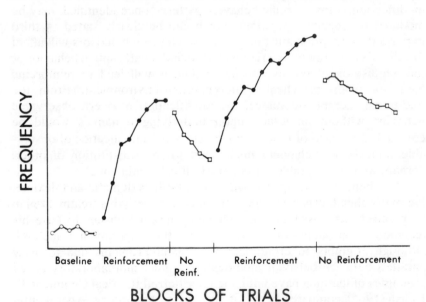

BLOCKS OF TRIALS

Fig. 1. The hypothetical data presented above could represent any class of socially desirable behavior recorded by frequent count.

---

[2]An excellent discussion of the single subject design has been presented by S. W. Bijou and his associates. Bijou, S. W., Peterson, R. F., Harris, F. R., Allen, K. E. and Johnston, M. S. Methodology for experimental studies of young children in natural settings. *The Psychological Record*, 1969, **19**, 177–210.

a child. The curves could represent an increase in frames per hour completed in a programmed learning course or an increase in eating behavior exhibited by a patient suffering from anorexia nervosa. The data are presented by frequency count, and represent a large amount of longitudinal data collected on one subject. Base line observations were recorded prior to the introduction of the experimental treatment. The continuous record across blocks of trials indicates that the experimental treatment led to increased subject responding and that withdrawal of the treatment variable led to an immediate decrease in the behavior under study. After the treatment procedure was reinstated and high rate stable responding had been maintained for a longer period of time, the experimental treatment was withdrawn permanently. In this particular example the desired behavior dropped somewhat in frequency during the nonreinforcement, or extinction period. How great a reduction in responding occurs during extinction depends upon a number of experimental variables, including the status of the organism studied and the manipulation of the parameters of reinforcement, e.g., amount, kind, schedule, temporal aspects, etc. Most important, perhaps, is whether or not the new desired behavior continues to be reinforced in the extra-experimental environment. A case described by Madsen, Madsen, and Driggs illustrates dramatically the failure of the environment to support a newly acquired behavior. A child who had been trained outside the classroom to hold up his hand in response to the teacher's questions was not called upon and soon stopped raising his hand. His newly acquired behavior had extinguished.

Case Studies and Clinical Practice

A number of elements of operant oriented case studies are congruent with existing biases of the clinician: the single case study is emphasized, the behavior of the single individual is studied over an extended period of time, and the concept of control groups is not considered essential since the therapist is primarily interested in the behavior of the individual in relation to his own past performance. Thus, frequently, the practicing clinician does not resist the behavior modification model in theory although he may find it extremely difficult to apply in face-to-face office therapy with the population of patients seen in outpatient clinics (Critical Comment 4). Putting it another way, behavior modification studies have interested the practicing clinician but he is not entirely convinced. This reluctance does not stem, it seems, from the more naïve accusations of behavior modification proponents. The clinician is *not* always unduly concerned about the necessity of dealing with underlying dynamics as opposed to the manipulating on surface behaviors, and he may not be overly concerned with the "spectre of symptom substitution." Nor does the clinician appear always to be bothered by the accusation that the behavior therapist "plays God" or the assertion that behavior modification techniques are cold and mechanical. The practicing clinician may be receptive, in general, to the concept of dealing with the overt patterns of behavior. On the other hand, he is extremely concerned about his ability to identify important patterns of behavior in the majority of patients in his case load, the likelihood of adequately identifying effective reinforcers to influence the behavior pattern, and particularly, problems of measurement and control (Critical Comment 5). The belief that members of the helping professions, in general, will be receptive to behavior modification techniques which can be applied to populations of individuals led to the compilation of this volume. Case studies are well established. It seems important at this point to illustrate the more general applicability of behavior therapy.

Overview

Engineering behavior change with one patient is quite different from daily confrontation with a population of patients exhibiting behavioral deviances. What has been the success of large behavior modification programs? Have they continued to exist over a span of time? Have they extended their sphere of influence and inspired the creation of similar programs? Do guidelines exist which would be helpful in establishing programs of behavior modification? Is behavior modification here to stay or is it a passing fad? Can generalization to the home environment be expected or must the clinician engineer the entire community after the patient's release? These and similar questions suggest themselves to the conscientious, harassed practitioner. He is interested in doing the best job he can with the time and resources available to him. He is interested in new techniques, perhaps even fascinated by them, but he needs some assurance that they are practical and can be engineered in a large program. A few years ago it was relevant to ask whether laboratory principles, gained primarily from experimentation with animals, would apply to deviant human behavior. Now the practitioner charged with developing a program in behavior modification is interested in knowing if findings from case studies and experiments in behavior modification can be applied in his more general situation (Critical Comment 6).

Each of the chapters in this book, beyond the introductory section, describes a program in behavior adjustment which has been in existence for two or more years. Each contributor presents the historical development of his program and describes the operations of treatment procedures in considerable detail. The programs describe the treatment of children, adolescents, and adults, ranging from mildly to severely disturbed. Several of the populations described are ordinarily considered outside the range of good psychotherapy risks, e.g., retardates, youthful prison inmates, and severely disturbed psychotics.

An important goal of the book is to illustrate the therapeutic commonalities found across the various programs in spite of great differences in patient populations, professional treatment personnel available, favorableness of prognosis, and types of behavior exhibited by the patients. These commonalities derive primarily from the theoretical position underlying each of the programs:

1. Socially undesirable behavior is focused upon rather than a pathological condition. Overt patterns of behavior are considered important and worthy of the best efforts of the patient and practitioner. In particular, efforts are made to strenghen adaptive behavior patterns that compete with undesirable behaviors.

2. The patient is usually actively involved as a participant in the therapeutic program. The words active and responsible should be stressed. The patient is actively involved and is expected to take responsibility for as much of his own behavior as possible. He is aware of the goals being worked toward and he is responsible for moving as directly as possible toward those goals.

3. The trained professional does not consider himself, necessarily, the most appropriate agent for behavioral change. When goals and treatment plans are clearly specified the actual management of the program can be left in the hands of the competent but less broadly trained personnel.

4. The principle of flexibility is very much in evidence. Behavioral goals change as the treatment process develops and at different stages in the program different treatment procedures are necessary. The object is to change a given pattern of behavior, not to prove a particular theoretical position or to operate exclusively within the confining framework of a "school."

5. All of the programs described are capable of objective evaluation. Some have progressed a long way in this direction while others are in the initial stages. The programs which have been evaluated most thoroughly are those dealing with more circumscribed, precise patterns of behavior. Those programs which are attempting a multidimensional approach to treating the individual are, typically, in a primitive stage of evaluation. However, the importance of evaluation efforts is

recognized in all of the programs, and in every case initial steps have been taken.

The chapter by Kennedy "A Behavioristic Community-Oriented Approach to School Phobia and Other Disorders" illustrates a number of directions important to the development and extension of concepts in behavior modification. The program is focused upon an outpatient population of children, involves the identification of a specific behavior pattern, and is oriented toward the involvement of community caretakers as well as mental health professionals. Kennedy's program differs from mental health work carried out by traditional child guidance clinics in a number of very important respects, perhaps the most important being his theoretical position in respect to the treatment of childhood disorders. A chapter on school phobia in a recent edited volume concerning childhood disorders exemplifies the traditional view in which the need to attack the underlying problems is stressed (Hammer & Kaplan, 1967).

Anxiety is said to be the causal force leading to all phobic behavior including school phobia. Techniques designed to alleviate the state of anxiety are advocated. By contrast, Kennedy has focused upon efforts to reinstate patterns of adaptive behavior which will be followed by appropriate consequences. Because of the strengths and abilities possessed by the typical phobic case, Kennedy presumes that the child's interactions with his environment will be followed by reinforcing consequences. That is to say, if the child remains in the classroom he will be caught up in the activities of the group and will respond to his own successful participation in classroom activities. In the Kennedy approach the parents are incorporated as agents who will elicit adaptive behavior from their children (doing what is necessary to get them to school) and who reinforce the child's school attending behavior by praise, attention, etc. Attendance supervisors, teachers, principals, and other adults important in the shaping and maintaining of the child's school attendance are advised of the treatment procedures and carry out their role in cooperation with the therapist and parents. The program has been evaluated carefully including the collection of follow-up data.

Summary

The behavior modification programs described in this book illustrate a rapprochement between *case studies* in behavior modification and existing *programs* in behavior adjustment. While the programs differ widely in staff, population, goals, and treatment procedures, they do employ a core of common concepts. Each contributor describes the historical roots of his program and discusses similarities to other programs in behavior adjustment. The immediate and ultimate goals of each program are identified along with a description of the operations employed to obtain those goals. Each program reports an estimate of success utilizing concrete criteria when possible: success is measured both in the attainment of the immediate subgoals and in terms of the ultimate goal of environmental adjustment in extraprogram situations.

The following criteria have been met by each of the programs described:

Uniqueness. A program utilizing predominately conventional interview therapy would not qualify. Neither would a less conventional approach such as Alcoholics Anonymous because it is an organization already well-known.

Systematic. A systematic, objectively verifiable approach to behavior change must be apparent. The operations of the programs are definable and teachable.

Wide scope. The programs are presently or potentially capable of treating large numbers of individuals. Major treatment roles are assumed by individuals not possessing advanced training.

Stability. The programs have been in existence for several years and show promise of enduring and/or widening their sphere of influence.

Emphasis upon the present as opposed to the past. The programs focus upon the current and future behavior of the individual.

Capable of evaluation. Programs were selected in which at least initial efforts at evaluation have been made. Evaluation efforts need not be complete at this time, but the operations of the program were judged capable of being evaluated.

While there are other well-established approaches to behavior modification,[3] the programs to be described rely primarily upon

---

[3]Prominent approaches to behavior modification include modeling (Bandura, 1968; Ullmann, 1968), implosive therapy (Stampfl & Levis, 1967), and systematic desensitization (Wolpe, 1958; Wolpe & Lazarus, 1967). In an informative review article, Rachman (1967) reports that systematic desensitization is the *most* widely used method of behavior therapy, and that its use is supported by some of the best available research (e.g., Paul, 1966, Paul & Shannon, 1966).

principles closely associated with operant conditioning, an experimental area pioneered by Skinner (1938, 1953). *A primer of operant conditioning* (Reynolds, 1968) provides a substantial background in operant methodology for the interested reader.

In the programs described, the focus is upon the modification of behavior through the control of the consequences of behavior. Thus the programs reported by Kennedy; Lewis; Madsen, Madsen, and Driggs; and Rickard and Dinoff are concerned primarily with programming the environment so that appropriate social behaviors of children meet with reinforcing consequences. As additional examples, the programs described by Cohen and Filipczak; Haring; and McKee and Clements, are oriented around strengthening the individual's educational repertoire through the provision for appropriate consequences (knowledge of results, points, tokens, etc.) following correct responses. The programs rely primarily upon mental health workers *without* advanced degrees; for instance college students, teachers, nursing assistants, parents, etc. These mental health workers traditionally interact with the individual in an extraoffice environment where the techniques based on operant procedures have proven flexible and easily adapted.

The second chapter by Brown, "Behavior Analysis and Modification in Counseling and Psychotherapy: A Review of Reviews", traces the vigorous development of behavior modification studies and experiments by tabulating the number of articles appearing in the *Annual Review of Psychology* from 1950 to 1968. It should be noted that his review included reports of studies in all areas of behavior modification including those with an operant orientation.

Section II describes behavior modification programs designed to increase socially desirable behaviors and to weaken socially undesirable behaviors in populations of children functioning in the home and school environment. The chapter by Kennedy illustrates the behavior modification stance which may be taken by an outpatient clinic. The chapter by Madsen, Madsen, and Driggs presents an illustration of a behavior modification program for children and teachers within the context of a school system.

Section III presents two programs (Lewis; Rickard & Dinoff) for emotionally disturbed children within the context of an enriched environment where every effort is made to provide rewarding consequences for the child's adaptive social and academic behaviors. In addition, Haring provides a concise analysis of behavior management in a well-organized classroom environment. Section IV presents a variety of programs aimed toward the rehabilitation of the legal offender. The chapters by Cohen and Filipczak and McKee and

Clements, emphasize behavioristic techniques designed to augment academic performance in groups of young offenders. Shah illustrates behavioristic techniques in the difficult outpatient treatment of legal offenders. Grant and Grant focus upon the offender as his own treatment agent, and as the major treatment agent for other offenders.

Section V includes programs of behavior control with institutionalized adults and children who present severely disturbed patterns of behavior. Slavin and Daniels report a variety of behavior modification techniques in their work with both inpatients and outpatients including the volume's only example of systematic desensitization therapy. Krasner and Atthowe illustrate the token economy approach to behavior control on a ward of severely disturbed psychiatric patients. Both the Attitude Therapy Program (Taulbee & Wright) and the Responsibility Therapy Program (Peyman) tend to strain the more traditional concept of behavior modification programs, but each contains related provocative concepts and procedures. Hamilton provides a good description of a behavior modification program oriented to the needs of retarded children.

CRITICAL COMMENT 1

Behavior Therapy in Historical Perspective

In a recent review article, Kalish (1965) credits Eysenck with the coining of the term, behavior therapy. Historical accounts of the growth of behavior therapy have been compiled by Eysenck (1960), Kalish (1965), Mowrer (1965), Ullmann and Krasner (1965), and others. The classical study of conditioned fear responses in a child by Watson and Rayner (1920) and the subsequent experiments with children exhibiting developmental problems (Jones 1924) are credited with laying the foundation for behavior therapy. In 1932, Dunlap published a book entitled *Habits: Their Making and Unmaking* in which he advocated negative practice for habits as diverse as stammering, tics, and thumb-sucking. Jersild and Holmes (1935) performed a series of experiments on the reduction of fear in children which could be properly called studies in behavior modification. Mowrer (1965) reviewed the early writings of Burnham (1924) and concluded that Burnham anticipated almost every technique employed by present day behavior therapists.

Nevertheless, after a short, vigorous burst in the late twenties and early thirties the direct conditioning approach to behavior modification lost impetus. The explanation for this marked decrease in interest is unclear. Failure to demonstrate effectiveness is an unlikely culprit, since published studies tended to report positive findings. Perhaps the trend away from direct treatment methods was partly a reaction against the global conclusions of the advocates. For instance, Dunlap stated: "Thumb-sucking is, in almost every case, the result of bad social treatment of the child in the first year of life. It is a sign the child has not been socially stimulated," (1932, p. 213).

Turning to alternate explanations for a decline in interest in direct conditioning, it seems possible that Freudian theory, Gestalt psychology, and Rogerian therapy may each have played a somewhat similar role in discouraging interest in the direct manipulation of behavior. Freudians focused upon the unconscious, the Gestaltists emphasized the organization of the total organism, and the Rogerians sought techniques for releasing the growth potential in clients. Each position implies that overt behavior modification is contingent upon a change in awareness, personality organization, or growth. Perhaps the simplicity of conditioning competed poorly with the romanticism of such inner-explanatory positions.

Eysenck (1960), as Kalish (1965) points out, probably influenced the present surge of interest concerning behavior therapy, providing the term itself, and editing a collection of classic and more contemporary behavior therapy studies. Bandura's theoretical article, "Learning Theory and Psychotherapy," appeared in 1961 followed by a review article by Grossberg (1964) and a critique of behavior therapy by Breger and McGaugh (1965). Ullmann and Krasner (1965) published a volume entitled *Case Studies in Behavioral Modification,* and a companion, more theoretical treatment, *Research in Behavior Modification* (Krasner & Ullmann, 1965).

Currently there are several journals devoted to experiments in behavior modification including, *Behavior Research and Therapy, Journal of Applied Behavior Analysis,* and *Behavior Therapy.* Section III, division 12 of the American Psychological Association was established to promote interest and research in this area. Each successive year since 1960 has brought an increasing number of references to behavior modification in the *Annual Review of Psychology.*

CRITICAL COMMENT 2

The Spectre of Symptom Substitution

Detailed discussions of the symptom substitution question have been presented (e.g., Bandura, 1959; Eysenck, 1960; Ullmann & Krasner, 1965). Briefly, psychoanalytic theory has assumed that unless underlying dynamic conflicts are resolved, it is useless and even dangerous to manipulate overt, undesirable behaviors. Thus a child's irrational fear of animals would be considered symptomatic and a displacement of an unresolved conflict. Helping the child overcome his fear through a direct conditioning procedure might well result in the exacerbation of other undesirable behaviors (symptom substitution). Such a simplified dynamic view of symptom substitution has found little support in the rapidly accumulating behavior modification literature.

However, the question of whether symptom substitution occurs is partly a conceptual problem. In considering symptom substitution it is helpful to drop the word symptom and substitute the term behavior or habit. Then, as Bandura (1961) points out, whether a given behavior is considered normal and acceptable or a symptom of disturbance depends upon a social interpretation. Parents may encourage aggressive behavior while school authorities view this same behavior as symptomatic of a disorder. To further illustrate, success has been reported in controlling enuresis using the conditioned response method. As soon as urination begins a wired pad sets off a loud buzzer which awakens the child. After a series of trials, bladder pressure becomes a conditioned stimulus for awakening. Bed-wetting is the symptom or old habit and awakening and going to the bathroom is the new habit. Here we have an instance of symptom habit substitution which is socially approved. On the other hand, a child may exhibit both enuresis and stealing behavior. It seems that after the enuresis has been successfully treated by the conditioned response method, stealing behavior may decrease, increase, or remain the same, depending upon the occurrence of adequate reinforcers for stealing. Both the stealing and enuresis may be treated as independent patterns of behavior, each controlled by environmental reinforcement. If the stealing behavior should increase in frequency one might be tempted to yell, "symptom substitution." In a facetious mood, one might suggest that if the stealing behavior decreased in frequency it could be described as "negative symptom substitution."

Lanyon, Manosevitz, and Imber (1968) report that fear reduction to spiders following systematic desensitization therapy generalized more to stimuli similar to spiders than to spider-unrelated stimuli, a finding which tends "to support a learning model (generalization of fear reduction) over a psychodynamic model (occurrence of symptom substitution)."

Barker (1969), in a well-controlled study, indicates that, rather than increased maladjustment, enuretic children successfully treated with a conditioning apparatus show subsequent improvement in parental reports, self-report scales, and drawings judged by experts.

To summarize, symptom substitution is widely accepted as a phenomenon that occurs when surface behaviors are modified and anxieties, angers, conflicts, etc., remain untouched. Evidence for symptom substitution exists mainly at the anecdotal level, strongly colored by the theoretical bias of the observer. The problem is simplified when symptoms are defined as habits or behaviors. As such they should follow established principles of learning. Indeed, in the last 10 years, an increasing number of case reports have reported direct manipulation of "symptomatic" behavior, mainly through counterconditioning techniques. While the available follow-up studies report little symptom substitution, it should be clear that determining whether symptom substitution has occurred is really an impossible task since the individual is constantly acquiring new habit patterns, and that society may well label some of these habits maladaptive "symptoms." Perhaps the experimenter who is interested in working with symptomatic behavior should, as Staats and Staats (1964) recommend, concern himself with clusters of behavior and develop a program of behavior control. A patient who is responding inappropriately to environmental stimuli by withdrawing, not talking, spilling food, etc., may respond to habit training directed at several of these symptoms. Thus the experimenter may well be modifying behaviors which society might focus on, judge maladaptive, and label "symptom substitution."

While the practitioner interested in behavior modification techniques must remain sensitive to the symptom substitution question, current information suggests that the dangers of direct behavior manipulation have been exaggerated.

CRITICAL   COMMENT   3

The "School" of Behavior Therapy:
A Functional Illusion

Breger   and   McGaugh (1965)   suggest   that   behavior   therapy has become a dogmatic school which makes unsubstantiated claims to methods derived from learning principles. They argue that behavior therapists fail to derive their operations from learning principles and, moreover, the learning principles which behavior therapists claim to follow are incapable of adequately handling the heterogeneous problems brought to psychotherapy. In effect, they charge that a "school" of behavior therapy has evolved which is dogmatic in its orientation and nonfunctional in its operations.

Conversely, it may be argued that a school of behavior therapy does not exist, but that the operations of behavior therapy, are, indeed, based on principles of learning and are extremely functional in the treatment of behavior disorders. Breger and McGaugh (1965) stress the fact that evoking terms like "laboratory based" and "behavioral" does not make behavior therapy scientific. They identify two major groups of offenders: the "Skinnerian group" and behavior therapists in the "Wolpe-Eysenck tradition."

It is agreed that the evocation of scientific terms is merely a labeling procedure and should be so understood. By the same reasoning to label therapists as operating in two arbitrarily defined classes is to suggest therapist identifications that need not exist. To design an experiment involving a single subject, to select an observable class of behavior for manipulation, and to attempt to control that behavior through its consequences does not make the therapist a Skinnerian. Reasoning analogously, adopting the technique of reciprocal inhibition for one or a series of sessions does not make one a behaviorist in the Wolpe-Eysenck tradition.

We suggest that there is no evolving school of behavior therapy. There exists, instead, an experimental practice of behavior therapy by practitioners of diverse training and affiliation. It is important to expose the illusion of a school of behavior therapy which Breger and McGaugh lament, but at the same time augment by their labeling. The importance of the protest lies in the fact that an individual practicing behavior therapy should be free to draw upon whatever techniques are available to him, including the freedom to utilize a variety of techniques in a given experiment. Thus classical conditioning techniques which

Breger and McGaugh identify as belonging to the Wolpe-Eysenck tradition frequently coexist in the same study with techniques which they identify as Skinnerian (Lazarus, Davison & Polefka, 1965).

Turning to the question of the utility of basing behavior therapy on laboratory principles, Breger and McGaugh indicate that conditioning may be no more simple or basic than other forms of learning. And further, they argue, S-R formulations have proven inadequate to handle accumulating data which is easily encompassed in a mediational framework. How then, they ask, can the conditioning paradigm be transferred to work with humans when there are major problems surrounding its use with animals? Criticisms of this sort, whether valid or not, should not be viewed as contraindications to the practice of behavior therapy. Behavior therapists expect conditioning paradigms to provide conceptual guides in the formulation of experiments in behavior modification. These guides need not possess perfection— only utility. In a similar vein Breger and McGaugh criticize the use of reinforcement by declaring that the Law of Effect is at best a weak law, pointing to latent learning studies to support their arguments. Again, the usefulness of a concept is attacked, this time reinforcement, because every instance of learning has not been demonstrated to depend upon reward. Such an argument is tangential to the clinical application of the principles of reinforcement. If reinforcement "works" in his particular experiment, the applied behavior therapist is most pleased.

CRITICAL COMMENT 4

Modeling Adaptive Behavior

The limitations of behavior modification are felt most by those who actually practice outpatient psychotherapy, a situation in which verbal interchange is the major modality through which therapeutic change is attempted. To utilize a conditioning approach within the framework of the interview, it is necessary to define undesirable behavior and then develop a treatment plan capable of modifying that behavior. Unfortunately, adequate dependent variables are not always immediately known to either patient or therapist. Usually the task of defining and modifying selected dependent variables within the therapy interview can best be accomplished by gaining the support of the patient himself and reaching an agreement upon a compatible course of action. The establishment of such a contract takes time and effort. What to do in the interim? Can the therapists best move toward his goal in a mechanistic, invariant progression of steps, or should he stop along the way and attend to the stumbling, self-exploration efforts of the patient? Is there a "type" of behavior therapy that can be unsystematically intermingled with the systematic identification, elicitation, and reinforcement of specific adaptive behaviors?

Perhaps the answer is yes. How the therapist goes about searching for appropriate dependent variables, how he structures himself as a person, how he interacts with a patient, and a multitude of other active *modeling* responses on the part of the therapist, provide an extremely important part of the learning complex within the therapy interview. For example, the existential school of psychotherapy values spontaneity and emphasizes the importance of the experience between patient and therapist. Behaviors on the part of the therapist which communicate empathy and warmth may be imitated by the patient. The social milieu rewards those who are warm, honest, and sufficiently attuned to the needs of others. The therapist who models socially approved behaviors is actively engaged in behavior therapy.

The implication of such an assumption is enormous. It gives the therapist freedom to do some of the things he likes to do and feels comfortable doing in the therapy situation; he can feel free to interact spontaneously with the patient. Obviously, that is not all he should do; frequently modeling behavior will not do all the job. A reticent patient might well receive positive feedback from spontaneous behavior in the presence of his girl friend—but only if he first manages to ask her for a date. Approaching single, attractive females might be one dependent variable for which both patient and therapist are searching. In the interim the therapist has modeled a very useful behavior pattern, spontaneity. The concept of spontaneity in psychotherapy is by no means new, but placing spontaneity within a modeling framework affords the advantage of offering a social referent. Complete spontaneity, complete self-disclosure, complete self-expression, are not accepted patterns of behavior in the framework of this society, and a therapist, as part of his role, must be concerned about the social adjustment of his patient. He will model spontaneity, self-disclosure, etc., to the degree that these traits are rewarded in the patients' social context. The therapist will refrain from modeling characteristics which will place the patient at odds with society and lower the probability that the patient will receive environmental reinforcements.

A number of the programs described in this volume touch upon the importance of modeling behavior. For instance, Kennedy cautions the parents regarding the stimulus they present to the frightened, confused child exhibiting school phobia. The parents are trained to adopt a composed attitude, thus becoming models for adaptive behavior. Rickard and Dinoff discuss the importance of the counselor's role as model within the context of a therapeutic camp. In group problem solving, for example, the therapist is expected to assume a verbally active role in the identification of behavior patterns in need of modification and in the proposal of useful, imaginative, alternative solutions. The child learns to engage in problem solving behavior, in part, by modeling his behavior after that of the counselor.

CRITICAL COMMENT 5

Criteria for Success

The importance of employing specific, overt behaviors as criteria for success in psychotherapeutic intervention has been emphasized by Pascal (1959). Rickard (1965) has suggested further, that the overt behavior patterns selected for modification should be stable, sensitive, and important. If fighting behavior occurred only one day per year, an 8-year-old boy would probably not be labeled physically aggressive. However, if the behavior pattern occurred several times a day for three months the criterion of *stability* would undoubtedly be met. Case studies in behavior modification (Ullmann & Krasner, 1965) indicate that behavior patterns such as fighting can be controlled by arranging proper environmental consequences, thus demonstrating *sensitivity*. A child might swing his legs excessively during class periods, and not receive negative feedback from either an accepting teacher or indifferent classmates, but he could not continually physically assault his peers without repercussions—excessive fighting behavior meets the criterion of *importance*.

It should be noted that the goal of a reduction in frequency of fighting behavior would constitute an acceptable criterion measure, whereas improvement in self-control would not. In fact, the whole range of higher order variables are unacceptable as criteria including: aggression, dependency, sexual conflicts, etc. Obviously, any of these gross personality descriptions which could be more precisely represented by one or more overt behaviors meeting the criteria of stability, sensitivity, and importance would be acceptable.

The concept of a partnership approach to behavior change has recently received considerable comment. Krumboltz (1966) presents the idea that the client should help decide what behaviors need to be changed. In an educational program for young offenders Clements and

McKee (1968) have made good use of performance contracts in which the individual helps set his own production goals. Dinoff and Rickard (1969) have developed the concept of therapeutic contracts in their work with emotionally disturbed children. Goals are decided upon in advance and the responsibilities of both patient and therapist are clearly specified, frequently in writing. Goldiamond (1965) states that "the weekly therapy sessions then become research conferences as between a professor and his research associate as to what has to be done next to bring the organisms behavior into line ... eventually, as in most relations, *S* may become an independent investigator, capable of tending to things on his own." In each case, the mutual responsibility of the patient and therapist is apparent, both in the delineation of specific, appropriate goals and the treatment plan decided upon.

CRITICAL COMMENT 6

The Range of Behavior Therapy

Practicing clinicians observe that patients frequently do not exhibit circumscribed patterns of maladaptive behavior which may be conveniently quantified. Breger and McGaugh (1965), in a critique of behavior therapy, stated that only a small percent of the patients coming to their particular clinic were candidates for behavior therapy. Part of the difficulty arises, it seems, from the fact that interview behavior therapy in which the problem area is both the immediate and ultimate criterion has only a limited role in the usual clinical setting. However, if the definition of behavior therapy is expanded to include indirect manipulation of the problem behavior, the door would open to the modification of a much wider range of problems. The danger lies in broadening the definition of behavior therapy until it encompasses all existing clinical modification techniques, thereby inheriting not only the clinical treatment throne but all of the problems surrounding it.

Direct Behavior Therapy

In direct behavior therapy the behavior manipulated is, typically, the symptom or response which prompted the therapeutic intervention in the first place. That is to say, the immediate and ultimate criterion responses are essentially identical. The direct manipulation of temper tantrums (Williams, 1959), delusional speech (Rickard, Dignam & Horner, 1960), and hyperactive behavior (Patterson, 1965) are cases in point. It should be clear that the experimenter may employ various modes of intervention and still be involved in the direct manipulation of behavior. For example, he may choose an extinction paradigm and withhold reinforcement following the occurrence of the response class to be manipulated (Williams, 1959), or he may elect to reinforce a response (Zimmerman & Zimmerman, 1962). Detailed discussions of the various learning principles utilized as models in direct conditioning have been presented elsewhere (Ullmann & Krasner, 1965). But in all forms of direct behavior modification, the experimental intervention is designed to immediately affect the dependent variable, usually to increase or decrease the frequency of a specific response.

Indirect Techniques

While the immediate and ultimate criterion has been identical in most behavior modification studies reported to date, it is of interest to examine studies which have not aimed their treatment at the presenting behavior. For example, Birnbrauer and his associates (1965) have used programmed materials to teach retarded children. The immediate criterion of adequate performance on the programmed tasks was presumed to relate to improved performance on tests, the ultimate criterion.

McKee, Masterson, and Rickard (1963) worked with a group of academic underachievers who were presenting behavior control problems in the classroom. Efforts were made to improve the students' academic standing rapidly through the use of programmed instructions. Teachers' ratings were obtained before and after 55 hours of programmed instruction. The immediate criterion was performance on the programmed material while the ultimate criterion was change in behavior as measured by teachers' ratings. It was presumed that catching up academically through the use of academic material, the immediate criterion, would be related to the ultimate criterion of improved classroom behavior.

At this point an important question suggests itself. If behavior is expanded to include indirect manipulation of the undesirable behavior, what characteristics distinguish behavior therapy from existing interview therapies? While far from a complete answer, the following comments seem relevant. The interview therapist might be interested in modifying the clients' self-concept, habits, values, etc., hoping thereby to influence an environmental behavior. Certain gross therapeutic manipulations may be identified in the various interview therapies both in the physical arrangement of the therapy environment, and the type of verbal intervention preferred by the therapist. But it would be difficult to identify response-reinforcement contingencies which had been programmed. Indeed, most interview therapists would hasten to deny the necessity or desirability of establishing conditions in which response reinforcement contingencies are clearly specified. In effect, the interview therapist seeks to modify intervening variables in an amorphous situation and without the benefit of clearly defined dependent and independent variables. On the other hand, the behavior therapist who wished to engage in indirect behavior change must attend to precisely just those conditions. He must clearly specify the immediate response he intends to manipulate and the environmental events he will bring to bear upon the response.

REFERENCES

Bandura, A. Psychotherapy as a learning process. *Psychological Bulletin*, 1961, **58**, 143–159.

Bandura, A. Modeling approaches to the modification of phobic disorders. In Ruth Porter (Ed.), *The role of learning in psychotherapy*. London: Churchill, Ltd., 1968, Pp. 201–217.

Barker, Bruce L. Symptom treatment and symptom substitution in enuresis. *Journal of Abnormal Psychology*, 1969, **74**, 42–49.

Barnard, J. W. & Orlando, R. Behavior modification: A bibliography. *IMRID papers and reports*, 1967, **IV**, 3.

Birnbrauer, J. S., Bijou, S. W., Wolf, M. M. & Kidder, J. D. Programmed instruction in the classroom. In L. P. Ullmann & L. Krasner (Eds.), *Case studies in behavior modification*. New York: Holt, Rinehart & Winston, 1965. Pp. 358–63.

Breger, L. & McGaugh, J. L. Critique and reformulation of learning-theory approaches to psychotherapy and neurosis. *Psychological Bulletin*, 1965, **63**, 338–358.

Burnham, W. H. *The normal mind*. New York: Appleton-Century, 1924.

Clements, C. B. & McKee, J. M. Programmed instruction for institutionalized offenders: Contingency management and performance contracts. *Psychological Reports*, 1968, **22**, 957–964.

Dinoff, M., & Rickard, H. C. Learning that privileges entail responsibility. In J. D. Krumboltz & C. E. Thoresen (Eds.), *Behavioral counseling: Cases and techniques*. New York: Holt, Rinehart & Winston, 1969.

Dunlap, K. *Habits: Their making and unmaking*. New York: Liveright, 1932.

Eysenck, H. J. (Ed.), *Behavior therapy and the neuroses*. New York: Macmillan, 1960.

Goldiamond, I. Stuttering and fluency as manipulable operant responses classes. In L. Krasner & L. P. Ullmann (Eds.), *Research in behavior modification*. New York: Holt, Rinehart & Winston, 1965. Pp. 106–156.

Grossberg, J. M. Behavior therapy: A review. *Psychological Bulletin*, 1964, **62**, 73–88.

Hammer, M. & Kaplan, A. M. *The practice of psychotherapy with children*. Homewood, Ill: Dorsey, 1967.

Jersild, A. T. & Holmes, F. B. Methods of overcoming children's fears. *Journal of Psychology*, 1935, **1**, 25–83.

Jones, M. C. The elimination of children's fears. *Journal of Experimental Psychology*. 1924, **7**, 383–390.

Kalish, H. I. Behavior Therapy. In B. B. Wolman (Ed.), *Clinical Psychology*. New York: McGraw-Hill, 1965. Pp. 1230–1253.

Krasner, L. & Ullmann, L. P. (Eds.), *Research in behavior modification: New developments and implications*. New York: Holt, Rinehart & Winston, 1965.

Krumboltz, J. D. Promoting adaptive behavior. In J. D. Krumboltz (Ed.), *Revolution in counseling: Implications of behavioral science*. New York: Houghton Mifflin, 1966, **1**.

Lanyon, R. I., Manosevitz, M. & Imber, Ruth R. Systematic desensitization: Distribution of practice and symptom substitution. *Behavior research and therapy*, 1968, **6**, 323–329.

Lazarus, A. A., Davison, G. C. & Polefka, D. A. Classical and operant factors in the treatment of a school phobia. *Journal of Abnormal Psychology*, 1965, **70**, 225–230.

McKee, J. M., Masterson, J. & Rickard, H. C. Programmed learning: An approach to the modification of undesirable behavior. Unpublished manuscript. The Draper project. Elmore, Alabama, 1963.

Mowrer, O. H. Learning theory and behavior therapy. In B. B. Wolman (Ed.), *Handbook of clinical psychology*. New York: McGraw-Hill, 1965.

Pascal, G. R. *Behavior change in the clinic—a systematic approach*. New York: Grune & Stratton, 1959.

Patterson, G. R. An application of conditioning techniques to the control of a hyperactive child. *Case studies in behavior modification*. New York: Holt, Rinehart & Winston, 1965. Pp. 370–375.

Paul, G. L. *Insight versus desensitization in psychotherapy*. Stanford: Stanford University Press, 1966.

Paul, G. L. & Shannon, D. T. Treatment of anxiety through systematic desensitization in therapy groups. *Journal of Abnormal Psychology*, 1966, **71**, 124–135.

Rachman, S. Systematic desensitization. *Psychological Bulletin*, 1967, **67**, 93–103.

Reynolds, G. S. *A primer of operant conditioning*. Illinois: Scott, Foresman, 1968.

Rickard, H. C. Tailored criteria of change in psychotherapy. *Journal of General Psychology*, 1965, **72**, 63–68.

Rickard, H. C., Dignam, P. J. & Horner, R. F. Verbal manipulation in a psychotherapeutic relationship. *Journal of Clinical Psychology*, 1960, **16**, 364–367.

Skinner, B. F. *The behavior of organisms*. New York: Appleton-Century, 1938.

Skinner, B. F. *Science and human behavior*. New York: Macmillan, 1953.

Staats, A. W. & Staats, C. K. Attitudes established by classical conditioning. *Human learning*. New York: Holt, Rinehart & Winston, 1964. Pp. 322–328.

Stampfl, T. G. & Levis, D. J. Essentials of implosive therapy: A learning-theory based on psychodynamic behavioral therapy. *Journal of Abnormal Psychology*, 1967, **6**, 496–503.

Ullmann, L. P. Making use of modeling in the therapeutic interview. In Rubin & Franks (Eds.), *Progress in behavior therapy*, 1968. Pp. 175–181.

Ullmann, L. P. & Krasner, L. (Eds.), *Case studies in behavior modification*. New York: Holt, Rinehart & Winston, 1965.

Watson, J. B. & Rayner, R. Conditioned emotional reactions. *Journal of Experimental Psychology*, 1920, **3**, 1–12.

Williams, R. I. Verbal conditioning in psychotherapy. *American Psychologist*, 1959, **14**, 388 (abstract).

Wolpe, J. *Psychotherapy by reciprocal inhibition*. Stanford: Stanford University Press, 1958.

Wolpe, J. & Lazarus, A. A. *Behavior therapy techniques: A guide to the treatment of the neurosis*. New York: Pergamon Press, 1967.

Zimmerman, E. H. & Zimmerman, J. The alteration of behavior in a special classroom situation. *Journal of the Experimental Analysis of Behavior*, 1962, **5**, 59–60.

CHAPTER 2

Behavior Analysis and Modification in Counseling and Psychotherapy: A Review of Reviews[1]

Daniel G. Brown

The purpose of this chapter is to present a brief review of recent developments in behavior analysis and modification in relation to research work and practice in counseling and psychotherapy. These developments, which have been variously referred to as operant and classical conditioning therapies, behavior therapy, learning theory therapy, reinforcement therapy, etc., may all be subsumed under the generic term, behavior analysis and modification. Evidence is now accumulating which suggests these developments may prove to be equal in magnitude to such revolutions or milestones in mental health as the reforms in the treatment of the mentally ill by Pinel in France in the last century, the establishment of psychoanalysis and psycho-dynamic theory and therapy during the first half of the present century, the psychopharmacological advances of the last 20 years, and the current national comprehensive community mental health center program under way in the United States at the present time. And as each of these epochal developments has affected the mental health field as a whole, this newest development may do no less; in fact, there is reason to believe it will have far-reaching effects in treatment, training, research, and preventive work in all aspects of mental health.[2]

[1]Revision of a paper originally prepared as an introduction to a Regional Conference on Behavior Modification for Departments of Psychology and Psychiatry and Schools of Social Work and Nursing, Georgia Mental Health Institute, Atlanta, Georgia, Nov. 2–3, 1967.
[2]Because of the importance and significance of such developments the Atlanta Regional Office of the National Institute of Mental Health sponsored or will have helped to spon-sor a number of regional conferences or workshops during the period, 1967–1970, all on Behavior Analysis and Modification. In November 1967, an interdisciplinary conference for faculty representatives of the accredited graduate training programs in the

The reluctance to accept new ideas and improvements in procedures and techniques in mental health practice was alluded to by Lebensohn in his introduction to a conference sponsored by the Group for the Advancement of Psychiatry on *Pavlovian Conditioning and American Psychiatry* (Razran and Bridger, 1964); he points out that many workers in the mental health professions have shown a singular lack of curiosity and remained unaware of the theoretical and practical aspects of conditioning phenomena in relation to clinical research and therapy. In this same connection, on the basis of a reivew of the literature on behavior therapy, Grossberg (1964) concluded that it is unlikely that substantial numbers of traditional therapists will begin to apply the behavior therapies regardless of their demonstrated economy or success. He adds that many psychotherapists are personally and professionally committed to personality theories and treatment methods that are in sharp contrast to those of behavior therapy and, hence, will find it difficult to change or modify their own therapeutic position and work.

The brief survey of the literature that follows is based on a study of each chapter on counseling and on psychotherapy in *The Annual Review of Psychology*, Volume 1, 1950 through Volume 19, 1968. Twelve volumes contain a summary chapter on counseling and all 19 volumes contain a summary chapter on psychotherapy. The cumulative number of references included in these reviews during the past 19 years is 1408 on counseling and 2140 on psychotherapy. The focus of the present review, then, is on the extent that developments in

---

four basic mental health disciplines from universities throughout the Region was held in Atlanta at the Georgia Mental Health Institute. In March 1968, a Workshop on Applications in Mental Hospitals was held at Central State Hospital, Milledgeville, Georgia, and attended by professional personnel from 20 state mental hospitals. In April 1968, a Workshop on Applications in Nursing was held at Vanderbilt University School of Nursing and attended by faculty members of schools of nursing and state consultants in psychiatric and public health nursing; in October, 1968, a Workshop on Applications in Social Work was offered by the University of Tennessee School of Social Work for faculty members and state consultants in social work. And in March, 1969, a workshop for psychiatrists in Departments of Psychiatry and in Community Mental Health Centers was held at the Medical College of South Carolina. A similar meeting is planned for faculty members in graduate programs in psychology and future conferences or workshops will be planned for other mental health personnel in community mental health centers, and in programs primarily concerned with treatment services for children. In addition, state-wide interdisciplinary conferences on Behavior Analysis and Modification have been held or are scheduled in Alabama, Georgia, and Mississippi. These meetings are all a continuing education effort to decrease the time-lag that has been created by the rapid and significant new developments during the past few years on the one hand, and the incorporation of these new procedures into the training programs of academic and institutional mental health agencies on the other.

behavior analysis and modification have been recognized or included among the more than 3500 references on counseling and psycho-therapy reported in *The Annual Review of Psychology* since 1950.

In the volumes for 1950, 1951, and 1952, mention is made of the early attempts of Shaw (1949), Shoben (1949), Dollard and Miller (1950), and Mowrer (1950), and others to conceptualize psychotherapy in terms of learning theory; at this time, learning theory psychotherapy as such did not exist but rather there were these attempts to explain psychotherapy within a learning theory framework. Despite the fact that these were initial, tentative efforts, the possible implications of such conceptualizations were explicitly recognized in Volume 2, 1951, in which reference is made to the identification of psychotherapy and learning as having aspects of a new movement and therapeutic system that might have considerable impact on both training and practice in psychology and other mental health professions: "If psychotherapy were to be identified as an educative process in increasing degree, psychology might undergo a kind of renaissance as a basic science to the practice of psychological healing." (Hathaway, Vol. 2, 1951, p. 264). As the present review will indicate, this predictive statement made nearly 20 years ago would appear to be at the threshold of validation; i.e., a renaissance in psychological healing science may very well be underway at the present time with the establishment of the behavior analysis and modification model.

In 1953 and 1954 Eysenck's (1952) critique of traditional psycho-therapeutic approaches is cited but promptly dismissed with one reviewer even suggesting that it be ignored. This critique by Eysenck was based on his survey of studies concerned with psychotherapy, the effectiveness of which he concluded, has not been demonstrated in the published reports. In this same connection, in a subsequent discussion, Eysenck (1961) concluded:

> With a single exception of the psychotherapeutic methods based on learning theory, results of published research with military and civilian neurotics, and with both adults and children, suggest that the therapeutic effects of psychotherapy are small or nonexistent, and do not in any demonstrable way add to the nonspecific effects of routine medical treatment, or to such events as occur in the patient's everyday experience. (p. 720)

In the 1955 volume, one of Wolpe's (1952) earlier papers on conditioning in psychotherapy is cited and described as provocative, but probably not one that would be taken seriously by the mental health professions because the conditioning-behavioristic approach was not in tune with the times. The implication is clear that even if Wolpe's method of conditioning-reciprocal inhibition therapy was demonstrated to be significantly more effective, it would still not be accepted because of the entrenched status and dominance of the older, traditional approaches in psychotherapy.

The volume in 1956 refers to a survey by Wolff (1954) of 43 experienced psychotherapists of various approaches which showed about three-fourths of them were dissatisfied with their own theoretical framework in psychotherapy; this group did not include learning theory or behavior therapists since at that time such a group did not exist. In 1957, reference is made to a trend toward more flexible, exploratory approaches in viewpoint and techniques among representatives of various systems of psychotherapy.

In 1958, three major theoretical approaches in psychotherapy are discussed: psychoanalytic, client-centered, and learning theory; this is one of the first recognitions of equal status of learning theory with other major systems of psychotherapy. The volumes in 1959, 1960, and 1962, however, emphasize the centrality of psychoanalytic theory in psychotherapy and tend to minimize learning theory developments. Thus, the 1959 volume includes the following summary statement: "Without a doubt, most of what we know about psychotherapy was presented in the work of Freud, and we have yet to learn how best to use the fruit of his excellent observations." (Luborsky, Vol. 10, 1959, p. 307); and in the volume for the following year: "It is still abundantly clear that the center of the stage is being held by writers who attach to themselves the label psychoanalytic, psychoanalytically oriented, or modified psychoanalytic in describing their method of treatment." (Rotter, Vol. 11, 1960, p. 381). An exception to these conclusions occurs in the 1961 volume which refers to one of the significant trends in the field as "the attempt to bring therapeutic theory into the mainstream of general psychology . . . ," specifically in the conceptualization of psychotherapy in learning theory terms; also, mention is made for the first time of the Skinnerian paradigm of operant conditioning in shaping the verbal behavior of psychotic patients (Seeman, Vol. 12, 1961, p. 157).

Beginning with Volume 14 in 1963 and extending through Volume 19 in 1968, there is full recognition of the impact of learning theory and behavior analysis and modification approaches in counseling and psychotherapy. In 1963, three and one-half pages of the chapter are devoted to a section on applications of principles of learning and reference is made to *innovations* in psychotherapy that were becoming widespread, as well as to the fact that less emphasis on insight and interpretation and more emphasis on applications of learning theory were being reported in the literature. In 1964, developments in operant and verbal conditioning are described as generating most of the new ideas in psychotherapy the preceding year and as forcing therapists who follow traditional approaches to reexamine their own therapeutic positions. In addition, a prediction is made to the effect that methods of operant conditioning would be increasingly applied to psychological disturbances in childhood.

In Volume 16, 1965, the conclusion is reached that psychoanalysis is no longer the most dominant theme in psychotherapy theory, research, or practice. The reviewer refers to the contention of Schofield (1964) that psychodynamic psychotherapy has been oversold in terms of its contribution to or need by society, its assumed complexity in training and practice, its insistence on the necessity of a very special interpersonal relationship, and its highly selective criteria of who should and who should not be its practitioners. In this same volume, behavior therapists are referred to as a "new breed" rapidly becoming known in England, the Soviet Union, and the United States. Behavior therapy is described as an important new force in psychotherapy that "is here to stay and probably will become increasingly dominant during the next decade" (Matarazzo, Vol. 16, 1965, p. 217). The volume in 1966 makes reference to the fact that those workers who identify themselves as behavior therapists exhibit all the characteristics of a new school complete with ideas, people to espouse, others to reject, and a new journal, *Behaviour Research and Therapy* (Dittman, Vol. 17, 1966, p. 68); mention is also made of Grossberg's (1964) review of the literature on behavior therapy from 1924 to 1963 and his conclusion that overwhelming evidence now exists that behavior therapy has widespread applicability to a variety of human maladjustments and produces generally successful and long lasting results.

In Volume 18, 1967, specific reference is made to developments in behavior modification which are described as having "real promise"; there is also recognition of the widespread and fundamental changes that were reported beginning to occur both in conceptions of and procedures in psychotherapy:

> The picture of psychotherapy as a condition in which two people sit privately in an office and talk about the thoughts and feelings of one of them with the expectation that changes in these will automatically produce changes in overt behavior outside that office has been shattered. A new generation is emerging in the field of psychotherapy. A much wider range of procedures is being used by people with a variety of theoretical persuasions. (Ford & Urban, Vol. 18, p. 366)

Finally, the most recent volume, Volume 19, 1968, includes a section on behavior therapy, which is one of six major divisions in the review chapter on psychotherapy; the preceding year is described as a

"very good" one for behavior therapy in terms of reports in the literature demonstrating its applicability and effectiveness. In addition,
reference is made to the decreasing acceptance of the illness model and
increasing acceptance of the learning model in psychotherapeutic work:

> ... with the dissipation of the view of the behavior disorders as
> illnesses and the replacement of this with the conception of these as
> learning distortions (Mowrer) all the literature on how persons break
> old, inefficient patterns and relearn better ones as well as that on the
> methods for instituting such changes becomes relevant to this review
> ... there is now a flavor to the literature that a new era has dawned
> .... (Cartwright, Vol. 19, p. 124)

The above review of the literature of the past 19 years yields an
interesting overall observation that is reflected in the volume just
quoted; namely, that a characteristic part of the behavioral model has
been the vibrant expression of confidence concerning the value and
utility of this approach in counseling and psychotherapy. This pervasive optimism is based, in part, on the assumption that, while not a
mental health panacea, in comparison with the more traditional therapeutic approaches, the behavioral model may have several important
advantages that may be summarized as follows:

1. Greater *effectiveness* as a treatment method; i.e., at least for
some emotionally disturbed behaviors the results are often clearly
superior.

2. Greater *efficiency* as a treatment method; i.e., in general, it
takes less time and fewer sessions to bring about desired changes in
the patient's life adjustment.

3. Greater *specificity* in establishing goals and outcome of therapy;
i.e., the specific end result of therapy is specified at the beginning of
therapeutic work.

4. Greater *applicability* to a wider segment of the population; i.e.,
it covers the broad spectrum of maladaptive behaviors rather than, for
example, being limited more or less to middle or upper class neurotic
patients with above average intelligence, etc.

5. Greater *utilization* as a treatment method by various groups; i.e.,
the behavioral approach can be used not only by the practitioners of
the basic mental health disciplines themselves but by public health
and other nurses, case workers, counselors, adjunctive therapists,
teachers, etc., and even by parents.

In short, in comparison to traditional therapies, the behavior modification approach may be more effective, more efficient, more specific
in therapeutic outcomes, applicable to more people, and can be used
by all of the mental health and mental health related helping professions and their related groups (Urban & Ford, 1967).

Another interesting observation that emerges from the present review is the fact that most of the work involving applied behavior analysis and modification has been published during the past five or six years, indicating the recency of this development in mental health (Brown, 1967).

There are a couple of concluding observations as to the implications of the learning-behavioral model in mental health. One of these observations has to do with the acute need that exists for more efficient and effective utilization of existing mental health manpower: Hoch (1962), who was Commissioner of Mental Health in New York until his death several years ago, wrote as follows:

> There is a tremendous waste of psychiatric resources in treating four or five persons for five or six or seven years with an indefinite outcome, while many of the others who seek help cannot have help and will receive no help or have perfunctory help ... we think that the clinics should use methods of treatment which are more flexible and more elastic, and that they should serve all the different psychiatric categories. To say ... 'I am treating only a limited number of persons in a limited group of conditions' because only these patients would benefit from a particular therapy around which the clinic is organized, is in my opinion an anachronism and will change and will have to change very rapidly. I will do anything to support this change and to adapt our treatments to the tremendous social need which is present in this field. (p. 3)

The other observation, which has to do with the primacy of learning theory both as an explanatory and operational system of psychotherapy, was made by Alexander (1965) shortly before his death. Although trained in the psychoanalytic tradition, after a lifetime of study, he wrote as follows:

> The therapeutic process can be best understood in terms of learning theory ... the principle of reward can be applied not only to a rat learning to run a maze, but to the most complex thought processes as well. The therapeutic process can be well described in terms of learning theory ... [which] appears to be at present the most satisfactory framework for the evaluation of observational data and for making valid generalizations in psychotherapy ... at present, we are witnessing the beginnings of a most promising integration of psychoanalytic theory and learning theory. This may lead to unpredictable advances in the theory and practice of the psychotherapies. (pp. 195–198)

There are some indications that these unpredictable advances, suggested by Alexander just a few years ago, are, in fact, occurring and that a new revolution in mental health may now be under way.

REFERENCES

Annual Review of Psychology, Volumes 1–19, 1950–1968, Annual Reviews, Stanford, California.

Alexander, F. The dynamics of psychotherapy in the light of learning theory. *International Journal of Psychiatry*, 1965, **1**, 189–198.

Brown, D. G. Selected bibliographies on behavior modification. Prepared for Regional Conference on Behavior Modification, Georgia Mental Health Institute, Atlanta, November 2–3, 1967. (Mimeo) Rev. 1969, NIMH, Publ. 5016.

Dollard, J. & Miller, N. E. *Personality and psychotherapy*. New York: McGraw-Hill, 1950.

Eysenck, H. J. The effects of psychotherapy: An evaluation. *Journal of Consulting Psychology*, 1952, **16**, 319–324.

Eysenck, H. J. *Handbook of abnormal psychology*. New York: Basic Books, 1961.

Grossberg, J. M. Behavior therapy. *Psychological Bulletin*, 1964, **62**, 73–88.

Hoch, P. Long range trends for New York State's mental health program. Invited address to the New York State Community Mental Health Boards, Albany, New York, April 30, 1962. (Mimeo)

Mowrer, O. H. *Learning theory and personality dynamics*. New York: Ronald Press, 1950.

Razran, G. & Bridger, W. H. *Pavlovian conditioning and American psychiatry*. New York: Group for the Advancement of Psychiatry, 1964, No. 9.

Schofield, W. *Psychotherapy: The purchase of friendship*. Englewood Cliffs, N. J.: Prentice-Hall, 1964.

Shaw, F. J. The role of reward in psychotherapy. *American Psychologist*, 1949, **4**, 177–179.

Shoben, E. J. Psychotherapy as a problem in learning theory. *Psychological Bulletin*, 1949, **46**, 366–392.

Urban, H. & Ford, D. H. Behavior therapy. In A. M. Freedman & H. I. Kaplan (Eds.), *Comprehensive textbook of psychiatry*. Baltimore: Williams and Wilkins, 1967.

Wolff, W. Fact and value in psychotherapy. *American Journal of Psychotherapy*, 1954, **8**, 466–486.

Wolpe, J. Objective psychotherapy of the neuroses. *South African Medical Journal*, 1952, **26**, 825–829.

SECTION II

Minimal Environmental Control Programs

As opposed to the control which may be exercised in an institution, the practitioner of behavior intervention in the clinic or in the school system has only minimal opportunity to program the environment. The trained mental health specialist must rely extensively upon those already designated as control agents of society, e.g., parents and teachers. The assumption is made that *most* teachers and *most* parents will profit from direct information and training, designed to help them function more efficiently in their roles. The socially undesirable, disruptive behavior exhibited by some children can be brought under control by these community agents of change backed up by professional consultation. The newly acquired adaptive social behavior frequently permits the child to function in the home and school environment and the new responses become self-sustaining through positive environmental feedback. The chapter by Kennedy, "A Behavioristic Community-Oriented Approach to School Phobia and Other Disorders" describes programs in which the parents are given the major treatment role. "Freeing Teachers to Teach" (Madsen, Madsen & Driggs) focuses upon training in behavior control for the teacher, an extremely important community agent of change.

CHAPTER 3

A Behavioristic, Community-Oriented Approach to School Phobia and Other Disorders

Wallace A. Kennedy

The purpose of the present chapter is to describe a behavioristic program of therapeutic intervention put into practice on a community basis. A number of problems must be faced in the development of such a program. How can a Psychological Service Center break out of the traditional doctor–patient relationship and establish innovative therapeutic techniques which are useful both in the treatment and in the prevention of serious emotional conditions? What kinds of restructuring are possible? What kinds of redefined roles are possible? Is it possible to maintain a laboratory-like stance in the community and still maintain the community's confidence and goodwill? These are representative of the questions which have been asked in the last 10 years as the Human Development Clinic at Florida State University has moved from a traditional psychological service to a broader community program where behavior oriented strategies are emphasized.

A primary concern of the Human Development Clinic is the training of clinical students in their second and third year on-campus practicum work prior to their internships. Thus, any innovative technique developed in this setting must, as a first criterion, be readily adaptable for students with relatively low-level professional training and personal maturity, but with high motivation to develop clinical skills, and with a sound theoretical foundation onto which practical skills can be grafted. While making allowances for the training level of its interns and clerks, the Clinic needs to maintain its second role as an innovative clinic. Clinic research should range from broad, normative studies on standardized intelligence and achievement tests and perceptual motor tasks that provide regional normative data on the population with which the clinic is primarily concerned, and epidemiological studies that provide information about the incidence of problems in the population, to the development of new treatment strategies.

In order for a university clinic to play a multidimensional role of training, research, and service, careful modification is required in the traditional role of a child guidance or psychological services clinic. In its break with tradition, it behooves the clinic to hold on to the best traditions of the past, those fringe benefits of the medical model which have encouraged people to seek help in a clinical setting, while trying at the same time to modify some of the attitudes which have seemed to be nonproductive. It seems important to inform the public, as well as one's professional colleagues, of the changes which this new role requires.

An Illustration:
The Treatment of School Phobia

The following discussion of a school phobia program illustrates the behavioristic, community-oriented approach of the Human Development Clinic. It is hoped that the success achieved by this particular strategy for relief of school phobia will supply a convenient model for the application of behavioral techniques in the community setting.

Of all the clinical problems which come to the attention of the psychological services worker, probably none has a longer, more consistent tradition than school-related phobic behavior in children. This dramatic and often puzzling emotional crisis has played a key role in the development of two major treatment strategies in general use today and has been the center of several important controversies. In fact, the history of the treatment of phobias spanning, as it does, the entire era of modern psychotherapeutic intervention, makes a convenient model for understanding the evolution of behavior oriented therapy and its contrast with more conventional therapeutic approaches, especially psychoanalysis.

In 1909 Freud presented one of his first case histories, his only case of child analysis, Little Hans. Often reviewed, this case represented a landmark in the application of the dynamic approach to phobias: an approach in which the symbolic significance of the phobia was uncovered and a cure was effected as a result of the development of insight. It is a landmark also because, although the follow-up was informal, Freud did report a follow-up after 12 years: an absence of follow-up evaluations has been one of the problems in psychoanalytic research.

In describing the reason for the change in Hans after treatment, Freud said, "analysis does not undo the *effects* of repression. The instincts which were formerly suppressed remain suppressed; but the same effect is produced in a different way. Analysis replaces the process of repression, which is an automatic and excessive one, by a temperate and purposeful control on the part of the highest mental facilities. In a word, *analysis replaces repression by condemnation.*" (1953, p. 285).

Later Freud writing on the origin of phobias, said, "on a previous occasion I ascribed to phobias the character of projection, since they substitute for an internal instinctual danger an external perceptual one. Such a process has the advantage that from an external danger protection may be gained through flight and the avoidance of the perception of it, whereas against a danger from within, flight is of no avail. This statement of mine is not incorrect, but superficial. For the instinctual demand is not in itself a danger, but is so only because it entails a true external danger, that of castration. So that fundamentally we have in the phobias, after all, merely the substituting of one external danger for another." (1936, p. 62). In his writings Freud made it rather clear that the term "castration" had the broadened meaning of retaliation by society in the form of punishment.

About the same time that Freud made the correction mentioned above, Broadwin (1932) had begun to identify among the phobias one particularly related to the process of going to school. From the case records of the Jewish Board of Guardians he chose two cases, a boy 13 and a girl 9. These children, who had stayed out of school almost a year, seemed to have slowly-developing obsessions and an intense love of their mothers. This love was almost smothering in nature; they feared for the safety of their mothers when separated from them for any period of time. The fathers played a confusing role in which their sex-role identity was not at all defined. Broadwin recommended that these children were in need of analysis aimed at revealing and expressing instinctive emotions, a position which followed the conception of Freud very closely.

There was, then, a very pronounced feeling among the child guidance therapists that although the symptom, failure to attend school, could be treated by brief psychotherapy, it was to be remembered that this problem was only a surface one, beneath which there were others far more difficult. As Alexander said, "the phobia is an attempt to localize the anxiety in a single situation, while keeping the ego from recognizing the real, unresolved conflict and touching it. Localized anxiety often gives way to a gradual, spreading anxiety and multiple problems develop." (1948, p. 217).

Johnson *et al.* (1941) presented to the American Orthopsychiatry Association one of the earliest papers on school phobia. She reviewed the literature and presented eight cases from her files. All of the boys in her sample were submissive and obedient; all of the girls were aggressively defiant, with a tendency toward temper tantrums. All eight cases had a history of night terrors, short phobic episodes, somatic complaints such as asthma, and other evidences of emotional upsets prior to the present illness. The most outstanding common symptom, however, was the evidence of acute and increased anxiety on the part of the mother, due either to sudden economic deprivation, marital unhappiness, or illness. There was also a poorly resolved, early dependency need, which seemed to affect both the child and the mother, and the mother's relationship with the maternal grandmother. Johnson reported that seven of her eight cases were successfully treated, using a technique involving the development of insight in much the same fashion as Broadwin before her. At this point a tendency seemed to be developing to be rather firm in getting the child back into school.

It was Klein, however, who originated the idea of the importance of getting the child back to school at any level which he could sustain. That is, the child should be taken back to school, even if only for a very few minutes with the mother in attendance. The importance of this procedure was emphasized even though Klein admitted some difficulties in the use of force. He said, after reviewing the difficulties involved with forced school attendance, "not getting the child back has almost equally bad results. If the child remains out of school for a while, there is quick development of primitive regressive fears — in young children, of an oral character; in older ones, of a paranoid nature simulating schizophrenia." (1945, p. 263). So, although he recommended the return of the child to school at the earliest time possible, he also recommended brief psychotherapy of a psychoanalytic orientation to bring about the removal of the symptom of non-school-attendance and intensive analysis to treat the underlying problem.

By the mid 1950's the psychoanalytic literature contained a fairly well-defined etiology. Two articles complete the clinical description, the first by Talbot (1957) and the second by Coolidge *et al.* (1957).

Talbot described six characteristics of the school phobia problem:

1. An inbred family constellation; that is, a large involvement between the child's parents and their parents, uncles, aunts, and grandparents.
2. A neurotic involvement of the mother with her own family.
3. A heavy involvement between the father and his family.
4. An immature relationship between the parents in their marriage.

5. A neurotic involvement with death.
6. A close, symbiotic relationship between mother and child.

Coolidge *et al.,* on the other hand, suggested that some of the confusion regarding the treatment plan of school phobia is caused by the existence of two types of school phobia, rather than only one. Although the two types share a common group of symptoms, they differ widely in other symptoms. The types are designated as Type I or the neurotic crisis, and Type II or the way-of-life phobia. The symptoms are listed below. both the common symptoms associated with all school phobias and the differentiating symptoms expressed by Coolidge *et al.,* and further refined by Kennedy (1965). A differential diagnosis can be made logically and empirically on the basis of any 7 of the 10 differential symptoms.

Common Symptoms

1. Morbid fears associated with school attendance.
2. Frequent somatic complaints: headaches, nausea, drowsiness.
3. Symbiotic relationship with mother, fear of separation.
4. Anxiety about many things: darkness, crowds, noises.

Differentiating Symptoms

Type I

1. The present illness is the first episode.
2. Monday onset, following an illness the previous Thursday or Friday.
3. An acute onset.
4. Lower grades most prevalent.
5. Expressed concern about death.
6. Mother's physical health in question; actually ill, or child thinks so.
7. Good communication between parents.

Type II

1. Second, third, or fourth episode.
2. Monday onset following minor illness, not a prevalent antecedent.
3. Gradual development.
4. Upper grades most prevalent.
5. Death theme not present.
6. Health of mother not an issue.
7. Poor communication between parents.

8. Mother and father well-adjusted in most areas.	8. Mother shows neurotic behavior; father a character disorder.
9. Father competitive with mother in household management.	9. Father shows little interest in household or children.
10. Parents achieve understanding of dynamics easily.	10. Parents very difficult to work with.

Throughout classic analytic literature is the often-expressed, always-implicit admonition to treat phobias by establishing a relationship of sufficient strength to encourage a flow of unconscious material except when phobias are a defense against a psychotic break, and not to deal directly with the symptom. In fact, Greenbaum, in a recent summary of the theory and practice of the treatment of school phobias, implies that a great deal of harm would be done if school attendance was forced. He best expresses this with the analogy, "no one has ever, to my knowledge, threatened claustrophobic patients with jail if they did not take the elevator, yet the literature reports just such threats being made if the child does not go back to school" (1964, p. 622). Regardless of the differences found in treatment strategy, one obvious fact in the literature on school phobia is that the prognosis is excellent, far better than for other emotional problems.

At about the time Freud published his work on a child's phobia, the effects of Pavlov's work began to be felt in the area of children's problems. Pfaundler (1904), a German pediatrician, arranged an apparatus to ring a bell when a child in a pediatric ward needed changing. This was conceived originally as a method to make the nurses more efficient in keeping their charges dry, but was soon discovered to have a therapeutic effect, and thus, the beginning of an application of learning theory technique to problems of children.

However, the application of Pavlov's findings to more complex problems awaited Watson's work, when he, along with Rayner and Jones (Watson & Rayner, 1920; Jones, 1924a, 1924b), demonstrated the application of conditioning to the learning and unlearning of phobias. Watson, in his classical demonstration, built up a phobia against rabbits which generalized to white furry objects and then to the color white itself. Finally, he and Jones demonstrated that the phobia could be reduced by deconditioning in the same way that it had been conditioned. The phobic object was paired with pleasurable objects and as the association built up the fear broke down. There did not seem to be any spontaneous recovery of the phobia, but the psychoanalysis-oriented psychologists generally responded that this abatement of the symptoms did not mean that the phobia did not still exist, but rather that it had gone underground.

Watson himself seemed to lose interest in the problem, and the resistance to the conclusion was so strong, that little application of the technique followed until the early 1950's, when some enormous changes took place in the thinking of psychologists and psychiatrists. One can rather sharply date these changes to the period from 1952 to 1954, for in this 2-year span, two dramatic events occurred.

First was the often-quoted, thoroughly reviewed, well-criticized and, perhaps, in places, somewhat inaccurate article by Eysenck (1952), in which he made his classic attack on the psychoanalytic approach, with his one-third-by-one-third-by-one-third analysis of the best and the worst the psychotherapist had to offer. Eysenck said, in effect, that understaffed, overworked, overcrowded, perhaps merely custodial mental hospitals in New York State indicated that approximately one-third of the people who entered their institutions stayed a minimum time and then walked out through those gray doors into life completely restored, never to need the services of the mental health field again; that one-third of the people who entered those gates left tentatively and though improved or much improved, nevertheless remained for the rest of their lives uncured; and that one-third of the people who entered those gates were diagnosed as unimproved or worse after treatment. He added that, nevertheless, the best of the Park Avenue psychiatrists find that a third of their patients are completely restored by psychotherapy, a third are improved, and a third are unimproved or worse.

Eysenck left some untidy ends here and there and Hans Strupp (1963), in his review, has done a commendable job at pointing up the limitations. The challenge was issued, however, and the burden of proof rested with the established psychotherapies. When the hue and cry had subsided, the fact remained that psychotherapy as practiced in 1950 could make only a very poor case for having a unique answer to emotional distress. Thus, although it still remains possible that a technique such as Watson's or Skinner's or Wolpe's (1958) may indeed be merely dealing with symptoms, the fear of doing something wrong in psychotherapy by not following the established psychoanalytic techniques began to subside and slowly, little by little, the application of symptom-oriented, behavior-oriented techniques began to gather momentum.

The second critical event of the early 1950's was the dramatic effect of the introduction of chlorpromazine hydrochloride. The large number of subsequent variations of tranquilizers, mood elevators, stabilizers, antidepressants, etc., gave the psychiatrist and general practitioner some way, other than psychoanalysis, of dealing with neurotic and psychotic problems. The effectiveness of chlorpromazine and similar drugs in reducing the misery of neurotic patients and making the management of psychoses and depressions feasible on an outpatient basis reduced dependency on the analyst and provided a healthy climate for skepticism to develop.

Up to this time physicians themselves still tended to consider psychoanalysis as the treatment of choice for those who could afford it. But, with the development of mood-swing, mood-stabilizing drugs, a whole new language began to emerge, and the public began to hear about metabolic disturbances, chemical imbalances, and reticular-activating systems, rather than ids, egos, and Oedipuses. This tack has been minimally helpful in understanding the processes of behavior change, but has tended to dilute the influence of psychoanalytically oriented therapy and has opened the door to research in the use of alternative techniques.

One of the very first of the new generation studies of school phobia was the Baltimore study by Leon Eisenberg, a physician who laid careful groundwork to make peace with the existing views, first by emphasizing the need for an intensive diagnostic approach and by mentioning the usual case of a child who was felt to have school phobia, but actually had hydropexis secondary to ureteral obstruction. That is, the school phobia was merely a secondary symptom of some serious medical problem.

But after this lip service to the Establishment, Eisenberg made a rather important and, for the times, unusual divergence from the traditional path. He recommended that once the diagnosis was established, the central focus in the management of school phobia was prompt return to school. Anticipating the criticism to follow, Eisenberg said, "This may seem at first glance a hazardous undertaking with a child who displays panic at the prospect of returning to school. The physician no less than the family may fear the precipitation of an acute breakdown. In fact, however, this does not occur with adequate support to child and family. The reasons for this therapeutic emphasis and its success require discussion." (1959, p. 761).

In the discussion which followed, Eisenberg stressed these points:

1. The longer the child is out of school, the more complicated is the process of return, what with the pile up of homework and missed work and the difficulty in explaining his absence to peers.
2. The child has learned to enjoy the additional attention which he has received as a result of his behavior; that is the secondary gain is rather marked.

3. He has been away from the healthy environment of school with its stimulation for growth and has been, instead, in the home situation which promoted his problem in the first place.
4. The fact that the adults around him tend to go along with his fears tends, in a child's mind, to give support to their reality.
5. The failure to return the child to school feeds the neurotic pattern within the family itself.

Eisenberg recommended, as had Klein, that the child should be returned to school to whatever degree he could sustain.

Eisenberg's results, considering the fact that some of the patients had been out of school for three years, were quite impressive. Of the total 41 cases treated, 29 were attending school regularly when seen for a 3-year follow-up. Of the 27 children younger than 11 years old, 24 were able to attend school regularly, while of the older children only 5 out of 14 were able to attend school regularly.

In the fall of 1957 the Human Development Clinic at Florida State University embarked upon an experimental procedure for the treatment of Type I School Phobia — a procedure similar to that of Rodriguez, Rodriguez, and Eisenberg (1959) with one major exception: whereas they made no distinction between types of school phobia and treated in the same manner all cases which came to the clinic, the 50 cases reported herein (Kennedy, 1965) were selected on the basis of the differential criteria mentioned above. The Florida State University Human Development Clinic, as a teaching and research clinic, does not generally see deeply-disturbed children but refers them to other agencies.

In the 8-year period covered by the report, there were six cases which would meet the criteria of Type II School Phobia. These six cases were treated by supportive therapy for the children and parents. None of the six Type II cases had more than three of the 10 Type I criteria and the results were completely dissimilar to those reported for the 50 Type I cases. All of the Type II cases were chronic in nature. All had family histories of one or both parents being seriously disturbed. Two of the cases were diagnosed as having schizophrenia; two were diagnosed as having character disorders with the school phobia being a minor aspect of the case. One of the six was hospitalized; one was sent to a training school; of the four remaining, two were able to go to college although their records were poor and their symptoms continued. These six cases were in treatment for an average of 10 months. In no instance was a school phobia case changed from Type I to Type II, or vice versa.

This experimental procedure for Type I School Phobia was begun with considerable caution with only one case in 1957 and two the following Spring. The treatment involved the application of broad learning theory concepts by blocking the escape of the child and preventing secondary gains from occurring. In addition, the child was reinforced for going to school without complaining. This rapid treatment procedure was followed with 50 cases.

Subjects for the 50 cases over an 8-year period were school-age children from the geographic area served by the Human Development Clinic of Florida State University, all suffering from the first evidence of a phobic attack. The subject distribution by year of treatment and sex is illustrated in Table 1, by symptom and sex in Table 2, by age and sex in Table 3, and by grade and sex in Table 4. The fathers' mean age for the male subjects was 36, the mothers' 35. For the female subjects the fathers' mean age was 38, the mothers', 36. The boys' mean age was 9, that of the girls, 10. There was no definite pattern in birth order of the subjects nor in number of siblings.

TABLE 1
Year of treatment and sex of 50 Type I School Phobia Cases

Year	Male	Female	Total
1957	1	0	1
1958	1	1	2
1959	4	2	6
1960	4	8	12
1961	6	3	9
1962	5	4	9
1963	4	5	9
1964	0	2	2
Total	25	25	50

TABLE 2
Symptom checklist and sex of 50 Type I School Phobia Cases

Symptom	Male	Female	Total
1. First attack	25	25	50
2. Monday onset – Thursday illness	24	25	49
3. Acute onset	25	23	48
4. Lower grades	22	18	40
5. Death theme	22	22	44
6. Mother's health an issue	23	21	44
7. Good parental marital harmony	24	23	47
8. Good parental mental health	23	24	47
9. Father helper in the house	21	21	42
10. Parents achieve insight quickly	24	25	49

TABLE 3

Age and sex of 50 Type I School Phobia Cases

Age	Male	Female	Total
4	0	1	1
5	3	1	4
6	2	3	5
7	3	2	5
8	3	1	4
9	3	5	8
10	4	3	7
11	1	2	3
12	3	0	3
13	2	4	6
14	1	2	3
15	0	0	0
16	0	1	1
Total	25	25	50

TABLE 4

Grade and sex of 50 Type I School Phobia Cases

Grade	Male	Female	Total
Nursery School	0	2	2
Kindergarten	4	0	4
First	4	4	8
Second	0	1	1
Third	6	4	10
Fourth	3	4	7
Fifth	2	2	4
Sixth	3	1	4
Seventh	2	2	4
Eighth	0	2	2
Ninth	1	2	3
Tenth	0	1	1
Total	25	25	50

Five of these 50 cases might be considered semicontrols because they were untreated Type I cases of some duration or they were Type I cases unsuccessfully treated elsewhere by other techniques before they were seen at the Clinic. One of these semicontrol cases had been out of school for one year, and the other four had been out for over three months. All 50 of the cases responded to the treatment program with a complete remission of the school phobia symptoms. Follow-up studies indicated no evidence of outbreaks of substitute symptoms or recurrence of the phobia.

In the follow-up schedule, the parents were phoned in about two weeks and again in six weeks to see if the progress had continued. They were then phoned on a yearly basis except in 1961 when follow-up interviews were conducted, reaching 19 of the 21 cases completed at that time. During the course of the eight years, six families were lost because of moving with no forwarding address. Of these lost cases none had been followed less than two years, two were followed three years, and one for four years.

The rapid treatment program for Type I School Phobia involves six essential components:

1. good professional public relations,
2. avoidance of emphasis on somatic complaints,
3. forced school attendance,
4. structured interview with parents,
5. brief interview with child, and
6. follow-up.

It is necessary to establish good communication with schools, physicians, and parent groups, such that cases are likely to be referred on the second or third day of the phobic attack. This groundwork involves the typical mental health consultation and case-by-case follow-up with the referring source.

If phobic qualities predominate, that is, if the child conforms to seven of the differential symptoms of Type I School Phobia, emphasis on somatic complaints should be avoided. The child's somatic complaints should be handled matter-of-factly with an appointment to see the pediatrician after school hours. Abdominal pains will probably require the pediatrician to make a prompt physical examination but this can be accomplished on the way to school.

It is essential to be able to require that the child go to school and to be willing to use any force necessary. In all of the present cases, simply convincing the parents of this necessity and having them come to a firm decision generally has been sufficient. The ability to be decisive when necessary has been essential. The following is a procedural outline of the treatment used:

1. Have the father take the child to school. These fathers are not unkind, and they can show authority when necessary.
2. Have the principal or attendance officer take an active part in keeping the child in the room.

3. Allow the mother to stand in the hall if she must or to visit the school during the morning, but do not allow her to stay.
4. Stressing the following points, conduct with the parents a structured interview designed to give them sufficient confidence to carry out the therapeutic program even in the face of considerable resistance from the child.

Lead the interview. The confidence of the parents is greatly increased by the interviewer's verifying the history rather than taking it. Correctly anticipating 7 out of 10 variables within a family structure is well-calculated to induce full cooperation.

Be optimistic. Stressing the transient nature of the difficulty, the dependable sequence of a difficult Monday, a somewhat better Tuesday, and a symptom-free Wednesday, tends to lighten the depression of the parents regarding their child's unwillingness to go to school.

Emphasize success. Type I cases always recover. Ninety percent of the Type I phobics stay at school most of the first day. Along with optimism, comes a slight mobilization of hostility, which helps the parents to follow the plan.

Present the formula. Simply but directly with repetition for emphasis, outline a plan for the parents to follow assuming that it is the end of the school week by the time of the referral and that the interview with the parents is conducted on Thursday or Friday.

Do not discuss in any way school attendance over the weekend. There is nothing a phobic child does better than talk about going to school. Don't discuss phobic symptoms. Simply tell the child Sunday evening, "Well, son, tomorrow you go back to school."

On Monday morning get the child up, dressed, and ready for school. Give the child a light breakfast to reduce the nausea problem. Have the father take the child matter-of-factly off to school. Don't ask him how he feels or why he is afraid to go to school or why he doesn't like school. Simply take him to school, turn him over to the school authorities, and go home. If the child's therapist has not seen the child the previous week, he may see him after school on the first day.

On Monday evening, compliment the child on going to school and staying there, no matter how resistant he has been, no matter how many times he has vomited, cried, or started to leave. If he has been at school for 30 minutes on Monday, progress is being made. Tell the child Monday evening that Tuesday will be much better and make no further mention of the symptom.

Tuesday can be expected to be a repetition of Monday, but with everything toned down considerably. On Tuesday evening, encourage and compliment the child strongly for doing so much better.

Wednesday should be virtually symptom-free. Wednesday evening with considerable fanfare, give a party for the child in honor of his having overcome his problem.

The child himself should be seen only briefly by the child therapist and only after school hours. The content of the interview should be stories which stress the advantages of going on in the face of fear—how student pilots need to get back into the air quickly after an accident and how important it is to get right back on the horse after a fall. In addition, the therapist can describe real or imaginary events in his own childhood, when he was frightened for a while, but where everything turned out all right; he also can stress to the child the transitory nature of the phobia. Follow-up by phone, being chatty and encouraging and not oversolicitous. In the long-range follow-up, chat with the parents about further school phobia, school attendance records, academic progress, and the occurrence of other emotional problems in the child.

Critique

Two legitimate concerns have arisen from preliminary reports on the rapid treatment of school phobia cases. The first is a concern about the claim of complete remission for all 50 cases—a claim inconsistent with the usual child guidance clinic success rate—and the consequent belief that the criterion for success is simply too narrow. Only self-report data and reports from school administrations were obtained regarding the symptom-free nature of these children, once this phobic episode had passed. No diagnostic evaluation was undertaken with any of these children during the follow-up. It must be remembered, however, that the definition of symptom remission was restricted to those obvious symptoms which might conceivably lead the parents or school officials to re-refer the children to the Clinic. In this regard, these 50 children in the Type I School Phobia group are symptom-free.

Because of the nature of the Human Development Clinic and the nature of this project, careful selection was exercised in accepting cases. Due to the relationship between the schools and the Clinic and the clear definition of cases suitable for the project, there is reason to believe that the majority of Type I School Phobia cases in the 5-county area the Clinic serves have come to our attention, whereas the local county mental health clinic has received a high percentage of the Type II cases. The success of the Type II School Phobia cases accepted by the Human Development Clinic for teaching purposes has not been remarkable.

The second concern is that perhaps what is called Type I School Phobia is not really a severe phobic attack at all, but borders on malingering of a transient nature which would spontaneously remit in a few days anyway. In fact, because of the apparent sound mental health of the family as a group, its middle class values which stress school, and the family's good premorbid history, including the academic record of the child, there is little reason to doubt that the majority of the cases would eventually return to school whatever treatment was undertaken.

This possibility was brought out with dramatic clarity at the regional medical meeting where we presented the findings of our first 50 cases, reviewed carefully the criterion for separating the two types of phobias, and stressed the very high success with this group. When we had finished the presentation and had experienced a rather positive response from the audience about the specific, describable clinical entity with a prescribed course of treatment and a high rate of cure, an old-time pediatrician in the audience raised his hand. Upon being recognized, he stood up and said that he would like to thank us for having expanded his vocabulary. He had never heard of the term, "Type I School Phobia." But it seemed to him that it was common enough when he was a boy when it was called by a more generic name: "Let me see now; what was it? Oh, yes. Hooky!"

However, our five semicontrol cases and evidence from other clinics of Type I cases who have been out of school for prolonged periods suggest that this method of treatment may accelerate or facilitate the remission. Recommendation for the use of this technique is restricted to those cases showing Type I symptoms which, in spite of their possible transient nature, present a rather serious problem to teachers, parents, and counselors.

The guiding principle of mobilizing parents to return the child to school at any level the child can emotionally sustain, which is the backbone of both the Eisenberg and the Kennedy treatment technique for school phobia, has met with the predictable mixed reaction. On one hand, there have been several successful replications (Altrocchi, personal communication; Leventhal *et al.*, 1967) even though there have been some problems noted in the distinction between the two types, both at the Human Development Clinic and in other settings. There now have been demonstrated mixed types, where the child seems to have only half of the Type I symptoms. In general, the higher the percentage of Type I symptoms, the greater the success obtained. The lack of success in the mixed cases seems to relate to a failure in the insistance by the parents that the child return to school. There have been no reports of children who reverted to more serious emotional problems as a result of the treatment strategy. Behavior oriented therapists have seemed to accept this principle and in general have been able to succeed in returning the child to school under the treatment plan outlined.

On the other hand, Greenbaum (1964) in a careful and temperate attack on the forced school attendance treatment method states that forcing a child into a feared situation does not relate to any known theory of the development of phobias. Greenbaum believes the reason for the attempt to push the child back into school is not based on any theoretical foundation but rather is based upon biases that are characteristics of middle class parents.

The first of these biases is the attitude of the psychotherapist, with his own educational history and his identity with the goodness of education in general, who is panicked by the thought of any child not going to school. He is committed to the idea of school as the proper place for children and, regardless of the consequence, feels that being out of school is such a dreadful thing that almost any expense is justified in returning the child to school. The second bias concerns the therapist and his need for easy, shortcut solutions, such that any system that purports to make a quick cure is adopted readily and perhaps negative results are not adequately reported. The last bias assumes that the school situation is a healthier situation than the home situation since the home situation really produced the phobia and, therefore, the strong need is to return the child to the school as rapidly as possible. Greenbaum states that, even though there is usually no question but that the school offers a healthier situation in which to function than does the home, an environment that is realistically better by objective standards does not aid in treatment if the patient's response to being placed in such an environment is an increase in terror.

One of the most important considerations in the application of this technique to an outpatient setting would seem to relate to the development of an expectancy. An activist role, such as that demanded in the outpatient application of behavior oriented therapy programs, needs some translation from the scientist laboratory model, and this would seem to be one of the most important aspects of the present program of treatment at the Human Development Clinic.

All of the cases in the first sample of 50 school phobic children involved a senior staff member with the interns serving mainly as participating observers rather than having the primary responsibility for the case. Students sat in on the initial interview with the parents of the phobic child and monitored telephone calls in the follow-up. They in turn were encouraged in the latter phase of their training, either while on their second clerkship or during their internship within a school setting, to try the technique on a case of their own, and those students in the school psychology program were generally able to complete two or three such cases.

This was possible, of course, because the staff of the Clinic also provided supervision within the school setting during the internship of student school psychologists. As a result the Clinic staff was able to establish, on the administrative level, the necessary permission and required public relations demanded by an experimental treatment program. To the parents and teachers the experimental nature of the program was minimized and its theoretical soundness and its effectiveness within the clinical setting was maximized.

Because of the social and political pressures with which the school has to cope, it is probable that many school settings would be unable to permit experimentation with an untried methodology within the school setting. However, it is possible that a secondary validation of a therapeutic innovative program can be made within the school setting and patients from the desired population can be obtained by referal from principals, guidance coordinators, and special education teachers in the school setting.

This relationship with the school also provides for an excellent opportunity to work with the parents through PTA talks and informal parent conferences, and for the prevention of school phobia through the application of the treatment program to borderline cases before they reach crisis proportion. And this, of course, is probably one of the major roles of a university-related clinic: that of adapting treatment skills and knowledge to the point where parents, teachers, nurses, and pediatricians can use these strategies in the early stages of symptom development. It is quite conceivable that treatment strategies, which would take a highly skilled professional many hours of intensive preoccupation, in a well-developed problem of long-standing, could be employed with great success by a person with a skill level no higher than that of the average parent upon the first occasion of the child's turning to a pathological response to meet a challenging situation in his life. Herein lies the great challenge: the possibility of preventive intervention in the lives of the community at a time when prevention is still possible.

Thus far, we have been talking entirely about a simple clinical entity about which there is some controversy but which is generally recognized as a problem with a favorable prognosis. It is favorable most probably for two reasons, the first being the readily identifiable phobic criteria. The presence or absence of the problem is obvious. It is most likely favorable, however, because the nature of the problem forces early attention such that treatment is obtained prior to the response pattern becoming habitual. The sooner a problem is dealt with in a systematic, effective manner, the better the prognosis. The symptoms of school phobia are generally looked upon as undesirable, their elimination warranting even drastic action. The "let's wait and see if he will grow out of it" attitude is rarely employed in a problem that prevents school attendance in a society where school attendance is highly valued.

However, the generally favorable prognosis for the Type I School Phobia program does not hold for well-established Type II cases. Most often the reason for failure with Type II cases revolves around problems which are encountered in soliciting strict cooperation from the parents. When the problem is well-established, as in a case showing more than eight Type II symptoms, we have found it impossible to secure the necessary level of cooperation from the parents. Instead such cases require a mixed treatment program with heavy outside pressure to get the child back into school and a rather extended, supportive treatment program for children and parents alike. Such a well-established behavior pattern requires much understanding on the part of the therapist and much insight on the part of the parents, and this cannot be accomplished in the 3-day program outlined above. In such cases a strict behavioristic approach is not as effective as a program which combines the best aspects of the two.

The best use of this combined treatment program can be made with the mixed-type school phobias with four to six Type I symptoms and where some difficulty exists in making a distinction between one or more symptoms relating particularly to parental adjustment and marriage adjustment. It was with these cases that a modification of the treatment program was most important. It was our feeling that the parents' cooperation was the weakest link and thus a change was effected in the program at the point of contact with the parents. In these cases the child was seen for a 2-hour diagnostic evaluation after school, and the parents were given daily support during the crisis.

Patience, repetition, and support, as well as time for catharsis, seem essential for the treatment of the mixed-type school phobias. Still the success rate of the cases showing less than three Type I symptoms or more than seven Type II symptoms was very low and represented little more than a slight improvement in the multiple symptom complex. Thus progress was measured in terms of better functioning on the part of the child rather than a complete remission of the symptom. In a typical case the child would still be subject to complaints about school, would express dislike or fear of the school setting, but would continue to attend without incident.

In these cases, where clearly there was at least a partial failure of the method, the focal point of the failure seemed always to be a break-down in communication and rapport with the parents. The parents lost confidence, if indeed they ever had any, and removed themselves from treatment. Some sought help from other sources but many continued to accept failure to attend school as an unresolvable conflict, and we had reports of some children of the Type II complex who never returned to school on a formal basis, although many finished on a home-bound basis or later went to night school to complete their education.

Current Clinic Programs

Now that the school phobia treatment program has become part of the routine operation, new applications of a conditioning program have been started on a pilot basis. These programs represent the direction in which the Clinic is moving as its next major focus of clinical research.

Enuresis

Following the research findings of Turner and Young (1965) in London on the use of a CNS stimulant and a Mowrer-type con-ditioning program for enuretics, the Human Development Clinic has undertaken a cross-validation of the Turner and Young program using both an outpatient and inpatient population. Since it is evident that one of the largest sources of error in the application of this conditioning program was the failure of parents to follow carefully the details of the conditioning plan, the Clinic proposes to replicate Turner and Young's program and admit the small percentage of failures to an inpatient program where the conditioning paradigm can be put into effect for a 3-week period under the direct control of the Clinic. If, as we suspect, those failures reported with the home treatment program are indeed resulting from the neglect of the parents to follow directions, it is likely that this demonstration will convince doubting parents that the program will succeed.

The program requires that the children be given medication three times a day for six weeks and that the conditioning apparatus be set each night and reset during the night if the child voids in his bed. The problem seems to come at the point of resetting the apparatus after the first nightly incidence with the result that many children who void more than once are not conditioned on the second voiding and are thus given partial reinforcement. There are various reasons for failure to reset the apparatus, but in general they seem to revolve around the parents' distress over their lack of uninterrupted sleep and consequent failure to sustain interest when the results are not instantaneous.

Again, the purpose of this program is to help in the translation of a research plan into a program that will be followed by the outpatient population. The importance of giving the parents adequate preparation and support such that they will follow a program cannot be overstressed. Without prolonged and accurate help from the parents, there is almost no hope that the program will succeed on an outpatient basis with a high degree of regularity. The rather high degree of failure with some of the commercially available conditioning apparatuses with enuresis is mute testimony to the need for an effective orientation program. These boxes and the treatment program outlined in the instructions are quite adequate for success, if the parent and child would only follow the directions. But we find many of the parents have one of these boxes on their shelves at home where they placed it upon experiencing failure after a short trial period.

Obesity[1]

Another program which has been initiated involves the application to obese patients of a conditioning paradigm using a noxious gas, butyric acid, as the unconditioned stimulus. The favorite gorging food of obese patients is paired to this aversive stimuli. So far, this is in the pilot stage with only two patients. Using a conditioning program with this population is particularly appropriate because the literature on obesity indicates that with any conventional treatment program, the prognosis is extremely dim. Following the pilot study, a more ambitious program will be undertaken to determine if an obese population will respond to an aversive conditioning program with some modification for the outpatient clinic setting.

It is obvious that the conditioning program will not work unless there is either full control of or full cooperation from the patient, and in an outpatient clinic it is hardly reasonable to feel that full control is possible. Thus far the highest success rate for conditioning programs has been in residential settings, where support for the program has come from the administration and where much of the patient care has been supervised directly by the investigators. In order for such a program to work on an outpatient basis, a modification in the program will be required to encourage cooperation.

---

[1]Other behavioristic approaches to the control of obesity have been reported by Ferster, Nurenberger, and Levitt (1962); Stuart (1967); and Moore and Crum (1969).

A supportive program of group therapy has been added to attempt to deal with the patients' feelings during the course of the conditioning program. The group therapy should permit ventilation of the obese patients' anger and frustration in a controlled emphatic setting. At the same time, the obese patient knows numerous tricks to "fool" himself into believing that he is staying on a low-calorie diet and the group therapy should provide the impetus for personal honesty needed to follow a conditioning program.

Hypochondriasis

Another problem under research in a pilot program involves the reduction of the use of professional time and medication by patients diagnosed as hypochondriacal. This program calls for the application of a verbal conditioning program in which the patient is seen in an interview situation for supportive therapy although the therapist is careful to avoid reinforcement of hypochondriacal statements. The patient is reinforced for talking about anything else. The expectancy is for the patient to condition to other expressions, as it is assumed he has been conditioned for hypochondriacal statements. The pilot data indicate that the use of medications and requests for medical consultations can be sharply reduced by regular verbal conditioning. Again, these pilot data deal with very few patients. But it appears that the program might well be modifiable with a group therapy, in which the leader controls the group's expression, such that hypochondriacal statements are extinguished in the group setting.

Summary

These, then, are some examples of the process by which the findings of experimental clinical research can be translated into clinical practice in an outpatient psychological services center setting. For too long the gulf has opened wider and wider between the laboratory and the clinic. A portion of the difficulty may be attributed to the widespread use of the medical model for illness as opposed to a learning model. There is obviously much to recommend the medical model for the treatment of certain emotional problems and the model of the healer-priest which has developed through the centuries does indeed have certain seductive qualities.

On the other hand, the behaviorist model offers obvious advantages: widespread applicability, teachability, and the potential for greater objectification and measurement. We owe it to ourselves and to the public to insist that the behavioral approach is given an adequate trial in the hands of therapists who understand the basic theory and the requirements of science for validation of a technique. At the same time, we must carefully guard against becoming so deliriously happy at our success that we join the ranks of our psychoanalyst brethren of the first half of the century and begin to believe that anyone who practices any other kind of treatment is unenlightened. Our success at this early date must not lead us into the trap of becoming the Establishment which will sit on progress in mental health for the next 50 years, when present technology is insufficient to do the job.

REFERENCES

Alexander, F. *Fundamentals of psychoanalysis.* New York: Norton, 1948.

Broadwin, I. T. A contribution to the study of truancy. *American Journal of Orthopsychiatry*, 1932, **2**, 253–259.

Coolidge, J. C., Hahn, P. B. & Peck, A. L. School phobia: Neurotic crisis or way of life. *American Journal of Orthopsychiatry*, 1957, **27**, 296–306.

Eisenberg, L. The pediatric management of school phobia. *Journal of Pediatrics*, 1959, **55**, 758–766.

Eysenck, H. J. The effects of psychotherapy: An evaluation. *Journal of Consulting Psychology*, 1952, **16**, 319–324.

Ferster, C. B., Nurenberger, J. I. & Levitt, E. B. The control of eating. *Journal of Mathetics*, 1962, **1**, 87–109.

Freud, S. A further consideration of infantile zoophobia. *The Problem of Anxiety.* New York: Norton, 1936, **3**, 59–68.

Freud, S. Analysis of a phobia in a five-year-old. In *Collected Papers.* London: Hogarth Press, 1953. Pp. 149–289.

Greenbaum, R. S. Treatment of school phobias — theory and practice. *American Journal of Psychotherapy*, 1964, **18**, 616–634.

Johnson, A. M., Falstein, E. I., Szurek, S. A. & Svendsen, M. A study of five cases. *American Journal of Orthopsychiatry*, 1941, **11**, 702–711.

Jones, M. C. The elimination of children's fears. *Journal of Experimental Psychology*, 1924, **7**, 382–390. (a)

Jones, M. C. A laboratory study of fear: The case of Peter. *Pedagogical Seminar*, 1924, **31**, 308–315. (b)

Kennedy, W. A. School phobia: Rapid treatment of fifty cases. *Journal of Abnormal Psychology*, 1965, **70**, 285–389.

Klein, E. The reluctance to go to school. *Psychoanalytic Study of the Child*, 1945, **1**, 263.

Leventhal, T., Weinberger, G., Stander, R. J. & Stearns, R. P. Therapeutic strategies with school phobics. *American Journal of Orthopsychiatry*, 1967, **37**, 64–70.

Moore, C. H. & Crum, B. C. Weight reduction in a chronic schizophrenic by means of operant conditioning procedures: A case study. *Behaviour Research and Therapy*, 1969, **7**, 129–131.

Pfaundler, M. *Menonstration eines apparatex Zu Selbsttatigen signalisierung Stattgehaber Bettnassung.* Verhandlunger Der Gesellschaft Fur Kinderkeilkinde, 1904.

Rodriguez, A., Rodriguez, M. & Eisenberg, L. The outcome of school phobia: A follow-up study based on 41 cases. *American Journal of Psychiatry*, 1959, **116**, 540–544.

Strupp, H. H. The outcome problem in psychotherapy revisited. *Psychotherapy*, 1963, **1**, 1–13.

Stuart, R. B. Behavioral control of overeating. *Behaviour Research and Therapy*, 1967, **5**, 357–365.

Talbot, M. Panic in school phobia. *American Journal of Orthopsychiatry*, 1957, **27**, 286–295.

Turner, P. K. & Young, G. C. CNS stimulus drugs and treatment of nocturnal enuresis. *Behavior Research and Therapy*, 1965, **3**, 93–101.

Watson, J. B. & Rayner, R. Conditioned emotional reactions. *Journal of Experimental Psychology*, 1920, **3**, 1–12.

Wolpe, J. *Psychotherapy by reciprocal inhibition.* Stanford: Stanford University Press, 1958.

CHAPTER 4

Freeing Teachers to Teach

Charles H. Madsen, Jr.,
Clifford K. Madsen and Don F. Driggs

As long as recorded history and very probably long before, there have been teachers—teachers and students. Most students profess interest in learning and most teachers in teaching, yet often little teaching goes on and perhaps even less learning. Some pupils begin complaining about teachers and teaching practices before they begin to seriously evaluate any other aspect of their lives. From the lower grades through graduate school one hears constant rumblings concerning educational practices which at best are deemed irrelevant, at worst spitefully vindictive. Only occasionally are reports of excellence voiced. The thoughtful person may look past apparent idiosyncrasies and trivia to ask some basic questions: Why is this educational situation extant? What happens in the teacher-learning process to elicit unhappy responses? Are most teachers committed to misery for themselves as well as their students? Do people enter the teaching profession to promote ineffectual learning? The authors think not; neither do we believe that educational processes are so complex as to defy analysis and subsequent improvement. It appears to us as true but unfortunate that several important changes occur with many teachers in that short period of time while passing from a "naïve idealist" to "practionaire." The desire to be a good teacher often gives way first to disillusionment, then to cynicism, and perhaps on to despair. The culmination is sometimes complete resignation and apathy.

It would seem that a first step toward ameliorating this problem would be to establish some hard and fast values in teacher training that would lead to different practices. We refer specifically to that genre of teacher preparation that would base teacher training on behavioral ingredients in addition to platitudinous clichés, for to think and even to know is not necessarily to act; to be concerned is not necessarily to effect positive change; and to desire change is not necessarily to produce it. A second aspect of improvement might come from giving teachers actual practice in behavioral shaping (teaching) with immediate feedback and individual instruction in the use of behavioral techniques. This chapter deals with a threefold program using the above rationale and activities in order to free teachers to teach.

Exercising Control Over Classroom Behavior

Individual research activities within classroom situations are continually in progress to determine what reinforcements are indeed effective in the classroom. In one classroom study, 10 pupils referred by their teachers as having severe problems were observed. Experienced observers trained in techniques of recording children's behavior participated. These observers recorded in 10-second intervals those children's behaviors that interfered with learning. The average inappropriate behavior level for these pupils during six weeks was 72 percent (talking, fighting, getting out of seat, etc.). After this initial recording (three sessions per week, 45 minutes each) the teachers were instructed in specific classroom strategies: (1) classroom rules were to be explicit and repeatedly stated; (2) minor behaviors which interfered with learning were to be ignored; (3) withdrawal of approval was to be used as punishment; (4) praise and attention were to be made to reinforce prosocial behavior incompatible with inappropriate social behavior. The participating teachers also were given a weekly workshop session in behavior modification during the experiment and were shown daily observation graphs concerning their own procedural effectiveness, based upon the above classroom strategies. Inappropriate pupil behavior decreased from 72 percent to 19.5 percent over eight weeks (Becker, Madsen, Arnold & Thomas, 1967).

Often research studies must continue over an extended period to determine if it is indeed the specific behavioral reinforcements which teach the desired responses. Therefore, in another study two second grade boys were observed during a complete academic year. These boys were referred by their teacher for inappropriate behaviors including unfinished assignments, bothering neighbors, and playing in class. Trained observers initially recorded 47 percent inappropriate behavior based upon total number of 10-second intervals during daily observations lasting 30 minutes. The teacher and class then formulated rules (e.g., we raise our hands before we talk) that were repeated orally by the class six times per day for two weeks. There was, however, little decrease in inappropriate behavior (average 40 percent). Apparently just knowing, i.e., being able to repeat rules, was not effective in reducing inappropriate behavior. The teacher next attempted to ignore inappropriate behavior but this procedure was also unsuccessful. Ignoring deviant behavior is a technique that takes much practice and is extremely difficult even for experienced teachers. This particular teacher was unable to completely eliminate disapproval responses following inappropriate behavior. She was, however, able to reduce the number of these responses through practice and decreased these comments considerably. The two boys' behavior was worse. That is, there was an increase in number of unfinished assignments, bothering neighbors, and playing in class. The average inappropriate behavior over four days' observations was 69 percent. The teacher was next instructed to praise prosocial behavior, repeat classroom rules, and continue in the attempt to ignore inappropriate behavior. This combination of procedures was indeed effective in reducing inappropriate behavior, which decreased to an average of 20 percent.

In order to determine if teacher praise was the most effective aspect of the teacher's responses, the teacher was instructed to act as she had in the beginning of the school year in September – that is, according to traditional teacher behavior which is often quite negative. On the same day both boys' inappropriate behavior increased and the average for eight days was 38 percent. Rules, ignoring, and praise were reinstated for the remainder of the school year during which time inappropriate behavior again decreased, averaging only 15 percent in the last 8-week period (Madsen, Becker & Thomas, 1968).

It is interesting to note that many teachers who believe they use more approval than disapproval actually do not. We have found that it is necessary for the teacher to give himself time cues written on the material being taught if he is to be effective in changing his own negative behavior.

In the above study it is observed that ignoring inappropriate behavior is difficult. Actually, if the teacher would have been able to ignore inappropriate behavior completely and teach the class to do the same the boys probably would have improved, for behavior that is not rewarded will finally be extinguished. The next study demonstrated the opposite principle that *any* behavior to which attention is paid may increase. The study occurred when two teachers who were team teaching a first grade class became concerned with children being out of their seats. Of course, the first step in any teaching is to establish what behavioral episodes are actually occurring and in what quantity. In this particular case, this constituted determining how much standing was taking place. If this initial recording is not done the teacher never really knows if the behavior is getting better, worse, or staying the same, especially when changes are gradual. During the initial observation children's standing behaviors were counted during 20 minutes for 12 days. It was observed during this time that teachers told specific children to "sit down" an average of 6.8 times per 20 minutes. Whenever a teacher told a child to sit down, that particular child complied. The average number of children standing was 2.91 per 10-second interval. The teachers were then instructed to tell any child who stood up without good reason to sit down. When the teachers did this (27.5 times per 20 minutes for 10 days) standing actually *increased*. Individual students sat down when told to sit down; however, others stood up and overall more pupils were counted standing (4.07 per 10-second interval). The procedures were reversed; i.e., children were told to sit down only six times per 20-minute period, the same as during the original observation. Standing decreased to approximately the original level, 2.95 per 10-second interval for 10 days.

To demonstrate that teachers' commands were associated with (caused) standing behavior, teachers again told each child who stood up without good reason to sit down (average 28.3 times per 20-minute interval for eight days. Standing up again increased to about the same level as the first time teachers paid attention by telling children to sit down, 3.94 per 10-second interval). At this point vicarious praise and modeling were introduced. Teachers began to praise good sitting. Whenever one child stood up or walked around, the teacher noted a sitting student working diligently and praised the "good" child. Standing decreased (1.89 per 10-second interval). Praise delivered to individuals for sitting and not standing was very effective in controlling the entire class. What teacher has not noticed 30 backs straighten when one child is complimented for sitting up and paying attention? In this study the "good child" was used as a model for the group: "Watch how quietly Susie gets her math counter." "See how nicely Jim writes while sitting," etc. (Madsen, Becker, Thomas, Koser & Plager, 1968).

The teacher may be deceived into believing classroom control is improving. The children actually sit down when told; that is, the short-term effect from the teacher's point of view is effective. The problem occurs in time as the long-term effect of the attention produces a more disruptive learning atmosphere.

Undergraduates As Classroom Therapists[1]

The second major aspect of freeing teachers to teach is demonstrated in behavioral research using so-called "untrained personnel"

[1]This section quotes extensively from a paper entitled "Schoolroom problems and nonprofessional therapists," by Madsen, C. H., Jr., Saudargas, R. A., Hammond, R., Lewy, M., Dockterman, C., Thomas, D. R. & Holtzworth, W. S. Presented at Southeastern Psychological Association, April 1, 1968.

as psychotherapists to teach correct associations. Behavioral investigators have trained *mothers* (Guerney, 1964; Wahler, Winkel, Peterson & Morrison, 1965;, Hawkins, Peterson, Schweid & Bijou, 1966), *housewives* (Rioch, Elkes, Flint, Usdansky, Newman & Sibler, 1963), *teachers* (Becker, Madsen, Arnold & Thomas, 1967; Madsen, Becker & Thomas, 1968), *nursing aides* (Ayllon & Michael, 1959), and *undergraduates* (Reinherz, 1963; Poser, 1966) as individual or group therapists. The results have been uniformly promising. Poser (1966) noted that the undergraduates in his experiment did as well or better than the trained professional staff, (psychiatrists, psychologists, and social workers). He concluded that "Traditional training in the mental health professions may be neither optimal nor even necessary for the promotion of therapeutic behavior change in mental hospital patients."

When we focus on therapy with children we must recognize that a major contradiction of opinion exists between the dynamic versus behavioral positions. Dynamic therapies imply that deviant behavior is maintained by something "intrapsychic" and generally rely on techniques of play therapy (Eissler, 1950; Erickson, 1963; Freud, A., 1946; Klein, 1932). Dynamic therapists specifically contend that rewards and/or praise and affection are rarely found to be useful or necessary methods with children (Allen, 1942; Moustakas & Schlalock, 1955). In sharp contrast, behavior therapists maintain that for an optimal change in behavior to occur, a direct manipulation of environmental contingencies is required (Krasner & Ullmann, 1965). Dynamic therapies do not typically deal with specific behaviors and do not utilize reinforcement contingencies as a matter of course, whereas behavioral positions work with both specific behaviors and reinforcement contingencies as a basic and necessary element of successful therapy.

For schoolroom problems specifically, therapists of all persuasions attempt to alter inappropriate schoolroom behavior either by dealing with nonverbal and verbal behaviors in a (nonschool) therapy situation or through structuring of contingencies within the naturalistic schoolroom setting. Successful transfer manipulations from laboratory to naturalistic settings have achieved many important classroom goals, among which are: emotional responses (reviewed by Paul, 1968), produced information seeking behavior in high school students (Krumboltz & Thoresen, 1964), eliminated school phobias (Kennedy, 1965; Patterson, 1965), decreased inappropriate behavior in nursery school (Holtzworth, 1968), and many more. It can be seen that since behavior therapy is based upon overt behavioral responses, undergraduates can be used to: (1) assess the behavioral deficits in the child's repertoire, (2) specify behaviors which are amendable to change, and (3) specifically program new behaviors incompatible with inappropriate behaviors.

Children used in the study were within normal IQ ranges and selections were made in consultation with teachers on the basis of extreme behavior problems which interfered with learning. Three children each were selected from a kindergarten, a first grade, and two fifth grade rooms. Subjects were referred by teachers and then observed for level of inappropriate behavior by trained observers. The teachers furnished daily schedules, posted classroom rules, and repeated them with the class four–six times per day for two weeks prior to baseline (preliminary) observations.

A general feeling for the behavioral problems evidenced by children who are generally referred for reported studies can be seen from classroom rules developed by teachers to regulate classroom behavior and descriptions of inappropriate behavior. The rules used by teachers during the observation periods for this study precede the pupil descriptions.

Kindergarten: (1) Find work, keep busy. (2) Stay in your own place. (3) Walk. (4) Small voices. (5) Clean up own work first—then help others.

Class demonstration rules: (1) Find a place to sit. (2) Stay in your place. (3) Keep hands in lap with legs crossed.

General: (1) At all times no hitting or shoving. Keep hands to ourselves. (2) No fighting. (3) Act like young ladies and gentlemen.

Cort was loud, blurted out, talked continually, hit others, moved around constantly, grabbed objects, knocked over toys, and refused to obey his teacher.

Henry demanded teacher attention, was distractable, wandered around, refused to obey orders, blurted out, talked loudly, and struck others. Occasionally he was very withdrawn, and refused to do anything.

Mark would suddenly scream and run from the room. He did not stay with the group, verbalized constantly, nagged the teacher, and made his own rules.

First grade: (1) No throwing. (2) No running. (3) No pushing or fighting during group instruction. (4) Stay in seats. (5) Raise hand to talk. (6) No private conversations.

Jerry had a short attention span, talked to his neighbors incessantly, played with work materials during demonstrations and instructions, distracted others, and used unusual seating positions.

Fred vacillated between quietness and severe problems in behavior, would walk around the room in a daze and then suddenly turn, talk to neighbors, and strike other children.

Dave stayed on tasks for very short periods, walked around, ran in class, left the room without permission, talked to others, scooted, crawled, and rolled around the floor, adopted odd and disruptive seating positions, stomped and shuffled feet, slid his desk around, talked to neighbors, burst out loudly, and took equipment belonging to others.

Fifth Grade: (1) Hold up hand to be called on. (2) Only leave seat with permission. (3) No talking or conversations with neighbors. (4) No fighting.

Bruce worked slowly, accomplished little, occupied his time with anything other than school work, copied from others, paid little attention, turned around continually, and talked loudly.

Bert worked fast, spent too much time looking round, walked around the room, talked loudly, copied from a girl next to him, sat in contorted positions, blurted out, and struck other children.

Mike had a hearing difficulty and refused to wear prescribed glasses in school, looked around, often took off shoes, played with small objects, wrote in notebook during discussion, made many disturbing noises (cracked knuckles, banged desk top, slid feet, dropped books, tapped pencil on desk), and ignored all commands.

Fifth Grade: (1) No talking or conversations with neighbors. (2) Raise hand if you need help. (3) Leave seat only with permission.

Tom walked around and talked incessantly, turned around continually, and during assignments spent time on other tasks.

Ray would not work in a group, sat at his seat and played with small items, drew continually in his notebook, walked around and out of the room without permission, and talked incessantly.

Ben was distracted by anything, talked out, turned around, doodled during work, flipped pages of books, stared at other people, walked to other desks during individual study, and made many noises by tapping pencil, crumpling paper, and sliding desk.

Therapy and observations were completed by four advanced undergraduates (psychology and sociology majors) who had worked as observers in other school projects. Each had been trained to observe problem behavior reliably but had no prior experience as therapists. Prior to therapy these undergraduate college students were trained weekly in reinforcement techniques and play therapy in four 2-hour training sessions which included role-playing techniques for three of the four sessions and demonstrations by trained therapists the fourth. After therapy began, training sessions consisted of discussing problems and reviewing recorded tapes of therapy. (It should be noted that this was not a traditional play therapy study. Children not in the behavior therapy group were used as contact and no-contact controls.)

Extrinsic reinforcers were M & M's in the first grade, jelly beans in kindergarten, and donuts and coke in the two fifth grades. For example, in a 15-minute session, 30 jelly beans and/or 30 M & M's were dispensed. Tokens were used in the fifth grades, and one token was worth a small cup of coke (two ounces) or one-eighth donut. Fifteen tokens were given for each 15-minute session. These reinforcers were dispensed contingently for obeying classroom rules and other tasks relating to classroom prosocial behavior.

When therapy began following the initial observations, a double blind procedure was used. That is, each teacher knew that two children were being taken out of her classroom, but she did not know which child was receiving behavior therapy. Observers knew when the conditions changed but did not know which children were in which condition (behavior therapy, contact control, or no-contact control).

The results of the study show that inappropriate behavior for the subjects in the behavior therapy condition decreased by approximately 16 percent. There was also a significant rank order change between conditions. The contact control remained the same and the no-contact control decreased 5 percent. Observational ratings of teachers indicated that the effects of behavior therapy in reducing inappropriate classroom behavior was directly related to the amount of approval for prosocial behavior the teacher gave in the classroom and inversely related to the amount of disapproval for inappropriate behavior. This represents much the same results as described in the sit down study.

It appears that undergraduates with a small investment in training can be used to offer effective behavior therapy for classroom behavior problems. Tape recordings of therapy sessions indicate that student therapists were indeed competent and able to follow directions explicitly. As was expected there were differences between therapists. These differences, however, appeared to be much less important than the teacher's reaction back in the classroom.

The study was extended to include 24 sixth grade boys and girls and 12 separate student therapists during a period of four months with much more complete teacher observational records. (In both studies all therapists gave both types of treatment.) One study took place in Illinois. The later extension was carried out in Florida. The results of the later study were nearly identical with the first (15 percent decrease in inappropriate behavior with a direct relationship between behavioral effectiveness and the teachers' approval to appropriate behavior).

The major conclusion to be drawn from the above series of studies reviewed is that the most important variable controlling the behavior of children in the classroom is the attention of the teacher. Behavior improvement is directly related to the amount of attention given by the teachers to appropriate behavior. The attention and reinforcing aspects of these studies is very important. It appears that if the classroom environment does not reinforce behavior, then whether it is reinforced or not reinforced in another situation (i.e., therapy) is not relevant. The child learns to discriminate between the two and extinguish those responses which are not reinforced. The idea that generalization is possible from therapy to the "real world" without specifically teaching for such transfer is extremely questionable. Observers' comments also support this contention. For example, one child was taught in therapy to raise his hand instead of loudly blurting out. The first day following behavior therapy he raised his hand (50 seconds); when the teacher did not call on him he slowly raised his hand less regularly and waited shorter periods of time (32, 23, 18, 7, and 1 sec.) until he was no longer raising it at all. He then began to "blurt out" again. Unfortunately, this blurting out did receive a response from the teacher! It cannot be overemphasized that attention to inappropriate behavior even in the form of a reprimand may increase the very behavior the teacher thinks is being punished.

Behavioral Management For Teachers

A logical extension based on the conclusions of behavioral research in the schools indicates that the final aspect of freeing teacher to teach should include a series of behavioral workshops for classroom teachers. At the present time workshops are being conducted in a number of school systems in Florida. A complete elementary school also was provided by the Leon County School System, Tallahassee, Florida, where data are being gathered continuously in order to more narrowly define the effect of behavioral principles in teaching and learning. All current teacher training projects demonstrate greater success than when using therapists to treat behavior problems. For example, compared to an average 15 percent decrease in inappropriate behavior resulting from one-to-one therapy with food rewards, teacher training has resulted in an average 25–40 percent decrease without the use of primary rewards in a shorter period of training and contact time. A recent study compared behavior therapy with teacher training in the same classroom with different children over time and also substantiated the same conclusion (Saudargas & Madsen, 1968).

The authors suspect that school counseling and/or therapy for classroom behavior problems are highly ineffective compared to training the classroom teacher. It seems questionable to give individual (or even group) treatment to behavioral problems outside the classroom by professionals or nonprofessionals, when training teachers in a fraction of the time not only benefits the problem children but the entire classroom as well. In addition, unless the behaviors which are reinforced in the contrived situation are also reinforced in the classroom environment, therapy may be totally ineffective. However, it should be stated that therapy outside the classroom may offer a positive contribution when the child does not have appropriate behavioral responses in his repertoire. In this instance, initial responses could be trained in the contrived settings and the teacher trained to reinforce appropriate behaviors when the child comes back in the classroom. With some children it may also be necessary to begin by making the teacher a positively reinforcing agent and/or instituting procedures which include classmates as reinforcing agents. All such procedures as well as other research argue for teacher training programs where the school psychologist serves in a consultative role (Bergen & Caldwell, 1967; Gray, 1963; Leton, 1964; McDaniel & Ahr, 1965; Morice, 1968). Teachers can function very effectively as behavioral managers. Perhaps the psychologist or other behavioral professional could train a large number of "behavioral engineers" with B. A. Degrees who could function under the direction of the psychologist and work directly with teachers. These personnel could be given training in Departments of Psychology and Schools of Education. The inadequacy of the psychological profession to sufficiently staff school systems is apparent (Morice, 1968; Schmidt & Penz, 1964) and teacher training programs would offer a solution to this problem.

It should be evident that teacher training projects need evaluation not only to help determine the best training procedures but also to find who can best do the training. One study attempted to check the effectiveness of a limited exposure of teachers to behavioral training by first year graduate students in psychology. Thirteen volunteer teachers from a rural area of North Florida participated in this classroom management teacher training program. The teachers taught in grades ranging from 1 to 12. Teachers' classroom behaviors were observed by trained observers measuring the frequency of approval, disapproval, and errors in reinforcement. Following the collection of preliminary data, a series of teacher workshops with eight hours of total training was initiated. During this period teachers were instructed in the use and application of behavioral principles in a classroom setting. The workshops included discussion, role-playing, and specific suggestions for the implementation of various techniques (Madsen, Saudargas, Koropsak & Madsen, 1969).

Post workshop observations in the classroom indicated a significant change in teacher behavior. There was an overall increase in the teachers approval following appropriate child behavior, a decrease in their disapproval following negative child behavior, and a decrease in the errors of reinforcement (27 percent overall positive change). A 6-month follow-up (next school year) on 10 teachers indicated further changes in the appropriate direction (2 percent additional overall positive change).

The above study extends a group of studies carried out in classroom management techniques attempting to pinpoint teacher training variables. Previously validated criterion measures involving classroom observations points toward objective measures for evaluation of teacher training workshops. The use of subdoctoral trainees as consultants indicates the effectiveness of using personnel on this level of training.

The favorable teacher training results, however, must not be taken as an indication that the task is simple. We have found that contrary to these teachers who were able to change dramatically following eight hours of training, other teachers have been unable to alter their habitual behavioral patterns even after many hours of in-classroom cueing and role-playing with consultants (Vanderbeck & Madsen, 1968). These teachers were volunteers and very excited about improving their effectiveness through the use of behavioral principles.

While we have never been able to find teacher training supervisors who admit to training prospective teachers to be negative, when results of over 200 teacher observations were analyzed (Madsen & Madsen, 1969) it was surprising to discover that there had been only two teachers who dispensed more approval than disapproval, plus errors upon initial observations. (An error occurs when a teacher responds inappropriately, for example, when attending to deviant behavior.) It should also be noted that many teachers had as much as four months to become accustomed to the observers.

A comparison of five experimental studies indicated that prior to training the average approval ratio (approval over approval plus disapproval plus errors) was 24 percent whereas the average approval ratio for 32 teachers who had a 2-week summer workshop in behavioral techniques averaged 78 percent over a 9-month period (Madsen & Madsen, 1969; Madsen, Madsen, Saudargas, Hammond, Smith & Edgar, 1970).

Substantial experience with a variety of teachers has convinced us that teacher training institutions should modify their curricula to include training in behavior modification. The time for selection, training, and evaluation of prospective teachers should be early in the teacher training curriculum. Behavioral technology is consistently being expanded and now waits upon innovative universities to make use of this technology to solve a severe manpower shortage.

This chapter is not intended to be a comprehensive review of behavioral research in classrooms. Additional current studies being conducted by personnel in school psychology from Florida State University concern the effectiveness of such learning-promoting activities as the use of a game center, early reading experiments, training preintern teachers, applying behavioral principles to curriculum, and so on. Reports of the above will be made elsewhere when specific research projects are completed.

In summary we have presented a selected chronology of behavioral research in the classroom. Initial studies of specific behavior modification were expanded to include research questioning the foundations of traditional therapy in schools. Results of teacher training experiments indicate that many teachers are extremely capable of achieving just about whatever they desire in teaching if principles of (1) *contingency* and (2) *consistency* are used in the application of effective reinforcers (Madsen & Madsen, 1970; 1971).

REFERENCES

Allen, F. H. *Psychotherapy with children*. New York: Norton, 1942.

Ayllon, T. & Michael, J. The psychiatric nurse as a behavioral engineer. *Journal of the Experimental Analysis of Behavior*, 1959, **2**, 323–334.

Becker, W. C., Madsen, C. H., Jr., Arnold, C. R. & Thomas, D. R. The contingent use of teacher attention and praise in reducing classroom problems. *Journal of Special Education*, 1967, **1**, 287–307.

Bergen, J. R. & Caldwell, T. Operant techniques in school psychology. *Psychology in the Schools*, 1967, **4**, 136–141.

Eissler, K. R. Ego-psychological implication of the psychoanalytic treatment of delinquents. *The psychoanalytic study of the child*, 1950, **5**, 97–121.

Erickson, E. H. *Childhood and society*. New York: Norton, 1963.

Freud, A. *The psychoanalytical treatment of children*. New York: International Universities Press, 1946.

Gray, S. W. *The psychologist in the schools*. New York: Holt, Rinehart & Winston, 1963.

Guerney, B., Jr. Filial therapy: Description and rationale. *Journal of Consulting Psychology*, 1964, **28**, 304–310.

Hawkins, R. P., Peterson, R. F., Schweid, E. & Bijou, S. W. Behavior therapy in the home: Amelioration of problem-child relation, with the parent in the therapeutic role. *Journal of Experimental Child Psychology*, 1966, **4**, 79–107.

Holtzworth, W. A. Efforts of selective reinforcement therapy in a miniature situation on nursery school children. Unpublished master's thesis, University of Illinois, 1968.

Kennedy, W. A. School phobia: Rapid treatment of fifty cases. *Journal of Abnormal Psychology*, 1965, **70**, 285–289.

Klein, M. *Psychoanalysis of children*. New York: Norton, 1932.

Krasner, L. & Ullmann, L. P. (Eds.), *Case studies in behavior modification*. New York: Holt, Rinehart & Winston, 1965.

Krumboltz, J. D. & Thoresen, C. E. The effect of behavioral counseling in group and individual settings on information seeking behavior. *Journal of Counseling Psychology*, 1964, **11**, 324–335.

Leton, D. A. School psychology: Its purpose and direction. *Psychology in the Schools*, 1964, **1**, 187–190.

Madsen, C. H., Jr., Becker, W. C. & Thomas, D. R. Rules, praise and ignoring: elements of elementary classroom control. *Journal of Applied Behavior Analysis*, 1968, **1**, 139–150.

Madsen, C. H., Jr., Becker, W. C., Thomas, D. R., Koser, L. & Plager, E. An analysis of the reinforcing functions of 'sit-down' commands. In R. K. Parker (Ed.), *Readings in educational psychology*. New York: Allyn & Bacon, 1968. Pp. 265–278.

Madsen, C. H., Jr. & Madsen, C. K. The extent of negative classroom interaction patterns. Paper presented at the meeting of the Florida Psychological Association, Orlando, May, 1969.

Madsen, C. H., Jr., Saudargas, R. A., Koropsak, E. A. & Madsen, C. K. Changes in classroom behaviors of teachers as a function of behavior modification training. Paper presented at the meeting of the Southeastern Psychological Association, New Orleans, February, 1969.

Madsen, C. H., Jr. & Madsen, C. K. *Teaching/Discipline: Behavioral Principles Toward a Positive Approach*. Boston: Allyn & Bacon, 1970.

Madsen, C. K. & Madsen, C. H., Jr. *Children/Discipline: A positive approach for parents*. Boston: Allyn & Bacon, 1971.

Madsen, C. H., Jr., Madsen, C. K., Saudargas, R. A., Hammond, W. R., Smith, J. B. & Edgar, D. E. Classroom RAID (Rules, Approval, Ignore and Disapproval) A Cooperative Approach for professionals and volunteers. *Journal of School Psychology*, 1970, **8**, 180–185.

McDaniel, L. J. & Ahr, E. The school psychologist as a resource person initiating and conducting inservice teacher education. *Psychology in the Schools*, 1965, **2**, 220–224.

Morice, H. O. The school psychologist as a behavioral consultant: A project in behavior modification in a public school setting. *Psychology in the Schools*, 1968, **5**, 253–261.

Moustakas, C. E. & Schlalock, H. D. An analysis of therapist-child interaction in play therapy. *Child Development*, 1955, **26**, 137–143.

Patterson, G. R. A learning theory approach to the treatment of the school phobic child. In L. P. Ullmann & L. Krasner, (Eds.), *Cast studies in behavior modification*. New York: Holt, Rinehart & Winston, 1965, Pp. 279–285.

Paul, G. L. Outcome of systematic desensitization. In C. M. Franks (Ed.), *Assessment and status of the behavior therapies and associated developments*. New York: McGraw-Hill, 1968.

Poser, E. C. The effect of therapists training on group therapeutic out-come. *Journal of Consulting Psychology*. 1966, **30**, 283–289.

Reinherz, H. College student volunteers as case aides in a state hospital for children. *American Journal of Orthopsychiatry*. 1963, **33**, 544–546.

Rioch, M. J., Elkes, C., Flint, A. A., Usdansky, B. S., Newman R. G. & Sibler, E. National Institute of Mental Health pilot study in training mental health counselors. *American Journal of Orthopsychiatry*, 1963, **33**, 678–689.

Saudargas, R. A. & Madsen, C. H., Jr. Individual behavior modification vs. classroom teacher attention in reducing inappropriate classroom behaviors. Presented at the meeting of the Florida Psychological Association, Clearwater, May, 1968.

Schmidt, K. M. & Penz, F. The psychologist as a consultant in the schools. *Psychology in the Schools*, 1964, **1**, 419–425.

Vanderbeck, D. H. & Madsen, C. H., Jr. An examination of the differential effects of positive and negative teacher attention on classroom behavior. Unpublished mimeograph. Florida State University, 1968.

Wahler, R. J., Winkel, G. H., Peterson, R. E. & Morrison, D. C. Mothers as behavior therapists for their own children. *Behaviour Research and Therapy*, 1965, **3**, 113–124.

SECTION III

Enriched Environmental Programs for the Emotionally Disturbed Child

Institutional programs for emotionally disturbed children have existed for many years. It is generally agreed, however, that in the past the focus has been too frequently upon specific psychotherapy administered by professionals (when such was available) and too infrequently upon the potential for learning available in the controlled institutional situation. The programs reviewed in this section, by contrast, view the school or camp environment as an opportunity for rich, varied learning experiences. The counselors and teachers who are in direct contact with the children are viewed as the important therapeutic agents of change. Program direction and sustained consultative service are provided by mental health professionals, but traditional psychotherapy is not practiced. It is presumed that the child can acquire skills and socially adaptive behaviors through reinforced learning trials which will permit him to readjust in the home situation. The program "Behavior Modification in a Therapeutic Summer Camp" (Rickard and Dinoff) is designed to provide mildly disturbed children a controlled summer experience in adaptive group functioning and cooperation, an area in which most of the youngsters show marked deficits. "Project Re-ED: The Program and a Preliminary Evaluation" (Lewis) avoids conventional mental health terminology almost entirely preferring instead to view both the learning of social responses and academic skills as a process of reeducation. Both programs emphasize the importance of learning within the framework of relationships — the peer group and the counselor-teachers with whom the children are in contact. The chapter by Haring, "Experimental Education: Application of Experimental Analysis and Principles of Behavior to Classroom Instruction", focuses much more specifically upon experimental control of the educational process. The chapter contains valuable information concerning the details of a classroom program based upon the operant paradigm.

CHAPTER 5

Project Re-ED: The Program and a Preliminary Evaluation

Wilbert W. Lewis

During the past decade we have witnessed an unprecedented interest in innovative programs for children designated as emotionally disturbed or mentally ill. The motivation for these programs is twofold: (1) increasing recognition of the gap between the number of children who need special help for behavior problems and the availability of mental health specialists to provide that help through conventional programs (Albee, 1959), and (2) increasing concern regarding the efficacy of traditional patterns of treatment through child guidance clinics and psychiatrically oriented residential treatment facilities (Lewis, 1965).

Project Re-ED is an attempt to construct a new mental health role and, in addition, a new institutional context for the implementation of that role (Hobbs, 1965). The role is that of an educator, broadly construed, working toward the attainment of limited, carefully defined goals related to increasing the social competence of emotionally disturbed children. The institutional context is a residential school that keeps its program and the goals it sets for children carefully articulated with the natural habitat of each child it serves. During the initial stage, Re-ED was an 8-year demonstration, training, and research venture jointly sponsored by George Peabody College and the States of Tennessee and North Carolina. Each State, through its Department of Mental Health, provided a small residential school for emotionally disturbed children and Peabody College provided general coordination, a training program for the staff of the schools, and a research program to evaluate the effectiveness of the demonstration. A grant from the National Institute of Mental Health helped support the project from 1961 until 1968 when the two States assumed complete operational and fiscal responsibility for the schools. Some of the early momentum for Project Re-ED came from a study of resources for mental health training and research conducted in 1954 by the Southern Regional

Education Board and the National Institute of Mental Health. The study highlighted the problem of inadequate services for emotionally disturbed children, particularly residential treatment facilities. There were virtually no such facilities in the region and when a child's problems became so grave that the community was compelled to find residential placement for him, it was likely to be grossly inappropriate, a detention home for delinquent children or an adult ward in a psychiatric hospital, for example.

During that same period of time, Nicholas Hobbs, the Principal Investigator for Project Re-ED, had been studying the institutional patterns of caring for emotionally disturbed children in Europe. Well-established residential programs in Scotland and France suggested what has now become the staffing pattern in Re-ED schools. One residential treatment center for emotionally disturbed children near Glasgow, in Scotland, is staffed by workers called educational psychologists. They are teachers who are given on-the-job training and who are responsible for around-the-clock therapeutic care of disturbed children. A similar staffing pattern was observed in France in residential programs for several kinds of exceptional children which are staffed by personnel called *educateurs*, a professional group with relatively little formal education but extensive on-the-job training in pedagogy, group dynamics, psychodynamics, and other skills required in a total therapeutic program for children.

The four essential elements that seemed transposable to residential care for children in this country were: (1) staffing by persons requiring less extensive professional preparation than for the mental health disciplines, (2) careful selection of workers on the basis of individual qualities indicating potential for effective work with children, (3) a residential setting in which the program for small groups of children is in the hands of these personnel, and (4) consultation by mental health specialists.

Project Re-ED was initiated in September 1961 with a 9-month training program at Peabody College for 13 carefully selected elementary teachers. The teachers were selected on the basis of unusual teaching competence, as judged by their supervisors and colleagues, adaptability and creativity in the teaching techniques they used, and an interest in the education of emotionally disturbed children. The training program for the first group of teachers, later called teacher-counselors, consisted of two academic quarters of graduate work followed by a 3-month internship in an established residential school for emotionally disturbed children including some placements in England and Scotland.

During the school year of 1962–1963, Cumberland House

Elementary School in Tennessee and Wright School in North Carolina began to operate on a limited basis, staffed by the group of teachers who had gone through the first year's training program. The training program at Peabody has continued to supplement the staff of both schools as vacancies have occurred and as the program has expanded. Each school is organized into groups of eight children who live and attend school together and who are the responsibility of two teacher-counselors. The average length of enrollment is six to seven months. The pattern that has been followed in both schools is a 5-day-a-week residential program, with children returning to their own homes on the weekends. The two teacher-counselors are responsible for designing and carrying out an intensive treatment program for each child based on his needs, and presenting problems and the common objectives shared by the child's family, the referring mental health agency, and the Re-ED school.

The demonstration is directed toward the development of a total educational milieu for troubled children. Traditional residential treatment centers provide a few hours each week with highly skilled and highly paid professional personnel interspersed among long periods of inactivity and idleness. They also tend to isolate the child from his natural environment—family, school, and friends—to which he must eventually return. The Re-ED staffing pattern is intended to address itself to both of these problems—first, to provide an engaging, goal-oriented educational climate during all of a child's waking hours and second, to keep him related to his own child-rearing systems by weekends at home and by careful liaison work that prepares the way for his return following a brief stay at the Re-ED school.

An Overview of the Program

The Re-ED schools emphasize the educational quality of their program in designation of roles—teacher, student, principal; in designation of activities—enrollment, recess, student council; and in designation of limited goals which lend themselves to direct teaching. The language of mental hospitals and clinics is intentionally avoided. This does not represent a denial of shared responsibility with the mental health professions. It represents, rather, an assessment of the potency of teachers and educational processes in the socialization of children, "disturbed" as well as "normal." While the staff of the schools are as comfortable in dealing with an outburst of negative feeling as with a problem in remedial reading, they prefer to define their role as educational rather than therapeutic.

The reason for making this distinction is the emphasis in the Re-ED program on short-term, specific goals toward which the individual child and his teacher-counselors work. There is no use of psychotherapeutic treatment for intrapsychic problems that characterizes many programs. With deep-seated emotional problems, psychotherapy may be necessary but it is a long and expensive route and may not be required with the less complex behavior and learning problems for which many children are referred to treatment agencies. The Re-ED demonstration has been exploring the extent to which direct educational programming can be effective in modifying relationships between children identified as emotionally disturbed and their families, schools, and communities.

The Re-ED treatment pattern assumes a basic validity in the traditional child-rearing arrangements in our culture, that they are on the whole effective and wholesome for a child's development. We refer to the primary groups responsible for a child's socialization as his "ecological unit." When there is a disruption of child-rearing functions and the child is identified as emotionally disturbed, it is looked upon as a disturbance within the ecological unit to which that child belongs rather than within the child himself. If the disruption is not completely enervating, the relief provided by a fairly rapid shift in symptoms or in demands on the child may allow the ecological unit to recover its potential for change and continue the socialization process relatively unaided. With this hypothesis in mind, goals are set for children at the Re-ED schools emphasizing reading skills, learning to tolerate sitting in a classroom for extended periods of time, trusting adults, and living with peers with a minimum of conflict. There is an effort to approach a child's behavior at an overt, symptomatic level and to see in what specific ways his behavior creates conflicts with the ecological unit of which he is a member. Then an attempt is made to construct a sequence of learning experiences that will influence, quite directly, the areas of concern in the child's behavior and responses to him by important people in his life.

The process begins with a referring agency – child guidance clinic, family service agency, school, or other community agency involved in the identification or treatment of emotional disturbance in children. A Re-ED school is not seen as a sufficient or autonomous treatment facility but as a resource for agencies in the community already working with children. In most cases an agency referring a child to a Re-ED school will continue to work with the parents while the child is enrolled in the school. The admission conference between the referring agency and the Re-ED school reviews the history of the child's problem, any treatment of the problem that has been attempted, and the current status of the child, his family, and school. Preliminary treatment goals are established at the admission conference, with an emphasis on specific changes that can be made rather quickly in the child's behavior or in his ecological unit within the realistic limits imposed by the intent to return him to his home quickly. Planning for the child's return, including additional community resources that need to be mobilized, is initiated at the admission conference and is an integral part of the treatment pattern. These plans remain flexible to allow for the unpredictable in human and institutional behavior and the thrust is forward, anticipating future behavior rather than explaining past events. There has been a gradually diminishing concern with the kind and degree of pathology in making the decision to enroll a particular child. When the schools were first opened, admission decisions reflected use of exclusion criteria like severe psychosis, brain injury, and mental retardation. As the confidence and skill of the staff have grown, the admission decisions have been based on a judgment that a child and his ecological unit can respond in specified ways to the group-centered educational program and mobilization of community resources. This attitude has resulted, of course, in the admission of children with a wide range of diagnostic labels although each child has some unique strengths that can be exploited.

Following the admission conference, the child is assigned to a particular group and the specific preparation for his enrollment begins. He visits the school with his parents and meets the children and teacher-counselors with whom he will be living for the next few months. The teacher-counselors begin to outline a specific program of remedial education and social living experiences, based on their analysis of the details in the clinical and educational records on the child. In addition, they prepare the other children in the group for the coming of the new child so that on the day of his enrollment he will be received warmly, on the basis of realistic expectations including what-ever problem behavior he is likely to present to the group.

The school day typically begins about 9:00 a.m., proceeds until noon with time out for a recess period and resumes after lunch until about 3:00 p.m. when the recreation period begins. The school day is heavily loaded with instruction in basic academic skills, reading, arith-metic, and use of language. Since the placement of children in groups is based more on social maturity than educational development, much of the academic instruction is related to skills that will have maximum utility for a particular child. However, units of instruction that will support heterogeneous educational abilities such as preparing for a field trip to the Smoky Mountains National Park are also a vital part of the school curriculum.

The nonacademic part of the school day also emphasizes competence that has social currency for elementary school age children but which, for some reason, has not been developed. The ability to kick a football, for example, or to roller skate, swim, or ride a bicycle may have a social utility as great as arithmetic skills in a child's reintegration into his normal school and home environment. Thus a program of planned instruction, reflecting an assessment of a child's need for socially adaptive skills, is extended beyond the bounds of the usual school day. This is true also of the evening program which emphasizes competence in living harmoniously with a group of peers and the adults to whom a child is responsible. It is one of the important strengths of the Re-ED staffing pattern that the afternoon and evening hours including the routine tasks of eating, dressing, and getting ready for bed are supervised by sensitive, competent adults. It is a time that is rich in opportunities for a child to learn skills in social living and to explore personal feelings. The way an adult responds to his refusal to eat or to go to bed or his strong impulse to hurt another child can make an important contribution to the child's social and emotional development. Each child's progress toward his goals is reviewed periodically, along with the progress being made in planning with his family, school, and community resources. As soon as a judgment is made that the child is functioning just well enough and/or his ecological unit is changing its tolerance thresholds and opportunities enough to support his behavior with a reasonable prognosis for his continued healthy development, plans will be made to return him to his own home and school. During this time the teacher-counselors become much more active in working with the child's parents and regular teacher. The Re-ED staff, the referring agency, the child's family, his school, and the child himself are all actively involved in planning the return.

Selection and Training of Staff

Central to the purpose of Project Re-ED is the development of a new professional role identity, the teacher-counselor. The teacher-counselor is an educator whose role definition has been radically expanded from that of a classroom teacher. He is, of course, first a classroom teacher with skills in teaching basic school subjects to elementary-age children. He is also a counselor, recreation supervisor, camper, parent surrogate, and general handyman. In addition to the multiple skills required for working effectively with children in a total educational milieu, he must be conversant with the language of the mental health specialists who refer children to the school and to whom he turns for consultation.

The teacher-counselor role is an attempt to provide one model that may ease the acute shortage of highly specialized mental health professionals. Our intention is to recruit successful young public school teachers, provide them with a brief but rigorous training program, and give them support from mental health professionals as they move into positions of responsibility in Re-ED schools. This plan of induction into a professional role has several advantages over training in the mental health professions. The first, obviously, is time; less than one year of graduate study is required. The shorter time in training is possible because the teachers selected for the program have already demonstrated competence with children in a public school classroom. The second advantage is that the experience these teachers have had in regular classrooms allows a realistic estimate of their capabilities that is based on actual work with children. It is an attempt to take advantage of the natural variation in behavior among teachers and to bring into a training program persons who have demonstrated empathy with children's problems, creativity in approaching human relationships, and so on, rather than depending on the development of these characteristics in a training program. A third advantage is in the efficient utilization of mental health professionals in training and consultation. The year of formal training launches the teacher-counselor on a course of experiences that brings him much later to mature, well-rounded professional competence in planning a total educational program for disturbed children. A key ingredient in their professional growth is the availability of frequent consultation from specialists in mental health and education.

The training for teacher-counselors consists of one academic year of course work and practicum that leads to a master of arts degree in special education with emphasis in the area of emotional disturbance. The program of study presumes an acquaintance with educational procedures for normal children and builds upon this background. Course work introduces students to concepts and procedures used by the mental health professions in working with emotionally disturbed children, educational procedures currently being used in school programs for emotionally disturbed children, and milieu treatment techniques used in residential settings. In addition to the courses that are aimed specifically at work with emotionally disturbed children, students take courses in remedial reading, clinical-educational diagnosis of learning difficulties, and techniques of counseling.

Each student is also engaged in a practicum throughout the academic year. The practicum emphasizes three kinds of experiences: (1) clinical education with individual children, (2) small group teaching, and (3) liaison work with families, schools, and community agencies. The practicum is centered in the program at Cumberland House, the

Re-ED demonstration school in Nashville. Each student has opportunities for observation and increasingly responsible participation in all parts of the program. While the work of the school does not depend upon students in training, all assignments are intended to provide a real service as well as an opportunity for the student to learn to do effective educational planning for disturbed children. The assignments vary with the needs of the student, but may include tutoring a child who is nearing the end of his stay, developing a remedial reading program for a nonreader, providing an enrichment program for a group of children in music, art, science, etc., or working as an assistant to a teacher-counselor or liaison-teacher.

The Staffing Pattern

There are three roles which in combination provide the unique operational pattern in a Project Re-ED school as it attempts to influence not only the behavior of a child, but the primary socializing systems in the ecological unit to which the child will return. These roles are: (1) teacher-counselor, (2) liaison-teacher, and (3) consultant.

The Teacher-Counselor Role

It will already be quite clear that the success of a Re-ED school is highly correlated with the success of individual teacher-counselors in planning and carrying on effective programs for children. Two teacher-counselors work as a team with a group of eight children, setting goals, planning daily programs, evaluating progress, and articulating their efforts with the plans for parents, home schools, and community agencies. In consonance with the objective of helping smooth the child's return to his home, school, and community, the teacher-counselors' initial goal-setting reflects an analysis of the locus of discordance which in the past has created problems and which needs to be given priority in the goals set for a child. Since most of the children referred have a history of academic difficulties, goals involving school achievement are likely to be given prominence and can be formulated quite specifically. Problems related to social responses or emotional reactivity are likely to be stated in more general terms at the time a child is admitted to the school and sometimes may require a period of observation by the teacher-counselor before particular goals can be formulated. There is a continuous application of two criteria: (1) goals must be articulated with goals for the social milieu to which the child will return, and (2) goals must be feasible in a program of brief educational treatment.

The program planned for a group of children by the two teacher-counselors reflects both individual goals and group process goals. The work toward individual goals takes place largely in the context of group interaction. Most children referred for residential treatment need to learn new techniques for relating to peers and to important adults in their lives. Planning for an overnight camping trip, a car-wash to earn extra money, or the building of a tree house provides a task orientation around which conflicts occur and problem-solving processes evolve. The teacher-counselors engage in a constant cycle of planning, carrying out plans, and evaluating results in giving direction to the group process as well as to the achievement of goals for individual children.

Two slightly different roles have emerged for the two teacher-counselors working with a group of children in a Re-ED school. Although both have come from an educational background and have received similar training, one works with the group during the day primarily in the classroom, and emphasizes the formal teaching aspects of the role. The other works with the group after school and during the evening, and emphasizes the informal counseling, group-work aspects of the role. They meet together each day to review goals and day-to-day planning in an attempt to maintain maximum consistency in the educational milieu for each child during his waking hours.

The Liaison-Teacher Role

The liaison-teacher has the same background of experience and training as the teacher-counselor; many are former teacher-counselors. His responsibility is to coordinate all aspects of the program for a child enrolled in a Re-ED school. Initially, this involves development of referral information with an agency or clinic and planning with the agency, family, and regular school for the child's enrollment. The total plan will involve four aspects: (1) the work of the teacher-counselors with the child, (2) the work of the referring agency with the child's parents, (3) the work of the liaison-teacher with the child's regular school, and (4) with any special community resources that need to be developed for a particular child, such as remedial tutoring, YMCA membership, a part-time job, etc. The total plan is cast in broad outline before a child is enrolled and is monitored and modified if necessary by the liaison-teacher. It is the liaison-teacher's responsibility to be especially sensitive to changes in the ecological unit and to articulate the several efforts as they interact in developing a mutually positive relationship between the child and the environment to which he will return.

The liaison-teacher makes a special investment in planning successful school experiences for a child. Initially, before enrollment in a Re-ED school, he makes a careful appraisal of the sources of discordance between a child and his school, ranging from specific reading disabilities to mannerisms that annoy his teacher or peers. This appraisal receives careful consideration in setting goals for the child. During the time the child is enrolled in the Re-ED school, the liaison-teacher maintains contact with the home school through conferences with teachers, the approximation of assignments where possible, exchange of letters with classmates, etc. As the planning for his return gets under way, the liaison-teacher discusses with the home school teacher the remedial techniques that have been used and any special management problems that may be anticipated. Following the child's return the liaison-teacher helps ease the transition by maintaining regular contact as an educational consultant to the classroom teacher.

The Consultant Role

The mental health specialist in the Re-ED schools functions as a consultant. One of the general aims of the project is to develop more efficient use of the available supply of psychiatrists, psychologists, and social workers. In line with this aim, the Re-ED schools use only educators in direct service roles with children; mental health specialists serve in consulting roles. After experimenting with a variety of consultation patterns, three have emerged as ways of integrating the body of knowledge of the mental health professions into the operational pattern of a residential school. First, consultants are used to help evaluate existing clinical records on a child before he is enrolled. Second, many kinds of specialists are on call to meet with teacher-counselors on unusual problems; these are not only mental health professionals but specialists in pediatrics, physical education, social group work, elementary education, etc. Third, the regular program consultant meets at least once a week with the two teacher-counselors to help evaluate goals and techniques for individual children. The consultant comes to each session with his background of professional skills and with specific knowledge of the child being discussed but with no authority to make decisions in program planning. Decisions are made by the two teacher-counselors and are clearly defined as working hypotheses to be tested in the program and continued or discarded on the basis of feedback from a child's behavior. The relatively heavy investment in consulting time is intended not only to provide teacher-counselors with whatever help they need in solving problems of the moment but to provide a learning experience that will allow teacher-counselors to develop into behavior specialists in their own right.

Intervention in Social Systems

The initial impetus for Project Re-ED came from a desire to create a staffing pattern that would substitute for the more expensive traditional patterns of treatment for emotionally disturbed children. In choosing to use educational personnel and techniques, we made an explicit choice not to use the psychotherapeutic model but to evolve our own conceptual framework from experience with the new staffing pattern. We were obliged to limit ourselves to specific goals relevant to a child's natural environment that could be achieved in a short-term program relying on direct teaching and on an educational milieu. The more conventional treatment programs do not always aspire to complete "cure" of a child's problems, but they do tend to set ambitious goals with respect to the development of new response patterns. They also tend to accept more or less total responsibility for modification of a child's behavior to allow him to cope with most of the stresses he might encounter as he moves back to his natural environment.

The emphasis on specific, short-term goals in the Re-ED schools has led to a different way of thinking about emotional disturbance. We began with the premise that the identification of a child as "emotionally disturbed" reflects a state of discordance between that child and the primary agents of his socialization, rather than a psychological condition within the child. It is a judgment that the normal process of socialization has been interrupted.

The natural ecology for any child includes at least his immediate family, his public school, and his habitual peer group relationships. For some children, the ecological unit would also include church groups, the family of a close friend or relative, special interest groups, or a treatment relationship with a mental health facility. Definition of membership in the ecological unit for any particular child is unique, depending on the degree to which a participant effectively imposes obligations and evaluations on a child. In our culture, a child's family and school do so. To the extent that other individuals and groups also do so at any stage in his socialization, they are at that time a part of his ecological unit. In this view, discordant behavior is seen in the context of a transaction between a child and the small social systems responsible for his socialization, that has resulted in a discrepancy between the child's competence and the evaluation of that competence relative to standards set for his performance. A child's task in the socialization process is to learn the valued attitudes and behaviors in his own ecological unit. Most children do. Those who do not, or who do not seem to be making reasonable progress toward the desired behaviors, may be identified as emotionally disturbed. Operationally, this takes place when a parent's assessment of the discrepancy between expectations and behavior is so great that home remedies are no longer sufficient and assistance is required from professional child-socialization agencies in the community.

A treatment program that implements this way of thinking about children's problems makes an ecological, rather than psychological, diagnosis by identifying specific points of discordance in transactions between the child and the other members of his systems. These points are located by statements of participants that indicate departure of behavior from expectations in highly valued role performances: "He's too bossy"; "He won't try to read"; etc. The cumulative discrepancies that get a child labeled as emotionally disturbed may be reduced either by increasing the child's competence in specific ways or by helping other members of his ecological unit modify their expectations and provide different opportunities for him. In a Re-ED treatment plan a combination of both strategies is employed with the expectation that minor shifts in several components can restore balance and capacity for continued development in the whole ecological unit. The objective is to enhance the social stimulus value of the child for those who will continue to evaluate and guide his socialization. The child learns to read a little better, stops picking on younger children in the neighborhood, and develops his natural skills in athletic games. The school provides a special tutoring program, the father moves to a job that allows him more time at home, and the mother learns to accept less than perfect grades in school. None of these changes is dramatic, and there is little emphasis on the objectives valued in most psychotherapeutic programs, but limited gains may get the child and his socializing systems above threshold for a mutually rewarding, growth-facilitating relationship.

The Re-ED Children

It may be helpful at this point to give some impressions of what Re-ED students are like from data on the first 250 children admitted to the two demonstration schools. The children range in age from 6 to 12 with a mean age of about 10.5 years. Diagnoses by referring agencies encompass the spectrum but the designation most frequently given is "adjustment reaction of childhood." Brain damage is mentioned as a contributing factor in about one-fourth of the cases, schizophrenia or schizophrenic processes for about one-eighth. Almost all Re-ED students have had problems learning in school, as well as behavior problems. By a criterion of administrative action, including retention, expulsion, or placement in a special class, three-fourths of the children had been identified as school problems by the time they were enrolled in the Re-ED school. On standardized achievement tests, the average Re-ED child is one and one-half years below his expected achievement level. Between 85 and 90 percent are functioning below grade level in both arithmetic and reading.

Measured intelligence and family socioeconomic level of the children approximate the population at large. Average I Q is about 100, and lower middle class is the median socioeconomic status classification, with a wide range of family income and living circumstances represented in the group. The children are atypical with respect to race and sex — most are white males — and with respect to stability of family organization — almost one-half do not now live with both natural parents, and a majority of these children have experienced more than one change of parent figures in their families. These descriptive statistics suggest what some readers might feel is self-evident, that the Re-ED schools serve a population of children similar to that served by community child guidance clinics, with some weighting toward the "more disturbed" end of the continuum of behavior problems. This observation is supported by the history that Re-ED children already have with mental health agencies at the time of their enrollment. The family of the typical child has made initial contact with a treatment facility at least two years prior to his enrollment and has been seen in at least two different agencies during that time, in addition to the agency referring the child to the Re-ED school.

Evaluation Methodology

Because of the ecological bias in appraising children's problems, in establishing goals and developing programs of reeducation, the data gathered to help evaluate the effectiveness of Re-ED schools lean heavily on perceptions of the child by those who are his natural evaluators, his parents and teachers. They are asked to describe him during the application process — before he is enrolled in the Re-ED school — on checklists, rating scales, and open-ended questions. They describe his behavior again after he has returned home from the Re-ED school and still again after he has been home for more than a year. These periodic assessments are aimed at plotting changes in the valence of the child for those who know him best and whose judgments about the adequacy of his performance are most potent. This emphasis in evaluation is based on the assumption that a more positive appraisal of a child's performance is essential to a reinstatement of mutually rewarding relationships that have been blocked during the time he was seen as "emotionally disturbed." In fact, from an ecological point of view, the discordant relationships *are* the problem rather than symptoms of the problem.

While the evaluation procedures give prominence to the social stimulus value of the child, we do not eschew more customary, sometimes more objective data regarding his progress. Achievement tests, teachers' grades, promotions, assessments by teacher-counselors at the Re-ED school and by staff members of the referring agency, and self-reports by the child are all included in an attempt to obtain a balanced appraisal of a child's progress following his experience in a Re-ED school. This chapter, however, will report only findings from the child's natural evaluators before and after residence in the treatment program.

To the extent that it is possible, data used in evaluation are collected as a part of service routines. Several rating scales are included in the application forms filled out by the child's parents and teacher as a part of the enrollment routine. This practice increases the likelihood that pre-enrollment, postdischarge, and follow-up information on each child will be available for later analysis. Specifically, the timing of data collection is: pre-enrollment information is obtained during the application process, usually within a few weeks of admission—first follow-up information about six months after discharge. Since the average length of stay is about seven months, the average time spanned between enrollment and first follow-up is a little more than one year. Another follow-up about two years after enrollment is in process but will not be reported here.

Results[1]

Before reporting the changes in perception of children over a period of time, it may be of interest to look at a single, global rating made by several persons of each child's progress soon after he leaves. Each child's mother, father, and the worker from his referring agency were asked to assess his behavior on a 5-point scale ranging from "worse" to "greatly improved." Each person, of course, was well acquainted with the child at the time of his enrollment, had followed his

---

[1]The data reported in this section have been collected and analyzed under the direction of Laura Weinstein, Ph.D. The results are based on information from both Re-ED schools. Tables in this chapter were prepared by Dr. Weinstein for a more detailed report in *Exceptional Children* (Weinstein, 1969).

progress with great interest, and was in a position to make a subjective, but well-informed judgment about changes in his behavior during and after the Re-ED experience. Table 1 is based on these global ratings.

TABLE 1
Ratings of Change of Child
Percent of Children Rated Moderately or Greatly
Improved

Rater	Wright School		CHES[a]	
	N	%	N	%
Mother	43	86%	92	80%
Father	29	76%	69	78%
Referring Agency	37	73%	43	89%

[a]Cumberland House Elementary School.

By combining the two most favorable categories, "moderately improved" and "greatly improved," one may arrive at an approximate index of the success of treatment as seen by these three interested observers. The three judgments prove to be consistent and quite positive for children from both schools, more than three-fourths being seen as moderately or greatly improved. In order that these favorable opinions of Re-ED children not be construed as a temporary "honeymoon" phenomenon, it should also be reported that a similar rating was obtained 20 months after discharge from mothers of 53 other Re-ED children and that 85 percent of these mothers felt that their children continued to be moderately improved or greatly improved from the time of enrollment.

Another general index of the effectiveness of a program for disturbed children is the ability of the children to remain in ordinary home and public school placements following treatment. Table 2 shows the placement of Re-ED children at the time of the first follow-up, about one year after they were enrolled in the Re-ED program. At enrollment, of course, many of the children were in danger of being expelled from their public schools and, had it been available, long-term residential treatment, or in some cases, placement in correctional institutions, would have been deemed appropriate. It is significant, therefore, that most of the Re-ED children, almost 90 percent, returned to their own homes and regular public school classrooms and continued to maintain themselves there six months later.

The periodic ratings, in the form of scales which summarize numerous judgments of discrete but related behaviors, reflect a similar

TABLE 2
Placement of Re-ED Children at First Follow-up

	Wright School ($N = 64$)	CHES ($N = 127$)
Residential treatment center	6	2
At home[a], but not enrolled in school	2	1
Correctional institution	0	3
At home[a], and in school, but in a special class	4	4
At home[a], and in school, in a regular class	52	117

[a]"Home" includes home substitutes such as orphanages, homes for dependent children, foster homes.

improvement in children's adjustment at home and at school. Table 3 reports the changes in parents' ratings at both schools from enrollment follow-up. The symptom checklist is a list of 36 behaviors often ascribed to emotionally disturbed children such as "thumb-sucking," "bed-wetting," "stealing," "running away," etc. Each parent is asked to indicate the frequency of each behavior, on a 4-point scale, during the preceding two weeks. The weighted score for each parent is intended to reflect both the number of current problems and their intensity. The means show a significant reduction in number and intensity of symptoms seen by both parents between enrollment and six months after discharge.

TABLE 3
The Parent Rating Scales
Change in the Child between Enrollment and First Follow-up

Rating Scale	Rater	Wright School				CHES			
		N	Enr	F#1	t	N	Enr	F#1	t
Symptom Checklist	Mother	29	34.4	21.7	4.75*	73	41.0	27.9	6.98**
	Father	24	27.6	20.7	2.32*	55	35.6	22.7	7.06**
Social Maturity	Mother	30	23.8	28.0	6.47**	71	22.4	27.1	10.05**
	Father	24	23.7	26.7	3.60**	53	22.3	25.9	7.03**
Semantic Differential Discrepancy	Mother	20	141.9	91.2	3.11**	65	138.6	95.1	4.78**
	Father	18	103.1	70.8	2.43*	42	125.3	71.7	6.45**

*Significant at 0.05 level, two-tailed test.
**Significant at 0.01 level or beyond, two-tailed test.

The social maturity scale is a brief adaptation of the Vineland Social Maturity Scale, in checklist form. Each parent is asked to respond "yes" or "no" to items like: "Washes hands before meals"; "Makes change properly"; "Makes telephone calls on his own"; etc. There is no attempt to establish any absolute level of social competence with these items, only to determine whether the child is developing greater responsibility in the eyes of his parents with respect to tasks usually performed by elementary school age children. The changes in mean scores reported in Table 3 show significant increments in social maturity, as judged by both parents, from enrollment to six months after discharge.

The semantic differential discrepancy, also reported in Table 3, is intended to provide a measure of disparity between a parent's aspiration for a child's behavior and his perception of the child's actual performance. A 6-point scale is used with each of 19 bipolar adjectives such as: "happy . . . sad," "tense . . . relaxed," "adventurous . . . timid," etc. The parents are asked to make two ratings for each of the 19 items, one describing the child's present behavior and the other describing their expectation of his behavior. The squared discrepancies are cumulated over the 19 items to obtain a score for each parent. There was a significant reduction in this discrepancy for both parents between enrollment and 6 months after discharge indicating that the children's behavior much more closely approximated parental expectations.

Analyses from a second follow-up two years after enrollment will be reported when larger numbers of children having all three sets of ratings are available. Preliminary analyses on small numbers suggest that parent ratings will continue to reflect improvement not only from enrollment to first follow-up, but also from first to second follow-up.

Additional analyses comparing enrollment ratings of the two parents indicated statistically significant differences between them on the symptom checklist and on the semantic differential discrepancy scales, with mothers indicating greater dissatisfaction with the child's behavior on both. Mothers also indicated greater improvement after Re-ED with the result that ratings by the two parents after Re-ED were more alike than they had been earlier.

Change in school adjustment over a similar period of time, enrollment to six months after discharge, is presented in Table 4. The student role behavior scale is a set of 27 questions, such as: "Is the child willing to come to school?"; "Does he usually listen well enough to understand directions?"; "Is he very careless or lazy about his work?"; etc., reflecting general expectations teachers have of elementary school children. Ratings were made by teachers in the child's regular home school. Their responses to this scale indicated significant improvement

TABLE 4
Teacher Ratings
Change in the Child between Enrollment and First Follow-up

Scale		Wright School				CHES		
	N	Enr	F#1	t	N	Enr	F#1	t
1. Role Behavior	39	12.6	17.4	4.57**	77	13.9	19.1	7.08**
2. Disruptiveness	39	1.6	1.3	3.02**	77	1.7	1.2	7.35**
3. Feelings of personal distress	36	2.3	1.8	3.08**	76	2.2	1.6	6.11**
4. Ability to face new situations	34	2.6	2.0	3.53**	71	2.4	1.7	4.51**
5. Work Habits	42	2.7	2.3	3.61**	96	2.5	2.2	4.11**
6. Relationships with other children	42	1.7	1.4	2.13*	85	1.9	1.4	6.25**
7. Ability	37	3.1	3.5	−2.46*	77	3.1	3.3	−1.98*

*Significant at 0.05 level, two-tailed test.
**Significant at 0.01 level or beyond, two-tailed test.

in student role behavior between enrollment and six months after discharge. It should be noted that usually two different teachers responded to this scale for each child because he had returned to a different public school classroom.

Items two through seven in Table 4 reflect ratings suggesting that in addition to more generally appropriate role behavior on return from the Re-ED school, the children were less disruptive, less subject to personal distress, better able to face new situations, had better work habits and relationships with other children but had less ability as compared to other children in the classroom. We are especially puzzled by the last comparison since it is clearly an exception to the generally favorable reception given Re-ED children on their return to regular classes. We wonder, since objective test data do not indicate any decline in academic performance relative to age peers, whether the prior public school teachers may have been somewhat more forgiving because the children were "emotionally disturbed" while the later teachers felt they had been relieved of their problems and more should be expected of them.

The ratings of teachers' comments about behavior and teachers' comments about achievement, reported in Tables 5 and 6, were made by members of the research staff[2] on the basis of the teachers' answers

---

[2]Inter-rater reliability was 0.92 for behavioral-emotional adjustment and 0.91 for the academic adequacy.

TABLE 5
Global Rating of Behavioral-Emotional Adjustment
Change in the Child between Enrollment and First Follow-up

	Wright School (N = 43)				
	Normal Range	Mild Problems	Fairly Severe	Very Severe	Mean
Enrollment	2%	7%	65%	26%	3.1
Follow-up	26%	35%	33%	7%	2.2
			$t = 6.04**$		

	CHES (N = 109)				
	Normal Range	Mild Problems	Fairly Severe	Very Severe	Mean
Enrollment	9%	25%	47%	20%	2.8
Follow-up	38%	40%	18%	4%	1.9
			$t = 8.76**$		

**Significant at 0.01 level or beyond, two-tailed test.

TABLE 6
Global Rating of Academic Adequacy
Change in the Child between Enrollment and First Follow-up

	Wright School (N = 43)				
	Normal Range	Mild Problems	Fairly Severe	Very Severe	Mean
Enrollment	16%	14%	23%	47%	3.0
Follow-up	19%	14%	33%	35%	2.8
			$t = 0.85$		

	CHES (N = 112)				
	Normal Range	Mild Problems	Fairly Severe	Very Severe	Mean
Enrollment	28%	15%	31%	26%	2.6
Follow-up	43%	16%	29%	12%	2.1
			$t = 3.52**$		

**Significant at 0.01 level or beyond, two-tailed test.

to open-ended questions about a child's classroom behavior. Two dimensions were used because most teachers seem to evaluate the adequacy of a child's social-emotional adjustment independently of his academic achievement. The research staff used a 4-point scale to reflect the teachers' judgments of each dimension:

1. Has very severe problems.
2. Has fairly severe problems.
3. Has mild problems.
4. Is within the normal range.

Ratings on both dimensions showed improvement from enrollment to follow-up with a more substantial improvement in social-emotional behavior than in academic achievement.

Discussion of Results

Evaluation of the significance of change in children's behavior, particularly children who have been identified as emotionally disturbed, is difficult at best. It is not surprising that children change in the eyes of those who are concerned with their socialization. As they grow older, they learn new skills and find new ways to cope with social demands. Children who have had serious problems may be more likely than others to be seen as "improving" simply because there has been a great deal of room for improvement. They have nowhere to go but up.

One reason for including the global rating of improvement by mothers, fathers, and clinic workers is that, while it is imprecise, it does allow a comparison with similar judgments made about children treated in clinics, the only baseline information currently available. Levitt (1957) has noted a consistency in outcome studies of children who have received psychotherapy. These studies typically report about two-thirds of the cases improved at the close of treatment and about three-fourths improved in follow-up studies extending two years or longer. While these figures are rough approximations based on averages of many reports from many different settings, they do give us some perspective on our own estimates of improvement. Using this global criterion, the Re-ED children are doing well, with less time spent in treatment than is customary. Three observers who have known them during their enrollment in the school agree, within fairly narrow limits, that more than three-fourths of the children are functioning much better than when they were enrolled.

The rating scales used by parents and teachers of the Re-ED children are a somewhat more careful measure of their changing social stimulus value. It has been rewarding to the staff of the schools that the reported changes are consistently in the direction of fewer symptoms, greater social maturity, meeting parents' expectations, and getting along better in school, both socially and academically. That the changes are statistically significant has been established. That the changes are socially significant may be moot. We are faced with the very real question of how much an emotionally disturbed child's behavior may be expected to change simply by getting a year or two older and having additional experiences and opportunities that had not been available before. The social maturity scale is the most extreme example of this source of uncertainty. One would be surprised if a child, even one who could be called emotionally disturbed, did not have significantly higher social maturity ratings after a year or two. Our concern in evaluating a program of treatment is the extent to which one may attribute the change to treatment rather than to maturation alone.

For this reason, the changes reported here, while encouraging, must be viewed as tentative and incomplete. Later reports will develop a more analytical treatment of the data available on Re-ED children, e.g., the relationship between type of problem, family situation, or community resources to improvement in a child's behavior and learning problems. The baseline question is also being addressed in studies that have identified children who have problems similar to those of the Re-ED children but who are receiving no formal treatment. These children will be periodically evaluated for three years in order to develop more precise expectations regarding how many, and what kinds, of children may "outgrow" problem behavior without intervention.

In summary, Project Re-ED is providing a demonstration of one method of serving emotionally disturbed children that does not require direct service by scarce mental health professionals. It is developing new mental health roles, teacher-counselors and liaison-teachers, educational methodology, and a conceptualization of children's problems that depart from conventional mental health patterns. The analysis of preliminary follow-up data reported here supports our more subjective impressions that children are being helped in significant ways to move back toward a trajectory of normal development in their own families, schools, and communities.

REFERENCES

Albee, G. *Mental health manpower trends*. New York: Basic Books, 1959.

Hobbs, N. How the Re-ED plan developed. In N. J. Long, W. C. Morse & R. G. Newman (Eds.), *Conflict in the classroom*. Belmont, Calif: Wadsworth, 1965.

Levitt, E. E. The results of psychotherapy with children: An evaluation. *Journal of Consulting Psychology*, 1957, **21**, 189–196.

Lewis, W. W. Continuity and intervention in emotional disturbance: A review. *Exceptional Children*, 1965, **31**, 465–475.

Weinstein, L. Project Re-ED schools for emotionally disturbed children: Effectiveness as viewed by referring agencies, parents, and teachers. *Exceptional Children*, 1969, **35**, 703–711.

CHAPTER 6

Behavior Modification in a Therapeutic Summer Camp[1]

Henry C. Rickard
and Michael Dinoff

The pressing need for treatment resources for emotionally disturbed children is well documented. Hobbs (1965) has suggested that we must have an array of services for emotionally disturbed children and adolescents, including short-term and long-term camping programs.

The general concept that camping in and of itself may be beneficial is not a new one. Since the inception of recreational camping it has been assumed that there is considerable benefit in "the great outdoors" which is enhanced by a carefully planned program. Partially because of the heritage of pioneering in this country, outdoor living has always been an accepted pastime for young people. Traditional camping as we know it in America began approximately 100 years ago. Therapeutic camping, however, is a relatively new concept.

Perhaps the most clearly established therapeutic camp is the University of Michigan Fresh Air Camp (McNeil, 1962). This camping program began in 1921 with 130 boys selected by welfare agencies and juvenile detention homes in Detroit and Ann Arbor. The University of Michigan camp was built upon an idea "imported from the University of Pennsylvania" where a similar program had been developed in 1919. Gradually the camp began to develop a systematic clinical rationale, imposed upon the existing therapeutic concepts of the day. In the late thirties and early forties, concepts of clinical diagnosis, team approach, and new concepts of psychopathology and psychodynamics were incorporated into the Michigan program. Soon

[1]The reported findings concerning evaluation sessions and group problem solving techniques were supported in part by University of Alabama Research Committee Grant No. 516.

after, the camp became a training program for various professional mental health disciplines.

In an effort to define therapeutic camping McNeil (1962) states:

> A therapeutic camp has more to offer the disturbed child than the enjoyable, but hardly curative, fresh air, swimming, and nature lore. In the diagnosis and treatment of emotional disorders of youth, a therapeutic camp has a number of singular advantages. It can provide a 24 hour-a-day controlled living situation without the drawbacks of permanent institutionalization and can eliminate the artificiality of 'office therapy' by substituting corrective guidance during the natural activity of camping and play. (p. 116)

Most therapeutic camp directors see their efforts as adjunctive to an ongoing treatment program for the child; the program must be carefully coordinated with the referral source prior to and subsequent to the camping experience. In some cases the camp may serve as the first step in a treatment program; only in rare instances is it viewed as terminating a treatment plan.

Camp Ponderosa was established in 1963 as a short-term summer treatment program for the emotionally disturbed child. A number of landmarks may be identified in the evolution of the Ponderosa program. One of the co-directors had an extensive background in recreational camping which provided impetus for the initial development of the program. Both co-directors were experienced in traditional evaluation and therapy with children; however, feedback from intensive camp experiences was soon to lead to a reorientation of philosophy and technique.

An attempt was made to integrate emerging experiential concepts with existing rationale, although a review of the literature (Dinoff & Rickard, 1964) revealed few generalizations which could be applied to the majority of therapeutic camp programs. Little uniformity exists, for example, in terms of recommendations concerning staffing, camper population, physical setting, or program philosophy. Precedence for therapeutic camping existed, but firm guidelines for program development were only vaguely suggested by the available literature. Another very important landmark in the development of the program was a conference for therapeutic camp directors sponsored by the Southern Regional Education Board. Loughmiller was a participant at that conference where he effectively shared ideas accumulated over more than 18 years experience in a full-time therapeutic camp program.

The Ponderosa Program shares numerous concepts with the Dallas Salesmanship Camp, formerly directed by Loughmiller (1965). The Dallas Program relies heavily upon the initiative of a small relatively fixed camper-counselor group which meets most of its basic needs in a primitive camp environment. It has not proven possible or desirable in a 7-week program to adopt all aspects of the Dallas Program but certain concepts and attitudes have transferred readily to the Ponderosa Program: the counselor's active involvement with the campers, camper initiative in schedule planning, and the philosophy that the camper must assume a high degree of responsibility for his own behavior. Emphasis upon small group subcultures and the handling of interpersonal difficulties through group problem-solving are further concepts adapted from the Dallas Program.

Philosophy of the Program

The conceptual biases of the Ponderosa Program may be expressed in a few phrases, suggesting emphases within the program rather than exclusive directions. For instance, the focus is upon *experience* versus *insight*, with the expectation that the camper will learn through numerous corrective experiences rather than through a dynamic consideration of why he behaves as he does. Linked with the emphasis upon experiences rather than insight is the stress upon *present* versus *past* events. *Control* is emphasized rather than a total *permissiveness*; linked to the emphasis upon control is the preference for *prompting* behavior as opposed to a more relaxed *following* and *waiting* process. *Group* techniques are emphasized rather than *individual* relationships although there is a place in the program for the latter. Finally, the philosophy of the program embraces a behavioristic point of view and, as much as possible, the treatment techniques and procedures are placed within a learning principle framework.

Again, emphasis rather than exclusive direction must be stressed. A youngster exhibiting encopresis (i.e., soiling symptoms) was treated by both behavior shaping techniques and a form of what could be considered self-control. "The camper was administered social and candy reinforcers for bowel movements under proper stimulus control, the benefits to be derived from bowel control were freely discussed, and attempts were made to help the camper verbalize and be aware of bodily sensations preceding bowel evacuation." (Rickard & Griffin, 1969). While no attempt was made to promote dynamic insight in terms of a relationship between past conflicts and the present soiling behavior, every effort was made to encourage the camper to recognize the effects of his soiling behavior on others. Group problem solving, therapeutic contracts, and evaluation sessions, techniques to be described, also emphasize awareness of one's present behavior and the likely consequences of that behavior. In the camp program the promotion of awareness is limited almost entirely to understanding present behavior. A camper who makes himself a scapegoat for his more aggressive peers finds his behavior interpreted to him on more than one occasion. Specific incidents are cited, making it clear that the behavior pattern does occur and that it is the responsibility of the camper to recognize it and to do something about it. Events which originally influenced and molded the pattern are not explored. On the other hand, the assumption is made that the ability to recognize current situations in which maladaptive behavior will be provoked and to appropriately visualize the consequences of that behavior permits the camper to control his responses through anticipated rewards and punishments.

Obviously, behavior patterns are evoked and reinforced in every camp environment, recreational or therapeutic. The question is one of specificity and control. What kinds of behaviors will be stimulated, under what conditions, and with what consequences? Seven weeks is a short period in which to attempt to influence established behavior patterns; following, waiting, and understanding may be of value but frequently are not enough. A 3-day hike might never get under way unless the counselors are enthusiastic about the trip and take every opportunity to reinforce momentum in the campers. A building project may be either a great accomplishment or a complete fiasco, depending upon the initiative shown by the counselors. At the same time, while we are convinced that control is essential to an effective behavior modification program, it is obvious that some of the best learning experiences occur when the camper is allowed to explore an enriched, stimulating environment. Again, the question is really not one of control versus no control, but when to control and under what conditions. The counselor may profitably follow and wait when the group is achieving its goals. He must be prepared to lead, to intervene, to do whatever is needed, when goals are no longer being reached and group disintegration threatens.

Group relationships are emphasized because so many emotionally disturbed youngsters exhibit their symptoms primarily in a family or other group setting; it seems reasonable to attempt to modify patterns of behavior in an interpersonal environment similar to the one in which they occur. The use of group techniques by no means releases the counselor from the obligation to develop individual relationships with his campers. There are literally hundreds of opportunities within the general framework of the group program for the counselor to form individual relationships. A rest along the trail, breaks during building and work projects, free periods during the day, etc., all provide opportunities for counselor-camper communications. In a sense, group techniques may be considered a framework for individual relationships.

Framework for a Program

A general framework for the Ponderosa Program is provided by the physical setting. The camp is situated on 80 wooded acres five miles from the nearest town. The rugged atmosphere of the camp was preserved by clearing only those areas needed to develop cabin space and necessary recreation fields. The cabins are spaced well apart, and each is a self-contained unit consisting of nine campers and three counselors. Each cabin group is expected to form a close knit subcul- ture and separation from other groups enhances this concept. Each of the groups is given an Indian tribal name and a group is first addressed by its tribal name in an effort to further develop feelings of group identification and cohesion. Recreational activities are available to the campers who, along with their counselors, may decide to swim, hike, engage other groups in a spontaneous ball game, or take part in one of the many available work and building projects. A back-stop for the ball field, an outdoor chapel, an outdoor museum containing relics from the remains of homes of early settlers in the area are among some of the many useful projects undertaken and completed by camper groups. A bus, christened the Ponda-bus, is available to the camper groups for once-a-week trips away from the camp property to explore points of interest on the mountain and in surrounding areas. For this purpose, a group budget is provided to plan trips, some as distant as 125 miles from camp. Each cabin group has the responsibility of getting together a Friday night dramatic presentation at least once during the camp season. Further, each group contributes to the weekly newspaper. There are certain events scheduled for the entire camp including Monday night movies, scavenger hunts, a water regatta, and a grand circus day near the end of camp, complete with recreational booths, prizes, and skits. The most popular circus booth has been one called "dunk the staff member" in which the campers delight in throwing balls against a triggering device, releasing floods of icy well-water upon directors and counselors.

Berry-picking, nature hikes, and campout nights far away from the cabin areas are activities enjoyed by traditional campers, and no less so by the Ponderosa camp population. In short, the camp environment provides a setting in which the campers may engage in a variety of activities, most of which have a great deal of appeal for children. One of the major goals of the camp program is to provide an opportunity for the youngsters to take part in activities available to children in non-treatment camps, but to do so under circumstances that will maximize the probability of success experiences and minimize the probability of failure. Cooperative behavior, for example, cannot occur in a vacuum but is a mode of interpersonal behavior tied to a specific task or situation. The camp environment offers many situations and many problems which require cooperation for a successful solution.

Staff

The program is directed by two clinical psychologists and staffed by a nurse and counselors. A counselor to camper ratio of better than one to three is maintained. The counselors are recruited primarily from graduate students in psychology and undergraduates with a wide array of majors. College students have acquitted themselves well working with emotionally disturbed individuals in a variety of settings (Greenblatt & Kantor, 1962; Beck, Kantor & Gelineau, 1963). While usually lacking extensive experience with emotionally disturbed children, college counselors are bright, enthusiastic, and possess the high energy level necessary to meet the demands of the program. As the season progresses the camp becomes an isolated community in which interpersonal interactions acquire an intensity difficult to describe; the assets and liabilities of each staff member stand out in clear relief by mid-season. However, in agreement with the reports of students working as volunteers in mental hospitals (Beck, Kantor & Gelineau, 1963), substantially all the counselors describe the emotionally charged camp experience as meaningful and worthwhile.

The counselor needs already-existing personality characteristics which give him reinforcement value and insure him the status of an adequate cultural model. He needs the ability to empathize with and understand the child, and the ability to interact with relatively little defensiveness. Like the ideal therapist, he should possess the characteristics of warmth and liking, empathy, and adequacy of adjustment (Bergin, 1966). In the fast-moving camp situation the counselor must possess still another characteristic—he must be able to set firm, consistent limits. Perhaps such a characteristic may be subsumed under good personal adjustment, empathy, experience, or even warmth and liking. However, even an experienced counselor who possesses these characteristics to a considerable degree may still lose control of the situation unless he is prepared to set firm limits.

Early in the history of the program, the camper population was quite small and the directors conceived of themselves as the major dispensers of treatment. Initially, each of the campers was scheduled for individual and group psychotherapy, but the directors' traditional therapeutic posture was quickly undermined. It somehow seemed more effective to take walks down the trail, chatting with a camper, rather than talking face-to-face in an "office" situation. By the same token, paddling a canoe up a river presented a relaxed and logical framework for the development of a relationship between camper and director. A cabin which had been structured for group play therapy proved much too confining, and a desperation hike to a nearby creek resulted in a fascinating dam building and boat floating project that consumed several hours a week for the remainder of the summer. What had started out to be a rather formal individual and group psychotherapy program with trained clinical psychologists as therapists had obviously become a situation in which environmental props were successfully utilized to promote adaptive behavior and enhance interpersonal relationships. A further extrapolation was not difficult to make: if hiking therapy, canoe therapy, and mud therapy could be practiced by psychologists hopefully possessing Bergin's relationship criteria, could not equally effective relationship therapy be performed by counselors possessing the same characteristics? Thus the focus of the treatment program passed from one in which trained professionals played a central role to one in which professionals in training and undergraduates became the recognized treatment personnel. The directors concentrated primarily upon working with the counselors through formal and informal teaching, crisis consultation, and various forms of staff training sessions.

The Counselor as a Model

Among the many therapeutic functions of the counselor, two roles stand out: the counselor as a model and the role of the counselor in controlling and shaping behavior. The role of the counselor as a model will be considered at this point, followed later by a description of techniques for controlling and shaping behavior.

The psychotherapist has been described as a new model of reality (Strupp, 1960), and is said to affect the patient's philosophy of life (Buhler, 1962; Rosenthal, 1955). The therapist influences the patient's behavior through his example (Menninger, 1958), his attitudes (Dollard, Auld & White, 1953), and even his physical and behavioral characteristics (Binder, McConnell & Sjoholm, 1957). Bandura and McDonald (1963) provide data which suggest that if an accepted model adopts a particular moral stance, this orientation is likely to be adopted by the subject.

Desired attitudes may be evoked by a counselor purposely structuring himself as a desirable model. Mowrer (1966) states that in conventional therapy the patient is expected to talk while the therapist remains relatively silent. As an alternative, he suggests that in some cases talking openly about one's own mistakes and concerns can have a beneficial modeling effect upon the patient. During group problem solving sessions, in particular, the counselor has an opportunity to verbalize his own feelings and demonstrate openness to his own experiences. The camper is exposed to another individual who is not always certain, right, and congruent, but who is attempting to arrive at the best approximations to the truth of the moment and the most rational, equitable, and meaningful solution to a problem.

Modeling procedures have been effective in working with specific patient symptoms, for example, fear of dirt (Levy, 1939), lack of assertiveness (Jack, 1934; Page, 1936), and low verbal productivity (Staples, Wilson & Walters, 1963). The camp environment produces numerous opportunities for the counselor to encourage adaptive behaviors through his example and stimulus value as a model. He uses a sharp tool with care and confidence, he speaks calmly and rationally in the face of explosive camper verbalizations, and he enters into group problem solving productively and enthusiastically. In these and dozens of other ways, the counselor structures himself as a figure worthy of imitation. Sometimes the modeling is planned and tailored to the needs of a particular camper but more often it is a part of the counselor's ongoing attitude and behavior.

In our society the handling of aggression is a problem of considerable magnitude, and the role of modeling in the acquisition of patterns of aggressive behavior appears to be substantial. Bandura and Walters (1959) report that the fathers of aggressive boys tend to be aggressive. Fathers who are stern disciplinarians, presumably modeling aggression as an acceptable pattern of behavior, produce aggressive sons (Glueck & Glueck, 1952). Kessler (1966) refers to an observation by Rexford suggesting that fathers of aggressive boys frequently equate aggression with masculinity and tend to encourage aggressive behavior. The counselor is expected to present himself as a nonpunitive, nonaggressive model. Occasional anger on the part of the counselor is obviously acceptable; constant or irrational uncontrolled anger would place the counselor on an undesirable generalization gradient with other aggressive individuals and serve to provoke at a high level the very behavior he is attempting to control. The counselor who attempts to reach "good" ends through "aggressive" means runs the risk of having the camper imitate aggressive actions and apply them indiscriminately to other interpersonal situations.

Population

Campers must be referred by qualified professionals. Major referral sources include mental health clinics, psychiatrists, social workers, psychologists, and special education personnel. Both boys and girls in the general age range of 7–14 are considered. Professional reports, and sometimes interviews, are used in helping determine the suitability of the program for the youngster's needs. The camper must be average in intelligence or his tests suggestive of average intellectual potential, and he must be able to function in a group situation. The intent is to select the mildly disturbed child who may be experiencing academic underachievement and disturbed peer, parent, and authority figure relationships. The frankly psychotic or autistic child is usually not accepted, the enrollment of older boys with marked psychopathic features is limited, and campers whose primary behavioral difficulties are attributed to brain damage are usually excluded.

One hundred and four different campers experienced the program during the first five seasons of operation; 13 girls and 91 boys. Approximately 20 percent returned for a second season; only two campers were enrolled as many as three seasons. While only a few of the campers had failed a school year, the majority were described as "academic underachievers." The mean IQ of the camper group over the 5-year period is 108.

While psychiatric diagnosis is not an objective of the program, a nosological description of the population may provide an additional basis for comparison with other programs. A small percentage of the campers had received psychiatric diagnoses prior to their camp experience. The reported diagnosis in the remainder of the group was agreed upon by the clinical psychologist directors, occasionally in consultation with a visiting psychiatrist: 60 percent situational maladjustments of childhood or adolescence; 20 percent fairly well-defined character disorders; 10 percent borderline psychotic; approximately 5 percent neurotic; and approximately 5 percent suspected brain damage and perceptual motor problems.

Behavior Modification

Techniques designed to promote behavior change will be discussed under two major categories: (1) those situations in which overt environmental events are brought to bear upon immediate behavioral patterns, and (2) those situations in which the goals are oriented toward the attainment of greater self-control. The first category includes both environmental stage setting to elicit desirable behavior and direct efforts to shape and maintain behavior through reinforcement procedures. The second category includes a discussion

of the self-control techniques of group problem solving, group evaluations, and therapeutic contracts.

Stage Setting and Shaping Environmental Behavior

Much of the adaptive behavior that emerges in the camp situation
must be attributed to gross stage setting rather than precisely controlled behavior evoking and reinforcing events. The camp environment itself is the most important element in stage setting. The camper
has an opportunity to explore and create. He fords the deep creek,
survives the electric storm, and finds that he can live in interpersonal
closeness with 11 other individuals. In stage setting efforts (e.g.,
scheduling an overnight campout) it is expected that once adaptive
responses have been prompted by the demands of the situation, they
will be reinforced by their environmental consequences, but there is
little emphasis upon the precise control of consequences. The child
who learns to swim, brave a high place, or use a sharp axe needs no
reinforcement directly under counselor control; the successful repetitive accomplishment of the task is enough.

Unfortunately, the occurrence of a response is not always followed
by a reinforcing event inherent in the environment; a little help from
the staff may be needed to provide reinforcing consequences. An
illustration seems in order.

Building projects frequently serve as a vehicle for camper interest
and cooperation. One group of boys discovered a large abandoned
slab pile, relics of an old saw mill, on the banks of a stream some
distance above the camp. The following description is paraphrased
from a staff progress note.

> The five boys in Cabin B chose raft building as their special
> project. Carrying nails, hammers, and twine, they disappeared down
> the trail shortly after lunch. When the long shadows fell and the boys
> had not returned one of the directors searched for and found them
> dragging the newly constructed raft into navigable waters. Schedul-
> ing was off and dinner was waiting but it seemed important to let the
> boys continue what had become a special and important task. The
> raft was crude and sank below the water under the weight of the five
> boys; yet their pride in their creation was obvious. Poling or paddling
> proved ineffective in moving the submerged raft so the boys slipped
> into the water and using newly learned lifeguard strokes propelled
> their raft a full quarter mile to the main area.

Initially the staff was dismayed by the scheduling problem presented by the successful raft project. Only brief consideration was
necessary, however, to realize that the project was more important
than precise scheduling. Reinforcing events were made possible in

two ways: the staff allowed the boys to complete the project and experience the natural rewarding consequences of their efforts and, secondly, a spontaneous reception was found at the camp site when the boys finally navigated their craft to shore. The entire camp, including the kitchen staff, turned out to welcome the craft and its crew. The event was later described as comparable to the landing of the Queen Mary.

In other instances environmental events and consequences are planned and controlled. Specific behavior modification studies regard ing encopresis, nonparticipation, habits of personal hygiene, and enuresis will be summarized in an evaluation discussion. Numerous other behavior patterns in individual campers, e.g., tics, loud talking, rowdy table manners, etc., have been controlled through the manipulation of environmental events. In fact, much of the program consists of identifying behaviors which the campers and counselors feel are in need of modification and then establishing a treatment plan tailored to those behavior patterns. For example, temper tantrum behavior and rage reactions to stressful situations have occurred in several of the campers. The general approach to temper tantrums was to insure that the camper did not manipulate the group and "get what he wanted" through the occurrence of the undesirable behavior.

Self-Control Techniques

Interpersonal Problem Solving

Brief references are made to problem solving as a therapeutic tool in social work, clinical psychology, and psychiatric literature, and group psychotherapy is frequently conceptualized, at least partially, as a problem solving process. Sherif and Sherif (1956) report a series of staged problem solving situations in which normal boys in a camp engaged in cooperative acts to obtain food, water, and recreation. While not designed specifically as interpersonal problem solving experiments, the studies indicate that, in addition to obtaining environmental goals, the boys made gains in interpersonal functioning. The interpersonal group problem solving techniques discussed here, however, were most directly influenced by Loughmiller (1965).

When an ongoing activity breaks down the stage is set for interpersonal problem solving. The group stops its activities, sits down in a circle, and led by a counselor or other group member, begins a verbal interchange designed to solve the inter-personal problem. The problem solving session is divided into two parts: (1) identifying the behavior which has led to the group breakdown, and (2) proposing alternative responses for the behavior which has proven inefficient.

All group members including counselors are urged to contribute, and the prime offender(s) is given a special voice. The identified disruptive behavior must be accepted as the problem behavior by the entire group. Likewise, a solution to the interpersonal problem must receive unanimous group support and must not be obviously superficial, insincere, or designed to escape the stress of the problem solving situation. Initially counselors exercise control over superficial solutions, but as the camp season progresses many campers become aware that unsolved interpersonal problems recur and a "pat" solution is really no solution at all.

The goals of a group are most easily obtained when each camper contributes to the task at hand. As a minimal requirement the non-participating camper must not jeopardize the group's chances of receiving reinforcement. Conflict is clearly evident when interpersonal interactions in the camp environment elicit behaviors which block avenues of reinforcement. These conflicts which occur during the various camp activities become, immediately, the subject of discussion in a problem solving session. A pattern of behavior which has been described as passive-aggressive behavior may be used as an illustration.

Case

J. worked slowly, refused to take part in activities, and would not make his bed or clean his cabin area. Consequently, his group missed meals and had less time available for recreational activities. As a result of J.'s slovenly behavior the group frequently failed to pass inspection and was required to spend extra time cleaning the cabin. In each of these instances J. was clearly exhibiting behavior which prevented the group members from receiving reinforcement. J.'s resistive behavior resulted in numerous problem solving sessions.

While the conflicts occurring in the camp environment are both on a motor and verbal level, new responses acquired in the group sessions are usually verbal commitments. For instance, J. might state, "Tomorrow I'll make my bed first and then whittle." Several alternatives to a particular pattern of disruptive behavior are usually presented by group members. Each of these alternatives is discussed and the counselors and campers focus upon those responses viewed as most workable. Thus when faced with a similar situation in the camp environment, the camper has in his repertoire of potential responses, alternatives to the habitual response.

On the following morning J. might remind himself of his verbal commitment and/or be reminded by group members. If he managed to control his behavior and cooperate with the group, reward would be forthcoming from self-reinforcement, praise from group members, and whatever reinforcement lies at the end of the sequence of events (e.g., eating breakfast). If he were unable to control his behavior another group problem solving session would be called in which the verbalization of responses incompatible with passive-aggressive behavior would again be evoked and reinforced.

Early in the season, groups were recognized for their problem solving efforts; the concept of problem solving was treated very seriously. Problem solving was considered more meaningful than completing a project, taking part in recreational activity, or even eating a meal. Additionally, by the end of camp every camper could verbalize and accept that he was in a "problem solving camp." It has been hypothesized that even a hippie is a conformist in his own society. By the same token our egocentric, bright, highly individualistic campers showed a gradual shaping and conformity to the norms of the problem solving society in which they found themselves. Rickard and Lattal (1969) have presented a more complete description of group problem solving.

Therapeutic Contracts

A more complete discussion of therapeutic contracts has been presented earlier (Dinoff & Rickard, 1969). A summary follows concerning the use of therapeutic contracts in the Ponderosa Camp Program.

The concept of contractual relationships to the systematic modification of human behavior in other than legal issues appears in the psychoanalytic (Menninger, 1958), guidance (Krumboltz, 1965), and behaviorally oriented educational literature (Clements & McKee, 1968). All describe their encounters as a contract between two individuals and strongly indicate that the contract sets the limits of the encounter, be it therapy, education, or behavior modification. A contract implies an equitable exchange based upon a common understanding. In a therapeutic encounter it is oftentimes difficult to establish a contract due to the client's practice of failing in his own personal contracts with other people. One could argue, however, that he is keeping his neurotic contract, i.e., his obligation to fail.

Within the Camp Ponderosa Program the group problem solving techniques themselves are in part a contractual arrangement. For example, the group is obliged to deal with problems as they emerge regardless of other planned activities and individual desires not to negotiate. Further, each problem solving session is ended with a plan or contract in an effort to assure that the problem discussed would not recur, or would be modified in intensity or form.

However, contractual agreements in the camp setting are not limited solely to problem solving. They are oftentimes used as motivational devices to encourage specific participation by an individual or the total cabin group. Dinoff and Rickard (1969) cite specific examples. An additional example combines the use of an individual and group contract. A youngster who had many ritualistic behaviors such as backing up before entering a door, and highly specified, detailed, and manneristic table behaviors had extreme difficulty in fitting in with his cabin group. He could not keep up with the group since his manneristic behavior kept him "running late," and, as a consequence, he became increasingly left out and even scapegoated. A vicious circle which encouraged self-defeating behavior was established, not only for the ritualistic youngster, but for the group as a whole. A problem solving session ensued in which the group saw the dilemma, and decided to accept a contract to reinforce the manneristic camper for adaptive behaviors and to encourage the extinction of maladaptive ritualistic behavior.

For several days the group encouraged the youngster to break his rituals by administering social reinforcement for adaptive, on-time behavior. Several days later, however, it was clear that the group was losing interest and the youngster who was the focus of the attention and who had made considerable progress was "losing ground." Clearly the other campers were not receiving adequate reinforcement for their efforts; therefore the contract failed.

Another problem solving session was called and all the issues were discussed in detail along with the behavior modification rationale. The group decided that all of its members had behaviors that should be modified. Each youngster and counselor in turn specified behavior which he wanted changed. The directors offered to establish a system where each individual, including the ritualistic camper, would be rewarded for working on his undesirable behavior (e.g., cursing, failure to participate, fighting, etc.). The Rules (a contract) were mimeographed and distributed to the group members. This agreement was the most successful of any attempt at cohesion and control for that group during the camping season, and stayed in effect for the last two weeks of camp. Each camper was both giving something and getting something. He was encouraging other campers and counselors and being encouraged by them; and if he kept his contract, extrinsic reinforcement was also forthcoming.

Prior experiences have indicated the comparative virtues of written contracts (Dinoff & Rickard, 1969). Children who experience difficulty keeping a verbal commitment will honor their written word. A written contract enables detailed assessment and withdraws the distortion of memory as to what one "thought" he agreed. Furthermore, it is easy to indicate the mutual responsibilities of both parties to an agreement when the contract is written.

It appears important that the campers control the terms of the contract as much as possible. The terms must be limited by the demands and goals of the total program and must not intrude excessively upon others' rights and privileges. When allowed to establish their own contracts they are reckless, initially, and are quite willing to promise more than can be delivered. These contracts are never accepted and are returned for reevaluation and modification. For example, if a child with obsessive-compulsive behavior promises that he will give up all mannerisms tomorrow, the contract would not be accepted. Such a contract must fail! If, on the other hand, he contracts to improve somewhat, and specifies how much, in exchange for certain appropriate reinforcement, the contract would be readily accepted.

Contracts are discussed on many occasions during each camp session. Emphasis on contracts as two-party interactions is repeated. The give-and-take basis of agreements is not clear initially to these youngsters and needs to be specified whenever possible. Written contracts are used often early in the summer. As each season progresses, the staff encourages increasing use of verbal contracts and implied contracts. Even handshakes and greetings are discussed and labeled implied contracts.

Evaluation Interviews

Evaluation of progress in which the camper himself participates takes numerous forms. In a sense, problem solving is one form of evaluation in which the group subculture encourages the camper to take a careful look at his ongoing behavior.

However, group problem solving is oriented toward immediate problems in living. By contrast, evaluation sessions may be considered a form of long-range interpersonal bookkeeping. If they occur too frequently during the session, they appear to lose effectiveness, perhaps becoming categorized by the campers as just another way for adults to cajole and threaten. When held as few as two or three times during the summer session, evaluation interviews spark a great deal of interest as evidenced by camper participation.

The counselor attempts to structure himself as an active but non-threatening participant. The counselor leads the discussion and is very active in attempts to identify positive changes which have occurred in the camper. He seeks help from the group both in the identification and reinforcement of positive changes made by a particular camper. The identified changed behavior is usually an approximation of the desired behavior change and efforts are made to join with the camper in setting additional goals for behavior change. The following excerpt from an evaluation session illustrates the self-evaluation interview. The evaluation session, held by a group of nine boys in the 11–12 year age range and three counselors, occurred during the sixth week of camp.

C_1 All right, shall we move on? Do you want to add anything? Everyone seems quite pleased with Tim's remark. All right, who wants to be next? Billy?

Billy   Well, I've learned from this camp this year how to hold my temper and not throw so many fits sometimes because I used to.

C_1 What else? Does someone want to point out some things that they've seen?

Bob   Well, Billy hasn't been giving so much attention back to Terry as he used to when Terry first came in.

C_1 Why is this good? Can somebody answer this? Jim can you?

Jim   Well, because Billy does give him the attention and it does cause a fight.

C_1 Billy used not to be able to tolerate Terry. He used to get very angry. And now what happens?

Jim   Well, he ignores him and he just walks away.

C_1 And this tells us what about Billy really?

Jim   He's learned how to ignore people?

C_1 To control his anger a little bit, and that controls Billy.

C_2 In the last couple of days, I've noticed that Billy has stopped pushing limits a lot since we made that contract.

C_1 This was something that came out later. Eddy, what is the biggest gain that you think Billy has made this summer?

Ed   How to get along with people.

C_1 Billy, what do you think about this?

Billy   Well, I think he is right.

C_1 Tom?

Tom   The biggest change about Billy is that he holds his temper down, now, and not just fly off the handle like he used to do.

Ed   We've passed that.

C_2 Well, this is definitely it. Billy used to have such a temper that he would explode, actually explode. I haven't seen this in four weeks.

C_3 The remarkable thing that I've seen in Billy — remember the night we had the powwow fire. Something happened that night. We sat there and just a couple of days before he would blow up. We sat there for 45 minutes (while Billy tried to start the fire) and he said, "I think I'll go get some more matches." To me that was the greatest gain right there. (Billy was the fire chief that night and it was his responsibility to start the fire.)

Tim   It was Billy who used to be very impatient, and he wouldn't wait more than two or three minutes for anything, but after that incident he could wait almost indefinitely. That night did something to him.

C_1 He certainly can tolerate a lot more, can't he, without getting angry? He can control it a lot. Anybody want to add anything else about gains that Billy has made? OK, who wants to speak next?

Parental Counseling and Follow-up

The problem of promoting the generalization of learned adaptive behavior to other settings is well recognized. While the majority of staff efforts are devoted to working with the campers in the camp environment, the problem of transfer of learned behavior back to the home environment must be considered. Efforts to deal with the transfer problem involve, primarily, parental counseling and follow-up reports to referral agencies. A portion of the campers are referred by a professional mental health worker who will continue to have contact with the camper and/or with his parents following the camp season. For some campers who have not had prior professional contact a post-camp referral is made to a treatment resource. The usual camper comes from a middle class family in which both of the parents are present and making efforts to deal effectively with the youngster. Consequently the stage is set for parental counseling which may produce gratifying results. Opportunities for counseling are limited, however, since most of the parents live a considerable distance from the camp. Counseling typically consists of two or three sessions during the summer session in which the behavior of the camper and the efforts made by the counselors in working with the camper's behavior are freely discussed with the parents. Sometimes the camper participates in these sessions. In almost every case, parents have shown themselves to be very good reporters of the behavior exhibited by their children. Frequently the behavior described by the parents does not emerge in the early days of the camp but as the stress level increases and the initial "honeymoon" wears off the campers exhibit clearly the same patterns of rebelliousness, fearfulness, manipulation, etc., which tended to create problems for them in the home environment. Much of the counseling session consists of discussing with the parents successful and unsuccessful procedures employed by the staff in working with the camper. Again and again a pattern of subtle manipulation has been detected in the camper population. One goal of the counseling sessions has been to make explicit the maneuvers performed by the camper to obtain certain goals. While aware of the campers' behaviors, the parents are frequently unaware of how they unwittingly contribute to the campers' problems by allowing maladaptive behavior to lead to consequences satisfying to the camper.

There is at least one other problem area shared by most of the parents. Although both parents are typically concerned about the child's behavior, they are often in disagreement in terms of how the child should be handled. One parent, usually the mother, will readily admit to overleniency with the child at the same time stating that a permissive attitude is made necessary by the excessively punitive attitude of the spouse. This conflict is discussed at length, and it is frequently possible to draw a direct analogy to the group situation where the camper may be attempting to set up a "good" and "bad" counselor. The assumption is made in this rather direct mode of counseling that the parents are reasonably well-integrated individuals who have a relatively clear focus on the problem, and who can profit from a frank discussion of parent-parent and parent-child relationships. The staff members' vast contact with the camper makes them extremely knowledgeable concerning the child's behavior patterns, a fact instantly recognized and appreciated by the parents. The parent counseling sessions are structured as a problem solving session with the goal of providing information useful to the parent in solving problems arising in relation to the camper in the home situation.

During the camp season the directors correspond with referral agencies. At the close of camp a summary is written on each camper and forwarded to the referral source. The reports contain a clear description of the camper's behavior during the season and a statement of successful and unsuccessful counselor efforts to influence the camper's behavior patterns. Recommendations regarding treatment and follow-up planning are made when appropriate. The most frequent recommendation, by far, is for follow-up care in the form of continued parental counseling.

Program Evaluation

Thus far research efforts have taken two major forms: program evaluation and studies utilizing the campers as a research population of emotionally disturbed children. Only the former will be discussed here.

One form of program evaluation has been attempted through questionnaire ratings. A brief questionnaire following the first season (1963) requested that the parents rate change along the dimensions of relationships with family members, relationships with peers, and quality of school work. The parents were asked to present a global impression of whether or not the child profited from his experience, whether they would send the child to camp if they had to do it over again, and whether they, themselves, profited from counseling with the directors. Ten of 11 campers were reported improved in behavior with family members, nine were rated improved with peers, and eight were reported to have shown improvement in quality of school work following the camp experience. All of the parents stated that their child had profited from the camp experience. Nine parents stated they would have sent their child "if they had to do it over again," while two couples reported that they might have sent their child. Seven couples reported that they had profited much from counseling with the directors while three couples reported that they had profited little or not at all. The results of the questionnaire have been reported in greater detail elsewhere (Rickard & Dinoff, 1967).

Case Studies

The major evaluation concern is not with gross outcome in terms of "better" or "worse," but in terms of whether or not the camper modifies old patterns and/or takes on new patterns of adaptive behavior. In some cases overt behaviors possessing stability, sensitivity, and importance (Rickard, 1965) have been identified and specific behavior modification experiments have been devised. The following case summaries will serve as illustrations.

Rickard and Griffin (1969) report a case of soiling behavior which was brought under control in the camp situation. The counselors identified the time of day in which the soiling response occurred with greatest regularity and sent the camper to the toilet during those periods. Candy reinforcers, later replaced by praise, were effective in bringing the behavior under control. An important part of the program consisted of enlisting the cooperation of the camper himself in becoming more aware of the sensations preceding and signaling bowel evacuation and more aware of the negative social consequences of his soiling behavior.

Rickard and Dinoff (1965) identified instances of overt, rebellious behavior in a 13-year-old camper: refusing to go to bed, not getting up at the proper hour, and refusing to take part in activities. The camper was moved into activities by small steps and reinforced for adaptive responses with praise and attention. A great deal of time and effort was expended by staff members in developing relationships with the camper and establishing themselves as effective dispensers of social reinforcement. The camper gradually showed more initiative and was responding to authority well and taking part in all activities by the end of the camp session.

Lattal (1969), aware of the difficulties involved in encouraging personal hygiene in preadolescent boys, made swimming, a favored activity, contingent upon toothbrushing behavior. A baseline period revealed very little spontaneous toothbrushing behavior. Initially, during the acquisition phase, it was necessary for the counselor to prompt toothbrushing by verbalizing the toothbrushing-swimming contingency, but after a short adjustment period toothbrushing behavior was maintained at a high level.

During the 1967 camping session the conditioned response approach to enuretic behavior (Mowrer & Mowrer, 1938) was used with a 10-year-old chronic bed-wetter. The youngster was referred to camp because of academic underachievement, poor peer relationships, immature "crying" behavior, and enuresis. A baseline record prior to the camp experience revealed that the youngster was enuretic 4–6 nights per week. The enuretic behavior was brought under control in the camp situation; bed-wetting did not occur the last 10 days of camp. It should be noted that enuretic behavior was discussed openly with the group and treated as no more unusual than patterns of aggression, passive resistance, etc. Tendencies on the part of some group members to ridicule the enuretic behavior were countered by the counselor's verbalized attitude that each of the campers was exhibiting problems requiring work and attention.

Systematic Estimates

Table 1 presents a summary of undesirable behavior patterns identified in a sample of 3 of the 11 treated during the 1963 season. The

TABLE 1
Behavior Evaluation (1963)

Camper	Home Environment	Early camp
1.	A. Frequent fights with peers	A. Same
	B. Scholastic underachievement	B. N.A.
	C. Inattentive, overactive, acts out fantasies	C. Same
2.	A. Enuretic	A. Same
	B. Scholastic underachievement	B. N.A.
	C. Behavior problem at school	C. Control problem at camp. Fighting, bickering, initiated sex play.
	D. Aperiodic stealing and manipulative behavior	D. Pushed limits, manipulated staff
3.	A. Reversed day-night sleeping and activity pattern	A. Same
	B. Poor peer relations	B. Same
	C. Extremely angry, resistive toward parental authority	C. Similar behavior toward staff

campers are represented by numbers. The first column lists undesirable behaviors exhibited in the home environment while the second column lists similar behaviors observed at camp. In most cases there was striking correspondence between home and camp adjustment. Existing problem areas were quickly elicited by the close and intense interpersonal situation. As Middleman and Seever (1963) have pointed out, " ... there is no place to hide at camp." A majority of the campers experienced difficulty in the give-and-take of the interpersonal interaction. As a group they exhibited extreme egocentrism. Their behavior was very much self-oriented, particularly during the early portion of the camping session; actions suggesting empathy and caring emerged infrequently. Approximately 50 percent of the boys "acted-out" aggressively toward fellow campers, engaging in much bickering, fighting, and practical joking. Resistance toward authority figures, e.g., rule-breaking and refusing certain activities, occurred in almost all of the campers. In fact, for some campers, resistance to authority appeared to be a practiced style of life in which they were most adept.

A number of large changes were obvious. For instance, a camper who had "turned night into day" both at home and at camp settled down into a regular routine and was taking part in all activities by the fifth week of camp. On the other hand changes in some campers were more subtle and difficult to detect. It was estimated by the directors that 10 out of 11 boys showed positive change by the end of camp on a majority of the indices selected. Assuming that the behavior had a 50-50 chance to change or not to change in a positive direction, expansion of the binomial indicates that such an event would occur by chance less than once in 100 times. However, it should be pointed out that such data do not represent precise, objective measures. For example, a precise record of fights was not maintained. The entire staff was biased in favor of positive change and this bias undoubtedly affected the perception of change. Further, it does not represent all deviant behavior manifested by each boy. In short, data such as those contained in Table 1 represent an attempt at systematizing subjective judgments rather than a tabulation of objective measures.

During subsequent seasons a similar analysis was made of camper behaviors. Again, the concept of tailored criteria of behavior change was employed (Pascal & Zax, 1956; Pascal, 1959; Rickard, 1965). Additionally, efforts were made to involve the individual, himself, in the identification of behavior patterns to be modified and in the estimate of whether or not progress was made, an evaluation strategy described by Krumboltz (1965). The excerpt from the evaluation session presented earlier illustrates the process of identifying disruptive behaviors and estimating change. It should be noted that a reduction in intensity or frequency is usually the goal rather than complete modification of a response. The behaviors recorded during evaluation sessions represent a composite rating by the camper himself, counselors, and the other campers. In some cases frequency counts were actually made but in other instances the behaviors identified did not lend themselves easily to quantification.

Recent research (e.g., Ullmann & Krasner, 1965) has made it apparent that specific overt patterns of maladaptive behavior can be modified. Enuresis, soiling behavior, tics, and nonparticipation in activities are among the behaviors which have been systematically identified and modified in the camp population. An extremely interesting question, and one that seems to be more relevant to the total camp population, is the question of teaching the camper to consider alternative behaviors, to let words act as cues or signals for acceptable behavior, to make decisions, and to evaluate events and situations carefully and realistically. While these loosely described concepts are ordinarily considered to be mediated, cognitive behaviors, it is believed that they can be made observational and operational through the self-control techniques of evaluation, problem solving, and therapeutic contracts previously described.

Tape recordings have been made of actual group problem solving sessions. A report of the group problem solving process (Rickard & Lattal, 1969) indicates that maladaptive behaviors, for instance, physical and emotional withdrawal, are readily identifiable patterns which are perceived by the campers themselves as undesirable. While the effects of group problem solving have not yet been separated from the effects of other treatment techniques, a questionnaire has been devised to assess the camper's attitude toward group problem solving. The questionnaire describes 12 situations in which a camper might find himself in conflict with members of his group. In each case the camper may choose a solution which emphasizes: (1) an authoritarian decision by the counselor, (2) punishment to the camper, (3) no interference by the counselor or group members, and (4) an attempt to reach a solution through group discussion. A sample of 22 Ponderosa boys chose the group discussion alternative more frequently than a control sample of 22 boys from a nearby recreational camp ($p < 0.01$), suggesting that a set for problem solving had been induced.

Prior to the 1968 camp season, academic underachievement was treated primarily as a lack of properly directed effort on the part of the camper. Alienation from peers, parents, teachers, and authority figures, in general, seemed to enter greatly into the camper's lack of school achievement. While questionnaire information indicated that the majority of the campers did subsequently improve in the quality of their schoolwork, 73 percent following the 1963 season, a substantial number rated as improved in interpersonal relationships, did not show academic improvement. Consequently, an experimental academic program was initiated in 1968 (Rickard, Willis & Clements, 1969).

Twenty-two boys and three girls were exposed to an 8-day baseline period consisting of one and one-half hours of programmed instruction per day. Following the baseline period, the awarding of points, which could be exchanged for edibles and prizes, was made contingent on productivity. The point incentive program was clearly effective in producing more work per class period for students in the arithmetic group. Subjects in the arithmetic group as compared to their controls showed significant gains on the Iowa Test of Basic Skills. Students in the language group made significant gains in some skill areas but their overall performance was less impressive. From the results of the pilot study it was concluded that an educational adjunctive program was feasible within the framework of the therapeutic camp and showed promise as a remedial device; the educational program will be expanded in subsequent seasons.

Future Directions

Six years of experience and experimentation have produced a well-organized and workable program. A set of very useful therapeutic "tools" have been borrowed, adapted, and improvised. Much refinement is needed, however, in the use, and particularly, the evaluation of the therapeutic techniques employed. More ingenious and systematic methods are needed to evaluate self-control techniques, and more precise recording of high frequency undesirable behavior will be necessary to remove the subjectivity presently involved in the evaluation of overt behaviors.

REFERENCES

Bandura, A. & McDonald, F. J. The influence of social reinforcement and the behavior of models in shaping children's moral judgements. *Journal of Abnormal and Social Psychology,* 1963, **67**, 274–281.

Bandura, A. & Walters, R. H. *Adolescent aggression.* New York: Ronald Press, 1959.

Beck, J. C., Kantor, D. & Gelineau, V. Follow-up study of chronic psychotic patients treated by college case-aid volunteers. *American Journal of Psychiatry,* 1963, **3**, 269–271.

Bergin, A. E. Some implications of psychotherapy research for therapeutic practice. *Journal of Abnormal and Social Psychology,* 1966, **71**, 235–246.

Binder, A., McConnell, D. & Sjobolm, N. A. Verbal conditioning as a function of experimenter characteristics. *Journal of Abnormal and Social Psychology,* 1957, **55**, 309–314.

Buhler, C. *Values in psychotherapy.* New York: Free Press, 1962.

Clements, C. B. & McKee, J. M. Programmed instruction for institutionalized offenders: Contingency management and performance contracts. *Psychological Reports,* 1968, **22**, 957–964.

Dinoff, M. & Rickard, H. C. Therapeutic camping: A review. Paper presented at the Southeastern Psychological Association, Gatlinburg, Tennessee, 1964.

Dinoff, M. & Rickard, H. C. Learning that privileges entail responsibility. In J. D. Krumboltz & C. E. Thoresen (Eds.), *Behavioral counseling: Cases and techniques.* New York: Holt, Rinehart & Winston, 1969. Pp. 124–129.

Dollard, J., Auld, F. & White, A. *Steps in psychotherapy.* Macmillan, 1953.

Glueck, S. & Glueck, E. *Delinquents in the making.* New York: Harper & Row, 1952.

Greenblatt, M. & Kantor, D. Student volunteer movement and the manpower shortage. *American Journal of Psychiatry,* 1962, **118**, 809–814.

Hobbs, N. Conference for planning comprehensive community mental health services—comments. Paper presented to the Conference for Planning Comprehensive Community Mental Health Services, Washington, D.C., February 18, 1965.

Jack, L. M. An experimental study of ascendent behavior in pre-school children. *University of Iowa Studies in Child Welfare, 1934*, **9**, 3–65.

Kessler, J. W. *Psychopathology of childhood.* Englewood Cliffs, N.J.: Prentice-Hall, 1966.

Krumboltz, J. D. (Ed.), *Revolution in counseling: Implications of behavioral science.* Boston: Houghton Mifflin, 1965.

Krumboltz, J. D. & Thoresen, C. E. (Eds.), *Behavioral counseling: Cases and techniques.* New York: Holt, Rinehart & Winston, 1966.

Lattal, K. A. Contingency management of toothbrushing behavior in a summer camp for children. *Journal of Applied Behavior Analysis,* 1969, **2**, 195–198.

Loughmiller, C. *Wilderness road.* University of Texas: The Hogg Foundation for Mental Health, 1965.

McNeil, E. B. Forty years of childhood: The University of Michigan Fresh Air Camp, 1921–1961. *Michigan Quarterly Review,* 1962, **1**, 112–118.

Menninger, K. A. *Theory of psychoanalytic technique.* New York: Basic Books, 1958.

Middleman, R. & Seever, F. Short term camping for boys with behavior problems. *Social Work,* 1963, **8**, 88–95.

Mowrer, O. H. The behavior therapies with reference to modeling and imitation. *American Journal of Psychotherapy,* 1966, **20**, 439–461.

Mowrer, O. H. & Mowrer, W. M. Enuresis: A method for its study and treatment. *American Journal of Orthopsychiatry,* 1938, **8**, 436–459.

Page, M. L. The modification of ascendant behavior in pre-school children. *University of Iowa Studies in Child Welfare,* 1936, **12**, 7–69.

Pascal, G. R. *Behavior change in the clinic: A systematic approach.* New York: Grune & Stratton, 1959.

Pascal, G. R. & Zax, M. Psychotherapeutics: Success or failure. *Journal of Consulting Psychology,* 1956, **20**, 325–331.

Rickard, H. C. Tailored criteria of change in psychotherapy. *Journal of General Psychology,* 1965, **72**, 63–68.

Rickard, H. C. & Dinoff, M. Shaping adaptive behavior in a therapeutic summer camp. In L. P. Ullmann and L. Krasner, (Eds.), *Case studies in behavior modification.* New York: Holt, Rinehart & Winston, 1965. pp. 325–328.

Rickard, H. C. & Dinoff, M. Behavior change in a therapeutic summer camp: A follow-up study. *Journal of Genetic Psychology*, 1967, **110**, 181–183.

Rickard, H. C. & Griffin, J. L. A behavioristic approach to soiling behavior in a therapeutic summer camp. In J. D. Krumboltz & C. E. Thoresen (Eds.), *Behavioral counseling: Cases and techniques*. New York: Holt, Rinehart & Winston, 1969.

Rickard, H. C. & Lattal, K. A. Group problem solving in a therapeutic summer camp: An illustration. *Adolescence*, 1969, **4**, 319–332.

Rickard, H. C., Willis, J. W. & Clements, C. B. Token reinforcement and programmed instruction in a remedial program for emotionally disturbed children. New Orleans: Southeastern Psychological Association, 1969.

Rosenthal, D. Changes in some moral values following psychotherapy. *Journal of Consulting Psychology*, 1955, **19**, 431–436.

Sherif, M. & Sherif, C. W. *An outline of social psychology*. New York: Harper & Row, 1956.

Staples, F. R., Wilson, F. S. & Walters, R. H. Increasing the verbal responsiveness of chronic schizophrenics. Unpublished manuscript, Ontario Hospital, New Toronto, Canada, 1963. Cited by Bandura, A. & Walters, R. H. *Social learning and personality development*. New York: Holt, Rinehart & Winston, 1963.

Strupp, H. H. *Psychotherapists in action*. New York: Grune & Stratton, 1960.

Ullmann, L. P. & Krasner, L. (Eds.), *Case studies in behavior modification*. New York: Holt, Rinehart & Winston, 1965.

CHAPTER 7

Experimental Education: Application of Experimental Analysis and Principles of Behavior to Classroom Instruction

Norris G. Haring

Principles of behavior and principles of instruction that are emerging in education promise to provide the precision and scientific base that educators have long urged. Substantial advancement in the arrangement of learning conditions that improve performance and in the use of measurement procedures to evaluate performance and instruction are at the threshold. Educators only need take advantage of (a) knowledge available from research in several disciplines and (b) precise procedures of investigation and evaluation that have provided the scientific base for more advanced disciplines.

Use of principles of behavior and instruction is visible in programs at the Universities of Washington, Oregon, Kansas, Illinois, and California at Los Angeles, and at Temple University. These programs have several features in common. First, they represent programs of instruction that are scientific in origin and direction, for they are based on known principles of instruction and principles of behavior. Second, they use refined measurement procedures. While the Experimental Education Unit at the University of Washington exemplifies, perhaps more than the other programs, refinement in measurement, each program is pinpointing behavior and keeping records of some form. Third, each adheres to experimental analysis designs for establishing control and evaluating the effects of various conditions. Fourth, intervention is regarded as the objective of instruction. Fifth, in program selection each attends to the criteria which specify behaviors to be developed. Finally, each program in some way employs reinforcement principles.

These programs, among others, function in both regular and special classrooms and use the teacher as the primary manager of contingencies. Insofar as they offer precision and effectiveness in instructional intervention, the above programs represent the best available approximation for better management of instruction, evaluation of educational resources, preparation of teachers, and education of children.

Major Influences in Education

The movement toward more precision in instruction and educational research has not come from education itself, but rather from behavioral psychology, which over the past 40 years has made significant contributions to our understanding and management of human behavior. Ever since Skinner began his scientific investigations of the behavior of organisms, the focus has turned to the relationships between observable behavior and temporally related environmental conditions. Research has demonstrated the dramatic changes that occur in a child's performance when all relevant conditions in his immediate environment are recognized and systematically presented. The considerable body of knowledge that is accumulating to elucidate the influence of specific types and arrangements of cues and reinforcers is being organized into principles of instruction and behavior.

Classroom conditions which accelerate desired social behavior and all types of academic performance have been of special interest with emphasis on the instructional variables which serve to reinforce behavior. These have a substantial effect on the acquisition, maintenance, or elimination of behaviors regardless of the educational setting, be it the laboratory, or among groups of children in institutions for delinquents, or among the mentally retarded, or in after-school settings for the culturally deprived, or in the experimental special classrooms of the Experimental Education Unit. Consequently, it appears mandatory that any child within a resource room, special class, or regular classroom who is experiencing learning or behavior difficulties should be viewed as a child who requires a systematic investigation of all relevant classroom conditions for learning.

Four factors can be designated as the cornerstones of experimental education: (a) an urgent desire for more precision in instruction, (b) the principles of instruction, (c) the principles of behavior, and (d) procedures of experimental analysis. Just as these sources have been the mainspring of development for experimental education, these four factors will continue to be instrumental in the acceleration of its rate of growth.

Before considering the broad program of the Experimental Education Unit as it represents the outgrowth of experimental education, the principles of instruction and behavior as well as the procedures of experimental analysis require brief review to clarify the present state of knowledge derived from research.

Principles of Instruction

Principles of instruction (Wallen & Travers, 1963) can be delineated as follows:

1. Events subsequent to the responses being measured can influence behavior and performance, just as antecedent events can.
2. When cues are introduced to optimize performance, motivation is at its maximum.
3. Practice in applying principles to a new problem facilitates transfer of training.
4. The child can only respond correctly to a task at his level of skills.
5. Practicing the response to be learned establishes the skill most efficiently.

Consequently, the ideal instructional environment, one where the truest assessment of variables is possible, is one where:

1. Design plans include specifications for control of subsequent events that may function as reinforcement variables.
2. Each child is motivated to work at maximum performance.
3. Response requirements of the task are at the appropriate level for each child.
4. Variables introduced for evaluation allow measurement of responses exactly like those to be required by the actual classroom task.

Principles of Behavior

Principles of behavior are statements of the lawfulness of behavior observed under specific conditions. These principles define the influence of specific environmental events on behavior. Environmental stimuli gain control over behavior in one of two ways. Some responses initially are conditioned to the presentation of a stimulus without any recourse to reinforcing events to maintain them. A response pattern of this kind is involuntary and respondently conditioned. Many emotional responses are initially of this type. Most responses with which educators are concerned, however, are not involuntary but rather are conditioned through reinforcement. That is, the patterns of response have been strengthened by the consequences of that behavior. Skinner has coined these "operant responses," for as they occur they operate on the environment producing an environmental change that acts as a consequence for the initial response. This consequence, when it functions as a reinforcer to the individual, serves to strengthen the response it reinforces. Behavior principles will be expanded upon later under a discussion of reinforcement.

Procedures of Experimental Analysis

In addition to principles of behavior and instruction, one further feature is necessary for effective instruction. Without the inclusion of the measurement procedures of experimental analysis, the application of these principles would be no more exact than instruction has been traditionally. Procedures of experimental analysis provide the framework within which conditions for instruction can be applied and evaluated, for they provide the type of control and precision which makes response measurement reliable.

Basically, experimental analysis is a set of procedures for measuring behavior in order to evaluate specific conditions introduced in a temporal relationship with it. All variables are first defined as observable movements. Environmental conditions present before and during the experimental treatment are defined and controlled. The condition that is to be the treatment variable is defined and systematically introduced. Before and during the introduction of the treatment variables, behaviors to be measured are counted as they occur in cycles of movement (the basic unit). These movement cycles are tallied and then calculated in terms of *rate* of occurrence, as rate provides a sensitive measure of the effects of the treatment.

The advantages of using experimental analysis accrue from two characteristics: precision in measurement and reduction of uncontrolled variables. Both factors are responsible for valid, reliable information. Valid measurement is obtained because the response data require no inferential interpretation, as responses are directly observed and are the same type of response to which the results will be generalized. The data are reliable because measurement of behavior is continuous through a set of baseline conditions and then under a new set, differing from the first by only one variable. From this point, any number of new conditions may be introduced systematically, one at a time, under the same procedures of continuous measurement. A major advantage of these procedures is that any uncontrolled variables, causing variability in the data observed, can be investigated by systematically manipulating them until the cause of variability is determined and controlled.

Experimental analysis, as a set of microscopic procedures, should be the first step in any experiment. The most efficient way to experimentally demonstrate the effect of a variable is to begin with an N of 1. Then, knowing its effect, one can present the condition for broader application and further investigation to a class of children. The single N design for classroom instruction is a powerful teacher tool and will greatly influence instruction. Through experimental analysis procedures, the teacher can assess the performance rates of each of her children and can design effective programs without the need for specialists, except for very extreme problems. In a class of 20 pupils, if the data show similar relative pattern changes for all pupils, 20 replications of a particular variable's effects are provided.

In summary, procedures of experimental analysis provide a technique for measurement which, because of the effective control possible, provides valid, reliable information about specific conditions evaluated, using response data recorded from direct observation. In addition, it is a set of procedures useful both in the laboratory for research and in the classroom as a framework for the evaluation of instruction and performance. Finally, the data it provides serve as a basis for making effective decisions for further instruction and research.

Program Components Basic to Instruction

Recognition of these three major influences has brought attention to the observable, measurable components of the learning process. But to understand the complexity of the learning process, its elementary components must be isolated and the variables which facilitate learning must be identified. Intervention in the process of learning requires continuous attention to four basic program components during research and instruction: (a) the materials for the task, (b) the responses to these tasks, (c) the reinforcing consequences immediately following performance, and (d) management of the contingencies between the responses and the reinforcing consequences.

Cueing Responses

Cues are stimulus events that evoke the occurrence of specific responses — verbal, social, and academic. Cues may be written on the board or in books, or they may be oral or gestural cues from the teacher or other children.

Proper cueing must meet four criteria. First, the cues must be appropriate to the task. Second, they must continuously increase the probability of response accuracy. Third, they must be presented in units which have similar response requirements for comparability of performance records from day to day. Fourth, if the method of cueing is changed, the change must be made without causing a change in the response unit to be measured.

The selection of cues and the arrangement of their sequence are essential considerations in any plan for research or instruction. In addition, to allow for reliable performance measurements, cues must (a) evoke specific responses, (b) provide ease in response counting, and (c) start the child at his own level and guide him through successive approximations toward the terminal objectives.

Measuring Responses in the Classroom

Precision in research and instruction requires effective measurement of performance in the classroom. Typically, standardized test scores have been used to assess the adequacy of pupils' daily performance and the effectiveness of instruction. However, as assessment tools for the classroom, standardized tests have not provided the educator valid information.

Measurement continuum. If functional procedures for measurement are viewed along a continuum from least to most precise, measurement procedures would be ordered as follows.

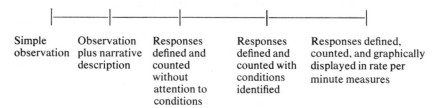

| Simple observation | Observation plus narrative description | Responses defined and counted without attention to conditions | Responses defined and counted with conditions identified | Responses defined, counted, and graphically displayed in rate per minute measures |

As shown, narrative description of the observed behavior provides slightly more precision than simple observation, if only because the record provides permanent information. More precise measurement comes from a definition and tally of responses, although such a tally provides no reliable information unless conditions in the environment are accounted for and held constant. Not until measurement procedures are used can we determine rate of responses, that control conditions in the environment, and that systematically introduce new conditions one at a time for evaluation, do we obtain precise information for decision making.

Precise performance measurement, the key to valid and reliable information concerning the variables of learning, is based on the rationale that the child's performance (the dependent variable) is *the index* of the influence of the conditions introduced. The precision of measurement tools springs from the requirements they impose on the investigator, including: (a) specific identification of classroom behaviors to be measured, and (b) specific identification and systematic manipulation of classroom conditions to be evaluated for learning.

Direct and systematic observation of classroom behaviors enables the teacher to obtain a record of any behavior of concern in the classroom. Practically all *behavior* from the child that is of relevance to the teacher is observable. All *events, objects,* and *conditions* in the classroom are also observable. Consequently, classroom behaviors can be defined specifically and counted. For example, *sitting* in a seat, *lifting* a desk top, *reaching* for a book, *turning* pages, *writing* letters or numbers, *reading* words orally, and *whispering* to a neighbor are all observable behaviors. These responses can be further classified as desirable or undesirable, or appropriate or inappropriate to cues presented. They also are classifiable as those which should be increased or decreased or eliminated. Regardless of their definition and frequency, they are all patterns of responding to particular cues being attended to.

Measurement procedures. The procedures for measuring responses require four steps: (a) systematic observation of behavior during the task, (b) a record of its occurrence, (c) determination of its rate per minute, and (d) a graphic display of the data. The graphic display of response rate provides patterns of performance from which to evaluate the conditions.

First, for a response to be valid and available for reliable measurement, its dimensions must be definable and observable. The characteristics of a response are largely determined by the response requirements of the cues presented (letter sounding, word recognition, addition, or spelling, for example), and by the physical movement involved (oral, kinesthetic or tactual, and graphic). Each task can be further defined according to specific types of responses—for example, specific types of word recognition such as recognition of short vowel *a* in 3-letter words; or specific types of addition, such as addition of 2-letter numbers requiring carrying; or specific types of spelling, such as 3-letter words and their plurals.

Second, responses must be measured as they occur in active cycles of movement (Kunzelmann, 1968) in order to be reliable. A cycle of movement begins as the movement begins and ends as the movement ends. A pictorial illustration of cycles of movement in writing the letter *A* four times in 1 minute represents a tactic for measuring all other alphabetic and numeric graphemes as well as a variety of other symbols. In fact, any unit of behavior, once identified by its basic cycle of movement, is measurable.

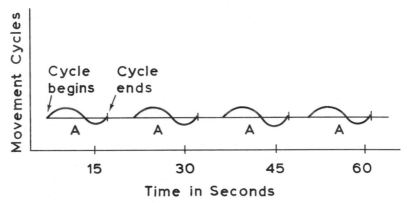

*After Kunzelmann, 1968.

Movement cycles, furthermore, must be basic enough to maintain comparable characteristics as materials become more complex and conditions systematically change. Otherwise comparisons of the influence of different conditions are not possible.

Third, recording the number of responses or movement cycles made per minute, as basic information, appears to be the best time unit for expressing response data, especially to account for any variance in session length at a time when all other conditions are constant. Finally, the record of rate of response is a visual display on graph paper, for which purpose 6-cycle semilogarithmic graph paper is becoming standard format, as it permits the charting of a wide range of performance rates, promotes consolidation of research data for more effective replication, and promotes growth for the field. This graph paper has the added advantages of (a) showing relative changes in rate of performance under different conditions, (b) allowing relative comparisons of the influence of different conditions without computations, and (c) retaining "the actual units of measurement of the raw data" (Kunzelmann, 1968, p. 144).

Precise procedures of measurement have the additional advantage of focusing attention on terminal objectives in skill development and the types of responses which are successive approximations to them. Achievement of such precision in identifying the specific skills, in identifying their hierarchy, and in specifying observable movement cycles as basic response units, will permit:

1. The specification of better criteria for evaluating instructional materials.
2. The development of better instruments and procedures for assessment of levels of skill development and degrees of deficit.
3. The identification of better criteria and tools for early identification of possible learning disabilities.
4. The identification of behavioral criteria that can be used as a scheme for identifying disorders in terms functional to the classroom.
5. The experimental testing of any and all methods of teaching basic skills.
6. The possibility of a more valid identification of those children who may be handicapped by some form of neurological involvement in a learning disability.

Programmed materials. The recent innovation of academic materials arranged in programmed format has easily identifiable requirements for active responses. Commercial materials which do not identify active responses can be modified to the point where they will. The only requirement is that responses for measurement must be active and observable and must occur at regular and frequent intervals.

Programmed materials have been especially designed to meet these objectives. With these materials, the child begins responding to the cues at a level where he makes few errors. Then he proceeds at his own rate through materials which become progressively more difficult and require responses which are successive approximations of the skills to be acquired. While all other classroom instructional materials are designed to meet the same objectives as programmed materials, the sequencing of these classroom materials for proper, efficient skill development has not proved as effective, unless the teacher has worked out an effective order.

These features of response measurement are as essential to daily classroom instruction as they are to research in the laboratory. If they are treated with the same care in the planning and application for instruction in the classroom as they are for research in the laboratory, procedures for performance measurement will be as effective for instruction as they will be for research.

Reinforcing Responses

Until recently, educators have credited the instructional curricula as *the* major influence in skill development and, consequently, have placed responsibility for learning directly on the child (Haring & Ridgway, 1967). Thus, past attempts to modify a learning problem have emphasized programs with built-in color cues, visual perceptual exercises, auditory perceptual exercises, and special organization and arrangements of materials. Furthermore, assertions from programmers, notably Holland (1960), Suppes (1964), among others, have emphasized programmed arrangement as the critical variable in the learning environment.

But research in behavioral psychology and education now can tell us how any behavior — including reading — comes under the control of relevant stimuli. This research states that the consequence of performance, when it is reinforcing and systematically applied, is a primary force in skill development. The independent variables functioning as reinforcers within the classroom are as crucial to improving the child's performance as the instructional materials presented to him. Reinforcement — whether in the form of verbal, social, academic, or other reinforcers extrinsic to usual classroom activities — when systematically used and relevant to the child, is the major variable in keeping the child at his task and working accurately once his level of skill is determined.

Through specific arrangements of consequences following a specified response, the rate of occurrence of academic, social, and verbal responses can be increased, decreased, maintained, or extinguished predictably. The principle of positive reinforcement explains the effect of a pleasant event in strengthening the probability of the occurrence of the response it follows. If the teacher's attention or reply of "good job" is a pleasant event for a child, the teacher can, by applying one of these rewards following a pattern of academic performance, predictably accelerate the child's rate of performance. *Positive reinforcement* can be viewed as a very general principle incorporating a number of subprinciples, all describing either (a) *types* of consequences which function as general positive reinforcers, or (b) *schedules* for presenting reinforcement which bring about precise patterns of behavior.

Specific types of stimuli which come to acquire strength as positive reinforcers can be described in terms of the strength and generality they predictably acquire to influence behavior. The subprinciples of *conditioned reinforcement* and *generalized reinforcement* explain the environmental arrangements which establish a wide variety of objects, events, conditions, and our own responses as pleasant events that can be used to increase the probability of responding. The human smile, the pat on the back, or the words in a book are not initially events which strengthen behavior, although for most individuals these stimuli gain strength when paired systematically with consequences already pleasant.

To establish a particular pattern of performance efficiently, it is not enough simply to present a pleasant event some time after a pattern of behavior or a set of responses has occurred. For example, acquisition of a response occurs most predictably when reinforcement is scheduled to be immediate and continuous. When a high rate of the behavior has become established, then reinforcement need occur only intermittently.

Negative reinforcement describes conditions that strengthen the probability of the occurrence of a pattern of responses through removal of an aversive stimulus after a response — arrangements which predictably produce escape and avoidance behaviors. Children in the classroom who do not begin working on an assignment until the teacher becomes very stern and scolds or nags have behaviors controlled through negative reinforcement. Under these conditions children typically stop work soon after the teacher stops prodding.

The principle of extinction describes environmental conditions that predictably eliminate a pattern of behavior. Arranging events so that a positively reinforcing consequence no longer follows a particular response pattern leads to the elimination of that behavior. For example, if the teacher ceases attending to a child when he is shouting or leaving his seat unnecessarily, these behaviors will decrease and eventually disappear, if it is the teacher's behavior that is maintaining them. Extinction occurs most effectively when a response incompatible with the response being extinguished is concurrently reinforced.

Without reinforcement, the human organism would never respond predictably to any stimulus. Technically, reinforcement establishes stimulus control. That is, a response immediately followed by an event which is reinforcing has a high probability of being repeated (Ferster & Skinner, 1957), and the environmental conditions present when the response was reinforced become discriminative stimuli that control the child's response in the presence of the same or similar stimuli (Terrace, 1966; Ferster & Perrott, 1968; Haring, 1968). Reinforcement, for example, can be credited as a primary factor in the discrimination of reading stimuli such as *b* and *d*.

Any stimulus can be made a discriminative stimulus so that when the word "hat" is presented, the child predictably says /hat/. Such stimulus control is no different from that observed when the child, hearing the recess bell, jumps from his seat and leaves for the playground. The child would not do this during his reading lesson, just as he would not use his spelling book to complete his math assignment or call the teacher "Mother." Specific stimuli control his responses because of past consequences of these responses.

The sensitivity of reinforcement as an influence on behavior can be readily seen when one considers that any stimulus has several observable dimensions. For example, the word "elephant" can be identified by its configuration; its length; its beginning, middle, or ending letters; its syllables; or by several or all of its sounds. Through reinforcement one or more of these dimensions may control the response which occurs in its presence; an effective sequence of cues will ensure that the relevant dimension(s) gain control. Once a dimension gains control, the child continues responding to that dimension, ignoring the other dimensions unless reinforcement contingencies change. Inappropriate stimulus control occurs when stimuli are not introduced to highlight their relevant dimensions in such a way that correct responses are made to them and reinforcement can follow.

The systematic presentation of reinforcement is such a powerful influence in the acquisition and maintenance of academic and social skills that even the scheduling of its occurrence will influence the level of performance achieved. For example, during the acquisition of a skill, frequent reinforcement promotes more accurate work in a given time than infrequent reinforcement. But when performance is occurring at a nearly maximum level of productivity, reinforcement is necessary only intermittently. For the purpose of this discussion, the reader needs to remember only that the systematic use of conditions and events as reinforcers contributes to the acceleration, maintenance, or elimination of behavior. Scheduling the occurrence of reinforcement is as important as the type of reinforcement presented.

These comments on stimulus control and reinforcement are emphasized here because it is urgent for the profession to attend to them in research and instruction. The application and further investigation of reinforcement variables have been a primary impetus for the experimental analysis of the learning process, not only because of the increasing awareness of the effects of reinforcement on behavior but more so because of the measurement procedures developed to investigate its influence. Dozens of books (Krasner & Ullmann, 1965; Ullmann & Krasner, 1965; Millenson, 1967; Haring, 1968) based on research are now available to describe this influence; yet, years of profitable research lie ahead for the further study of this major variable in human development.

Managing the Contingencies of Responses

The use of the influence of reinforcement in the development of academic skills cannot be haphazard, for precise management of the relationship between behaviors and their consequences is as essential in research and instruction as the proper sequencing of cues. Effective use of reinforcers — their amount, their timing in relation to the length of responding or the number of academic responses, and the changes in amount and frequency of reinforcement — is contingency management. Although the major focus of contingency management is on reinforcement, management of contingencies also requires attention to the presentation of cues relevant to academic responses. Secondarily, contingency management implies attention to the logistics of managing the reinforcement procedures.

Effective contingency management implies that all the cues and consequences impinging on the child's performance are identified and held constant while the child's pattern of responding to the task is measured over several sessions. This measurement produces a picture of the child's *baseline* performance pattern which can then be used for later comparison of performance when one change in conditions is introduced.

The procedures and rationale for the systematic manipulation of materials, conditions, or events deemed relevant to learning are best understood by considering several examples of basic designs in which procedures of contingency management are most effective. The designs obtain, in several different ways, a picture of performance under one set of conditions before a new condition is introduced to influence performance. These designs allow for conditions to be changed systematically after baseline measurement, as measurement of performance continues, thus providing response data for comparison of effects.

Obtaining a baseline measurement of performance is not difficult if well planned. A setting is first arranged whereby the conditions present for instruction are identified and controlled so as to promote the occurrence of a stable pattern of responses. When one of the conditions for instruction is changed, the rate of correct and incorrect responses may change (transition state) until the rate again stabilizes (a new steady state) under the second set of conditions. Because of the predictable nature of behavior in relation to environmental conditions, these steady states and transition states are replicable. Therefore, the influence of other conditions for instruction can be investigated against the known patterns of performance.

For example, consider that the investigator is interested in studying several variables which might influence the number of words learned from word lists having comparable characteristics. The variables might be the tape recorder, assistance from peers, and "no instruction at all," each compared to group instruction. Group instruction would be the baseline condition; performance records would be obtained in a number of sessions using group instruction. When the number of words learned daily appeared to stabilize for each child, one of the new variables would be introduced as the instructional procedure for learning the list of words and continued over a number of days while performance patterns were observed to determine if and when this new condition influenced a change in rate of word learning. Then the instructional condition would be reversed back to group instruction to note whether or not performance returned to the original pattern.

Second, the investigator might select one of several multiple baseline designs. Using group instruction as the baseline condition, he could introduce, one at a time, each of the other three conditions for teaching reading and evaluate their effects on performance.

Third, he could obtain baseline measures of performance on three different types of reading responses made under group instruction. Then he could introduce one of the new instructional procedures to one type of reading response, while continuing group instruction for the other two types of responses. This design is best for evaluating the effects of any type of reinforcer, such as evaluating the influence of the teacher's praise compared to time earned for self-directed activities.

If performance patterns change systematically as the conditions change, the investigator knows which of the instructional conditions is most effective and for which children. The value and strength of these designs comes from knowing the pattern of performance under one set of conditions so that it can be compared to a change in performance under another set of conditions. If performance patterns change for most students in a similar way under these probes, they serve as replications of the effects of these variables. Furthermore, reliable information concerning methods for individual children as well as for the group is obtained. Contingency management represents teaching at its best and research with widest control of influencing variables.

The product of contingency management is reliable response data from the child which serves as feedback on the effectiveness of contingency management. When the teacher or experimenter has manipulated variables according to an experimental analysis design with repeated demonstrations of the relative effects of specific conditions, when he has identified and controlled by systematic manipulation the extraneous conditions which may be affecting the performance data, and when he has systematically replicated the effects of these specific conditions, the information provided by the graphic display of data is as definitive as that which might be provided by statistical analysis of group data.

Response data obtained through this type of management are typically analyzed visually from a graphic display of data. Since the teacher or investigator is interested in the relative effects of conditions where the data are viewed in terms of the type of acceleration or deceleration or maintenance (Kunzelmann, 1968) resulting from a change in conditions, one of the following patterns of performance is sought. The experimental condition introduced upon a baseline measure of performance is evaluated in terms of relative changes in rate of performance: (a) a decreasing acceleration in rate of response, (b) a constant acceleration, (c) an increasing acceleration, (d) a maintenance of constant rate, (e) an increasing deceleration, (f) a constant deceleration, or (g) a decreasing deceleration. Quantitative changes in rate of responding can be described but the generalizable data come from the relative changes in rate of responding.

Statistical procedures are also available for determining the significance of the change in performance rate. If a visual analysis of data is not definitive enough, the recently introduced R_n statistic (Revusky, 1967), a nonparametric procedure, might be used for comparisons of individual mean data from condition to condition. Using a statistical experimental design, permitting a rank order analysis of the data of six subjects, each of whom performs as experimental subject once and control subject five times, one can determine the significance of the experimental treatment.

Experimental analysis designs might be considered short-term probes which allow the investigator a brief but reliable consideration of the feasibility of a method, materials, or procedures for effective teaching. With the availability of procedures for short-term probes, the investigator or teacher is able to look at the influence of more well defined variables than has typically been possible. These procedures offer the additional advantage of direct application of results. Because of the functional nature of the procedures, one investigation leads to the next as a search is conducted into the influence of other conditions or into parameters of the same conditions.

One of the major values of these experimental designs for contingency management will be their usefulness in evaluating various classroom conditions for motivating maximum performance, after a determination of the child's level of skills and selection of relevant academic materials. Studying the effects of various types of reinforcing consequences and the scheduling of their presentation is ideally suited for such designs. Since reinforcement variables are one of the two major conditions for skill building, it is essential that the investigator and teacher have at their command measurement procedures and designs functional for use in classroom.

Paradigms of the Learning Process

The basic components of the learning process that are observable during the teaching-learning act can be viewed from paradigms presented by Lindsley (1964) and Skinner (1953). They define the relationship of specific environmental conditions to behavior. In viewing either paradigm it is important to remember that a response immediately followed by an event which is reinforcing has a high probability of being repeated. In addition, reinforcement of that behavior in the presence of a particular stimulus gives a degree of control to that stimulus which comes to control the type of response made in its presence. For example, using Skinner's paradigm, if a child is smiled at by the teacher after he has made a correct response in arithmetic or is complimented while painting a picture, the probability is high that the child will again make that response in the presence of the same or similar materials.

$$S^D \dashrightarrow R \dashrightarrow S^r$$

arithmetic	adding or	teacher's
art materials	painting	smile or
		compliment

The arithmetic or art materials become a *discriminative stimulus* (S^D) in the presence of which the child will make that specific *response* (R) again as a result of his past experience with receiving a compliment — with receiving *reinforcement* (S^r) for making that response.

Lindsley presents his paradigm in two parts and adds one further symbol to account for the fourth component of the learning process which Skinner subsumes under reinforcement (S^r). Lindsley diagrams the specific variables of a learning situation first in terms of the four components which might be functioning as a unit, and, second, in terms of those four components which do form a functional unit for learning.

The initial diagram of the four components identifies the antecedent event (E^A), the movement (M) — the response to be measured, the arrangement (A) of reinforcement — the schedule, and the event which is a consequence of the response (E^C), all of which may or may not have a functional relationship.

$$E^A \dashrightarrow M \dashrightarrow A \dashrightarrow E^C$$

| antecedent | movement | arrangement | consequential |
| event | | | event |

Any one of these components can be investigated systematically for its influence in the learning situation if a known baseline of performance has been obtained. When a functional relationship has been identified between the components, the events, response, and scheduling of reinforcement can be more specifically diagrammed.

The functional paradigm cites the specific antecedent stimulus (S) which has demonstrated stimulus control over the response (R). In addition, the schedule of reinforcement (K) is precisely identified in terms of the ratio or interval on which reinforcement is supplied following the responses. This is the precise contingency between the behavior and the reinforcing consequences of it. The final component identifies the specific reinforcing consequence (C^R).

$$S \text{ -----------} \rightarrow R \text{ -----------} \rightarrow K \text{ -----------} \rightarrow C^R$$

stimulus   response   schedule of   reinforcer
                                    reinforcement
                                    (contingency)

This view of the components of the learning process is extremely relevant to research and to teaching. Investigating the learning process by systematic analysis of its components in research is considered experimental analysis of learning. The same process for instruction is considered precision teaching. Whether his activities originate in research or instruction, the educator must systematically attend to these four components.

Educational Technology

Educational technology, as its tools become more refined, will accelerate progress in the investigation of each component of the learning process. Like experimental education, educational technology also offers to extend precision of measurement and individualization of instruction. Progress will be especially evident in the further identification of terminal objectives, in the identification of subskills and responses which are successive approximations of these terminal objectives, in the development, selection, and ordering of cues, in response measurement, and in program modification based on these data.

Educational technology offers the control of conditions, the specification of variables, and the precision of measurement that educators have been searching for. It will be powerful as a research tool for the investigator, as an evaluative tool for instruction, and as a learning tool for the student. Over the next few years educational technology will become as responsible for the learning process as the teacher is now.

Currently, technology is providing a variety of ways to display instructional materials through functional teaching machines. In addition, it is providing a number of ways by which the child's performance can be measured. Numerous sensing devices have been developed and are coming to the aid of the educator for sensing and recording movement cycles. Many of these devices, developed at the Universities of Illinois, Pittsburgh, and Washington and Stanford University, are being used to record a variety of types of movement cycles, from epileptic seizures to hyperactive behaviors.

The current level of development in technology ranges from rudimentary equipment to the rapidly developing field of computers — hardware and software — providing very functional assistance for instruction in academic skill areas as well as in the content areas. Through the computer it is possible for the educator to receive quite accurate records of academic performance, accurate in terms of correct and incorrect responses which can be used to make further instructional decisions. These technological aids are significantly strengthening the skills of the technical educator as well as sharpening the results of his research.

Experimental education might best be characterized as: (a) a comprehensive strategy and set of objectives which encompass its total direction, (b) a set of measurement procedures for research, classroom instruction, and teacher and pupil evaluation, (c) an opportunity to extend the scientific base of education through the systematic use of common measurement procedures, and (d) a young and growing body of knowledge based on scientific research to be delineated as principles of instruction and principles of behavior. The extension of behavioral and instructional principles over the next few years, with the impending advancements of technology and the further application of experimental analysis procedures, will cause them to bloom as the guiding principles of teaching.

The Experimental Education Unit

Objectives and Strategy

The broad program at the Experimental Education Unit of the Child Development and Mental Retardation Center, University of Washington, is an initial and primary example of the emergence of experimental education. The broad program of the Unit includes research, professional preparation, service, instrumentation, and dissemination of information. All the activities of the Unit are directed toward organizing, developing, and evaluating the broad range of variables relevant to child performance in the classroom. The focus is on the development and testing of procedures, methods, instructional materials, and instrumentation that will promote the attainment of the fullest learning potential for each child, whether mentally retarded or handicapped in some other way.

Objectives

One of the major objectives of the Unit is intervention—changing classroom conditions in order to improve pupil performance. This objective includes continuing evaluation of those conditions most effective for improving performance, extending this knowledge to the didactic and practical experiences provided in programs of professional preparation, and guiding teachers in the reliable application of these findings in the classroom. Systematic observation is used to gain information for improving instruction. This information is then used in the continual refinement of programs, procedures, and materials. This is the orientation of research, professional training, and pupil instruction.

Specifically, the objectives are:

1. To apply and extend the principles of behavior and instruction in order to build upon previous knowledge.
2. To use procedures of experimental analysis in all endeavors of research and classroom evaluation to enable direct and systematic replication, without which a body of knowledge cannot grow.
3. To investigate the total resources of the classroom environment, including all curricular components of the learning environment and all other independent variables within the classroom which may affect pupil performance.
4. To develop and refine modern educational technology and instrumentation for obtaining efficient and accurate information within all areas of investigation.
5. To investigate the variables of preservice and inservice professional training programs and the procedures for evaluating teacher performance as a potential resource in learning.
6. To introduce laboratory research findings to applied settings for individuals and groups.
7. To translate the evaluations from field application back to the laboratory for further investigations.
8. To disseminate widely the results.

These objectives are designed to increase the amount of replicable information relevant to the education of children and youth.

Strategy

The strategy of the Experimental Education Unit springs from a desire to obtain better information about the child in the classroom in order to make more effective educational decisions. It is directed toward the investigation of observable variables of the learning process, through the use of measurement procedures that promote and extend a basic body of knowledge on the science of instruction.

The strategy designed to meet these objectives comprises three major programs: research, professional training, and service to children in the special experimental classrooms of the Unit. The research program is organized into teams in order to coordinate activities and to concentrate and conserve effort in the systematic investigation of a large area of research. All research activities of the Unit reflect the major concern of experimental education: to evaluate the interaction of the dependent variables of performance and the temporally related independent variables of classroom instruction.

The program of professional training, directed toward equipping the professional with necessary tools, is also concerned with the development of procedures and tools for the continual assessment of the teacher's performance and the evaluation of training procedures. The training program, like the service program, deemphasizes the exceptionality which labels the child, and instead, emphasizes the behavior and learning deficits exhibited and the classroom conditions which will promote growth.

The program of service to children is in many ways inseparable from the other two programs. for it is an essential component of both. The classrooms provide practicum experiences as well as direct teaching experiences for professional training. They provide. in addition. a source for the application of research findings from the laboratory as well as a source for initial, applied research. At the same time, the children receive a fully individualized and total curriculum, planned, implemented, and evaluated within the framework of experimental education.

Jointly, the programs comprise the beginnings of a multidisciplinary effort because the personnel represent a wide range of disciplines, including art, physical education, dental hygiene, dietetics, education, medicine, nursing, pediatrics, physical medicine and rehabilitation, psychiatry, psychology, social work, sociology, and speech pathology and audiology.

Physical Facilities

All three programs are conducted primarily within and through the physical facilities of the large, 1-story structure, except for those parts of each program specifically designed for other educational settings. Great care went into planning 41,000 square feet of facilities, starting with criteria the building should meet upon completion. Some of the criteria which influenced the design were: (a) safety for children, (b) indoor-outdoor relationships not only within the Unit, but in relation to the Clinical Training Unit, (c) separation of adult traffic flow from child traffic flow, and (d) flexibility to permit rearrangement of classrooms and other facilities to accommodate future change and innovation in programs. One overall concern was to provide a facility which afforded a school atmosphere rather than a hospital atmosphere.

Among the unique features of the building is the network established between the Instructional Center, Instrumentation, Data Photography, and the Data Processing Laboratory. The 100-seat capacity Instructional Center affords an opportunity to use multimedia projection, closed circuit TV, and an ultramodern telectern which has extensive capabilities and flexibility for use in demonstrations and in instruction of adults in professional training programs. This package for communication and training will be augmented by facilities for telephone conferencing to permit hook-up to distant institutions, school districts, and other research and demonstration facilities. As soon as funding is available, a computer-compatible response panel system will be installed to make possible feedback from each individual in the Instructional Center. Analysis of such data will be used in the study of the variables relevant to the improvement of instruction. The system will also permit the individualization of certain types of instruction at the adult level.

Along with the facilities for administrators, psychologists, social workers, speech therapists, and medical personnel, the Unit houses 14 classrooms with a student population projected to be approximately 170 by 1971. The classrooms are arranged in sets of two: one for a small number of children, especially exhibiting severe behavioral deficits, the other for a larger number of children primarily showing learning deficits. These classrooms for children 2.5 to 21 are provided at the levels of preschool, primary, intermediate, junior high; and a high school level having an orientation primarily prevocational and vocational. In addition, two classrooms have been set aside for children profoundly deaf and hard of hearing. Each classroom is equipped for closed circuit television in direct line with the Unit's large instructional center, and capabilities for automatic response measurement through cumulative recording and computer analysis. Each classroom has its own enclosed outdoor play area, as well as a large covered play court available to all classrooms. These associated outdoor classrooms enable activities for developing certain skills and learning taught better in the out-of-doors than in the indoor classroom environment. Each classroom has a connecting teacher's office and an observation booth which permits students in professional training to observe and take data through a one-way glass window.

In addition to classrooms and offices for staff and faculty, laboratories are available for behavioral research and other types of investigations.

Program of Research

The broad program of research at the Experimental Education Unit is being influenced by the program planning strategy of the Convergence Technique (Carrese & Baker, 1967), a technique for organizing major programs, subprograms, and individual research projects in an operational matrix.

For planning large scale research activities, this technique, as a modification of other network approaches, is more appropriate to the needs of a research program which, by its nature, comprises activities more tentative than nonresearch activities and requires flexibility for program modification over time. Use of this technique, when an adequate information base and technical capability are available, derives a number of benefits. First, it provides a framework for determining and ordering objectives. Second, it is a means to integrate the basic parts of the research program and to determine their interrelationships. Third, priorities and resource needs can be determined clearly. Finally, requirements for disseminating information, monitoring activities, and making decisions can be described.

With the convergence technique, the research activities, the information flow, and all the required resources (personnel, materials, equipment and facilities) are arranged in a matrix in an order logical to the research in a hierarchy of phases, steps, and individual projects. Each of these phases and steps has specific objectives, although not all the individual projects need be achieved in order to accomplish them. Accomplishment of certain projects, however, may be prerequisite to the commencement of others.

The matrix design, in addition, provides for the timing of information, the requirements for resources, and the points at which program activities converge on the objectives to be accomplished.

Such a convergence chart represents a "valid model of the scientific content of the program to be conducted, and if the sequential order of the program elements is accomplished on the basis of this logic, then, in reality, as research performance moves in the matrix from left to right in time, the intermediate objectives of each step and phase will be achieved and the scientific scope of the program will become narrower until all efforts converge on the end point which has been established as the overall program goal." (p. B-423-3)

To meet the commitments for building a scientific foundation of educational data at the Unit, research at three levels of investigation — basic, developmental, and applied — is necessary. Basic research is the level where the dependent and independent variables are the most precisely defined and most accurately controlled. The direction of research at this level is to discover laws, to refine procedures of experimental control, and to investigate the fundamental features of the processes of learning.

Research activity at the second level — developmental — is designed to develop and refine procedures, materials, display methods, instrumentation, computer-assisted instruction, and other forms of modern technology directed toward more precision in instruction. This level of research necessarily produces a product, an independent variable of performance directly applicable to instructional settings. Such development, then, necessitates a third level of research activity — applied research.

Applied research activity, which tests the independent variables developed and refined at the second level, requires measurement procedures enabling continuous evaluation of the experimental innovation in the setting where the variables will be used. Here at this level, as at the other two levels, measurement procedures are those of experimental analysis. Information is gained in the applied setting through continuous measurement of the child's performance during the application of the product. The performance data, used for evaluation of the product, are fed back immediately to the setting of developmental research where the product is further refined to permit more precise, functional application.

As a total strategy, these three levels of research have become visible in seven major areas of activity at the Unit. Over the past several years this activity has provided the groundwork for continuing research in communications, preschool behavior, social and academic behaviors, instrumentation, and vocational education. Within each area a team of researchers, directed by a coordinator, was organized. The activities of each team are based on the objectives, strategy, and measurement procedures of experimental education. Investigators within each team share a common interest as well as related individual research experiences. Team membership overlaps and is also quite flexible. The major objectives of each team are the subobjectives of the research directions of the Experimental Education Unit. The subobjectives of each team are directed toward satisfaction of the major objectives, and are in turn the major objectives of individual investigators whose interests they reflect.

Communications Research Team

Review of research activities. Research in this area has centered on two problems. Rieke (1968) has investigated the use of teacher and peer attention in the acquisition of gestural and verbal behaviors of speech deficient children in the communication classrooms. She and her associates have also directed attention to the identification of behavioral criteria in the language development of normal early childhood.

The research team in this area is concerned with two types of exceptionalities: severe hearing losses and communication deficits not a function of hearing loss. With both types of disorders the child's abilities to respond to auditory events and/or to express himself verbally are below norms for chronological age. Consequently, the direction of the research is to identify the variables critical to deficits in communication and language reception. The team first plans an investigation of the small steps necessary and sufficient for the development of a language scale as a curriculum guide. Second, they plan to study the variables of transfer from the communications classroom to the regular classroom in the field without a loss of acquired language behavior. Third, evaluation of components of a training program essential to the development of clinical research specialists will be made. The influence of an inservice training program for the field teacher of the deaf child will also be studied. Finally, the variables of very early language training in the establishment of early and effective language in the deaf child will be determined.

Preschool Research Team

Review of research activity. At the preschool level, the use of social reinforcement has been of special interest. Allen and her associates (1964, 1966, 1967a, 1967b) have studied the influence of teacher and parent social interaction in the acquisition and elimination of appropriate and inappropriate social behaviors in the more normal preschool setting. In addition, Nolen and her associates (Haring, Hayden &

Nolen, 1969) have investigated the systematic application of social reinforcement for changing deviant and deficient social and pre-academic behaviors of disadvantaged children. Their research under-scores the use of teacher and peer social reinforcement for establishing desirable social and preacademic behavior.

Proposed research activity. This team recognizes the need for refined experimental analysis of antecedent and consequent stimuli that function as variables to increase social, verbal, and preacademic skills. Consequently, their intentions are to: (a) investigate the variables in the classroom which function as cues and reinforcers of normal preschool behaviors, (b) study the effects of reciprocal peer interaction, (c) examine response generalization from the preschool setting to other settings in which the child functions and examine the variables which promote this, and (d) measure behaviors in the classroom with procedures extended and refined from the laboratory. Experimental designs relevant to the school setting are an underlying concern in all the work of this team.

Academic Research Team I

Review of research activities. Team members have concentrated their activities in three directions: program evaluation, response measure-ment, and evaluation of reinforcement variables. Activities in program development and evaluation (Lovitt, Kunzelmann, Nolen & Hulten, 1968) in an instructional resource center to date have emphasized evaluation of the content and sequence of commercially prepared programs in reading and arithmetic. These evaluations have been guided by three educational objectives: (a) the acquisition and refine-ment of basic skills, (b) the acquisition of knowledge of content, and (c) remediation which may be required for modifications in the develop-ment of skills and the acquisition of knowledge. At all times the response data of both correct and error rates serve as the basis for evaluation. Terminal objectives of these efforts include the develop-ment of a large resource center for continuous evaluation of all educational stimuli as they relate to the child's performance.

Response measurement in the special classroom (Kunzelmann, 1968) has involved a search for valid units of responding basic enough to enable reliable assessment of performance and evaluation of variables over time as response requirements necessarily become more complex. Identification of movement cycles, ranges of rates of per-formance, types of graphic performance patterns, and other measure-ment techniques have been emphasized.

A large number of investigations within both academic teams have concentrated on the effects of reinforcement variables which function to strengthen, weaken, or maintain patterns of performance. Establishment of reading skills through the systematic use of reinforcement variables has been investigated by Haring and Hauck (1969). A thoroughly programmed environment for reading in a resource room setting was presented to four severely disabled readers. The sequence of reading materials was programmed commercially, while the systematic use of token reinforcement was continually monitored, using daily performance data. This individualized approach to reading with specific attention to the reinforcement of correct responses doubled daily performance and changed the levels of reading skills by one and one-half to four years in only five months of daily 75-minute sessions.

This basic set of procedures for contingency management in programming the reading environment was extended to the regular classroom with 24 poor readers (Haring & Hauck, 1969b). Procedures were developed for framing basal readers, measuring reading responses, reinforcing individual performance with activities natural to the classroom, and evaluating pupil progress which totally individualized the reading environment. This form of contingency management provided the teacher with a reading program which students eagerly sought, where discipline problems were eliminated for the duration of each session, where no student ever handed in an incomplete assignment, and where students performed their tasks so efficiently that they read themselves right out of materials.

Proposed research. Six types of research activity are planned. The first concern will be the identification of types of movement cycles made to academic tasks defined by their topography, rate limits, and ranges of rate. An extension of the work on self-contingency management will also be made. Other research will be directed toward the identification of the cues and their sequence, as well as the reinforcers which facilitate development of phonic skills. Two other investigations will focus on the effects of group contingencies on academic rate and the effects of the availability of reading materials on the switching and choice rates of young readers. Programming the academic environment for errorless learning of reading and math skills for children mentally retarded who live in the central area of the city will be another major effort.

Academic Research Team II

Review of research activities. The investigations of this team have centered on cooperative behavior, assessment of antecedent events, especially preference responses with conjugate reinforcement, and classroom management procedures. Burgess and Lovitt (1968) have been exploring the conditions under which two individuals will emit reciprocally reinforcing behavior. This work thus far indicates that individuals will engage in such behaviors to the extent that they are dependent upon one another for reinforcement.

Lovitt (1968) has directed his attention to the technique of conjugate reinforcement, especially for the purpose of assessment of preference of different variables functioning as continuous reinforcement contingent upon responding. Using such variables as different narrative rates of storytelling, sex of narrator, types of music, and rate of response as a function of reinforcement, conjugate reinforcement has been demonstrated as an effective procedure of determining reinforcement preference.

Within the special classrooms at the Unit, Lovitt (1968) has systematically explored several types of contingency management, two of which have been reinforcement contingent upon a specific rate and self-management of contingencies. Results indicate that when reinforcement is graduated to provide increasing increments in reinforcement as rate increases to three progressively faster yet accurate rates of performance, the most efficient rate predictably occurs. Investigating self-management of contingencies as opposed to teacher management, reveals that contingencies set by the child are more effective for improving performance.

Projected research. Research in this area will primarily expand upon that already begun. Based on the initial work of Burgess and Lovitt which established rate of exchange as the basic datum for the analysis of cooperation, these investigators intend to study the acquisition and maintenance of exchange rates as a function of a variety of social relationships and reinforcement histories. A number of independent variables of exchange rates will be investigated. Cooperative behavior will also be measured by verbal and nonverbal instruction in terms of rate of exchange. Then, using the baseline exchange rate data from this study, as well as the same subjects, other variables will be investigated. Applied research on contingency management in the regular classroom will be extensively investigated.

Social Behavior Research Team

Review of research activities. Concentrating on the variables of the social process, team members have especially been concerned with measurable social responses identifiable as competition, cooperation, and exchange, and the reinforcement variables instrumental in their development. Mithaug (1968) defines competition between any two subjects as "behavior that is increased and maintained by a comparison of its consequences with that of another's behavior consequences." Exchange he defines as "interaction in which the behaviors are reciprocally reinforcing." Cooperation is defined as "organized or coordinated behavior that produces and is maintained by progress on a common task." These investigators have determined that cooperation on single task requirements appears when: (a) the interdependency of the task requires each group member to cooperate to achieve the task, (b) reinforcement is provided to the individual upon completion of the group task, and (c) feedback is provided on accuracy of responses to the task. When cooperation is required under conditions of alternative tasks, it is necessary for the above conditions to be in effect and for more individual reinforcement to be provided for task achievement than for alternatives (Mithaug & Burgess, 1967, 1968). Cooperation also emerges when each member knows the contingencies for cooperative responses (Mithaug, 1969).

Projected research. Using both normal and mentally retarded subjects, the team will investigate the variables which function with cooperative, competitive, and exchange behaviors. The information obtained will then be applied to the instructional setting in order to develop and change social behaviors. The latter phase has as its terminal objective the development of social behavior chains in the classroom, with academic work as the group task.

Instrumentation Research Team

Review of activities. The instrumentation team has directed itself toward three primary activities: development and evaluation of devices and processes for collecting response data from the classroom, production and evaluation of teaching films in which the viewer actually participates, and the use of data photography to facilitate analysis of results. All endeavors represent forms of response measurement which will provide information as well as techniques for the display of visual and auditory stimuli and the presentation and scheduling of reinforcement.

Projected research. The application of computer-assisted instruction in the special classrooms of the Unit, as well as in several specially selected local schools, will be a major activity. Attention will be given to response measurement of handicapped children, program evaluation of the language arts and mathematics curricula for these children, and physical modifications necessary for ease of use by, for example, children who are orthopedically handicapped.

The activities for developing data photography will be concerned with units of film which train the teacher to observe children, to specify behaviors, to select relevant materials for instruction, and to evaluate the effectiveness of teaching using the performance data of the child. These activities will also attend to the measurement devices sensitive to the participant's responses. In addition, evaluation of educational media and equipment designs will be systematic and regularly available to the local schools.

Vocational Education Research Team

The Vocational Education Research Team recognizes the need to investigate the skills that are necessary for successful performance in the vocational setting. At the same time, it also recognizes the lack of a continuous sequence of experiences from the academic emphasis of the classroom to the vocational emphasis of the job setting for mentally retarded youth. The variables which motivate task performance to criterion level are also considered essential to investigate. The team intends: (a) to isolate and specify the essential skills necessary for maintaining a vocation and for making the required responses necessary to face individual and family responsibilities in the community, and (b) to investigate as precisely as possible, within a controlled environment and within the community, those variables which can be applied to improve performance as an employee, as a family participant, and as a citizen active in the community. The investigators will especially conduct a task analysis of various kinds of vocational and prevocational subskills that must be taught in order to acquire the necessary final skills. Performance rates that may be predictive of success at employment will be studied. Variables of wage payment will be evaluated for their function as reinforcers. In addition, materials will be developed that are designed for the acquisition of specific sequences of vocational tasks. All of these activities are directed toward the establishment of broad programs of research, professional and semiprofessional training, and demonstration in the prevocational and vocational training of the retarded. The vocationally oriented unit will provide facilities and equipment where professionals can view and evaluate effective techniques.

The vocational unit plans a Learning Laboratory to meet the academic needs of the student in addition to his regular school work. The lab will consist of four separate units, each serving a particular developmental or skill level, i.e., grades K-3, 4-6, 7-9, and 10-12. These labs will allow each student to obtain supervised, successful experiences appropriate to the subject matter of both prevocational and vocational skills. The training program for teachers and counselors will occur prior to the establishment of the lab settings. Prevocational instruction will be incorporated into the K-6 curriculum while the junior high level through twelfth grade will include the vocational-technical curricula.

At all times, concentrated effort will be directed toward developing, testing, and evaluating programs, techniques and procedures for vocational training.

Other Research Activities

Research in professional training. In addition to these five areas of investigation, the professional training program is an adjunct of the program of research. In this area, the effort has been to train teachers from the regular classroom to use procedures of experimental education (Haring, 1968). When fully trained after two years, these teachers will then become resource teachers with the skills not only to use these procedures to improve child performance, but also with the skills to train other teachers within their own buildings to use these procedures. The variables specifically investigated have been the criteria for an entering assessment of teacher skills, specification of the components of an effective training program and their sequence, criteria and measurement procedures for teacher performance evaluation, and administrative variables in the effective functioning of a resource teacher. A listing of the specific content objectives of the training program has been left to the section describing the program of professional training. Although an evaluation of these variables has not been completed at this writing, results promise to identify many specific response components of teaching and the training variables which should be introduced for their acquisition.

Program of Professional Training

The teacher is a tremendous coordinator of all resources for learning. It is the teacher's task to coordinate the wide variety of curricular materials, to coordinate the technological media effective for instruction, and to coordinate the exploration of temporal arrangements of events which effectively reinforce performance. In addition, the teacher must evaluate these effects, using reliable procedures of measurement. These skills must be learned.

The program of training encompasses the areas of mental retardation, learning disabilities, emotional disturbance, the deaf and hard of hearing, and speech and hearing. Although instruction is not based on these labels of exceptionality, several of the programs are identified in this traditional form because of the dictates of legislation pertaining to fellowship and trainee funding. The larger focus is on training professionals to work with children exhibiting any kind of deficit in behavior or learning. The total program is a comprehensive approach, not only to the instruction of teachers, but also to the evaluation of teacher performance and program effectiveness.

The overall purpose training is to provide didactic and practicum experiences that help the professional acquire the knowledge and procedures of experimental education. Special emphasis is given to experiences which develop skills: (a) to observe and measure behavior and performance as it occurs in the classroom, (b) to establish and maintain experimental control, (c) to manipulate instructional conditions that appropriately cue and reinforce specific types of performance, and (d) to make decisions for further instruction based on response data from the child.

Objectives

The comprehensive purpose of the training programs is to develop competencies and skills of professional educators in the following areas:

1. Assessment of child performance in four areas: academic, verbal, social, and physical requirements in the classroom.
2. Establishment of systematic procedures for observing, recording, and analyzing behaviors.
3. Determination of child preference for activities available to the classroom.
4. Familiarity with the presently available instructional materials within the broad range of content — reading, science, math, language, and social studies — and their sequence for skill development.

5. Establishment of task initiation based upon initial assessment.
6. Development of systematic procedures for maintaining ongoing task performance.
7. Utilization of measurement procedures which permit continuous assessment of performance which guides ongoing instruction.
8. Implementation of systematic contingency management to promote efficient performance as well as effective discriminations.

The acquisition of these skills is complete when the trainee demonstrates them on both individuals and groupings of children.

Didactic and practicum experiences are concurrent. Laboratory exercises, which begin the trainee early in the program with teaching a child, provide step by step guidelines for the acquisition of new teaching skills. In addition, they provide the guidelines by which teacher skills can be measured.

Teacher performance is evaluated through pupil progress and through systematic observation of teacher responses to the instructional tasks she must perform. Assessment of the trainee's professional skills, i.e., responses which must be made before, during, and after the act of teaching, are based on the terminal objectives of the training program.

As with the service program, the broad program of training shares a common commitment to the idea that all children learn and behave in a manner consistent with behavior principles. In addition, as with the research program, it shares the common commitment to continual evaluation of the conditions sufficient and necessary to effective instruction. The contiguity of these latter two programs is underscored by the concern for tactics to evaluate teacher performance as well as tactics to evaluate the components of training.

Demonstration Project

The training program (Haring, 1969) which probably best illustrates the efforts of professional training at the Unit was that begun Autumn Quarter, 1967, with the support of the U.S. Office of Education. The program was designed to teach regular classroom teachers to use the procedures of experimental education as a remediation process for children in the regular classroom who exhibit learning disabilities and behavior disturbances. The first objective was to train a small cadre of teachers to function as resource teachers within school buildings where they would apply their skills through the modification of child behavior through the regular classroom teacher, while at the same time, teaching the regular class teacher the same skills learned through the program. The project, under which teachers from four surrounding school districts are being trained, has sought to demonstrate the importance of training teachers to apply the principles of instruction and behavior and to use scientific measurement procedures in order to evaluate the interrelationships between the variables of the teaching-learning act. More importantly, this project was designed to demonstrate that teachers so trained can assist regular and special classroom teachers to: (a) specify behavioral problems, (b) design remediation plans to alleviate these problems, (c) arrange conditions to implement the procedures, and (d) evaluate the effectiveness of the arrangements of conditions for learning.

The trainees were taught to directly observe and measure social and academic behavior, to specify and evaluate classroom variables relevant to performance, to assess academic skills, and to program the environment for modification of behaviors. From direct assessment of the child's performance, the teacher learns to evaluate classroom resources, and thus to make effective educational decisions, all based on the child's response data. The objectives of these teachers are those of the training program itself: precision teaching for efficient learning.

Before the intensive training began, each trainee was assessed in her skills relevant to the objectives and components of the training program. As she entered the program, each was presented with four tasks to conduct, during which time permanent records of her performance were obtained through video tape, magnetic tape, and written records from the trainee as well as from the classroom teacher with whom the tasks were conducted. During each phase of the evaluation, the specific responses of the teacher relevant to her task were specified, observed, and recorded from observation of her ongoing performance and from her written records of procedures and evaluations.

Each trainee was evaluated from responses exhibited while: (a) assessing the skills of a child, (b) assisting another teacher arrange a remedial program in class for a child new to class, and (c) assisting a classroom teacher to make an assessment of the performance of a child with a learning problem who was not new to class, as well as with a child new to class. Comparison of the types and number of responses the teacher made relevant to prespecified performance criteria was the basis of evaluation. Essentially, the prespecified performance criteria were the terminal skills expected to be developed through the program.

Teachers in this program spend a concentrated two years in training, first under direct instruction within the classrooms of the Experimental Education Unit, then under intermittent supervision as they assist teachers and children both within the experimental and regular classrooms.

The project demonstrates the feasibility of:

1. Immediate feedback to the teacher in training on her accuracy of performance in the program, and immediate feedback to the instructors of the program on teacher skill acquisition and readiness for the next step in training.
2. Experimental analysis for behavior modification within the child's own classroom environment.
3. Precision teaching for efficient learning.
4. Resource teacher assistance to the classroom teacher to assist the child.
5. Direct evaluation of teacher performance.

The uniqueness of this approach to professional training rests on four features. First, terminal behavioral objectives guide the entering assessment, instruction, and evaluation of the teacher in training. Second, training experiences start the teacher immediately with the child in the classroom. Third, the skills taught are exactly those useful in classroom instruction. Finally, wherever feasible, modern technology is introduced to facilitate instruction and the evaluation of training.

End results of the efforts of the program of training will be the redirection of professional training to focus on the further training of experienced regular classroom teachers to provide them the skills to manage and prevent learning and behavior problems within the regular classroom.

Projected directions. Future activities of these programs are directed at more precision in identifying, implementing, and evaluating the components of training. To accomplish these objectives will require further evaluation of the teacher responses that are sufficient and necessary for effective instruction. To accelerate this overall direction, a progressive increase in the utilization of education technology is especially anticipated.

Program of Service

One of the three principal functions of the Experimental Education Unit is to provide service (Haring & Kunzelmann, 1966) to children and youths between the ages 2.5 and 21 years, who, having problems with learning or behaviors which interfere with the acquisition of skills and impede progress in school, are referred by clinics, physicians, school districts, or parents. While the primary objective is to provide service to mentally retarded children, many children placed in the Unit have other neurological dysfunctions, physical handicaps, and sensory handicaps. As retardation is only relative to normal development, the focus of instruction is diffused over the total range of development to include even children environmentally disadvantaged. All of the children, however, can be viewed as retarded in one or more aspects of development or performance, such as motor skills, language, speech, academic achievement, emotional maturity, or social behavior.

Generally, children for whom appropriate classes can be located in public or private schools are not admitted to the classes within the Unit. In addition to the service programs provided within the Unit, cooperative programs are maintained within the community, with emphasis on inner-city, suburban, and rural schools.

Objectives

The program of service is designed to implement a total educational management program that:

1. Presents sequences of cues to facilitate errorless, individualized development of skills.
2. Motivates maximum performance.
3. Provides instructional programs which at all times enable active responding from children, permitting daily program evaluation and modification based on the response data of the child.
4. Involves the parents, the Experimental Education School, and the community school programs in this total effort.

Organization for Instruction

The five major classroom divisions are organized according to the age of the child: preschool, primary, intermediate, secondary, and vocational. Special programs at the preschool level are also available for children profoundly deaf or hard of hearing and for children exhibiting communication disorders.

Within each instructional division two classrooms are provided. One classroom serves up to 12 children who have rather severe deficits in verbal, social, preacademic, and academic behavior. Placement for this group is a maximum of two years. The second classroom within each division manages approximately 18 children having moderately handicapping deficits — primarily academic. Placement for these children is shorter, not to exceed one year, at which time they are returned to more natural placement in the community.

Each division is staffed by an instructional team comprising a coordinator, two master teachers, one assistant teacher, and one teacher intern. In total, this cadre is responsible for: (a) service to approximately 160 children, (b) coordination of professional training in the classroom, and (c) cooperation in research projects designed by a variety of investigators from the number of disciplines. In addition to these services, educational services are also provided by psychologists, pediatricians, speech pathologists, and sociologists.

All teachers in the Experimental Education Unit School participate in regular teachers' meetings, parents' meetings, inservice training programs, multidisciplinary training and research programs, special conferences and seminars, and meetings of professional organizations. In the classrooms they are continuously concerned with the selection, modification, or development of instructional materials appropriate to the individual child's educational diagnosis; they evaluate procedures and teaching methods to determine their effectiveness; they record data on children's performances and graph this information to determine implications for individualizing instruction or modifying behavior.

Instructional Team Coordinators participate in meetings of the Consultant Advisory Committee when children are being considered for admission to the particular program they coordinate. If a child is to be transferred to another program, the Team Coordinator will assist in effecting a successful transfer and in following the progress of the child in his new placement. They also assist in developing new special instructional programs, either in the University or in the community. In addition, they work with the faculty in the assignment and training of University students placed at the Unit for practicum experiences.

Instructional Management

Instructional management in the Experimental School is best described by: (a) the physical facilities available, (b) the curriculum, (c) the response measurement procedures, (d) the basic form of reinforcement used, (e) the types of contingency management provided, and (f) the entering assessment procedures.

Physical facilities. Each classroom is divided into two sections without a physical partition. In one area the students respond at their desks to academic tasks. In the other area the students respond to a wide variety of activities in art, crafts, and science, for example. The large, carpeted classrooms easily accommodate both areas of activity. From each classroom a door leads to an adjacent, enclosed outdoor play area. At the entrance to each classroom from the large hallway are two smaller rooms: a teacher's office with one-way glass, and a larger observation room also with one-way glass. The structure of the observation room is designed to accommodate the observer with a ledge and inset lights at sitting height for ease in recording data.

Facilities at the preschool level provide for communications classes, Head Start programs, normal preschool, and programs for children profoundly deaf and hard of hearing. Facilities for children at the primary, intermediate, and initial junior high levels are primarily the self-contained classrooms described previously. At the high school level, extensive vocational facilities are being organized to include full shop operations as well as a complete home economics area. In addition, a large gymnasium with an adjacent outdoor court is provided for physical education.

Curriculum. The curriculum, totally individualized for each child in class, is primarily comprised of programmed material, commercial or teacher made. For the preschool classes, the curriculum centers on cues which facilitate the development of social, verbal, and pre-academic skills regardless of the program. In addition, cues for the communications classes as well as classes for the deaf and hard of hearing are selected and arranged to enhance the acquisition of receptive and expressive speech. Above the level of preschool, each child is presented a broad curriculum in reading, math, spelling, geography, writing, science, and social studies. For automatic display of stimuli, the several devices used before the introduction of computer-assisted instruction included the language master, the MTA scholar, the cyclo teacher world book and systems 80. The application of computer-assisted instruction, currently in the initial stages of a pilot project for teaching mathematics, is planned for extensive use.

Curriculum for vocational education, in its developmental stages, will focus on cues which can be sequenced to promote each response component of the final skill, as identified from task analyses. The parameters of this curriculum will also embrace cues necessary to prevocational skills. In addition, the overall school curriculum includes, for each child, experiences in home and family life, physical education, and the fine arts.

Response measurement procedures. Procedures have been designed which implement the requirements of effective response measurement, as described earlier in the chapter. Measurement procedures are necessarily concerned with responses, movement cycles, and rate of response. As described earlier, the occurrence of one movement cycle of a particular behavior is counted as one response. Over a period of time, a number of these responses can be observed and counted. When the amount of elapsed time is known, as well as the count of responses, the rate of the occurrence of these responses can be determined.

For ease of record-keeping, a set of event records is on the desk of each child at all times. Either the teacher or the child (if trained) records the response data and specific information on events temporally pertinent to these responses. The Event Record (Figure 1) at the Unit provides a place to record: (a) time of recording, (b) pupil or teacher initiation of contact, (c) academic subject, (d) errors, (e) correct response data, (f) points earned, (g) consequences chosen, (h) number of minutes of earned time used, (i) time remaining to be spent, (j) total errors, (k) total correct responses, (l) total points earned, and (m) ratio of correct responses to errors. This event record is usable for one hour of data at which time a new data sheet is begun.

From these event records each day, performance records are graphed on 6-cycle log paper to show the pupil's correct response rate to each of the academic tasks presented. His error rate on these materials, and any other target behaviors, may also be graphed from these records. In addition, data are used to evaluate the number of times the teacher interacts or assists the child, how many points he earns, when he redeems the points for free time, and how he uses these minutes of earned free time.

The modes of responding that require analysis in order to determine the total effectiveness of a program are being discovered from these initial explorations in the classroom, with further refinements to follow later from the laboratory. Measurement from the classroom in the future will be ongoing as computer-assisted instruction becomes incorporated into the school program.

Basic forms of reinforcement. Reinforcement procedures are based on the Premack Principle (Premack, 1959), the principle on which the physical organization of the classroom is also based. Premack generalized that any behavior with a higher probability of occurring than another can be used to reinforce the less likely one if it is made contingent on the performance of the less likely. Any high probability behavior, such as coloring, listening to music, or building models, will reinforce any preceding low probability behavior, such as reading, mathematics, or spelling (Haring & Lovitt, 1967). Translated into classroom operations, this temporal arrangement of activities provides the child who has successfully completed a certain amount

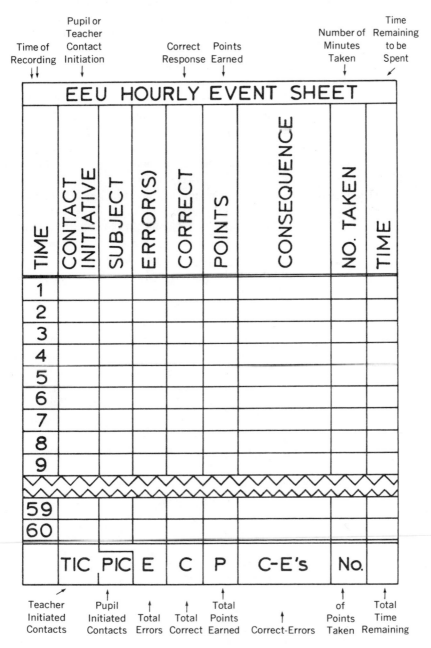

Fig. 1.

of work with a certain number of points that may later be redeemed for leisure time pursuits. For example. for every two correct math responses, the child might be given one point or minute of free time.

This form of reinforcement, especially when points are used for correct responses, is a token reinforcement system, whose planning and implementation is just as carefully laid out as the sequencing of academic materials. In fact, at the present stage in the development of more precise instruction, educators who systematically use reinforcement for performance are probably more effective in their sequencing of reinforcement than educators have managed to become with academic cues.

The high strength areas arranged for reinforcing performance contain a wide variety of activities from which children can choose to spend their earned time. Activities both indoors and in the outdoor play area are available. Plans include arrangements to change gradually the types of available reinforcers, from those which are far removed from academic pursuits to those very similar, as specific types of performance rates are acquired and maintained at a high level over a period of time.

Contingency management. From the graphic displays of daily performance record of correct and error rates of response. the teacher is able to determine the effectiveness of cueing and the strength of the reinforcers for performance. The child's pattern of errors, of correct responses, of points earned, spent, and saved, and of activities engaged in during the use of earned time all reveal the effectiveness of the conditions for learning. With this information the teacher can plan changes in instructional programming for the child and can commence to evaluate the effectiveness of the new decision for modification. again using the response data to be collected from performance.

Contingency management in the classrooms takes a number of directions. It focuses on:

1. The scheduling of reinforcement.
2. Changes in types of reinforcers.
3. Changes in the timing of the availability of high strength activities in relation to the timing of points earned.
4. Self-contingency management as opposed to teacher-imposed contingencies.
5. The interrelationships introduced between the types and scheduling of reinforcement and the patterns and levels of criterion performance.

Entering assessment. Following the completion of admission procedures, the collection of data on the referred child, and the recommendations for placement made by the Unit's Consultant Advisory
Committee, the child enters a classroom containing a population of
children primarily his age mates. At this time he undergoes a thorough
analysis of his learning and behavior difficulties as they occur in the
instructional situation.

Based on the information obtained. a more functional analysis of
his skills and the variables for instruction is possible. Because the
assessment procedures entail the use of precisely specified materials
and events relevant to instruction as well as precise measurement of
the responses made to the assessment tasks presented. an effective
program can be implemented directly. Because the procedures allow
repeated measurement of performance to these conditions a number of
times before their effects are evaluated, more meaningful information
for instruction is obtained. Having an evaluation of both the product
as well as the process of instruction, the teacher can implement a better
initial program.

From this initial assessment. educational objectives are established
for the child. These behavioral objectives are generally specified in
terms of direction—to increase or decrease specific behavior. The
objectives may be to increase the child's skills in certain areas—more
specific reading or mathematics skills or more involvement with
peers. Or the objectives might be directed toward decreasing the
occurrence of such behaviors as hitting or talking out of turn. In
addition, the extent of expected improvement is also specified.

Following detailed assessment and specification of objectives, the
teacher can incorporate the child and his instructional program into
the ongoing management system of her class. First, academic materials
that correspond to the child's current level of performance are selected
—programmed wherever possible. Second, the child is placed on
contingencies which specify the relationships that will operate between
his performance and the opportunities for time to engage in leisure time
activities. Third, the conditions arranged for instruction based on the
initial functional assessment are held constant over a period of time
while their effectiveness is evaluated from response data obtained
from the child's performance.

The process of decision making by the teacher in the classroom.
which begins with measuring performance, differs very little from
that of the scientist in the laboratory in that the more carefully the
information is collected about interrelationships between conditions
set up and the behavior measured, the better the decisions about the

next procedures are likely to be. Thus teaching becomes more precise, more scientific — a parallel to effective research.

Projected Activities

The future plans for the program of service at the Unit include continued refinements in the application of environmental control on programming, behavior measurement, and contingency management. The results of service thus far are promising in that the behavior of the children at home. at school, and in the community has changed in line with specified educational goals.

This program will witness many advancements and refinements in educational technology and instrumentation for response measurement and stimulus display. Experimentation in each of the areas at all times precedes application. Testing of procedures and programs before their application in public school settings forms the basis for the development and refinement of instructional practices.

Conclusion

The overall viewpoint of research, training. and service within the Experimental Education Unit (Haring & Hayden. 1968) is that, although the response deficits children exhibit may have a biological basis, the temporal relationships between the response patterns and the conditions and events within the environment become the critical factors in learning. That behavior occurs predictably has been well documented and is not at all restricted to "normal" behavior. The patterns of behavior exhibited in mental retardation or any other handicapping condition have also come about in predictable ways.

Any program of activities which seeks to apply known principles and to extend them through the use of scientific procedures facilitates the growth of a field. The Unit, through its broad program, is seeking to make this contribution, as are other similar programs around the nation. These contributions are building what might be considered a discipline of experimental education.

Education in the form described here is experimental because of the degree of control over classroom conditions that is possible with the use of procedures of experimental analysis. Common use of these measurement procedures will facilitate the growth of a science of instruction.

Research educators can do well to build on behavior principles readily available from the behavior laboratories and apply these principles to the classroom setting. Academic learning in any form obeys behavior laws. This provides the teacher with an important set of rules that can assist immensely in instruction and classroom management. These are the beginnings of experimental education, an end product of the concern for a more scientific approach to research and an opportunity to improve child performance through more effective instruction.

Through the growth of experimental education. principles of teaching are developing. At the present stage, six basic statements can be made. Primary to all the other principles is the necessity to identify. record. and evaluate performance based on specified and well-defined responses to classroom tasks. Second, because child performance data is the most sensitive index of the effectiveness of instruction, measurement procedures must be used that obtain valid and reliable data are the most sensitive index of the effectiveness of instruction, mance data of the child. Fourth, for purposes of planning. instructing. and evaluating performance, terminal objectives must be defined behaviorally and their successive approximations must also be specified. Fifth. cues to academic tasks must be sequenced in an order which develops skills efficiently with a very low error rate. Sixth, as the consequences of behavior are the critical variables for developing discriminations and for motivating performance, reinforcement procedures must be used as carefully and systematically as educators have come to use cues. For research or instruction these principles underscore the importance of systematic attention to the responses of the task requirement and to the two major variables of performance: cues and reinforcers. Educational technology, as it comes to offer more precision in the measurement and presentation of these variables, will facilitate the refinement and extension of these principles.

REFERENCES

Allen, K. E. Improvement in verbal behavior of two preschool children through systematic social reinforcement. *Paper presented at American Educational Research Association Annual Meeting, New York City, February, 1967*. (a)

Allen, K. E. & Harris, F. R. Elimination of a child's excessive scratching by training the mother in reinforcement procedures. *Behaviour Research and Therapy*, 1966, **4**, 79–84.

Allen, K. E., Hart, B., Buell, J. S., Harris, F. R. & Wolf, M. M. Effects of social reinforcement on isolate behavior of a nursery school child, *Child Development*, 1964, 511–518.

Allen, K. E., Henke, L. B., Harris, F. R., Baer, D. M. & Reynolds, N. J. Control of hyperactivity by social reinforcement of attending behavior. *Journal of Educational Psychology*, 1967, **58**(4), 231–237. (b)

Burgess, R. L. & Lovitt, T. C. The experimental analysis of social exchange. Unpublished manuscript, University of Washington, 1968.

Carrese, L. M. & Baker, C. G. The convergence technique: A method for the planning and programming of research efforts. *Management Science,* 1967, **13**, B420–B438.

Ferster, C. B. & Perrott, M. C. *Behavior principles.* New York: Appleton-Century-Crofts, 1968.

Ferster, C. B. & Skinner, B. F. *Schedules of reinforcement.* New York: Appleton-Century-Crofts, 1957.

Haring, N. G. *Attending and responding.* San Rafael, Calif.: Dimensions, 1968.

Haring, N. G. & Hauck, M. A. Improved learning conditions in the establishment of reading skills with disabled readers. *Exceptional Children*, 1969, **35**, 341–352. (a)

Haring, N. G. & Hauck, M. A. Contingency management applied to classroom remedial reading and math for disadvantaged youths. In *Proceedings of the Ninth Annual Research Meeting Co-Sponsored by the Department of Institutions, Division of*

Research, State of Washington and the University of Washington, School of Medicine, Department of Psychiatry. Seattle, Wash. University of Washington Press, 1969, **2**, 41–45. (b)

Haring, N. G. & Hayden, A. H. The contributions of the Experimental Education Unit to the expanding role of instruction. *College of Education Record,* 1968, **34**, 31–36.

Haring, N. G., Hayden, A. H. & Nolen, P. A. Accelerating appropriate behaviors of children in a Head Start program. *Exceptional Children,* 1969, **35**, 773–784.

Haring, N. G. & Kunzelmann, H. The finer focus of therapeutic behavioral management. In J. Hellmuth (Ed.), *Educational Therapy,* Vol. 1, Seattle, Wash.: Special Child Publications, 1966. Pp. 225–251.

Haring, N. G. & Lovitt, T. C. Operant methodology and educational technology in special education. In N. G. Haring & R. L. Schiefelbusch (Eds.), *Methods in special education.* New York: McGraw-Hill, 1967, Pp. 12–48.

Haring, N. G. & Lovitt, T. C. The application of functional analysis of behavior by teachers in a natural school setting. Final Report. U.S. Department of Health, Education, and Welfare, Office of Education: Bureau of Research. Project No. 7–0376, Grant No. OEG–0–8–070376–1857(032), 1969.

Haring, N. G. & Ridgway, R. W. Early identification of children with learning disabilities. *Exceptional Children,* 1967, **33**, 387–395.

Holland, J. G. Teaching machines: An application of principles from the laboratory. *Journal of the Experimental Analysis of Behavior,* 1960, **3** 275–287.

Krasner, L. & Ullmann, L. P. *Research in behavior modification.* New York: Holt, Rinehart & Winston, 1965.

Kunzelmann, H. P. Academic and social classroom measurement. In N. G. Haring & A. H. Hayden (Eds.), *Workshop in instructional improvement: Behavior modification.* Child Study and Treatment Center, Fort Steilacoom, Washington, June 17–July 17, 1968. Pp. 115–151.

Lindsley, O. R. Direct measurement and prosthesis of retarded behavior. *Journal of Education,* 1964, **147** (1), 62–81.

Lovitt, T. C. A contingency management classroom: Basis for systematic replication. In N. G. Haring & A. H. Hayden (Eds.), *The improvement of instruction.* Seattle, Washington. Special Child Publications, in press, 1971.

Lovitt, T. C. Diagnostic implications of conjugate contingencies. Final Report. U.S. Department of Health, Education, and Welfare, Grant No. OEG–1–7–070017–4269. Office of Education: Bureau of Research, Washington, D.C., 1968.

Lovitt, T. C., Kunzelmann, H. P., Nolen, P. A. & Hulten, W. J. The dimensions of classroom data. *Journal of Learning Disabilities*, 1968, **1** (12), 20–31.

Millenson, J. R. *Principles of behavior analysis*. New York: Macmillan, 1967.

Mithaug, D. E. A behavioral analysis of social process, theory, and research. Unpublished manuscript, University of Washington, 1968.

Mithaug, D. E. The development of cooperation in alternative task situations. *Journal of Experimental Child Psychology*, 1969, **8**, 443–460.

Mithaug, D. E. & Burgess, R. L. Effects of different reinforcement procedures in the establishment of a group response. *Journal of Experimental Child Psychology*, 1967, **5**, 441–454.

Mithaug, D. E. & Burgess, R. L. The effects of different reinforcement contingencies in the development of social cooperation. *Journal of Experimental Child Psychology*, 1968, **6**, 401–426.

Premack, D. Toward empirical behavior laws: 1. Positive reinforcement. *Psychological Review*, 1959, **66**, 219–233.

Revusky, S. H. Some statistical treatments compatible with individual organism methodology. *Journal of the Experimental Analysis of Behavior*, 1967, **10**, 319–330.

Rieke, J. B. The application of research techniques in the communications classroom. Speech given at professional staff meeting at Experimental Education Unit, University of Washington, Seattle, Washington, March 29, 1968.

Skinner, B. F. *Science and human behavior*. New York: Macmillan, 1953.

Suppes, P. Modern learning theory and the elementary-school curriculum. *American Educational Research Journal*, 1964, **1**, 79–93.

Terrace, H. S. Stimulus control. In W. K. Honig (Ed.). *Operant behavior: Areas of research and application*. New York: Appleton-Century-Crofts, 1966.

Ullmann, L. P. & Krasner, L. *Case Studies in behavior modification*. New York: Holt, Rinehart & Winston, 1965.

Wallen, N. E. & Travers, R. M. W. Analysis and investigation of teaching methods. In N. L. Gage (Ed.), *Handbook of research on teaching.* Chicago: Rand McNally, 1963. Pp. 448–505.

SECTION IV

Programs for Legal Offenders

There is no doubt that the legal offender learns while in prison; apparently, many learn to be more competent, able offenders. Fortunately the environment *may* be programmed so that socially effective behaviors are learned. The first three programs described in this section describe educational programs for the young offender based upon principles of direct behavior management. The chapter by Cohen and Filipczak provides an excellent sample of almost complete environmental programming. Although the major criterion of success was academic gain, it is obvious that many adaptive patterns of responding (cooperation, dependability, responsibility, etc.) were strengthened in the process. The Draper program (McKee and Clements) provides an additional sample of a behavioristically oriented educational program for institutionalized offenders. The Draper program has both used and advanced the technology of programmed instruction and has experimented with a variety of interesting reinforcement operations. "A Behavioral Approach to Outpatient Treatment of Offenders" (Shah) presents an excellent introductory section describing the principles of behavior control which he has found most useful in working with offenders. Shah illustrates these principles through the case study approach. The chapter by Grant and Grant, "Contagion as a Principle in Behavior Change," is less experimentally oriented than the other chapters in this section, but develops a specific point well: offenders can serve effectively as change agents both for themselves and other offenders.

CHAPTER 8

Programming Educational Behavior for Institutionalized Adolescents[1]

Harold L. Cohen and James A. Filipczak

One of the major objectives for professionals engaged in human research is the development of a state of "health" for their clients. The material that mental health researchers, clinicians, therapists, and educators direct toward that end is *human behavior.*

To describe the actual objectives for each client's desired state of mental health, the professional researcher finds that broad generalizations and blanket prescriptions are not useful. Also, what may be a useful objective for one individual may be either of little use or totally inappropriate for another. Similarly, and after some goal has been specified, procedures for the modification of existing, or the learning of new behaviors cannot be accomplished with a "broad-spectrum" behavioral antibiotic. In a very real sense, those of us concerned with the analysis and modification of behavior play a variety of roles in research and therapeutic settings. Two of these roles may be likened to the fictional characters of Goldilocks and Alice in Wonderland.

Like Goldilocks, we attempt to specify, usually by some valid method of testing and evaluation, exactly what we consider normal, "just right,"—not too much behavior and not too little. The result of this evaluation usually contributes to our definition of behavioral objectives for our client. Clearly, this evaluation is imperative if we are to define "normal" behavior. Also, like Alice in her Wonderland, we are concerned with the appropriateness of behavior to its local environment and we want our subjects to become aware of their own behavior. Through "awareness," we hope that the subject will develop

[1]Based on research performed under grants #66003 and #67007, entitled, CASE II—MODEL, and sponsored by the Office of Juvenile Delinquency and Youth Development. Welfare Administration. U.S. Department of Health, Education, and Welfare.

or maintain these appropriate behaviors. Without question, we are not merely concerned with topographical definitions of behavior, but with an analysis of the ecology that functions to maintain a variety of behavioral performances.

When a young man screams at the top of his voice, jumps up and down, and waves his hands wildly, what message does he impart to the researcher? Is this problem of the Golidlocks or the Alice in Wonderland variety? Is this behavior exaggerated or is it inappropriate? To settle this question, we must analyze more than the limited behavioral topography we have described thus far. Such behavior at a college football game is viewed as "good school spirit." In a public library, a high school classroom, or a suburban home, this same behavior will more likely be considered both disruptive and inappropriate. Yet, it may persist. Certainly, the consequences of this behavior as displayed in these various settings will differ. It appears, then, that the roles we fill in our research multiply and that we now are involved in questions regarding behavior, the environment in which the behavior takes place, and the consequences that result from that behavior occurring in that environment.

Every research project concerned with human behavior, including those on which this material is based, is supported, by design or default, by a complex behavior facilitating environment. This environment is composed of the selected subjects, the staff and administration, the physical space controls, the procedures for behavior analysis or modification, and the operational system of consequences (or payoffs). To determine what is initiating, maintaining, or attenuating any specific behavior, the researcher must be able to examine the ecology that supports his project. Such a project must be designed to deal with the variables noted above, and the researcher must be able to assess those variables that appear to be contributing to the results he finds. Further, the research methodology must include the means for gathering the objective information needed to determine whether the goals of the research are being fulfilled.

To design a research project for human subjects that produces objective, or objectifiable data that are of value in analyzing or modifying behavior is an overwhelming assignment. Man is not merely a chemical and physiological specimen and there has been a tendency for human researchers to avoid research strategies that required detailed, rigorous, and systematic study of man's complex and confounding behavior. The strategies that are rejected tend to be those typified by procedural and environmental control and the investigation of a limited number of human subjects. This strategy is most traditionally associated with operant (or behavioral) psychology. The researchers that reject this type of investigation often turn to a strategy based upon prediction, statistical, and chance controls, dealing with a large number of subjects. The second type of strategy is most often employed by educators and social scientists. This choice of strategy is frequently to the detriment of both research and modification programs, particularly where basic behavioral questions must be answered. At best the second type of strategy is useful in assessing the effects of various well-researched modification procedures upon particular behavioral performances. At worst it may be wasteful of both critical time and energy when a more individually-based strategy could be employed to provide answers to basic questions.

The basic premise for any human research project should be that behavioral objectives can be stated and that behavior is related to both the environment in which it occurs and the consequences it produces. Further, by setting up an ecology in which appropriate consequences are made contingent upon changing behaviors and behavioral requirements, specific behaviors can be established, altered, maintained, and transferred to other situations. Although the setting may be a penal facility, a mental institution, a half-way house, a court system, a high school, a Job Corps center, or the street, research objectives must be clearly specified and methods chosen that will enhance the likelihood of satsifactory programs of analysis and/or modification.

An Environmental Design/Operant Approach

During the past few years, the authors have been involved in behavioral research and modification programs with juveniles in both a private mental hospital and in a federal penal institution. In both situations, the youngsters were committed because of refractory (excessive or inappropriate) social behavior—the behaviors of the group housed at the penal institution were, of course, those expressly forbidden by law. Their histories of deviant social behaviors were certainly diverse and, it often appeared, exemplary of a broad range of learning deficiencies and misdirection. There was, however, one common facet to the varying behavioral pathologies of all these juveniles: their behavioral skills in traditional academic subjects were severely deficient in some major dimension. The activities in the penal environment, the National Training School for Boys, were more deliberately oriented toward research and behavioral analysis. Two principal projects were conducted at the NTS. These were termed the CASE I and CASE II projects, and their methodology was based on the environmental design and operant psychological considerations generally described above. The earlier CASE I project has been described at length elsewhere (Cohen, Filipczak & Bis, 1967) and it served to lay the operational and research guidelines for CASE II. In CASE II, a number of desirable research conditions were available, not the least of which was that the subjects were under the control of project management on a 24-hour per day, 7-day per week basis. Most of the discussion presented here will be drawn from the CASE II project.

The main task of CASE II was to *develop procedures that could be used to establish and maintain educational behaviors in a controlled penal setting.* The special 24-hour controlled environment was designed from an unused dormitory at the penal facility. Systems for the continuous recording of behavioral data were developed and instituted to assess the behavioral change and the efficacy of the procedures employed.

Although the results were obtained with an institutionalized deviant population, the procedures and their relation to the results appear to be of more general applicability. First, stemming as they do from research in the experimental analysis of behavior and environmental design, the results are consistent with a body of data currently being obtained, using similar procedures, with populations in other types of institutions ranging in degree of custodial control from a mental hospital (Ayllon & Azrin, 1965) to a midwestern college (Cohen *et al.,* 1964)—ranging in population from psychotics (Goldiamond & Dyrud, 1968) and from mental retardates (Sidman & Stoddard, 1968) to bright college freshmen (Cohen & Filipczak, 1968). The results are also consistent with results in basic laboratory research where promising procedures are being developed to alter deviant human behavior in a programmed manner (Lovaas *et al.,* in press). These same procedures are currently being extended to alter human behaviors of clinical relevance (Ferster & DeMyer, 1962). Establishing an educational system in which student and system behaviors are continually monitored and assessed may have implications for research procedures in general which transcend the specific limitations of the CASE research projects.

The Case II Contingency System

Students were involved in the CASE II project on a 24-hour basis and most of their institutional activities were confined within the project. Architectural and behavioral controls were provided to fulfill the students' requirements of rest, nourishment, hygiene, and recreation. A complete educational system was also provided. These activities as well as family visits and furloughs were integrated into a system organized for the purpose of maintaining educational behavior.

Among the procedures which have been recognized as maintaining behavior is reinforcement. Reinforcement involves making a certain consequence contingent upon a performance. Reinforcement will not be available unless the specific performance occurs. The ideal situation, of course, is one in which the intrinsic consequences of the task itself maintain the behavior. For example, one reads a novel to follow the development of the characters or plot which cannot be followed unless the book is read; or, one reads in order to learn. However, we were neither dealing with ideal situations, nor with students who have had a history of such an approach to learning. Therefore, a system of extrinsic reinforcements was developed which did maintain the student's educational behaviors. The extrinsic reinforcements chosen were those that were already strong in these students' repertoires. These also were chosen because they lent themselves to being altered gradually into the generally more desirable form of intrinsic reinforcement. These extrinsic reinforcements became available (purchasable) through points. These points were given for correct answers to programmed or semiprogrammed educational problems, tests, and other academic performances. Augmenting the system of using gold stars, to which they are analogous, the points could at any time be converted to material or social reinforcers. For example, each point is worth $0.01 and could be used to buy material from a mail order catalog or to buy entrance into a lounge where a jukebox and one's friends were.

These points were tied into the current system of values of the student-inmates and were used to establish and maintain learning so that after an initial educational repertoire was mastered, other reinforcers and systems of intrinsic values might then take over.

The program was voluntary and individualized. The student-inmate did not have to do academic work. Once he earned his points, for being correct in his subject matter exams, he did not have to convert them into any specified reinforcer. He could choose how he wished to spend them. He could also save them. He worked at his own pace on individualized curricula, based on the results of his pretesting. The major way he could earn points was to engage in studying and completing the educational material recommended to him. A grading system was developed which gave the student-inmate immediate access to his own progress and the adequacy of his understanding. A grade of at least 90 percent correct was required on all programmed instruction. Upon completion of a unit of study at 90 percent correct responses, the student was given an exam which earned him points. The students soon learned to achieve 90 percent on all programmed work.

The model for the project was that of a student research employee, who checks in and out of the various activities for which he is paid or for which he pays. The boys were actually hired to do a job. As student educational researchers, they were to be paid for learning. The immediate goal was to test the various programs, academic and nonacademic. Whether there was more to be gained for themselves was up to them, but they would have to work for it. There were no free handouts.

An excerpt from the SER Handbook explains the student's role as a researcher:

> Your title as a CASE II student is STUDENT EDUCATIONAL RESEARCHER and as a researcher you will be paid for the work you do for CASE II. Your payment (salary) will be in points. These points can be used just as you would use money. You will be able to pay for a private room, buy your meals, buy clothing, use the Lounge, and make purchases from the CASE Store. Your position as a Student Educational Researcher will also enable you to take vacations from the National Training School and will hopefully provide you with those academic and social tools which will be valuable to you as a citizen of these United States.
>
> As a STUDENT EDUCATIONAL RESEARCHER you are a free citizen within the project. You will have choices in what you do but your choices will also carry responsibilities.

Points were also available for part-time employment in kitchen and dining room, janitorial and maintenance, and clerical work. Students, who wanted to supplement their incomes from the educational work, could apply for a vacant position. Pay was proportional to the complexity of the job. The janitorial job became popular on a short-range basis; typically, students who were having difficulty with educational programs would request the position and keep it only until they were able to sustain themselves on their educational income.

The correctional officers could also award points as bonuses for exemplary social behavior. This opportunity to award bonuses was a distinct change in the officer's role. In conventional institutions, he uses aversive control over social behavior. In CASE, the officer's relationship to the student was enhanced by his awarding points, and several officers experienced great pleasure — and relief — at this opportunity to assume a positive rather than threatening role. This was not a universal reaction. The usual conception of the correctional officer's job guarantees that a certain number of punitively oriented people will gravitate to it. Because all bonuses had to be recorded in the students' bankbooks and in the officers' records, it was possible for the CASE staff to examine what student behavior an officer considered constructive. It became evident that one officer was particularly reinforcing to those students who consistently made their beds or straightened their rooms. Another officer noted good language. One officer was noted to be concentrating bonuses on a particular student, and an investigation led to the discovery of a mutually exploitative relationship between officer and student. The officers, themselves, had the opportunity to earn extra pay by attending special seminars at which they could not only learn constructive reinforcement techniques, but could propose new programs of their own design.

By not physically giving the points in a form such as money or tokens, the transference of negotiable points from one student to another was avoided. Consequently, points could not be acquired in any way unrelated to the learning specified by the CASE staff.

One of the major effects of this contingency management system was a sharp increase in academic skills as measured by national tests. The student's own success became a major source of reinforcement. A surprisingly high degree of violent social behavior came under control without using traditional punishment techniques (lockup, isolation, reduction of calorie intake — old penal means of control). Consistent with a sharp increase in their scores on a Revised Army Beta test, the students accepted more responsibility for self-control. All eight students who took the Tests of General Educational Development passed and received a high school equivalency certificate.

Backup for Points

Points were not the only reinforcing consequences available to the students, nor was academic learning the only kind of behavior reinforced. The points, themselves, were the equivalent of money, and could be used in many of the same ways we all use money. The various services and activities for which points could be spent not only maintained the reinforcing effectiveness of the points, but made it possible for the students to acquire possessions, skills, and the prestige which, in turn, opened up new opportunities for continuing development.

At first, the students used the points to purchase soft drinks, milk, potato chips, Polaroid snapshots, entrance and time in the lounge, entrance and time in the library, smoke breaks, rental of private rooms, rental of books and magazines, purchase of additional classroom time, private tutoring, and material from the outside world through the use of mail-order catalogs. By the catalog system, the student was able to purchase articles such as sports jackets, white shirts, ties, pants, Mother's Day cards, candy, flowers, and other desired items.

Money, and the physical service world it represents, is not the only thing for which man works. Respect, approval of one's peers, and correctness describe some of the most powerful areas of human reinforcement. These reinforcers help maintain human behavior in social groups, whether inside a prison or in a free society. Although our form of society is run on a powerful generalized reinforcer (money), each of us also works for doing good work, work we like, work we do well and/or work recognized by others, and work which brings us in contact with people we like. In a free society it is a social and judicial right to be with people we love, like, or respect. It is difficult for a young adult to learn how to obtain some of this form of reinforcement, i.e., praise in educational areas, when he has little or none of the repertoire required to achieve competence and success in these educational and socially accepted areas. By using teaching machines, the programming of special classes, devising new testing methods, and planning a supportive environment based upon the generalized reinforcer of points, most of the students were able to enjoy that reinforcement which comes from the excitement of being right 90 to 100 percent of the time. They also experienced approval for "good" work not just from the CASE staff, but from the other students.

Outline of a Typical Project Day

A typical day began between 6:00 a.m. and 8:00 a.m. The students were responsible for waking and preparing themselves for a day of school. Breakfast began at 7:30 a.m., when freshmen (Grades 1–4) were served. Sophomores (Grades 5–7) were served at 7:40 a.m., juniors (Grades 8–10.5) at 7:50 a.m., and seniors (Grades 10.5–12) at 7:55 a.m. The cafeteria closed at 8:15 a.m. At its closing all remaining students went into the lounge, which had also opened at 7:30 a.m. During the period from 7:30 a.m. until 8:30 a.m., the students had free admission to the lounge and free television. At 8:00 a.m., those students who wanted to go on "sick call" were taken to the NTS hospital.

When the educational area opened at 8:30 a.m., the students went directly from the lounge to spend the remainder of the morning on the various study programs. They worked on programmed instruction, took tests, went to classes, spent time in tutorial sessions with teachers, or went into the library/free area. At 11:45 a.m. the students moved downstairs to the home floor. They had 15 minutes to relax, tidy rooms, or clean up before lunch was served at 12:00 noon. Procedures at lunchtime were similar to those at breakfast, except that the order in which the students ate was reversed. The students entered the cafeteria at 5-minute intervals, with the seniors starting at 12:00 noon. The cafeteria closed at 12:45 p.m. and, as they had done after breakfast, all students went to the lounge. The lounge opened at the start of the lunch period, with free admission. From 1:00 p.m. until 1:30 p.m., the students could choose to remain in the lounge, to return to the home floor, or, when weather permitted and staff was available, to go outdoors for recreation.

School began again at 1:30 p.m., and the students continued the routine of the morning academic session. They also could leave the educational area at 3:00 p.m. and go into the lounge. However, the lounge charged a rather costly hourly admission of 100 points. The lounge remained open until 5:00 p.m. when any students remaining there went either to the cafeteria for their dinner or to the home floor. Although the educational area remained open until 4:30 p.m., several days each week the students had the option of leaving the educational floor at 4:00 p.m. for approximately one hour of outdoor recreation. All remaining students left the educational floor at 4:30 p.m. and went downstairs to the home floor. During this half hour before dinner, the students attended to a variety of personal activities. Shortly before 5:00 p.m., the students who had been outside returned to the home floor. The seniors ate at 5:00, juniors at 5:10, sophomores at 5:15 and freshmen at 5:20 p.m.

From the time the cafeteria closed at 6:00 p.m. until "lights out" at 10:00 p.m., the students chose their own activities. The store opened for any over-the-counter sales at 6:00 p.m. and at 6:30 p.m. the storekeeper supervised operations of the lounge which reopened. The library opened at 6:00 p.m. and provided book browsing and checkout, scheduled educational television programs, supervised hobby and craft activities, and, starting at 7:00 p.m., supervision and assistance with some study activities in regular program work. Unless a scheduled television program was in progress, the library closed at 9:00 p.m. On certain nights of the week the students were able to participate in activities at the NTS gym from 6:30 p.m. until 8:00 p.m. Several students also held part-time jobs within the project and worked from 7:00 to 9:00 p.m.

From 4:30 p.m., at the close of the educational area, the home floor remained open and all students were to be there by 10:00 p.m., "lights out." The shower room opened at 6:00 p.m., and the students also had an opportunity to use the washing machine that was on this floor. By 10:00 p.m., students were to have taken care of their hygienic needs, room-cleaning chores, and any other type of activity that required them to be outside their individual rooms. After "lights out," students were expected to remain in their rooms until the following morning, except for bathroom use and smoke breaks.

A typical Saturday provided some changes to the weekday schedule. Breakfast began at 9:00 a.m., permitting the students a later awakening time. However, since the home floor remained open all day, the students could skip breakfast and remain in bed for as long as they desired. Some students often chose to remain in bed all day on Saturday. The cafeteria and the lounge remained open until 10:00 a.m., at which time all the students returned to the home floor. An NTS barber came to the project for the remainder of Saturday morning to give haircuts to those students who wanted and could pay for them. Recreational activities were available from 10:30 a.m. until 12:00 noon, when lunch was served. Student entrance to the cafeteria according to educational grade levels was enforced as it was on weekdays. At 1:00 p.m. the cafeteria closed and the students chose between staying in the lounge or returning to the home floor. Both the store and the lounge opened at 1:00 p.m. on Saturday and students remaining in the lounge were required to pay an entrance fee. An outside recreation schedule ran from 1:30 to 4:30 p.m., depending upon weather conditions and staff availability. Dinner was served from 5:00 to 6:00 p.m. Thereafter, the cafeteria was closed.

Saturday evening activities were similar to those during the week with two major exceptions: the educational floor was not opened except for the 7:00 to 9:00 p.m. showing of the "CASE II Saturday Night Movie," and the students returned to the home floor at 11:00 p.m., one hour later than during the week. This later "lights out" schedule was employed on Friday, Saturday, and any night that preceded a holiday.

The schedule for a typical Sunday was basically a "free" schedule. However, religious services were available during the morning period. Visiting hours were between 1:00 p.m. and 4:00 p.m., and a gym period was scheduled from 6:30 to 8:00 p.m. The students voted for a two meal schedule on Sunday: 10:30 a.m. and 4:30 p.m. Unlike Monday through Saturday procedure, all students were served on a first-come-first-served basis at both meals.

All legal holidays were observed, and activities followed a Sunday schedule. In addition to special trips taken off-site, two parties were held, the first in the Jefferson Hall Lounge and the second at a church sponsored facility in the District of Columbia.

Some Examples of Educational Behavior

Computation of mean weekly student study hours for three distinct data-gathering periods in the project was completed. These data periods were denoted Periods I, III, and IV. Each period was approximately two months in length and corresponded to different kinds of learning activities available to students. (See Table 1)

TABLE 1
Techniques Used During Four Project Data Periods

	Learning Methods Employed	Weekly Daytime Hours Available for Study	Payment System Employed
Period I	Programmed Instruction Only (night classes)	28.75	Hourly Pay plus "Piecework" Bonus
Period II	Programmed Instruction Only (new programs introduced)	Changed from: 28.75 to 31.25	Hourly Pay dropped during this period
Period III	Programmed Instruction Only	31.25	"Piecework" Pay only
Period IV	Programmed Instruction and Classes during Day	31.25	"Piecework" Pay only

Data Period II was not included in this analysis of mean weekly student study hours as it was a transitional period that incorporated a number of procedural and study material changes.

The results of this analysis show that mean student study hours during Period IV were significantly greater than during either Periods I or III. However, this could have been the result of the changes in any one or all three of the techniques employed. Student study hours during Periods I and III were compared to determine the effect of the two payment systems used. During Period I, students were paid for hours spent studying and for correct answers on programs and tests. During Period III, students were paid only for correct answers on programs and tests, but their total pay was comparable to that earned during Period I. This change in payment procedure appears to have been a major influence on the daily hours that students actually studied.

Data from Periods I and III have been reduced to show this change in student study hours (Figure 1). Two 6-week series of data have been reduced to show the change: one series occurring during Data Period I, immediately after the increase in available study hours,

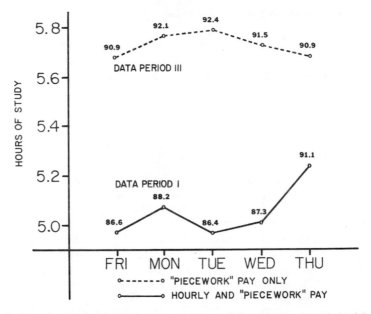

Fig. 1. Mean hours of active study, by days of the week, in two separate periods of time.

but after two months of 28.75-hour weeks; the second series occurring during Data Period III, three months after the increase in available study hours. By precluding the effect of learning method variables, these two data series most accurately reflect the impact of the increase in available study hours and the change in *pay method* on actual daily hours of student study.

During Data Period I, the mean number of hours studied during each week day was erratic, with a dramatic increase in measured study activity on Thursday, the day before payday. The individual data reduced for this presentation also show a wide range around the mean for Period I. In general it may be said that Period III indicates a more consistent work pattern than Period I. The small numerals above the graphic intersection points refer to the mean percentage of time spent studying by students during the total study time available. During Data Period I, a grand mean of 87.9 percent of available time was spent in study, or 5.06 mean hours per day. During Period III, students spent 91.6 percent of the available time in active study, or 5.73 mean hours per day. This was an increase of 0.66 mean hours per day in study (or 40 minutes) after an increase of 30 available minutes per day. The students appear to have been working both actually and proportionally longer and more consistently during Period III, under the "piecework" pay system.

This change of work patterns influenced other project operations. One of the most dramatic was the required rescheduling of teaching assistants from Thursdays (when the rush for program completions and checking was greatest) to more general (yet, as active) coverage for the entire week.

A record of the points that students earned for academic study was available, in weekly totals, for the entire project. Unlike hours studied, point earnings over time show more of a relationship with a number of other project variables. Although these relationships are marked, some of them may well be only coincidental (i.e., no functional relation has been established through control procedures) or the result of seasonal (weekly, monthly, yearly) cyclic variation.

There is generally one consistent pattern of earnings within each of the three data periods: high earnings at the beginning, lower earnings in the middle, and higher earnings at the end. The principal cause for this was the administration of Stanford Achievement Tests, tests (with high point payoff) at the beginning and end of each period. Inter-period variation was often associated with specifiable project variables other than student study activity. The variation in point earnings did, however, approximate a normal distribution. Further, the only mean weekly point payments which fell beyond two standard deviations were at the start of the project and during December when high point payoff in classes (as incentive for maximum achievement and in preparation for purchasing Christmas gifts) coincided with the administration of SAT tests.

Some Tangible Results

The mean educational hours studied, earnings, and the mean grade score changes on the five SAT subtests for Data Periods I, III, and IV are presented with their standard deviations in Table 2.

It was originally planned for these time periods to be of approximately equal duration. Exigencies of administration, however, led to one of the data periods, Data Period IV, being notably longer than the others. Direct comparisons among the means could not therefore be made. Data Period IV had approximately 1.34 times as many days of educational activities as did Data Periods I and III. A quality control approach was attempted, but the hazards of estimation precluded much of the value that this method was originally hoped to have.

The 95 percent confidence limits were calculated for the educational hours, achievement earnings, and grade level changes associated with Data Period I. These confidence limits could then serve as norms with which to compare and contrast some of the findings of the later

TABLE 2

Means and Standard Deviations for Educational Hours, Point Earnings, and Grade Score Change for Data Periods I, III, and IV

Variable Number and Name	Mean	S.D.
1 Educational Hours, Period I	147.56 Hours	39.13
2 Educational Hours, Period III	129.86 Hours	41.08
3 Educational Hours, Period IV	173.70 Hours	59.89
4 Point Earnings, Period I	133.89 Dollars	61.43
5 Point Earnings, Period III	153.81 Dollars	73.23
6 Point Earnings, Period IV	247.36 Dollars	104.24
7 Grade Score Change, Period I	+.21 Grades	0.48
8 Grade Score Change, Period III	+.37 Grades	0.64
9 Grade Score Change, Period IV	+.63 Grades	0.73

data periods. The results are presented in Table 3. In short, for every 150 hours (average) of recorded study behavior, a student gained from two to four months in grade level—approximately three times the standard expectancy for public school children.

TABLE 3

95% Confidence Limits Associated with Three Variables for Data Period I (as baseline period)

Data Period I	Confidence Limits
Hours of Educational efforts	132.93 to 162.19 Hours
Educational Achievement Points	110.53 to 157.25 Dollars
Grade Score Gain	0.2 to 0.41 Grades

On the basis of these estimates, a form of quality control could be set up to assess the findings of later data periods.

Analysis of variance techniques were used to analyze the grade changes in SAT scores for 16 students within four time periods of approximately two months each. Each of these periods was characterized by a different procedural or methodological approach in implementing a programmed instruction curriculum. Seven subtests of the Stanford Achievement Test battery were analyzed separately.

Statistically significant differences were found to be associated with treatment periods for paragraph meaning, language usage, and social studies. The greatest gains in paragraph meaning were recorded for Period IV, the period characterized by achievement pay, a stable curriculum, and classroom courses supplementing programmed instruction.

The average monthly rate of grade level gain for these students in each curriculum area is presented in Table 4 (normal public school increase approximates 0.08 levels per month):

TABLE 4
Average Stanford Achievement Test Grade Score Increases Per Month (16 Students)

Curriculum Area	Grade Levels per Month
Paragraph Meaning	0.17
Language Usage	0.28
Spelling	0.20
Arithmetic Reasoning	0.16
Arithmetic Computation	0.10
Science	0.16
Social Studies	0.11

Army Revised Beta: Group Evaluation

Whether increased scores on IQ tests reflect a true change in basic intelligence or simply a higher level of acculturation, less "test anxiety," or the acquisition of test-taking skills, the fact remains that of the 24 students tested at entry to the NTS and retested in the CASE project, 23 demonstrated an increase in IQ scores and only one remained the same.

Scores for IQ at entry were available for 40 of the full complement of 41 students who participated in the project's activities at any time during the period between February 4, 1966, and February 3, 1967. No IQ score was available for one student who escaped very shortly after his arrival.

For these 40 students, the mean of the IQ scores on the Revised Beta was 93.5 with a standard deviation of 9.98. The lowest IQ score of any of the 40 students was 67. The highest was 112. With an interval of 10 IQ points specifying the width of a frequency class, it was found that the modal class for IQ scores at admission was the 90.0 to 99.9 range. Seventeen students had IQ's recorded within these limits.

On December 20, 1966, 24 students were retested on the Revised Beta. These were all the students present for testing at that time, and did not constitute a selected group. Their original testing had been done at the time of their entry into the NTS and antedated the December testing by at least six months in almost all instances.

The frequency distribution of IQ scores recorded for these 24 students at entry to the NTS indicates that IQ scores from 90 to 99.9 was once more the modal class. The class of next highest frequency was the 100–109.0 category. The general pattern was similar when the distribution of the 24 students' scores was compared with the distribution of the 40 students' scores.

However, there were, at entrance, a number of students scoring in the 90–109.0 who were not present for the second administration of the Revised Beta in December 1966. This was not judged to have compromised the results of the later administration of the test, but served as a frame of reference for the results which follow.

A comparison between the mean IQ scores at entry and the mean of the IQ scores for the same 24 students on December 20, 1966, shows their mean gain was *12.5 IQ points*. These results represented statistically significant changes in their IQ scores at the 0.001 level. There were no students who failed to show gains. One student gained 27 IQ points. The range of the scores in the testing of December 20, 1966, extended from a low of 83 to a high of 121. The mean interval of time which had elapsed between testings was approximately seven months.

The pattern of change in frequency distribution of IQ scores for these students from entry to December, 1966, emphasizes the dramatic increase in scores (Figure 2). *Sixteen* of the 24 had scored below 100 at entry to NTS. In December, only six of the 24 registered an IQ score below 100. In the December testing the IQ score modal class was between 110 and 119.9, an increase from the entrance testing in which the modal class had been between 90 and 99.9.

On March 20, 1967, 19 of the 24 students were again tested. This group had a mean entry IQ of approximately 92.1, with a range from 67 to 112. The March mean score was 108.3, and the range of scores extended from 77 to 126.

The results of the testing of March, 1967, tended to confirm the reliability of the gains recorded in December, 1966. The changes in both instances had high statistical significance beyond the 0.01 level.

The December testing showed an increase of 12.5 IQ points for 24 students. The March results showed a mean increase of 16.2 IQ points for 19 students from the time of their admission testing.

Both the literature of clinical psychology and the personal experience of the psychologists associated with CASE II would support the hypothesis that practice effects on the three test administrations of the revised Beta were negligible in the generation of the increasing scores. It was felt, however, that an analysis of individual students' results and of the differences within and between subtests should be undertaken.

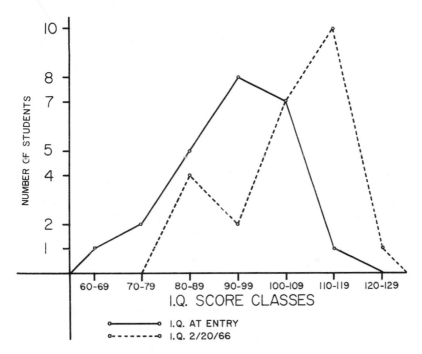

Fig. 2. Frequency distribution of IQ Scores on the Revised Beta for 24 Students of CASE II from the Time of Their Entry to December 20, 1966.

Subtests # 2, # 3, and # 5 were considered to be those most readily influenced by memory and practice and were given particular attention. Results of the analysis indicated that neither these subtests nor any others could be said to account for as much as one half of the average gain in IQ score.

It was also found that in no case could the increased score of any one student be attributed to better production in only one or two areas of mental functioning as measured by the Revised Beta. In the absence of evidence to the contrary, these IQ changes were taken to reflect across-the-board increases in the demonstration of ability. This applied to such areas of mental functioning as attention to detail, frustration tolerance, deductive reasoning, and acculturation.

General speculation as to why a steady increase in IQ scores was evident for these students brought out a number of possibilities. It was suggested that the students responded to the second and third administration of the test with greater enthusiasm and determination, since high scores were rewarded by a generous point payoff in proportion to the score; also, it was suggested that they were able to score higher because they had been exposed to a wider variety of intellectually stimulating material. The most important implication for the investigators was that there exists a large group of people in our society who fail to qualify for military service, further education and training, jobs, promotions, and so forth, not because of congenital disability but because of inadequate preparation and poor representation of chains of consequences. CASE II would seem to have refined certain procedures which showed promise for the overcoming of these obstacles.

Some Intangible Results and Reflections

Along with the students' tests, records, time spent, money earned, and behaviors learned (the objective products of the research), there is another part of the CASE II story that will not be found in any "Data and Results" analysis.

The interpersonal and attitudinal changes, which were reflected in the change in test scores, were also reflected in the group's social behavior. The change from harshly punitive prison custodial techniques to a positive reinforcing system of "earn while you learn," created behavioral changes in both staff and students. Although no concerted attempt was made to accurately measure these behavioral changes at the project's inception, the increase in wealth and "know-how," which was measurable, gave us an initial grid to subjectively assess each student's new "sense of worth." Purchasing power, an essential ingredient in any society, is, in itself, a powerful change agent.

Generally, the CASE students were from poor and uneducated families. These two factors, poverty and ignorance, generally produce a tight subculture which has little or no means to change economically. The inability to purchase and to have the educational skills necessary to participate in the mainstream of the American life have forced these young people to "self-ghetto" themselves and to absorb themselves into small communities which are on the periphery of the larger society. This circular dilemma produces a group of adolescents who not only drop out of school, but who in a real sense drop out of life.

The CASE II project dealt with these dropouts of life. These were the young men who had not "made it" in our society. They lived with frustration and anger, the results of failure. In fact, their schools had programmed them for failure. The question asked in the project was, "How can these youths be programmed toward success in a penal environment which has historically been aversive and restrictive?"

The project did not force an individual to do anything. This was against its basic philosophy. The reason for this concept was that the young man had to recognize that through his own efforts he could change himself. When the students first came, they always asked the simple basic question, "Man, what's in it for me?" To the students' surprise, the staff agreed. It was pointed out that "If there is nothing in it for you, don't do it." There was something in it for them. At the beginning it was points—money. It was necessary to have points because each student had to pay for his own room, board, and clothing. He could have chosen to go on relief, but that was neither dignified nor reinforced by the peer group's activities when he had the opportunity to work and to earn.

Extrinsic reinforcements were used to initiate behavior and "motivate" the student. Usually, after about four months' stay in the project, the student found that he could easily negotiate the CASE II environment. The project procedures enabled the staff and students to divert a large amount of the aggression to productive work and learning. Soon after the project opened, it was possible to remove the correctional officers from duty during the weekly day shift. In all cases, it was possible for each student to learn to read and write and to become deeply involved in the academic system. They had been, literally, programmed for success.

Further, the ability to purchase can lead to pride of ownership. This becomes obvious in the student's rented room. The amount of time spent in, and money spent on, furnishing each student's private room was a clear indicator that privacy and ownership were strong reinforcers to them. When the students first rented the rooms all the cubicles looked alike. Then the store began to put items on sale for their rooms: bedspreads, brightly colored pillows, art plates, etc. The rooms began to change. *Playboy* centerfolds were pinned up, paint was selected for the walls, rugs were purchased for the floor. Radios, TVs, books, and magazines were added. The rooms took on each student's personal "character." Comments indicated possessiveness: "Get out of my room; this is my room." "I paid 800 points for this room; this is my room." For most, this was the first time they could call a space their own—and tell others to "get out." As a result, they tended to stay in their rooms more and more. The inducement of the lounge with the pinball machine and pool table, games, etc., started fading, as their own rooms became a place to have friends in, watch TV, do homework, write a letter, etc. The students had begun to acculturate towards the middle class adolescent life—and they seemed to enjoy it. They were willing to pay a high fee for that privilege.

When one young man first came in during the early part of the program, he said that there was something wrong with him. He felt that he was a misfit and he couldn't do anything well, except the antisocial behaviors, and even then he wasn't very bright. He had gotten caught. In less than one year's time, he learned to succeed. And when he started to succeed in academic subject matter, English, algebra, etc., those subjects he could not do in the last eight years in public school where he had considered himself incapable and stupid, his whole approach, not only to education, but towards other things changed. He became a man who enjoyed the sweet smell of success. An important fact of life that all people have come to recognize is that success is one of the most powerful reinforcers for more activity, for more success. The CASE project made it possible for this reinforcer to operate with these youths.

The staff's premise in dealing with a student was that the individual student's behavior was always appropriate because it was a response to the system in which it occurred. The thief is working for the reinforcer — the payoff — the stolen goods. The care-worn statement, "Crime doesn't pay," cannot be supported by incisive evidence. Most of these youngsters had a higher ratio of theft than conviction. One young man had stolen 18 cars before he was caught. A successful car thief keeps stealing. This payoff and the peer reinforcement maintained his behavior. If it is possible to change the cues and the system which have maintained his performance, change the reinforcer and extinguish (or punish) the antisocial behavior, it is possible for the young man to "change." The CASE II project was a subculture, a miniature society designed and programmed to effect this self-change.

In the traditional training school, or any other penal environment, where an individual has been incarcerated, he is told what to do and how to do it. He lives by the aversive penal rules that have been established. He is told when to get up in the morning, when to go to eat, how to clean up, how to make his bed, where to walk, and how to march. He often learns better the antisocial lessons of his peers than the proper modes of societal conduct. He is never given an opportunity to make decisions on his own. The society is operated by "Do what we say or be punished," and is so programmed that the establishment makes all decisions for the youth. This premise could admirably prepare the youth for his release into a fascist police state where everyone is told what to do and how to do it. It does not prepare him for a life in a democratic society.

In the CASE II program, the individual made his own decisions: how he should dress, what he should wear, when he went to bed, and how to spend his time and money. Whether he was to work or not was his decision. This maximization of choice was essential. It was critical that the young man learn to make these decisions because, in a democratic society, he has to accept the consequences of his own decisions. Those programs, schools, penal, or mental institutions, that do not give the youth an opportunity to make decisions, and to fail or succeed in these decisions, do not prepare him for coping with "reality." It is through this system of decision making and experiencing his failures and successes that an adolescent can begin to evaluate his own performance, and prepares himself for a world which is not under constant parental, penal, or political monitoring.

REFERENCES

Ayllon, T. & Azrin, N. The measurement and reinforcement of behavior of psychotics. *Journal of the Experimental Analysis of Behavior*, 1965, **8**, 357–383.

Cohen, H. L. & Filipczak, J. An application of contingency programming to mass education in a college classroom. In Cohen, H. L., Goldiamond, I., Filipczak, J. & Pooley, R. *Training professionals in procedures for the establishment of educational environments*. Silver Spring, Md.: Educational Facility Press – IBR, 1968.

Cohen, H. L., Filipczak, J. & Bis, J. *Case I: An initial study of contingencies applicable to special education*. Silver Spring, Md.: Educational Facility Press – IBR, 1967.

Cohen, H. L., Filipczak, J., Bis, J., Cohen, J. E. & Larkin, P. CASE II-MODEL: Contingencies Applicable to Special Education – Motivationally Oriented Design for an Ecology of Learning. Final Report, November 15, 1968, Institute for Behavioral Research, Inc., Grant 66003 and Grant 67007, Office of Juvenile Delinquency and Youth Development, H. E. W.

Cohen, H. L., Goldiamond, I., Filipczak, J. & Pooley, R. *Training professionals in procedures for the establishment of educational environments*. Silver Spring, Md.: Educational Facility Press–IBR, 1968.

Cohen, H. L., Kibler, R. & Miles, D. A. A preliminary report on a pilot study for educating low achievers. *The Superior Student*, 1964, **6**.

Ferster, C. & De Myer, M. K. A method for the experimental analysis of the behavior of autistic children. *American Journal of Orthopsychiatry*, 1962, **32**, 89–98.

Goldiamond, I. & Dyrud, J. E. Some applications and implications of behavioral analysis for psychotherapy. *Research in Psychotherapy*, 1968, **3**.

Lovass, O., Freitag, G., Gold, V. & Kassorla, I. Experimental studies in child schizophrenia. *Journal of Experimental Child Psychology*, in press.

Sidman, M. & Stoddard, L. Programming perception and learning for retarded children. *International Review of Research in Mental Retardation*, 1966, **2**, 151–208.

CHAPTER 9

A Behavioral Approach to Learning: The Draper Model

John M. McKee and Carl B. Clements

The Draper projects[1] have, for eight years, been engaged in experimental programs in the education and rehabilitation of the public offender. The purpose of these projects has been to develop methods of enabling prisoners, upon release, to meet their material, social, and emotional needs without further resort to criminal activity. Programs designed to achieve this objective of discovering means of engendering overall social competence have provided prisoners with academic and vocational education, social skills training, counseling, and job placement. Post-release intervention in the form of follow-up services and intercession at crisis points was also a program element.

The current Draper projects are subsumed under the Experimental Manpower Laboratory for Corrections. They include a manpower training project, the evaluation of this project, other research studies such as determining employment barriers for ex-offenders, and an experiment designed to develop a method of modifying the offender's spoken English.

In a broad sense, the projects can be classified as experiments in behavior modification. They are attempting to modify human behavior, and the systematic application of the principles of behavioral science has been the goal in every phase of the activities — from the classrooms with their emphasis on individualization of instruction, learning contingencies, reinforcement, etc., to follow-up activities geared to meeting individual needs in the community. The projects have not, however, typically dealt with discrete and specific behaviors as do many behavior modification ventures. Rather, it has been a matter of treating whole classes of behavior, of enhancing and increasing a

---

[1]These projects have been conducted by the Rehabilitation Research Foundation under grants from the Departments of Labor and of Health, Education, and Welfare.

variety of skills and achievement. This approach seems to be in accord with Ullmann and Krasner's prediction that "one likely further development will be work with larger units of behavior with increasingly general social application" (1965, p. 61). There has been no systematic attempt to fully effect the application of behavior modification techniques in all areas of the program. Certain components lend themselves more readily to this approach. For example, in the area of academic education, a workable model which provides for the management of learning contingencies has been developed. This model is built around programmed instruction which is itself a concrete product of the application of the reinforcement principles of operant psychology.

The model is a learning system in which every student is pursuing an individually developed course of study designed to overcome his own academic deficiencies. He advances through this course of studies at his own rate of learning without regard to his classmates' course content or progress. There is simultaneous provision for any level of need from literacy training through college preparatory study. The instructors function as learning managers and counselors. The model provides a method for the management of learning contingencies which not only increases and sustains productivity but also involves the learner in the management of his own learning behavior. The need for professionally trained teachers is reduced since the system is subject to monitoring by indigenous, paraprofessional or subprofessional personnel. The system is expensive, but it succeeds with a population for whom traditional methods of instruction have failed.[2]

In describing the learning system, little attempt is made to distinguish between the several separate but related projects through which it was developed. The first section of this chapter contains a description of the inmate trainees for and with whom the model was developed and a discussion of environmental factors which shape the inmates' behavior and thus the model. The second section traces the development of the model and discusses the results achieved through its use.

Inmate Characteristics

The inhabitants of Draper Correctional Center share many characteristics with other disadvantaged populations. Generally, they are from the lower socioeconomic levels of society. They are under-

---

[2]Comprehensive findings and detailed procedures for implementing this system are given in Volumes I and III, respectively, of "The Draper Projects: Final Report" available from the senior author, Box 1107, Elmore, Alabama.

educated and have been either unemployed or underemployed. Coming as they do from broken homes, most have lacked adequate male role models. They are indifferent to responsibility, living in the here and now, unable to tolerate postponement of gratification. The majority has a long history of difficulties with the law. If they are not outright recidivists, the current confinement is apt to be the culmination of a long series of skirmishes with the law. They have been arrested for minor offenses, picked up for questioning, suspected of crimes for which they were not convicted, maybe sent to the state reformatory for juveniles.

The characteristics which are of major concern here, however, have to do with levels of education and attitudes toward formal learning situations. The following discussion of grade levels and scores on standardized achievement tests deals with 331 trainees who were graduates of the manpower training projects. There is no reason to believe, however, that there would be significant differences in the some 1500 other inmates with whom the projects have used pro- grammed instructional materials and related techniques.

These trainees reported that they had completed an average of 8.8 years in the public schools. Scores on standardized achievement tests indicated an average grade placement level of 7.8. It was, of course, the extremes, not the averages, which helped to shape the system of individually prescribed instruction. In one class of 80, grade placement levels ranged from the third grade to the second year of college. This variability of performance on standardized achievement tests scores is an individual as well as a group characteristic. It makes individually prescribed instruction an absolute necessity.

The averages are mentioned because they are indicative of two things. Either trainees perform at a level which is an average of one year lower than the norm established for the grade they have completed or they claim to have more education than they actually have. It is probable that both alternatives are true, and both were important in the evolution of the learning system.

It has become apparent to the Draper projects' staff that the inmate trainees accept the middle class belief that education is the high road to a better life. The first hint that they have done so comes when they exaggerate their claims to education. Further evidence that they have accepted this belief comes during the counseling and planning sessions which are a part of the education programs. They believe in the value of education; they seek status for themselves by claiming education they do not have; but they believe that the doors to education are barred to them.

These beliefs have been fostered by their experiences in the public schools, where they undoubtedly did (or would) perform below grade level. These men came from homes which generally are not supportive of educational endeavor. Their families only expect that they will "do their time" in school until they reach the age of 16 and are no longer required by law to attend school. Lacking the approbation, assistance, and support which the family should provide, they begin to fall behind. They earn failing grades, and they come to expect failure of themselves. Then the reinforcers which the school can provide — good grades, commendation, special awards, promotion, advancement toward the goal of college entrance — cease to be delivered to them. Eventually these events and expectancies cease to be reinforcing. The school environment grows yearly more aversive. The potential prison inmate at first withdraws by refusal to try or by truanting. At this point, he begins to verbalize the concept that "schools are no good." Eventually he escapes outright by dropping out. The damage has been done. To mask his feelings of inadequacy, he attempts to convince himself that the schools offer him nothing but drudgery which leads only to failure. In his thinking, teachers and school officials are lumped with the authority figures he has been learning to hate in the streets.

This, then, is the Draper inmate when he enters the projects: failure-prone, resistant to authority, lacking a background which is conducive to educational achievement, and ambivalent toward education. Beneath his veneer of scorn or indifference is the belief that education is important. Yet, because of aversive experiences in public schools, he avoids formal education settings — a classical approach avoidance reaction. Furthermore, the experience of imprisonment has exposed him to powerful forces which all too frequently have reinforced and strengthened the maladaptive behaviors he brought to prison with him.

The Prison Setting

The prisoner lives in a grim, cheerless setting which offers little or nothing in the way of recreation, education, or mental stimulation. Work assignments seldom rise above the deadliness of common labor; and leisure time is to be killed, not filled.

In Alabama, appropriations to the prison system are not sufficient to meet its operational needs; consequently, the system must use its inmate manpower to close the gap. Work assignments must meet the needs of the prison, not the prisoner. Rehabilitation programs have always had to take second place to this overriding concern, and little by way of education and training had been offered in the system before the Draper projects began.

The Alabama prison system includes the women's prison, and the following institutions for male offenders: two maximum security prisons, the youth center, the trusty barracks, the cattle ranch, a number of road camps, and Draper Correctional Center, a prison which handles all levels of security. It is the latter institution in which the projects are conducted and from which they take their name. Inmates from other institutions may be transferred to Draper to receive training.

Draper was built to house 650 prisoners, but it can accommodate up to 800 and has had to do so on occasion. The average population, however, ranges from 650 to 700. The prison is enclosed by an 18-foot chain link fence with five guard towers. The building contains four cell blocks which are arranged in dormitory style and equipped with double-decker bunks. Food is served cafeteria style. There is a gymnasium which is used for recreation, movies, and other activities. Laundry facilities within Draper serve all the State's penal institutions except the road camps and the women's prison. The only other industry at Draper is farming.

Draper was the first reformatory-type institution for adults in the state. At the time it was constructed, it was considered to be a step forward in prison reform. Actually it remains an archaic institution patterned on the 19th century human warehouse concept despite the Warden's almost single-handed efforts to change it.

The Prison Staff

Draper's administrative staff consists of the Warden, deputy warden, classification officer, captain of the guards, and chief clerk. Supervisory personnel include a steward, a laundry superintendent, and a farm supervisor. There are 87 correctional officers (guards) who work in three shifts. (The Warden states there should be a minimum of 125.) All staff members are State Merit System employees.

To qualify for employment as a correctional officer a man must be between 21 and 53 years of age, be at least 5'6" tall, weigh a minimum of 130 pounds, have completed the eighth grade, and hold a current Alabama driver's license. Obviously, correctional officers are not trained for their jobs, and such on-the-job training as may be provided must receive consideration secondarily to the demands of operations, particularly security. Well-formulated theories about or philosophies of corrections are almost beyond their ken. Nevertheless, they do develop their own notions about the nature and function of a correctional institution. A situation is created wherein inmates are dealt with by many people who have widely divergent views about how prisoners may best be prepared for their return to society.

Suppose a scale could be constructed. At one end would be placed the philosophy which holds that punishment is of no avail, that the correctional process should be one of helping the prisoner learn how to fit into free society, that the prisoner's every activity in the prison environment should be relevant to his task of getting ready to cope in the world outside the prison walls. At the other end of the scale would be the school of thought which says that prisoners are "different", that they must be under surveillance at all times, that they are never to be trusted, that punishment will cause them to repent and therefore "reform." Work is used as punishment, as is isolation; and prisoners are exhorted to reform, forced to do their keepers' bidding.

If the Draper staff could be placed on this scale, all of its points would doubtless be occupied. And the occupants, who are shaping the behavior of prisoners, would not all understand that they are often reinforcing behaviors they are attempting to extinguish.

The Convict Culture

Another force which shapes inmate behavior is the "convict culture." A prison is a cultural island. Within the prison walls is a small, complete society which has all the attributes of any other society: a code of behavior, an economic system, a "pecking order," the means and the will to punish deviants from its code. Even if an inmate does not embrace the convict culture, he may have to conform to its dictates just to survive. Unfortunately, its dictates are usually anti-society, anti-administration, and anti-rehabilitation (Clemmer, 1958; Cressey, 1961; and Watkins, 1964).

The convict culture at Draper is much weaker than those in other similar institutions — chiefly because it has been systematically undermined by the Warden. With his anthropological training, he has employed many techniques to weaken the contraculture, such as relaxation of rules (the tighter you squeeze them, the stronger the culture), never selling out to the strong guys to keep order, participation of the inmates in the affairs of the institution, converting the leadership to a new and humanistic value system, and many other measures. Even so, the convict culture affects both the individual inmate and any program designed to change his behavior. The effect is usually harmful.

Preliminary Experimental Study

The one common denominator of the forces described is this: each has its separate and often detrimental effect on men who are undergoing compulsory confinement in an institution which is a throwback to the last century. With few exceptions, the untrained keepers have a punitive philosophy upon which the convict culture thrives. To the Draper projects, the importance of the factors which have been discussed is threefold: First, the projects are made possible by the presence in the prison system of such men as the Commissioner of Corrections and the Warden. Second, the projects meet with varying degrees of support and acceptance from inmates and employees alike. Third, there are forces, diametrically opposed to the projects' aims, which compete for control of the inmate-subjects' behavior.

The first inmates to enter a Draper project were partners in a small pilot experiment designed in part "to demonstrate the administrative feasibility of an entirely self-instructional education program within Draper." By self-instructional, it was meant that programmed learning materials would be the method of instruction. Programmed instruction was at that time (1960) a new application of behavioral technology. And the Warden and the Director of the Draper projects had been impressed with the results obtained from its use with individual inmates.

Programmed Instruction (P.I.) functions as a tutor, providing instruction, testing for understanding, and giving feedback. It is self-pacing, that is, the user progresses through materials at his own rate of learning. Material is said to be programmed when it presents subject matter to the learner in a logical sequence in which concepts and/or behaviors are broken down into steps which are small enough to be easily learned. The learner is required to respond actively to each step. That is, he is asked to apply information or perform skills immediately after they are introduced to him. The learner receives immediate feedback as to the correctness of each response.

The pilot project succeeded beyond the expectations of its originators. In addition to indicating that large-scale utilization of self-instructional programs in a correctional institution would be practical, there was much evidence that the inmates not only learned from P.I., but that the experience of success in learning reinforced learning behavior. These and other findings were the basis for a proposal to conduct a large-scale project to develop further the procedures for establishing and operating a self-instructional school within a correctional center. The decision was made also to employ a vocational educator to experiment with the development of a

limited vocational training curriculum, using programmed instructional
techniques.

This venture was followed by the first of four experimental and
demonstration manpower training projects. The original manpower
project drew heavily on the findings and experience of its predecessor
in setting up its training program. The model which will be described
in the next section was developed, tried out, modified, and used in this
and all succeeding programs.

It was recognized early that P.I.'s intrinsic motivating capability
eventually diminishes and will not, of itself, sustain the performance
rate which is necessary for substantial educational achievement. One
project was, therefore, largely devoted to the development of effective
methods of continuously motivating students who are using P.I. The
findings of this project are incorporated into the model as a system of
managing learning contingencies.

Development of the Educational Model

Individually Prescribed Instruction

In the pilot phase and even in the early months after the programmed instruction project was funded, the number of commercially
available programmed materials was quite limited. Those courses
which were available were very lengthy and optimistically purported to
teach such broad and advanced topics as "first year algebra" and
"English grammar." This type of programmed text was fairly appropriate for pilot subjects who were capable of achieving at a high school
level. But such subjects constituted only a small minority of Draper's
600-plus population. Fortunately, commercial firms began producing
P.I. at all levels, and by 1965, some 400 distinct programmed lessons
were in the project's library.

Assignment to programmed courses was based on standardized
achievement test scores. As previously mentioned, these incarcerated
youths display quite a bit of "scatter" on achievement profiles, and one
student was likely to have been taking courses at several different
grade levels. The method of matching student with programs was
admittedly gross. But since P.I. lessons were still predominantly
lengthy and quite broad, about the best that could be done in the way
of prescribing materials was to match grade level on achievement
subtest to grade level of the individual text. Assignment of entire
programmed courses, however, has certain obvious disadvantages.
Since there is a large number of permutations of correct and incorrect

answers that will lead to the same score on achievement subtests, this resulting numerical grade level may be considered only a general estimate of student deficiences. Courses assigned on this basis may have been generally appropriate but did not meet the specificity later found to be necessary. The novelty of P.I. allowed the investigators to continue at this unrefined state of assessing weaknesses and prescribing programs for over a year. Students suffered both the boredom of repetitive and already-mastered material and the frustration of trying to learn material that was just beyond their grasp There were apparently many reinforcers operating which attenuated these internal conflicts and the predictable behavioral manifestations. For example, working as a subject in the project was, for a time, the only assignment in the institution in which some sort of physical labor was not required. Studying was preferable to working on the farm. Also, the students were passing tests on course content — a rare experience for these dropouts. But because of motivational considerations (to be discussed later) and the unrefined nature of the diagnostic and prescriptive techniques, many subjects began to "bug out." They often could not articulate reasons for their inability to sustain their learning behavior with P.I. lessons or to pass criterion tests. The first step toward enhancing performance was to look more carefully at procedures for diagnosing academic deficiencies.

Improving Assessment Procedures

The inefficiency of the diagnostic procedure had been due in part to a lack of staff. Employment of paraprofessional staff (College Corpsmen — upperclassmen who work in the project for a quarter or a semester) made possible a more careful appraisal of educational deficits. College Corpsmen have worked in two general areas: guidance and counseling, and basic education. In the latter areas they have provided technical assistance in diagnosing deficiencies and prescribing instructional materials and in managing the learning activities. The Corpsmen also played a valuable role as peer models for the inmate trainees.[3]

One immediate improvement was available in the form of the item analysis offered by the test manufacturer. Each question was keyed to signify the concept or skill that it presumed to test. Thus, in addition to a grade level score of 6.5 in arithmetic computation, for example, the performance of the student in areas such as "addition of like fractions"

---

[3]The use of paraprofessionals is treated more fully in Volume 1 of the report cited in footnote 2.

or "long division" could be assessed. Such assessment techniques are unfortunately tinged by subjectivity. For example, does missing three out of six questions on long division indicate more of a deficiency than missing two out of four on addition of fractions? The conservative approach is to give instruction in areas for which 30 percent or more of the specifically related test items are missed. Thus, while not eliminating the problems associated with the earlier grade-level approach, the investigators were hopefully reducing such problems and coming closer to the goal of completely individualized instruction. No further refinement of this particular diagnostic step has been developed.

Using the Diagnosis

Diagnosis of deficiencies and prescription of instructional materials are necessarily interrelated. Weakness in either link of this sequence will set an upper limit on the effectiveness of any remedial program. It would seem hardly worthwhile to have a highly specified description of the student's academic repertory if one could not then tailor the materials to meet the needs. In this particular project, "tailoring" meant adapting for our purposes the often hastily produced commercial programs. (As part of the commitment of the manpower training projects, a programming staff was trained to develop lessons not available commercially.)

Skill in prescribing materials is often related to nothing more than degree of familiarity with available resources. As inmates progress through programs, data are collected concerning degree of difficulty (i.e.. is the program suitable for grade levels cited by the publisher?), test performance at intermediate points and upon completion of the lesson, and the subjective evaluation of the program by students. One rather distasteful chore led to even further familiarity with many of the programmed materials—the necessity of devising tests to accompany the course work. Less than half of the publishers supply tests in any form; some offer only a final exam to cover a large body of material. If one assumes the feedback inherent to P.I. to be important, a commitment to frequent and periodic tests on a limited number of concepts logically follows. In designing such tests, staff members must determine what concept each group of frames is trying to teach. Something just short of actually going through the lesson as a student is required. This type of invaluable familiarity leads immediately to more skillful matching of materials to deficiencies.

Use of Criterion Tests for Diagnosis and Prescription

If programmed materials are correctly constructed, identification of "criterion" frames is fairly straightforward. These are frames which test the concept taught by the preceding frames. As implied earlier, a group or sample of such criterion frames might constitute a good intermediate or final examination, and indeed this technique has been used. At the same time, it became apparent that a complete listing of these criterion or test frames could serve as a valuable diagnostic instrument. To the extent that these items were identifiable and representative of the program content, students could, after taking this test, be directed to precisely those groups of frames for which they missed the criterion test frame. This practice has proven beneficial particularly for the longer, more comprehensive courses. Whereas a student might be assigned an entire section of a course based on achievement scores alone, the diagnostic pretest for the particular course would suggest that he complete only one-third of the material. In one pilot study, two subjects who made the same score on the diagnostic pretest for a particular programmed grammar text were selected. One worked through the entire course and the other worked only those portions for which the need was indicated by the test. Upon retest, both showed marked gains, and the subject who studied only selected parts of the program actually scored a few points higher. Though admittedly deficient in terms of number of subjects, these findings have been confirmed repeatedly in the practical application of this technique. The time-saving factor is apparent and is consistent with the goal of reducing academic deficiencies as quickly as possible. The inmate-subjects recognize the value of attempts at diagnostic refinement and are notably cooperative in any effort that will reduce the amount of material needed to achieve a specified goal.

Although the use of diagnostic pretests is particularly desirable in the case of the more lengthy programs, the advent of shorter, more restricted programmed lessons often made it possible to bypass this step. Assessment of deficiencies could revert to a former stage of dependence on the standardized achievement test results and the item analysis key. The use of these short lessons which are designed to teach a few highly specified concepts serves the same function as the prescribing of portions of more lengthy P.I. materials. But it has been observed by the staff that successive completion of several short lessons is likely to keep the student more motivated than his plowing through a weighty volume. Diagnostic effort is also simplified.

Definition of Goals

Refinement of goals has also been a major objective. The contrast of the aims of traditional psychotherapy to those of behavior therapy is perhaps an appropriate analogy to the progress made in this area. Early goals were stated in sweeping terms; there was little agreement as to which techniques were crucial and which could be dispensed with in attaining objectives; and evaluation of results was likewise fairly subjective. In recasting the aims of the projects, the overall commitment to education, socialization, and "rehabilitation" has not been sacrificed. Modification of many identifiable and circumscribed behaviors is assumed to contribute to successful re-entry and adjustment to the free world. The process and results remain essentially the same. But attention must be focused on specific portions of the inmate's repertory; deficiencies are tackled one-at-a-time; and evaluation at each intermediate step becomes more manageable than, though not a substitute for, long-range program evaluation.

Formula for Diagnosis

In the preceding few pages, the writers have been reviewing the development of techniques that allow for implementation of a more completely individualized instructional system. Implicit in this discussion has been an obligation to identify terminal objectives, to specify the academic, vocational, and personal-social deficiencies, and to intervene with appropriate materials and techniques. One might conceive of this sequence as $M - I = D$, or simply mastery skills (terminal behaviors) less the initiate's entry skills (existing repertory) equals deficiencies. Though no profound conceptualization, this guide has been meaningful and helpful in implementing concrete and individually tailored intervention techniques.

An Illustrative Case

D. H., who claimed to have completed the tenth grade in public school, scored at the 7.8 level on the standardized achievement test administered when he entered training. Scores on the subtests were as follows:

Word Knowledge	10.8
Reading	9.7
Spelling	5.9
Total Language	6.2

Arithmetic Computation	6.6
Arithmetic Problem Solving Concepts	7.8

Following item analysis of his test score, D. H. was assigned parts of English programs at the appropriate grade level in this sequence:

Basic Sentence Patterns
Punctuation
Spelling, Part I
Spelling, Part II
Vocabulary Building
Punctuation

On his first attempt, he failed the posttest on Part II of the spelling course, but after further study and reviews, he passed the test with a score of 90. The vocabulary building course proved to be too advanced for him, and he was permitted to drop it. He passed the other courses, with scores on final exams ranging from 88 to 100.

He was assigned Book II of a seventh grade math course and made a score of 94 on the final test. He then completed Book III, scoring 88 on the exam.

At the end of six months during which D. H. devoted eight hours a week to his studies, he was retested with a different form of the achievement test. His overall grade placement score was 8.5. Subtest scores were:

Word Knowledge	9.9
Reading	9.9
Spelling	8.5
Total Language	7.3
Arithmetic Computation	7.5
Problem Solving Concepts	7.7

Since he was enrolled in a 12-month occupational course, D. H. continued to spend eight hours a week in communication and computational skill development courses for another six months. He completed seven units of an English course, seven units of a basic math course, and a 40-hour reading improvement course which stresses vocabulary development. When he was tested at the end of the second six months, he achieved a 9.7 overall grade placement score. Subtest scores were:

Word Knowledge	11.4
Reading	10.8
Spelling	7.1
Total Language	8.1

Arithmetic Computation   10.8
Problem Solving Concepts   9.7

With 400 hours of instruction, D. H.'s placement level increased by almost two grades. There is, however, still significant subtest "scatter," which is frequently the case with the disadvantaged. Although the gain is uneven, it follows the usual pattern of significantly raised weak entry skills.

Motivational Adjuncts

A second phase in the development of the general educational model has been experimentation with and utilization of various motivational techniques. Operant conditioners, from whom the general model has been adapted, are notably disinclined to speak of motivation. They prefer instead to talk about discriminative stimuli and reinforcement contingencies. The Draper projects have had this orientation since their inception though the word "motivation" is not so easily dismissed from one's vocabulary. It was uniformly acknowledged that attempts to insert internal motivators were simply not productive. After years of extinction training and the resulting failure to incorporate the usual middle class reinforcers for learning, one lecture or one heart-to-heart talk could not supplant or negate the reinforcement history of inmate-trainees. In a very few cases, a true process of identification with a significant other occurred and seemed to provide the incentive for learning without elaborate contingency arrangements.

In many institutions which have rehabilitation and training programs, the philosophy of the staff often goes something like this: We are providing the inmates with an opportunity to get an education and learn a trade — but if they don't have the motivation to take advantage of it, we can't be concerned with them. This approach is, of course, the easy way out, though it is quite natural to harbor such feelings.

At Draper, however, the orientation has been to manipulate the consequences of learning behavior, to slowly rebuild the notion that learning pays off not only in the long run but right now. Far-reaching statements concerning the relationship of education to potential earnings are rarely effective. But when successful completion of a specific learning task is immediately followed by coffee and donuts, things begin to happen; students get "motivated." Throughout the remainder of this chapter, therefore, the term motivation will be used not to connote any internal condition but as a convenient summary term signifying the result of adroitly arranged contingencies.

Motivating Capability of P.I.

It was initially felt that programmed instruction would provide the incentives to sustain failure-prone inmates in efficient learning behavior. Indeed, this feeling was a major reason for selecting P.I. as the instructional vehicle. P.I. is purposely designed to maximize the student's success. While actively responding to specially constructed questions and statements, the learner is receiving continuous feedback, and almost exclusively positive feedback. Being right 90 percent of the time is sweet for these success-deprived subjects. But to speak of satiation on a steady diet of right answers may be as legitimate as speaking of satiation for grains of corn. Few students could perform effectively for long periods of time without additional reinforcers.

The Experimenter-Subject Role

One technique which (while not a reinforcement procedure as such) has been apparently successful is the establishment of a unique experimenter-subject role. Minimal reference is made to teachers and instructors; instead, such terms as experimenter, learning manager, and behavior technician are applied to staff members. The mere verbalization of these terms seems to enhance the overall research orientation. Inmates are sensitive to the differences between traditional teachers, techniques, and roles, and the innovative atmosphere of the Draper projects. They view themselves as subject-participants in meaningful, ongoing research studies in education and human development. This role appears to be more palatable than the student status with which they have experienced much discomfort. Other experimenters have shown this approach to be a useful substitute for the traditional teacher-student or therapist-patient relationship established in treating youthful delinquents (Slack, 1960; Schwitzgebel, 1964).

The Hawthorne Effect

An additional technique has been the harnessing of the Hawthorne effect. Much has been said about the need to be aware of and to control this phenomenon in educational research (Cook, 1962). However, it seems that if increased responding occurs as a simple artifact of changing conditions, this relationship should be systematically exploited. Teachers do this continuously with varied techniques and methods of classroom presentation. Naturally, the effects of change itself must be controlled if results of a new technique, as such, are to be more precisely assessed. This methodological consideration has been characteristic of the many small-scale experiments performed within the larger project framework. However, utilization of change for the sake of increasing performance is practiced and is seemingly defensible, particularly if one of the objectives is accelerated learning. In an analogous situation, Krasner and Ullmann (1965, p. 230) speak of the prevalence and legitimacy of placebo effects in treating psychological disorders. If one remains sensitive to the operation of such phenomena and if such effects enhance the treatment outcome, they may be used and maximized without apology.

Contingency Management Experiments

In studies (McKee & Clements, 1967; Clements & McKee, 1968) aimed specifically at increasing the productivity of inmate-subjects studying programmed materials, the writers have attempted to gain precision in identifying and administering reinforcers and arranging contingencies for learning. Much creative work in this area has come from Homme and his associates (Homme, C'deBaca, Devine, Steinhorst & Rickert, 1963; Homme & Tosti, 1965; Addison & Homme, 1966; and Homme, 1966) particularly regarding the teaching of preschool disadvantaged children. In working with nondeprived subjects, it is often difficult to identify suitable and stable reinforcers. Candy works well with children but not equally well with all children; money is reinforcing for youthful offenders but causes certain problems. Traditional thought has viewed one set of events as being reinforcing and another distinct set of events as being reinforceable. Food (and eating) reinforced running, bar pressing, or studying, but the converse was assumed not to hold. However, Premack (1959, 1963, 1965) has demonstrated that the relationship can be reversed and that, for example, drinking (lick) rate of rats can be increased by making the opportunity to run contingent upon it.

This and similar findings have led Premack to a rather innovative position concerning the important property that reinforcers have in common — namely, that reinforcers permit the organism to engage in high probability behaviors. As Premack states, "of any two responses the more probable will reinforce the less probable (1965, p. 132)." This generalization may be restated as follows: If behavior B is of higher probability than behavior A, then A can be strengthened by making B contingent upon A's occurrence. In animal studies, deprivation guarantees that eating, for example, will be at high probability strength. Even though behavior probabilities vary unpredictably for human subjects, the Premack hypothesis may be readily applied. Whatever a subject is doing on his own may be considered his high probability behavior at that moment. A contingency manager need only demand a small amount of low probability behavior which he wishes to strengthen; he then allows the subject to continue in his high probability behavior. Homme and associates have taken the Premack principle to heart and their search for reinforcers has been greatly aided. One unique application has been the development of a reinforcing event menu which presented a variety of high probability behaviors (Addison & Homme, 1966). Upon completion of a chunk of low probability behavior, the subject was rewarded with a block of time during which he could engage in any activity offered on the menu. In this situation, much of the guesswork of administering reinforcers is removed since the subject chooses his own reinforcing activity.

In a recent study (Clements & McKee, 1968), the writers attempted to incorporate many of the above-cited techniques. The behavior to be strengthened was rate and quality of performance in working programmed lessons. Inmate-subjects were questioned regarding what type of permissible activities they enjoyed. Insofar as possible, such activities (reinforcing events) were provided and the opportunity to engage in these presumably high probability behaviors was made contingent on completing segments of programmed materials. It seemed consistent with operant methodology that small units of work be required initially and that subject and experimenter contract for more low probability behavior as S gained experience. In operant laboratories, the contract is implicit and the increasing requirements are inserted without S's permission or awareness. In the study at Draper, amounts of work to be done to gain admission to a reinforcing event (RE) area were specified daily by means of a written performance contract. Each unit of work was followed by opportunity to engage in a menu activity for 15 minutes (RE period), and completion of the entire contract resulted in being dismissed for the remainder of the day. Contract requirements were increased each week for a 4-week period. One important distinction between this approach and traditional educational programs is that reinforcers do not accrue simply on the basis of time spent with materials and activities — inmates must produce to gain rewards. Payoff is not "by-the-hour" but by the unit of work — reinforcement is contingent upon specified amounts of desirable behavior. In a later segment of the study, subjects arranged their own contracts and agreed, as a minimum, to do as much work as each had done during a baseline period. This phase seemed particularly germane since the ultimate success of any behavior change program must be evaluated in terms of transfer to self-management conditions.

Results of this experiment were uniformly encouraging. Briefly, rates of performance were significantly higher during contingency management periods than during baseline. Moreover, under self-management conditions, neither rate nor total work decreased perceptibly from weeks in which the experimenter arranged contingency contracts. Test performance on unit and final exams actually improved even though inmate-subjects were progressing through material at a rate twice that of baseline. Data collected concerning the reinforcing activities selected by subjects as the study progressed suggest that "drinking coffee" was the only stable reinforcer. When an option was inserted, some subjects began to forego their 15-minute RE periods so that the total contract might be completed earlier. Such a sequence might be thought of as a chain in which the recording of starting and ending times at the beginning and end of each unit of work served as both a discriminative stimulus for the next segment of the contract and as a conditioned reinforcer for the just completed portion. Completion of the final contract unit resulted in dismissal for the day which, by inspection, is near the top of any list of behavior probabilities for inmate-subjects.

Current Applications

The ongoing manpower training project is a 5-step differential diagnosis paradigm which borrows heavily from diagnostic and prescriptive techniques developed earlier. Within this rubric, vocational and social skills training becomes as highly individualized as possible. Whereas in earlier projects certain training classes were set for six months or a year, course duration is now dependent on the subject's entry skills, his ability to learn, and his perseverance (i.e., the staff's skill at arranging learning contingencies).

Basic education. The basic education phase of the manpower program is charged with the task of getting the educational skills of inmates to a level where vocational training may become a realistic goal. In its essential elements, it is a replica of the model which has been described. However, the motivational system presently being investigated is a blend of the earlier mentioned contingency-contracts technique (Clements & McKee, 1968) and a token or point system. The efficacy of awarding tokens for completion of programmed lessons and accompanying tests has been demonstrated in another setting with emotionally disturbed children (Rickard, Willis & Clements, 1969).

The present system at Draper is employing performance contracts but no longer rewards each unit of work with a reinforcing event period. Instead, completion of daily contracts has a certain point value. Additionally, test performance is differentially reinforced by giving additional points for higher scores and for passing tests on the first attempt. Points are then accumulated and can be used to buy time during which reinforcing activities can be engaged in. Cohen has carried such a system to its logical conclusion at the National Training School for Boys by implementing a completely autonomous token economy in which income is achieved only by educational pursuits and in which the inmate has to pay his way for everything, including room and board above the minimum subsistence level. In the present design at Draper the cost of each activity is based on its ranking in a list of high probability events. Adjustments in this small-scale economic system are being made as data are gathered on the earning potential of inmate-students and on the actual frequencies of selection of reinforcing activities. This system will potentially lead to faster, more efficient learning, since both completion of more work and higher test scores lead to accumulation of more points. Competition between students is again avoided because each individual's daily contract is based on how much work he has been able to negotiate comfortably. Earlier experiences suggest that steady but slow increases in contract requirements can, up to a limit, be handled effectively.

Speech modification. An experiment in speech modification also has its roots in the system of individually prescribed instruction. The elements of speech which each subject will attempt to modify have been selected on the basis of his own oral usage. Drill and study materials and learning activities will be constructed to treat specific errors of specific students. Motivation will be maintained through the use of contractual agreements, money payments for daily participation, frequent feedback, and a variety of social reinforcers. The objective of the experiment is to produce a training package to improve English usage.

Summary and Conclusion

The procedures cited herein have evolved largely from a project supported by the National Institute of Mental Health, which was committed to exploring the economic and administrative feasibility of an educational system for offenders using programmed instructional materials. This project came to be known as the Self-Instructional School. The name was rather descriptive in that heavy reliance was put upon programmed instructional materials and each inmate-student became his own principal behavior change agent.

The series of manpower training projects at Draper have benefited from the onset from findings of the earlier academic project. Programmed instruction has been used almost exclusively in the remedial and basic education components of the manpower programs. While the Self-Instructional School devised and evaluated motivational systems, implementation in the manpower phase followed quickly wherever possible. ·

Findings from the studies and other related experiences have led the project staff to feel increasingly confident about administering an education and training program for institutionalized offenders. Progress made by the learners under their supervision has been substantial. Trainees in the manpower projects have averaged a gain of 1.4 grades per 208 hours of programmed instruction. Gains of as high as 4.8 have been registered. Certificates of high school equivalency were earned by 95 percent of the trainees who took the GED tests. Nine former students entered college after leaving the prison.

A workable model has been generated and refined. In review, the model consists of a number of interrelated but distinct components. Initially, one must decide on the terminal objectives — what knowledge, what behaviors, what skills are determined to be important in the adjustment of an offender upon his return to a free environment. Quite obviously included in the objectives are academic and vocational competence, which include occupational and social skills, attitude, job habits, and other more subtle behaviors. The next step may be thought of as diagnosis of behavioral deficiencies. Granted that factors related to successful adjustment can be isolated, where and by how much does the inmate fall short in these various areas? When deficiences have been identified, remediation techniques subsequently become the center of attention. Opinion may differ as to what methods or materials to prescribe. Only controlled observation and evaluation will resolve the issue. At many points in the remedial program, deficiencies must be reassessed and prescriptions modified and updated.

Overlaid on this cycle of diagnosis, prescription, and evaluation is a motivational system designed to ensure that subjects will interact with materials and other techniques in a meaningful and sustained way. Many of these procedures have been described in the foregoing pages. Instructional materials such as programmed instruction often contribute to more motivated performance. Additionally, an experimenter-subject relationship has proven to be a sound vehicle for securing cooperation. In bringing other procedures to bear on learning behavior, the philosophy has been to arrange and manipulate the contingencies for specifiable units of work. Thus, the methods requisite to a program of individually prescribed instruction in conjunction with empirically derived motivational components would appear to lead to an effective remedial or behavior modification system within almost any setting.

REFERENCES

Addison, R. M. & Homme, L. E. The reinforcing event (RE) menu. *National Society for Programmed Instruction Journal,* 1966, **5**(1), 8–9.

Clements, C. B. & McKee, J. M. Programmed instruction for institutionalized offenders: Contingency management and performance contracts. *Psychological Reports,* 1968, **22**, 957–964.

Clemmer, D. C. *The prison community.* New York: Rinehart, 1958.

Cook, D. L. The Hawthorne effect in educational research. *Phi Delta Kappan,* 1962, **43**, 116–122.

Cressey, D. R. *The prison: Studies in institutional organization and change.* New York: Holt, Rinehart & Winston, 1961.

Homme, L. E. Contiguity theory and contingency management. *Psychological Record,* 1966, **16**, 233–241.

Homme, L. E., C'deBaca, P., Devine, J. V., Steinhorst, R. & Rickert, E. J. Use of the Premack principle in controlling the behavior of nursery school children. *Journal of the Experimental Analysis of Behavior,* 1963, **6**, 544.

Homme, L. E. & Tosti, D. T. Contingency management and motivation. *National Society for Programmed Instruction Journal,* 1965, **4**(7), 14–16.

Krasner, L. & Ullmann, L. P. (Eds.), *Research in behavior modification.* New York: Holt, Rinehart & Winston, 1965.

McKee, J. M. & Clements, C. B. Experimental project to increase educational achievement of institutionalized offenders through programmed instructon. Progress Report, February 1967, Rehabilitation Research Foundation, Grant # 7–R11 MH 02529–02, National Institute of Mental Health.

Premack, D. Toward empirical behavior laws: I. Positive reinforcement. *Psychological Review,* 1959, **66**, 219–233.

Premack, D. Prediction of the comparative reinforcement values of running and drinking. *Science,* 1963, **139**, 1062–1063.

Premack, D. Reinforcement theory. *Nebraska Symposium on Motivation,* 1965, **13**, 123–80.

Rickard, H. C., Willis, J. W. & Clements, C. B. Token reinforcement and programmed instruction in a remedial program for emotionally disturbed children. Paper presented at the meeting of the South-eastern Psychological Association, New Orleans, February 1969.

Schwitzgebel, R. K. *Street corner research: An experimental approach to the juvenile delinquent.* Cambridge, Mass.: Harvard University Press, 1964.

Slack, C. W. Experimenter-subject psychotherapy: A new method of introducing intensive office treatment for unreachable cases. *Mental Hygiene,* 1960, **44**, 238–256.

Ullmann, L. P. & Krasner, L. (Eds.), *Case studies in behavior modification.* New York: Holt, Rinehart & Winston, 1965.

Watkins, J. C. The concept of Convict Culture and the Draper experiment in dealing with it. In *Proceedings of the ninety-fourth annual Congress of Corrections,* Kansas City, Mo., September 1964.

CHAPTER 10

A Behavioral Approach to Out-Patient Treatment of Offenders

Saleem A. Shah[1]

One of the more vexing problems confronting psychotherapists and others concerned with the treatment of maladaptive behavior has been that of treating offenders. As a group, offenders and delinquents have long been considered rather difficult subjects for psychotherapy. Such views have generally been based upon the fact that these persons are often lacking in what has been regarded as suitable motivation: they do not respond well to traditional therapeutic techniques, they frequently fail to continue in such treatment encounters, and, as would be suggested from the above remarks, success has been difficult to attain.

The therapeutic efforts to be described in this chapter were conducted in an out-patient psychiatric clinic[2] which provided diagnostic, treatment, consultative, and training services to a number of agencies within the criminal justice system. Except for a few cases referred by the Domestic Relations Branch of the local court, all persons referred to the clinic for evaluation and/or treatment had either been charged with or convicted of law violations. The criminal charges ranged from various misdemeanors, such as petty larceny, drunk and disorderly behavior, and simple assault, to more serious offenses, e.g., aggravated assault, robbery, criminal homicide, and various sexual offenses such as carnal knowledge, incest, rape, and indecent acts with minors.

The clinic setting was rather typical of such mental health facilities. It had the usual complement of psychiatrists, clinical psychologists, psychiatric social workers, and students in training. The theoretical orientation at the clinic was heavily psychoanalytic, with

---

[1]Chief, Center for Studies of Crime and Delinquency, National Institute of Mental Health.
[2]Legal Psychiatric Division, D.C., Department of Public Health, Washington, D.C. The author was with this clinic from 1957 to 1966.

most of the psychiatric staff either undergoing formal psychoanalytic training, planning such training, or undergoing personal analysis.

The author, while initially somewhat eclectic in his approach but with a psychoanalytic leaning, gradually shifted to a behavioral and learning theory approach. This shift was brought about because of the apparent unsuitability, ineffectiveness, and general inefficiency of the traditional psychotherapeutic approaches with the offender population. Although the shift toward a behavioral therapeutic approach began in 1960, experience, trial-and-error innovations, and study of the developing literature, led to continued refinements during subsequent years at the clinic. A behavioral treatment orientation was limited to the psychologists at the clinic and while evoking curiosity and interest, it did not appear to have any significant influence on the psychoanalytically oriented staff.

Overview

This discussion starts with some general remarks concerning treatment issues and problems with offenders in order to provide a conceptual framework for a behavioral approach. The general treatment program and specific behavioral treatment approaches employed will then be described. Examples and cases will be relied upon to illustrate the actual techniques used in working with a variety of adult criminals in an out-patient setting. In order to make the examples more meaningful, the conceptual framework and rationale for the therapeutic approaches will also be provided. In conclusion, evaluative comments about the treatment program and implications for future development of such treatment approaches are also provided.

Some General Issues Concerning the Treatment of Offenders

Traditional psychoanalytic and related psychotherapeutic techniques have been developed and used for the greater part with middle and upper class, educated, verbal, motivated, introspective, and essentially neurotic patients. The neurotic individual typically enters treatment voluntarily, the behavior is regarded as troubling or troublesome by both the therapist and the patient, and in addition, the maladaptive behavior is usually not so visible as to involve large segments of the community in its alteration.

In contrast, offenders typically do not present themselves voluntarily for treatment; they often do *not* feel very troubled, nor do they usually regard their behavior as necessarily indicative of any maladjustment. These general comments are true for a sizable proportion of lower social class offenders—this being the group which more frequently comes to official attention.

When the aforementioned psychotherapeutic approaches have been applied, or perhaps misapplied, to lower class people who are often not very educated, are nonintrospective, "unmotivated," and who "act out" character disorders, the results have not been very satisfactory. Experiences of this sort seem to have led to the belief that offenders were untreatable or at least extremely difficult to treat.

As Hollingshead and Redlich (1958), among many others, have demonstrated, there is much evidence to indicate that middle class values, expectations, and attitudes tend to influence diagnostic evaluations and the goals and practice of psychotherapy. In addition, it has been suggested (Hunt, 1960) that the very *principles* and *concepts* of psychotherapy may be class-linked—since these have been developed mainly by middle class practitioners in the course of their work with largely middle class patients. Also, it was as long ago as 1938 that Kingsley Davis (1949) contended that mental hygiene principles were little more than secular statements of the prevailing middle class (Protestant ethic) morality.

The requirements of traditionally oriented intensive psychotherapies for the patient to talk freely, to have motivation, to forego immediate alleviation of distress for later understanding and resolution of the "deep-seated causes" of the maladjustments, to tolerate and not act out anxiety, etc., are all deeply imbedded in a middle class value system (Shah, 1963). It would appear further, that the problem presented by the offenders' lack of motivation for treatment is often compounded by the fact that many therapists are equally lacking in interest and motivation to work with such persons. There is in addition the possibility of the self-fulfilling prophecy, in that therapists who perceive and evaluate certain subjects as poor prospects for therapy and as resistant to such endeavors, may well be less likely to establish sound rapport, to consider modifications in their approach, and thus help to bring about a validation of their initial hypothesis.

A Behavioral Conceptualization of Treatment

The manner in which we conceptualize problems tends to determine to a large extent the particular procedures to be used in the treatment process. The type of interventions applied—be they intensive psychotherapy, remedial education, group counseling, or vocation training—carry implications about the nature or determinants of the deviant behavior being addressed. If remedial education, firm discipline, and particular work assignments are seen as necessary and appropriate forms of treatment and rehabilitation, then the implication is that the lack of certain education, interpersonal, and vocational skills was related directly or indirectly to the person's law violations and related problems. Certainly, there is some expectation or hope that such procedures will influence the deviant behavior; else why use them? However, to the extent the treatment programs do not relate to some understanding of the determinants of the deviant behavior, no guidance is provided for treatment. "Treatment" then becomes a sort of umbrella word meaning all things to all people.

A Definition and Conceptualization of Behavior

Behavior can be viewed as involving an interaction between an individual and a particular environment. Behavior is neither fixed nor absolute, and rarely does it involve only the individual. For example, one does not behave on the job as he does at church, the New Year's party, the poker group, or in the privacy of the home. To varying degrees the environment influences and controls the kind of behavior displayed. It is not surprising, therefore, that certain offenders described as highly impulsive, explosive, and dangerous while they are in the community, may be described as "model inmates" within correctional institutions. Such observations concerning the variability of behavior are surprising only if one views behavior as an emergent and somewhat fixed quality of the individual. A conceptualization of behavior which considers only the individual variables would appear to be both inadequate and erroneous.

If behavior is viewed as involving an interaction between the individual and a particular environment, efforts at its modification have to be directed not only at the individual but also to alterations of the relevant environment. In contrast to the concern with presumed "intrapsychic" factors and with uncovering "basic causes" of the problem in the individual's remote history, a behavioral approach places a great emphasis upon understanding the variables *currently* maintaining and influencing the behavior. Much emphasis is also placed upon control and manipulation of various aspects of the physical and social environments (independent variables) to bring about the desired changes in the behavior of concern (dependent variables).

Human behavior in large measure is shaped by the individual's experience, i.e., by learning. Various patterns of behavior are produced by particular personal histories. While learning is seen as a major variable in the acquisition of behavior patterns, this does not deny the influence and contributions of biochemical, organic, pharmacological, and other variables. Indeed, to the extent that functional (lawful) relationships can be established between such variables and the behavior, these factors must be considered in the treatment process. The patient's behavior can be seen as being disadvantageous and/or dangerous to himself or others. Such a pattern of behavior is viewed as having been produced by a particular personal history.

The task of the therapist is to supplement the individual's expreriences through interventions designed to modify the behavior so that it does not have the aforementioned maladaptive characteristics

A Behavioral Approach to Treatment

The term *behavior modification* is one which encompasses many types of behavior change — including reading, language acquisition, and similar educational, athletic and other programs. The term *behavior therapy* is used more specifically in a clinical sense to describe the applications of principles derived from learning theory and the experimental analysis of behavior to the treatment of maladaptive behaviors. Since there are several kinds of behavior therapy, it would be more accurate to speak of *behavior therapies*.

There are two important aspects of the above definition of behavior therapy. First, the focus is upon principles of learning as the basis for treatment methods. The term learning is used to refer broadly to the effects of experience upon the organism. There is also the further implication that the behaviors referred to cannot be attributed to growth or temporary changes in the individual as a function of drugs or other organic factors. This by no means implies a dichotomy. As noted earlier, biochemical, organic, pharmacological, and other such variables may well influence behavior. However, while such variables may provide certain constraints they do not necessarily eliminate the acquisition of new behaviors. The second major feature of the aforementioned definition is the clear focus on behavior — whether the behavior is verbal or motor, whether it reflects immediate social needs or is highly symbolic and idiosyncratic. Moreover, the behavior should be definable, it should be amenable to observation, or reliably measurable in other ways.

Thus, if the concern is with strengthening the person's ego, one would need to know the specific behaviors which indicate poor ego functioning, as well as to know what specific things the person would have to do in order for it to be determined that the ego had indeed been strengthened. In other words, we would need to have the concepts made specific and relevant to observable behavior. Likewise, if the concern is to bring about "emotional maturity" or "self-actualization," one would need to know the specific behaviors which could be used to define these terms.

The above comments should not be taken to imply that behavioral therapy consists simply of changing discrete aspects of behavior. Human behavior is indeed very complex and its modification typically involves addressing a large number of interrelated variables. Further, some degree of understanding about the variables influencing one's behavior (which is one way of defining insight) may indeed be an important element in the treatment.

Evaluation of Behavior and Treatment Implications

The above conceptualization of behavior is also important in assessing the adequacy of a person's skills in coping with a particular situation. The individual's behavior may be inadequate or deficient in reference to some specific task or situation. Inadequacy of behavior relates both to the available skills (repertoires) possessed by the person, and also to the complexity of the situation (environment) in which he has to function. An individual may be able, for example, to function quite well as a farm hand in a rural setting, but may find it very difficult to find suitable employment and to cope with a complex and demanding urban community. Behavioral skills adequate to functioning as a farm hand will not be adequate when a high school education and certain levels of verbal and social skills are required, and more complex environments are involved. Likewise, satisfactory performance as an athlete, automobile mechanic, dancer, or even "con artist," does not ensure adequate functioning in some different situations, e.g., as a musician, carpenter, computer technician, or even as a husband. A college professor's behavioral repertoire, while most adequate in many academic, intellectual, and social situations, may be nevertheless quite inadequate when the task requires performing minor repairs on his automobile or television set. In the latter situations the professor may indeed display exasperated and frustrated behavior. Similarly, the young man described as lazy, shiftless, lacking in ambition, and with low tolerance for frustration may in some other situations display remarkable patience, persistence, interest, and ingenuity, e.g., when working on his hot rod, training as a boxer or ball player, courting a girl, or planning a heist.

The treatment tasks to be undertaken relate to the specific characteristics of the problem behavior involved. Some of the relationships between assessment of problems and the treatment tasks may be subsumed under the following interrelated categories:

1. Behavioral deficits. Many problems in functioning may be attributed to the absence of certain repertoires when circumstances call for them. Lacking various verbal, educational, social, and other skills, the individual will not be able to obtain the rewards and positive reinforcements contingent upon such behavior. In addition, the lack of adequate repertoires might also bring a variety of punishing and aversive consequences. A child or adult with noticeable behavioral deficits can expect to receive less positive reinforcements and more aversive or punishing consequences. Under such conditions it would be difficult to develop other adjustive responses and even to maintain those already acquired. A vicious cycle may thus be engendered and the individual may develop alternate repertoires which do manage to influence the environment, i.e., succeed in obtaining positive reinforcements, but in ways that are defined as socially inappropriate or antisocial.

The treatment focus in these instances would involve addressing the behavioral deficits and establishing more adequate and socially approved repertoires, which could effectively compete with and re-place the deviant responses. Educational, vocational, and a wide range of social and interpersonal skills may be needed. In these cases curbing or controlling the deviant behaviors themselves would not suffice; new repertoires would have to be developed and strengthened, or else the deviant responses may remain relatively strong (prepotent) in many situations.

2. Inappropriate behaviors. In these instances behaviors which can produce critical consequences may well be present in the repertoire, but they occur at the wrong time, with the wrong people, or in socially inappropriate situations. Many sexual offenses may fall in this category, e.g., pedophilia, rape, and incest. Problems may also relate to inappro-priate reinforcing systems. For example, many forms of sexual devia-tions are based upon stimuli which have become inappropriately effective reinforcers for the individual, e.g., voyeurism, exhibitionism, frottage, and fetishism.

The treatment task in such cases may focus around discrimination training in order to bring the behaviors under the control of socially appropriate stimuli. Some measure of attention also has to be given to developing sufficient behavior control as well as to the acquisition and strengthening of repertoires necessary for more appropriate behaviors. For example, the pedophile often will need to learn the complex inter-personal skills necessary for more adaptive adult heterosexual behaviors.

3. Improper or inadequate behavior control. In these instances the behaviors may be appropriate and the repertoires adequate, but the individual does not exercise sufficient control over the behaviors. Thus, inability to curb and control behavior may lead to a whole range of problems. Inadequate self-control would seem to be involved in a wide range of problems — especially in the case of delinquent and criminal behaviors.

One of the main treatment tasks in dealing with problems in this category is to develop effective behavior control, self-controlling repertoires, proper stimulus control, and various measures which are discussed later in more detail.

Other assessment and classification arrangements have been suggested by Staats and Staats (1964), Kanfer and Saslow (1965), and Ullmann and Krasner (1965).

Goals of Behavior Therapy with Offenders

In the treatment of delinquents and offenders one of the primary goals in most instances is to bring about a cessation of the antisocial activities. To the extent that the individual faces social and legal sanctions, may well face serious penalties for future law violations, and the particular behavior may cause harm to the person or property of others, such behavior becomes an important focus of treatment. In addition, it is necessary to develop a more constructive personal and social adjustment in terms of improved occupational, social, familial, and other interpersonal behaviors.

Value judgments are explicitly involved in the treatment and rehabilitation of offenders — as indeed such judgments are involved in all treatment of behaviors judged to be deviant or problematic. Thus, in dealing with offenders it is obvious that rather explicit value judgments have already been made by the larger society, in that the behaviors engaged in by the individual have not only been defined as deviant, but are regarded as "crimes" which are subjected to clearly stated penalties. Criminal sanctions and various correctional and rehabilitative programs are aimed, at least in part, at making the offenders' subsequent behavior less deviant and antisocial. To the extent that therapeutic efforts are designed — explicitly or implicitly, directly or indirectly — to bring about changes in attitudes, feelings, and behaviors, such changes are viewed as desirable and as improvements. Such determinations or evaluations of needed improvements in functioning involve certain value judgments. The values may be largely social, ethical, mental health oriented, philosophical, or ideological.

The Treatment Program

Offenders were referred to the Legal Psychiatric Clinic for treatment under a variety of circumstances. Often, the offender at the presentence stage, i.e., after he had entered a plea of guilty or had been found guilty after trial and just prior to the imposition of sentence by the judge, might indicate to the judge his awareness of his problems and his desire to obtain psychiatric help. As might be expected, and was demonstrated in actual experience with many offenders, often such expressed interest in and requests for treatment were specifically designed to obtain probation rather than incarceration in a correctional institution. In other instances, an offender already on probation or parole would request such referral through his supervising probation or parole officer. Or, the officer would become aware of serious problems in the course of his supervisory efforts and would encourage the offender to obtain treatment at the clinic. There would also be instances where the sentencing judge would place the individual on probation, but, in view of the nature of the offense, e.g., various sex offenses, or a previous history of psychiatric problems, would recommend that the probationer receive treatment. Understandably, such recommendations coming from the sentencing judge were often perceived as implicit requirements.

One of the frequent problems encountered in working with offenders in an out-patient setting is the lack of interest in treatment. Often, there would be marked reluctance to subject oneself to the "head-shrinking" process. It was almost as though the person felt that to be labeled a criminal was bad enough without also being perceived as and treated for being "crazy in the head."

An important initial task, therefore, was simply to arrange to have the offender come to the clinic for therapy. While the visit for an evaluation could be controlled fairly well by the authority of the court and/or the probation officer, regular attendance at therapy sessions was another matter. A large proportion of the persons seen at the clinic would fail to continue after the first three or four visits.

While traditional psychotherapeutic approaches tend to view discomfort and anxiety in the patient to be essential prerequisites for treatment, such expectations are based largely upon experiences with middle class persons with neurotic or other related problems. Since the bulk of offenders needing modifications of their maladaptive behaviors appear not to experience the kind of discomfort which would bring them to and keep them in therapy, it is obvious that other approaches have to be considered. Ascribing or interpreting the reluctance to come for therapy to various psychological *resistances*, perhaps does no more than reiterate the fact that the person does not wish to come. This reluctance to receive help may indicate many things: the person may not actually experience or perceive any problem for which he wishes help; there may be some discomfort and a realization of the need for help, but a concurrent apprehension about the enterprise vaguely described by others and known commonly as "head-shrinking"; also, it may be that when some initial therapy sessions are attended, the person's experiences in the encounter are unpleasant and aversive, thus further attendance is not desired.

Slack (1960), Schwitzgebel (1964), and Schwitzgebel and Kolb (1964), have demonstrated that in the absence of intrinsic (internalized) motivation for therapy in hard-core delinquents, extrinsic (external) motivation by way of payments for visits and a "subject-experimenter" type of relationship instead of the usual psychotherapeutic one, quite effectively overcomes the problem of getting the person to come to the sessions. It would appear that at least some of the criticism of Slack's approach of paying such persons to come for appointments, and of related behavior modification strategies, springs from the clear reversal of the direction of the flow of money and its implication for the conventional private practice of psychotherapy. In addition, there is the very clear and strong cultural norm that payments for services are to be made by the recipients and not by those who provide the services. Correctional rehabilitation is one exception to the above general norm, in that the State assumes the cost of rehabilitating those who are typically involuntary recipients of such services.

In the absence of the availability of extrinsic reinforcements in the usual clinic setting, various other approaches had to be used. Since there was not much to be done without at least the physical presence of the client, various pressures and external constraints available to the probation officer were at times utilized to bring the offender to treatment for at least the first several sessions. For example, when an individual who had fairly obvious problems, e.g., pedophilia, exhibitionism, incest, or other personal maladjustments, expressed an interest in and desire for treatment at the presentence stage, an explicit recommendation would sometimes be made that treatment be made a part of the probation. In this situation the probation officer could exert the necessary pressure to at least bring the person to treatment for several sessions. The task for the therapist would then entail the gradual extinction of the avoidance behavior, the development of appropriate rapport and relationship, and the provision of various specific forms of assistance so that the sessions could take on a positive and reinforcing quality for the individual.

In terms of what is known about the modification of behavior, and especially in view of the societal interest in changing the behavior of the offender, it would be preferable if a system of extrinsic reinforcers (money or other tokens) could be utilized to involve the individual in treatment or in other vocational and educational programs as, for example, has been done by Slack (1960), Schwitzgebel (1964), and Cohen (1968). However, as noted above, prevailing societal attitudes would not likely provide broad professional and agency support for the idea.

Another approach used to establish and maintain initial contacts with offenders was to structure the visits on an *ad hoc* basis, often with the specific objective of assisting with problems such as vocational guidance, job placement, help regarding family or marital problems, or just an opportunity to discuss personal things of concern.

After the initial contact with the patient had been established, it was necessary to develop an overall treatment plan. The task of assessment and planning of treatment was focused toward answering the following three questions: (1) What behaviors are maladaptive, i.e., which behaviors displayed by the individual need to be changed in terms of being increased, decreased, or otherwise influenced? One must obtain some understanding of how much maladaptive behavior was acquired; (2) What environmental variables currently maintain or otherwise influence the behavior—either to support undesirable behavior or to reduce the likelihood of performing more adaptive responses?; and (3) What are the available practical means which can produce the desired changes, i.e., manipulations of the environment, of the behavior itself, or the attitudes and feelings of the patient?

As early as possible after the beginning of treatment, several sessions were typically devoted to obtaining a detailed family and developmental history designed to obtain information about the acquisition of various behaviors, the *current* situations and circumstances in which particular behaviors were most likely to be displayed, information about current familial, social, occupational, interpersonal, and other significant influences on the patient's behavior. On the basis of such information and assessment of the patient's problems, a number of treatment goals were determined. Since the process of assessment was a continuing one and had to consider periodic changes in the client's behavior, his work and home situation, and other events in the environment, the treatment goals and subgoals were flexible and subject to change.

A systematic and graduated sequence of therapeutic tasks was set up with explicit criteria for ascertaining progress. For example, the following sequence of treatment goals might be established: (1)

strengthening the response of coming to therapy; (2) developing a "therapeutic relationship" in order that the therapist's responses begin to provide appropriate social reinforcement for the client; (3) establishing environmental controls and developing self-control repertoires in order that various criminal behaviors be curbed and better regulated — failure to do this could often lead to abrupt termination of therapy due to apprehension for new offenses; (4) specifically building up and improving a variety of social, interpersonal, educational and vocational behaviors; and (5) fading out the influence of the therapist, assisting in generalization of new behaviors, and bringing the new behaviors under the control of natural reinforcers in the client's environment.

Each of the above major goals consisted of several subgoals. These subgoals assisted in the application of various shaping procedures utilizing the principle of "successive approximation." Also, the particular subgoals provided almost weekly indication whether progress was being made. It could, for example, readily be determined whether the patient was coming regularly for therapy sessions and whether he was punctual, the amount of time spent in addressing specific problems as opposed to talking generally about the work situation or other such topics, the extent to which self-control was being developed, and whether there were other movements toward clearly specified subgoals.

The above graduated sequence was viewed as a sort of "programming" of the therapeutic steps so that at each stage only a slight amount of change was sought. As in any shaping procedure, a critical element is the patience and perceptiveness of the therapist in selecting steps that are not too big, the reinforcements sufficiently effective, and the timing of the move to the next step. Phillips and Wiener (1966) have referred to such a graduated sequence of therapeutic tasks as a process of "programmed behavioral change."

The subgoal during these initial sessions was to set the patient at ease, to extinguish his apprehensions about therapy being an unpleasant situation in which one was required to talk about his "problems," and generally to make the interaction pleasant, helpful, and nonthreatening. No effort was made to arouse or mobilize anxiety. On the contrary, efforts were specifically directed toward the alleviation of anxiety and to put the patient at ease.

Thus, depending upon the particular individual and his possible apprehension of therapy, an important therapeutic approach in the earlier sessions was to avoid discussion of psychological problems and inquiries about the criminal behavior (which may already have been labeled by the police, probation officer, or examining mental health professionals as "disturbed" or "sick"). The patient was allowed to discuss almost any topic he chose. Particular emphasis was placed on providing help with a number of more pressing needs and problems, such as obtaining employment, assistance with marital and family difficulties, vocational training, and related matters.

Assistance With Immediate Problems as Reinforcement

Help with specific and immediate problems—even though un- related to the offense—was found to be a powerful means for alleviat- ing anxiety and fear about the therapy situation, bringing about a fairly explicit reinforcing effect relative to the therapist and the therapy session, and also for establishment of coming to therapy as a condition- ed reinforcer since this was the occasion for obtaining various specific assistance in reference to immediate problems.

Through the therapist's various contacts with other agencies, patients could be directly referred for assistance in finding employ- ment, for providing vocational rehabilitation and related services, and for help in regard to public housing and other such matters. Instead of using the common method of furnishing the patient with a referral note, telephone contact with the agency would be made right then— and in the patient's presence—and arrangements made for an early appointment.

Some Basic Treatment Priorities and Strategies

It has already been noted that the basic assessment process in a behavioral approach to treatment involves three basic steps: (1) determination of the specific maladaptive behaviors which require change; (2) determination of the environmental and related variables which currently maintain the behavior; and (3) finding the best practical means which can produce the desired change through manipulation of the environment, of the behavior itself, or the attitudes and feelings of the client.

Having ascertained the particular behaviors to be made the target of the treatment efforts, it is essential to learn about the precise variables influencing the behavior, i.e., the settings, circumstances, etc., in which the problem behavior tends to occur. It is also necessary to determine the temporal, interpersonal, social, and ecological con- straints on the behavior.

A variety of priorities and strategies might be developed based upon the particular characteristics of the deviant behavior—frequency, seriousness, dangerousness to self and others, and other related features. When the maladaptive behaviors pose a serious threat to the individual himself, or can endanger others, e.g., sex crimes against minors, dangerous assaults, armed robberies, etc., the establishment of environmental control and self-control over the behavior becomes an important priority. The procedures used to develop and strengthen behavior control will be discussed in the following section.

In many instances, especially when working with patients having long-standing and multi-problem behavioral patterns, a useful therapeutic strategy involved selecting a discrete problem area and directly and rather quickly influencing behavior change. To do this it was important to select variables which appeared most amenable to and available for manipulation. Such prompt and observable improvement can provide positive feedback to the patient and to other significant persons in his environment, and can trigger off a "snow-balling" effect (generalization) to other areas. The reinforcing effects of such improvement also tend to increase other efforts related to treatment.

Case

Harold S. was a 35-year-old married man, the father of four, who was convicted and placed on probation for indecent exposure to a minor. Patient had been masturbating in his car in the middle of the afternoon while parked at the curb. He had been observed by two teenage girls who reported him to the police. It had been assumed that patient had intended to expose himself to the girls, but patient denied any such intention. Harold told of having had a problem with masturbation since his teens; such behavior had continued even after his marriage with a frequency of about once or twice a week. However, patient claimed to have a good sexual relationship with his wife and stated that there was no effort by her to deprive him sexually. It was noteworthy that Harold had a very good occupational and social adjustment, and had no previous history of trouble with the law, was very upset by the charge against him, and was anxious to get help.

On the basis of information obtained during the first three therapy sessions it became very apparent that Harold played a rather compliant role to a dominant wife, and that he was particularly bothered by and resentful of her interference in his supervision of the children. Periodically, the wife would clearly and blatantly undercut his supervision or discipline—sometimes in front of the children. Harold would be very hurt and resentful, but would generally go off and brood rather than express himself.

Since the wife appeared to be a generally well-meaning person, was very concerned about her husband's problem, and was most anxious that he receive therapeutic help, it appeared most likely that the above problem area for Harold was very amenable to direct instigation of certain behavior changes. This problem area was also considered important because the pent-up anger and resentment, and the resulting tension experienced by Harold, seemed to be related to his pattern of masturbation. The wife's obvious interest in her husband's therapy, patient's discussion with her of his therapy sessions, and the wife's desire to help in any way she could, were all factors favoring prompt and effective modification of the above problems.

The undesirable effects — both on the patient and the children — of the wife's undercutting of patient's discipline were discussed with him. He in turn, discussed this matter with his wife. Harold was then given specific assistance regarding the manner in which some general rules about discipline could be discussed by both parents, and also about the importance of freely discussing and arriving at agreements about such supervision with undercutting of the other parent's discipline — especially in front of the children — very definitely to be avoided. Simultaneously, Harold was given training in assertive behavior, helped to practice such behaviors through role-playing and behavioral rehearsals, and also instructed about carefully noting the situations in which the assertive behaviors could best be carried out, i.e., avoiding times when his wife was moody, irritable, and upset about something, and thus likely to respond negatively to his assertiveness.

Within a period of three weeks, more assertive behavior by the patient and marked improvements regarding the children's supervision had most satisfactorily been accomplished. The very positive effects on Harold's self-esteem and the more respectful and pleased response by the wife, were extremely important reinforcements which helped very quickly to establish the new behaviors in the natural environment.

As indicated in the above illustration, an important consideration in the choice of problem area for focus of treatment effort was to start with behaviors which could rather readily come under the influence of natural reinforcers in the patient's environment. Indeed, unless the changes achieved through therapeutic efforts came under the control of reinforcements available in the environment, the durability, generalization, and strength of the changes would be limited and short-lived.

In using the strategy of directly instigating behavior change in delimited areas, it was essential to carefully gauge the likely responses of significant persons in the relevant environment. The initial steps in the behavior change program had to be in areas and situations where the most probable environmental responses would very likely be positive and success almost assured. Behaviors initially developed under such relatively optimal conditions would then gradually be shifted to other situations in which more effort and persistence were required and where the environmental variables were not likely to be as supportive. In such a fashion the behavior was gradually strengthened and brought increasingly under the control of the wider range of stimuli and natural reinforcers in the environment.

Failure to carefully gauge the response probabilities and related variables in the environment can lead to undesirable consequences — even when the patient's response has been most appropriate. For example, a colleague of the author's had begun to use behavioral methods in his treatment of a young offender. This young man had a history of law violations involving unauthorized use of cars, a very impatient manner, low tolerance for frustration, and unstable employment adjustment. He had finally found a job as a bartender. Since the patient had problems with alcohol it had been suggested that some other job might be sought while he continued to work at the bar. With the therapist's assistance another and better paying job was found. Patient had planned simply to announce to his boss one day that he would not come in the next day. However, it was suggested by the therapist that he consider using a socially more appropriate response and give his boss a week's notice. The patient considered the suggestion and informed his employer that he would leave at the end of the week. The boss, however, got rather annoyed, told the patient that he was very ungrateful, and added that instead of waiting a week he could in fact leave right then — he was fired!

Another important consideration in using direct instigation of behavior change was to make very sure that the patient was helped to carefully weigh and evaluate the alternatives for himself and, in the final analysis, make his own decision. Often, offenders having had the direct experience of not being treated very considerately in employment and other such situations, may have sound reasons for not being as socially polite as persons in other circumstances. This knowledge and experience — even though often it may be distorted or exaggerated

—still had to be used by the individual in evaluating various courses of action.

Establishment of Behavior Control

As noted earlier, the primary therapeutic objective in the treatment of the typical offender is to bring about cessation of the criminal activities and replace them with a more constructive personal and social adjustment. In working with offenders, and also with persons whose deviant behavior is likely to cause serious injury to themselves or to others, it often becomes necessary to attempt to establish some degree of *behavior control* as a first step in the treatment process.

If the antisocial behavior is not under improved control there is the strong possibility that recurrence of such behavior will result in various serious consequences to the patient, namely, confinement, and that such antisocial acts may also harm the victims of such behavior. The development of behavior control and improved self-control is important for another reason. The immediate reinforcements provided by the deviant behavior usually offset any later guilt, anxiety, or regrets. Thus, the behavior continues to be maintained. Likewise, involvement in such deviant activities also decreases the opportunities for engaging in more constructive activities. For example, if regular housebreakings enable the individual to support himself and his family quite satisfactorily, there will be little economic necessity for seeking employment, vocational training, and other skills leading to socially approved forms of obtaining money.

It should be mentioned that the word "control" has come to have rather unpleasant connotations for some people. The word appears to be associated with an authoritarian, unfeeling, and even nontherapeutic program. Indeed, frequently the word "control" is used with distinct pejorative connotations. One might well wonder why this situation exists when in many situations the therapist's primary task and responsibility may well be to establish necessary controls so that the patient does not injure himself or others. Interestingly, the term "control" does not commonly occur in describing the involuntary commitment of persons to mental hospitals when they are judged likely to injure themselves or others. While the discussion in the above situation may be in terms of the need for more intensive treatment, the obvious social control features implicit in the involuntary commitment and the realities of institutional confinement seem not to get explicit mention.

It would appear that as used above the term "control" involves a variety of ideological and value judgments which appear to give surplus meaning to the word.

This discussion of behavior control and self-control will relate to the earlier basic conceptualization that behavior is not an emergent property of the individual nor a property solely of the environment. Behavior was defined as involving an interaction between the individual and a specific environment. Such an interaction may be described by a functional relationship between the two.

As Skinner (1953) has pointed out, implicit in the functional analysis of behavior is the notion of control. Thus, when we discover an independent variable which can be manipulated to influence some behavior of concern, we have indeed discovered a means for *controlling* the behavior which is a function of the manipulation. Such a functional analysis has both theoretical and practical significance. Theoretically, one can prove the validity of a functional relationship by the actual demonstration of the effect of one variable upon another. This is the essence of experimental science. Practically, the implications of a functional analysis are even greater. An analysis of the manner in which behavior can be influenced shows clear possibilities for its modification through manipulating the appropriate independent variables.

The problems raised by the control of human behavior cannot be avoided by a refusal to recognize the possibility of control and its implications. In any society there are numerous explicit controls to influence and regulate behavior: criminal laws, traffic laws, rules and guidelines of administrative and regulative agencies and even of professional groups, are all efforts to regulate and control behavior. The term *control* is used here simply to indicate that if behavior can be influenced, in that sense it can also be controlled. Such a functional relationship with its possibilities for controlling (influencing) behavior is neither good nor bad—it simply is. How, when, and for what purposes such influence is to be exerted does, of course, clearly involve issues of social policy and other value judgments. These issues are important and need to be faced squarely.

Essential to an understanding of the notion of control of behavior is the manner in which antecedent variables are conceptualized as determining behavior. While clearly acknowledging the importance of early experience upon later behavior, behaviorally oriented psychologists have difficulty with the long time span over which certain childhood experiences are postulated to influence adult behavior.

If we wish to learn about the variables which influenced an individual to exhibit his genitals to a woman in a public place, it becomes difficult to understand this act largely in terms of variables in the remote history of the person. Since these variables, i.e., early childhood influences, have been present all along, knowledge of such variables does not help us to understand why the offense occurred on that particular day and in that particular situation. Some knowledge of early history would be of value in learning about the determinants which may facilitate (predispose) engaging in such behavior. However, we would still need to look at the variables which currently elicit and maintain the behavior. Conceptually and also for practical treatment purposes, knowledge of currently important variables is of much importance. Since early developmental information is now mainly of historical value, interventions aimed at influencing present and future behavior have to be focused at those environmental and personal variables which are of current relevance and concern.

The experimental analysis of behavior has provided several principles for the establishment of improved controls over behavior (Ferster *et al.,* 1964; Goldiamond, 1965; Ulrich, Stachnik & Mabry, 1966; and Ferster & Perrot, 1968). The following are some of the major principles useful in clinical situations: (1) development of competing and incompatible behaviors, (2) development of delaying sequences, (3) establishing control under conditions of low drive, (4) utilization of deprivation and satiation variables in the operant paradigm, (5) manipulation of the emotional variables related to the particular behavior, and (6) increasing the effectiveness of aversive stimuli in controlling the behavior.

Ferster *et al.* (1964) have used the above principles in assisting overweight persons to control their eating behavior, Goldiamond (1965) has described in detail several cases where such procedures have been used, and Shah (1965) has applied such procedures in behavior therapy with offenders.

In order to establish some degree of control over a particular behavior, it is essential to study very carefully the numerous variables which currently operate to elicit, provoke, make possible, maintain, and otherwise reinforce the behavior. The following cases illustrate how these principles have been applied.

Case A

Harold S. is the same individual referred to earlier.

It will be recalled that this 35-year-old married man had been masturbating rather frequently since early adolescence; this behavior had persisted even after he had been married. The urge to masturbate, patient reported, was not always related to strong sexual arousal. At times when he felt the urge to masturbate he would not have an erect penis and would not be aware of a high state of sexual arousal. The urge often would be rather imperious and patient obviously had difficulty controlling his behavior. As was noted earlier, Harold had been convicted of indecent exposure to a minor because he had been observed by two teenage girls while masturbating in his parked car on a public street.

As far as trouble with the law was concerned, masturbation in some public place had been and appeared to be the only relevant behavior. Harold's occupational, social, and general interpersonal functioning was rather good. Although physically a big man he was rather passive, compliant, and unable to assert himself or express feelings of anger or annoyance. Detailed information regarding the urge to masturbate and the occasions for such behavior indicated that masturbation had over the years come to be more of a general tension-reliever than a means for obtaining sexual gratification. Thus, in situations where he felt angry, frustrated, resentful, and also tense because of the pent-up nature of these feelings, he would frequently experience the urge to masturbate. After such behavior he would feel very guilty and ashamed of himself. It was quite evident that although masturbation in public situation was a very low-frequency and episodic behavior, the possible consequences for any recurrence were indeed serious. Hence, the development of better control over the masturbation generally and improved discriminative control for public situations became an important initial goal.

Harold was asked to write out an exhaustive list of the various situations, incidents, moods, and emotional states in which the urge to masturbate was likely to arise. This list was to be studied, added to, revised, and otherwise used to make himself extremely alert to and self-conscious of the variables preceding the urge to masturbate. Likewise, he was asked to make a complete list of all the possible aversive consequences which would result from future convictions of the type for which he was on probation. These various aversive consequences were then discussed with the patient in much detail, he was asked to elaborate on them, and further implications and complications were suggested. Such detailed discussions of the various penal sanctions and other punitive consequences of further trouble with the law, were utilized as a sort of verbal aversive conditioning. The aim was to attach anxiety cues to the various situations and events which were likely to preceed and to lead to masturbatory behavior.

Patient was also trained in the use of progressive relaxation (Wolpe, 1958) and asked to practice this diligently so that he could learn to relax himself in the various situations where he felt very tense. To control and regulate the possibility of masturbation in public situations, explicit procedures were suggested for various competing and incompatible behaviors to be engaged in at the earliest indication of the desire to masturbate while in some public situation. For example, when he experienced anything more than just a passing urge to masturbate, he was to stop his work — driving a beer delivery truck — and go into the nearest restaurant for some coffee or other refreshments. He was to order whatever he liked — in his case vanilla ice cream — and was to eat and relax. He was to involve himself in conversation with people to control any fantasy activity, and was to stay there until the urge was gone or its strength had greatly diminished.

The rationale for the above procedures was as follows. First, it was important that, when the masturbatory urge became strong, the patient should not remain in a situation where public masturbation could possibly take place, namely, in his truck or car while on a public street. Going into a restaurant would remove him from such a public situation. While in the restaurant the eating and general relaxation would assist in allowing the tension-related urge to pass. Likewise, engaging in conversation with other persons, if this was possible, was designed to further prevent fantasizing or ruminating about masturbation. Finally, even if all this failed to control the urge to masturbate, the ready availability of the rest room would allow the above behavior to take place in a private situation without incurring any trouble with the law. Concurrently, the patient continued to receive training in becoming more assertive in the home situation in order to decrease in that relatively protected setting the number of tension-arousing situations.

Patient reported that the masturbation had ceased entirely right after his apprehension, but had started again after he had been placed on probation. The once-a-month masturbation continued for a while, but only at home. The urge to masturbate was markedly reduced after the start of treatment. There was not a single instance of public masturbation. Gradually, masturbation at home stopped and the urge to masturbate became a rare occurrence. Concurrently, the frequency of marital intercourse initially increased in frequency, but then returned to the previous frequency of about twice a week. For the last six months of follow-up patient reported no masturbation at all. It should be added that after the public masturbation and urge to masturbate had been controlled, focus was shifted to the home situation. Harold was seen for 12 weekly sessions, four bi-weekly sessions, and five once-a-month follow-up visits.

Case B

Mike S.[3] This was a 26-year-old man who had been involved in homosexual activities since about the age of 10. He had been married for six years and had three children. Prior to his marriage he had dated several other girls but had had only two heterosexual experiences – one, when patient was 16, involved a group of four boys who took turns with a girl who had run away from home; the other experience, when he was about 18, occurred when he came across a very drunk woman and was "helping her home." After about a month of marriage the homosexual behavior recurred with a frequency of about twice a month. Intercourse with his wife was reported to average twice a week, and masturbation about once a week. Mrs. S. was an epileptic whose grand mal seizures had been controlled effectively by anticonvulsive medication. However, she had a low threshold for frustration and would periodically have explosive bursts of anger at the patient and the children. Therapy with the patient was started shortly after the wife had discovered his sexual problem. Mike indicated that he was very ashamed of his homosexuality, loved his wife and children, and stated that he wanted very much to stop his homosexual activity.

In view of the circumstances under which patient would meet his homosexual companions (a sleazy part of town with fairly close police patrols), it seemed likely that trouble with the police could easily occur. Detailed information was obtained about the situations in which the desire to engage in homosexual behavior was noted to increase, and about the circumstances which made such behavior possible. Mike was asked

---

[3]This patient had not been in trouble with the law and was seen by the author in a private practice situation. The case is used for purposes of illustration since the problems were very similar to those seen in clinic cases.

to keep detailed daily notes of upsetting incidents and his various activities. It was quickly noted that a number of events seemed to relate to increased desires for homosexual activity. These events were as follows: sexual frustration caused by the wife's prolonged menstrual bleeding or her refusal to allow intercourse, serious marital arguments and fights in which typically he would receive quite a tongue-lashing, being scolded and reprimanded at work by his foreman, feeling very low in self-esteem when his behavioral inadequacies or immaturities occured in some obvious manner, e.g., persistent problems in getting to work on time, errors in his work, etc. In reference to the tongue-lashing he would periodically receive from his wife, the following was a choice sample patient had recorded verbatim in his daily notes: ". . . irresponsible, sloppy, cowardly, miserable, son-of-a-bitch jellyfish!"

Mike's moonlighting job provided him with the kind of freedom which made his homosexual activities much easier. His hours were flexible on the evening job and he could vary them from day to day. In addition, patient had not informed his wife of his working hours at this job, nor about his precise earnings. And, since he handled the budget, his wife did not have any clear idea as to how the money was being spent. Mike's homosexual behavior typically would be initiated in a part of town notorious for its cheap bars and strip-joints. Patient would have several drinks, then pick up or be picked up by some homosexual, and later return home as though just finishing his second job.

Verbal aversive conditioning was used as in the case of *Harold S*. It was pointed out that if, as claimed, he really wished to control the homosexual behavior, then a first step was to control the arrangements which made such behavior so very possible. Thus, it was necessary that his wife be informed of his exact working hours on the night job and also about his earnings, that the budget-keeping be shared with the wife, and that the amount of money he kept on his person be markedly reduced. Patient was instructed to keep a detailed list of the situations which increased the urge to engage in homosexual behavior, and to study and even memorize this list, thereby making himself very alert to and self-conscious about such events. Reduction of levels of sexual deprivation as a function of marital intercourse and masturbation was related to Mike's urges for homosexual activity. Such effects were discussed with him in regard to their possible influence on the homosexual contacts. Progressive relaxation training was provided as well as assistance in better self-regulation in regard to problems which led to marital and work upsets, such as getting up late, being late for work, and "forgetting" to do the various chores around the house.

While the above efforts were specifically directed toward control of the homosexual behavior, various other efforts were subsequently undertaken to remedy some of the glaring deficits in patient's heterosexual skills. Mike was remarkably ignorant about matters of marital sexual relationships, and did not have too clear an idea of female sexual anatomy; in six years of marriage his wife had never achieved an orgasm.

On the basis of later reports by the patient and also the wife's comments about his regular working hours, handling of money, the absence of drinking, etc., it appeared that the homosexual behavior had been controlled. While homosexual urges and fantasies continued for a period of time, patient reported that no homosexual behavior had taken place. (The period of time from start of treatment to the follow-up contact was slightly over four years.) The fact that marital sexual relations had markedly improved for both, the wife was now able to experience orgasm, and several other improvements in patient's behavior and self-esteem had also been accomplished, suggested that the control of the homosexuality was more than temporary. Mike changed jobs and displayed markedly improved functioning; after two years on the new job he was made foreman.

Ready Availability and Crisis Intervention

A treatment approach often used with offenders during the initial period of therapy, particularly in cases where poor controls and social judgment were significant problems, consisted of providing a structure within which patients could maintain close telephone contact. Patients were encouraged to call when faced with crises and other situations in which some prompt assistance was needed. This ready contact with the therapist, or with other significant persons in the social environment, was believed to be essential in order to influence the patient's social judgment and behavior at times of stress, and to assist in the establishment of better self-control. Such telephone calls and conversation also served as a delaying sequence between some upsetting event and the patient's response to it.

A patient who had in his past behavior demonstrated remarkably poor social judgment and self-regulation was faced with a situation in which his landlord, a member of the police force, had made a pass at patient's wife. Patient was enraged upon learning of this and among the courses of action he had angrily contemplated were: knocking on the landlord's door with baseball bat in hand to assault him, making a formal charge for "conduct unbecoming a police officer," undertaking some serious vandalism of the landlord's property, and informing the landlord's wife about the incident. With much persuasion from his wife to drop the matter, and in view of his own confusion about just what he wished to do, patient had called the therapist.

In the course of a 45-minute telephone conversation several things occurred: the patient was provided an opportunity to ventilate his feelings, given support and verbal reinforcement for having made the telephone call at such a time, and was assured that he certainly was "man enough" to protect his wife. More importantly, as the patient gradually calmed down, he was able more realistically to consider the possible consequence to his wife of the various actions he had been contemplating. Considering the fact that the patient was on probation, that he had a criminal record, and that his general reputation was not the best, the discussion quickly brought out that the patient's angry and impulsive actions could very well have the consequence of his *not* being able to provide his wife the very protection he sought. Specifically, the landlord could easily take a number of retaliatory steps which could lead to revocation of his probation.

In the above instance, as in many others of like nature, such telephone calls seemed to help in providing some measure of control in the immediate situation. As a patient's social judgment, self-control, and other adjustment improved, such telephone calls were gradually faded out. In other instances, such calls were channeled to close friends, relatives, and other persons more readily available in the social environment.

The Therapeutic Relationship and Other Reinforcements

In dynamically oriented and most other forms of psychotherapy, much importance is placed on the establishment and use of the therapeutic relationship with the patient. Behavior therapists, however, often do not appear to give sufficient attention to the importance of such a relationship in influencing the patient's behavior.

A common problem in the treatment of delinquents and offenders is that many of them do not respond to the usual social reinforcements. Thus, verbal and other social reinforcements used by the therapist often have little or no influence with such persons. In view of this, treatment techniques which rely heavily on social reinforcements mediated through the therapeutic relationship may not be very effective with such offenders.

Attempts to establish a therapeutic relationship through a friendly, cordial, and warm manner are not indicated unless there has first been some assessment of the patient's likely perception of and response to such therapist behaviors. Many offenders display marked suspiciousness, distrust, and apprehension about close involvement with people — especially those whom they perceive as authority figures. Such persons tend to respond negatively to premature attempts to relate with a cordial, friendly, and warm manner. In such instances a more formal, reserved, but politely interested manner is indicated. The initial therapeutic effort with such persons is directed at trying to gradually extinguish the distrust, apprehension, and hostility.

Like most mental health facilities, the clinic in which this behavioral treatment was conducted did not have any facilities for providing extrinsic reinforcements to patients for coming to therapy — as done by Slack (1960) and Schwitzgebel (1964), for example. On the contrary, there was a flexible fee schedule according to which small fees could be charged for clinic services, but often were not.

In such a situation a variety of other means had to be found for providing something resembling extrinsic reinforcements to patients whose interest in therapy was minimal and who, in addition, were non-responsive to social reinforcements. It was found that this could be done by providing patients with concrete and specific help in regard to a number of day-to-day problems possibly quite unrelated to their psychological difficulties. Thus, through agency and personal contacts, patients were often provided with help in finding employment, in obtaining services from vocational rehabilitation, welfare, housing, and other social agencies. Also, it was explicitly mentioned to patients that, contingent upon evidence of their efforts and progress in treatment, the therapist would be willing to make various recommendations to the probation and parole officers when such were felt to be indicated. For example, recommendations could be made about: change of employment and/or living arrangements, out-of-town trips, and earlier termination of probation or parole supervision. In the case of young adults sentenced under provisions of the Federal Youth Corrections Act, recommendations could also be made about the setting aside of their conviction when progress had been satisfactory. The latter was a statutory provision for persons whose good adjustment indicated that supervision could be terminated prior to the maximum period so that the conviction could legally be set aside. This was of tremendous value in terms of the various undesirable consequences which often can plague an ex-offender because of his criminal record.

At other times, help was also given to patients in reference to a spouse or child who had some problems. On many occasions the wife would also be seen periodically for therapy for her own problems and/ or in conjunction with the offender's treatment. There were several instances where the patient was assisted in the handling of a problem child, with the patient usually being placed in the role of the "change agent" for the youngster.

The approach to the treatment of children through the parents as the primary change agents has been used quite effectively (*see*, for example, Ullmann and Krasner, 1965; Shah, 1967). Placing the parent in the role of change agent is not only a useful way of assisting the child, but it can also be of much value in modifying the parents' behavior. In order to influence the child's behavior the parents have first to change some aspect of their own behavior; i.e., changes in their handling of the child are essential to modifying the child's behavior. While in the role of "therapists" for their children, parents can often make changes in their own behavior which may otherwise have been more difficult.

Case

William J. was a 35-year-old married man who had been convicted of indecent assault of his daughter and placed on probation with the condition that he receive treatment. Actually, the patient had been involved in an incestuous relationship with his daughter who subsequently was placed in a residential treatment facility for girls. Patient also had a son 10 years old who had a variety of problems. The boy had been doing very poorly in school, was a disciplinary problem, and was periodically encopretic. This latter problem was of much concern to patient and to his wife — the boy's stepmother.

Patient had a longstanding problem with alcohol. Both he and his second wife were alcoholics and had numerous other problems. Patient and his second wife had lived together more than two years before they decided to get married. The day before their marriage, during the course of a typical argument while both had been drinking, the wife had torn up the marriage license. The patient later gathered up the pieces and pasted them together in time to proceed with the marriage ceremony. The couple's friends were persons who also had obvious drinking problems. The social gatherings of this group would often involve parties in which consumption of alcohol and a variety of sexual activities provided the major forms of entertainment.

Following his conviction patient attended Alcoholics Anonymous meetings, managed to curb his drinking, and his work adjustment improved. He continued to have serious problems with his wife. Mrs. J. continued her heavy drinking, suffered from alcoholic cirrhosis of the liver, would often leave patient to stay with some alcoholic friends for several days, threatened to harm patient with knives, and had actually attempted such assaults on several occasions.

Mr. J. made rather rapid progress during the course of therapy, but frequent turmoil with his wife and the continuing encopresis of his son were sources of much distress to him. As a "favor" to the patient, his son was seen for a couple of interviews and subsequently patient was placed in the role of serving as the change agent for his son. Patient proved to be an excellent recorder of his son's daily behavior, his own response to the boy, and his wife's behavior. It seemed evident that the wife was an extremely disruptive and undesirable influence on the son. Her response to the boy would range from outright and blatant pampering of the boy by treating him as a baby, to episodes when, under the influence of alcohol, she would become very hostile and belligerent, would order the boy to leave the apartment, and had even threatened him harm. In one of the few interviews arranged with the wife, she told the therapist that even though she tried to be consistent in her discipline with the boy, when he looked at her with "those big, beautiful, blue eyes" she just did not have the heart to discipline him.

By utilizing a precise reinforcement schedule for the son and by making a wide range of reinforcements readily available but contingent upon proper bowel movements and the absence of encopresis, the patient was able to markedly influence his son's behavior. Discussions with the school teacher, and assistance with the youngster's schoolwork, enabled the patient to help his son to improve his classwork as well. However, the wife's drinking and other problems continued to be regular sources of difficulty.

In view of the patient's concern for his son and his plans also to get his daughter out of the institution once he had stabilized his own life, Mr. J. realized that he had to take more decisive action in reference to his marriage. Since the wife managed to exercise tremendous control over him through sexual and related reinforcements she was able to dispense, Mr. J.'s ability to anticipate and to respond with better self-regulation to his wife's behavior became an important treatment concern to him. Patient decided to consult a lawyer in regard to possible steps toward a legal separation or even divorce. He made efforts to again enlist his wife's cooperation in attending AA meetings and also about getting necessary medical and psychiatric help for her cirrhosis and severe alcoholism. When his wife continued her drinking, refused to obtain medical and psychiatric help or to join AA, and once again left the home on one of her drinking binges, Mr. J. finally moved to another apartment and decided to terminate the on-again-off-again pattern of their married life. At the time the above actions were taken patient had developed a very stable work adjustment, had a markedly improved relationship with his son, and had established very good and close social and interpersonal ties with his AA group.

Numerous other aspects of the therapeutic approach with Mr. J. will not be detailed; the point illustrated is that as a therapist for his son he began to see the destructive influence of the whole family situation on the boy and was able to take necessary action to improve the home situation.

In summary, as the therapeutic contacts with the patients continued, concrete assistance in immediate problem areas was provided, initial distrust gradually extinguished, and a more typical therapeutic relationship was generally developed. Once such a situation was established and the person became more responsive to social reinforcements, the relationship could then be utilized more systematically as an important therapeutic tool to influence behavioral changes.

Involvement of Other Change Agents

The primary objective of a behaviorally oriented treatment is to bring about desired behavior change. The behavior to be modified is not the verbal interactions occurring with the therapist in the office. In the main, the patient's problems lie in various situations and settings in his social environment—not in the treatment office. Clearly, therefore, the objective is to change the patient's behavior in his natural environment.

As indicated in the preceding pages, therapeutic efforts and interactions were designed to facilitate and otherwise assist the patients to adapt better to problem situations in their lives. To develop such change it is essential not only to know about the pertinent and significant aspects of the social environment, but also to include wherever feasible and possible significant persons in the patient's life in the behavior modification efforts.

It was noted earlier that it is essential to evaluate very carefully the environmental situations in which the patient attempts to modify his behavior. Such knowledge can indicate how, when, and under what set of circumstances specific changes in behavior can most appropriately and successfully be attempted. To the extent that the response of significant persons in the patient's social environment can also be influenced, the elicitation, support, reinforcement, and/or extinction of particular patient behaviors can more effectively be influenced.

The bringing about of new behaviors through shaping and other procedures is a first step toward other treatment objectives. It is essential also to strengthen such new responses in the natural environment so that they may be maintained under a variety of circumstances, with nonoptimal reinforcement schedules, and in the face of disruptive environmental stimuli. It is also desirable that these new behaviors become prepotent in reference to previous and competing response patterns.

The use of other change agents as important, if not the primary treatment agents, has most often and perhaps most effectively been used in treating children (Ullmann & Krasner, 1965 and Shah, 1967). However, other behavior therapists have used a variety of change agents in several settings. Ayllon and Michael (1959) have used psychiatric nurses in mental hospitals; Burchard and Tyler (1965), Patterson *et al.* (1965), and Tyler and Brown (1967) have utilized attendants and correctional staff in juvenile correctional facilities; Davison (1965) has used college undergraduates to work with autistic children; and Shah (1965, 1966) and Thorne, Tharp, and Wetzel (1967) have worked with probation and parole officers in the treatment of offenders.

Probation-Parole Officers

In view of the particular setting in which the therapeutic efforts described here were utilized, it was both possible and indeed most desirable to work closely with the probation and parole officers who were responsible for supervision of the offenders. The official relationship with the probation and parole agencies, the physical proximity to the office of these agencies, and the close personal contacts developed with these officers made various collaborative treatment efforts quite feasible.

There were three types of situations in which probation-parole officers were often involved in the treatment program: First, in assisting and facilitating the offender's initial contacts at the clinic, and in maintaining such behavior during the early sessions; Second, collaborative and joint treatment efforts by therapist and the officer — the latter using weekly group counseling sessions, periodic individual counseling, regular supervision, and home visits and contacts with the offender's family; Third, treatment efforts were also made entirely by the probation-parole officers but with close and regular consultation and assistance provided by the therapist. (The above situations refer only to treatment efforts which jointly involved the above correctional personnel. These agencies also had their own treatment and rehabilitation programs consisting of general supervision, orientation groups, individual and group counseling, and other related activities.)

A large number of referrals were made by probation parole officers for the purpose of treatment. Often, the officers would seek consultation regarding offenders who indicated various social problems and whose behavior was obviously maladaptive, but who seemed apprehensive of or unwilling to accept a referral to the clinic. Following discussions with the therapist concerning the particular case, the probation officers often played an important role in alleviating the offender's apprehensions and in providing information about the kinds of therapeutic and related services needed and available.

For example, in light of consultative discussions, the officers would casually mention the availability of the clinic as a special service resource to them and their clients, would provide information about the various services available, e.g., vocational guidance, individual and group therapy, help in reference to job and family problems, and the posibility of *ad hoc* or more regular contacts with the clinic staff. Sometimes the officers would simply bring the probationer along just to meet the therapist and to get acquainted. At other times the patient would be interested in a single appointment to discuss a specific problem. Such appointments were readily provided and a general climate created in which the person could himself seek other meetings when and as the need arose.

At other times, patients apprehensive about involvement in "treatment" would nevertheless wish assistance relative to vocational guidance or vocational training. In other instances the contact would be in reference to a marital problem, the offender's problem youngster, or for referral to some other health or related public or private agency.

In all the above situations, the probation-parole officers not only were important change agents in modifying the patient's apprehensions and uncertainties about seeking treatment for rather obvious problems, but they were also of much help during treatment, and particularly during the follow-up period after treatment at the clinic had been terminated.

In the second situation referred to above, the probation-parole officers would assist the therapist in regard to specific treatment goals. For example, the supervising probation officer could support efforts to get a patient involved in related therapeutic, educational, and vocational programs (Alcoholics Anonymous, Manpower Training and Development, vocational rehabilitation, etc.) by virtue of his official role and contacts with various community agencies. Likewise, on the basis of periodic field trips to the patient's home, the officer could learn about other treatment needs, and could also assist in regard to involving the spouse in the treatment efforts where this was desirable.

When treatment at the clinic was not feasible, the probation-parole officer would work with the offender himself and would receive periodic consultation from the therapist. Aside from the constraints of limited clinic staff and facilities, there were occasions when the patient would be reluctant to come to the clinic or the nature of the problems was such as to make the probation officer a more likely and appropriate change agent.

Spouse and Relatives

Previous sections of this presentation have emphasized the importance of becoming aware of and also utilizing significant persons in the patient's natural environment in the treatment program. Persons such as the patient's spouse, parents, and relatives can be of considerable help during the treatment program. These persons are particularly important to behavior modification efforts since their influence is available in the natural environment and thus more critical in maintaining and facilitating behavior outside the therapy session.

When agreeable to the patient, and also when otherwise feasible and appropriate, periodic contacts with the spouse were sought. Since much of the patient's behavior was often in interactions with the spouse, or could in other ways be influenced by the spouse, such contacts were rather essential aspects of the treatment.

The previously cited case of *Harold S.* indicates the indirect fashion in which the patient's wife was an important element in Harold's treatment. In that situation the therapist did have a couple of telephone contacts with the wife in reference to her interest and concern about her husband's treatment. Since the patient lived about 40 miles away, although working in the city, it was not feasible to arrange periodic interviews with the wife.

In the case of *Mike S.* the wife was also seen, initially in reference to her own problems, but later in reference to marital and family problems. Thus, Mrs. S. was utilized as a rather direct change agent in reference to certain of her husband's problem behaviors.

Case

It was learned from Mrs. S. that the problems in their sexual relationships were seriously influenced by Mike's behavior just preceding and during intercourse. She pointed out that Mike's behavior generally was fairly "masculine" despite his homosexual problem. However, at certain times when they would be "kidding around" in a somewhat amorous mood, Mrs. S. indicated that Mike's manner would take on distinctly "feminine" features. His verbal manner and voice would change, he would become somewhat "prancing," and would not behave in a strong and self-assured manner. Likewise, during precoital sex play, Mike would snuggle up to his wife, often lay his head on her bosom, and then wait for her to stimulate him and take a more aggressive role. While she had not been particularly bothered by this behavior before, being quite inexperienced prior to her marriage, Mrs. S. found herself very irritated by this behavior after she became aware of Mike's homosexual problem. On some occasions, she would become so annoyed and angered by the aforementioned "feminine" manner displayed by Mike that she would push him aside, abruptly terminate sexual relations, and leave him very frustrated and herself very angry. This situation had further complicated the marital relationship.

During the time that Mike was being assisted specifically in regard to improvements in his sexual repertoires, Mrs. S.'s help and cooperation became especially important. Mike was given general information about sexual anatomy, male and female physiology, and various sexual responses more appropriate to the masculine role. He was especially trained to become aware of "passive and feminine" behaviors, to curb and control them, and to replace them with a range of more appropriate responses. Alternate repertoires were learned from reading materials suggested to Mike and from discussions during therapy sessions. A graduated series of steps was also developed for the practice and establishment of the new behaviors in the marital situation.

In order to ensure success for Mike's new efforts and also to orient Mrs. S. to the treatment program, she was informed about the general steps and asked to try to be patient with her husband as they both worked toward establishment of a more satisfactory sexual relationship. It was also recommended that they both try to increase and improve communications during sexual relationships so that both could provide and receive more feedback about the effects of their responses on each other. Several joint sessions were held in order to clarify the suggested steps, to answer questions, and especially to facilitate direct communications between the couple on these and related matters.

Mrs. S. proved to be a most significant factor in the rapid improvements in her husband's behavior. Less apprehensive of his wife's angry outbursts and periodic tongue-lashings, Mike was able to assume a more self-assured and aggressive sexual role, while also trying hard to meet his wife's sexual needs, thereby further developing a positive picture of himself as an adequate husband.

It was during this period of therapeutic effort that Mrs. S. experienced her first orgasm — after almost six years of marriage. Needless to say, this experience was an extremely positive and significant one for both. It helped to further improve the frequency and quality of their sexual relationship, and facilitated other improvements in their overall marital and family adjustment. The feedback from the above improvements seemed very much related to Mike's increased self-esteem and confidence, as well as to improved respect and regard for Mike by his wife.

On some occasions various other significant persons were also involved in specific treatment situations. Such persons included the offender's pastor, other relatives, and in a few cases, the offender's employer. In all instances where other persons were involved as part of some specific treatment effort, the patient's explicit consent, agreement, and understanding was always first obtained. Typically, the offender would bring up problems in these areas and would ask if the therapist might be able to talk to such significant persons in reference to specific problem situations. The nature of such contacts would be explained to and discussed initially with the patient and the confidentiality of various other therapeutic contacts and communications would be safeguarded.

Evaluation of Treatment

In view of the typical constraints of an understaffed clinic with a heavy service obligation, facilities were not available to undertake systematic follow-up and evaluation of the treatment efforts described in this chapter. As a result, no definite statements can be made about the actual long-term effects of the therapeutic program described. The brief case studies have been used simply to illustrate the use and application of specific therapeutic procedures. The discussion in this section will, therefore, deal with more general issues relating to some of the complications involved in the evaluation of treatment efforts with offenders.

The conceptualization and approach of treatment described in this chapter allows for fairly explicit and objective assessment of the results of the therapeutic procedures. Since the primary goal of treatment with offenders was stated in terms of bringing about a cessation of the antisocial behaviors and also developing a more constructive personal and social adjustment, several specific criteria can be used to evaluate results.

Cessation of law-violating behavior—while a fairly specific criteria —is nonetheless not very adequately assessed in terms of officially noted and adjudicated criminal acts. While recidivism data can certainly provide one measure of subsequent law-violating behavior, as has clearly been pointed out by the report of the President's Commission on Law Enforcement and Administration of Justice,[4] and also by numerous other criminological studies, such information only covers a small proportion of the law-violating behavior which actually occurs.

The Federal Bureau of Investigation's *Uniform Crime Reports* and other police records can indicate if an individual was subsequently arrested and convicted. An arrest record alone does not mean very much. A conviction clearly implies a finding of guilt for the offense of which the person was accused. However, legal decision rules being what they are, i.e., acquit unless convinced beyond a reasonable doubt that the accused committed the crime, a finding of not guilty (acquittal) may in many instances simply mean that the jury had a "reasonable doubt" regarding the person's guilt. Thus, absence of subsequent convictions cannot be taken to mean that no law-violating behavior has in fact occurred. It could mean that such behavior has not taken place, or that such acts are markedly reduced in frequency and hence less likely to come to official attention, and/or that the individual is being

---

[4]President's Commission on Law Enforcement and Administration of Justice. *The challenge of crime in a free society*. Washington, D. C.: U.S. Government Printing Office, 1967.

more circumspect and using "improved" judgment and alertness in connection with such behavior. However, since a major social concern is with repeated and officially noted criminal acts, an absence of recidivism is commonly used as an index of improvement and rehabilitation in offenders.

Improvements in social and personal adjustment can be evaluated in a number of specific ways. Changes in educational, vocational, occupational, marital, and other interpersonal situations can be assessed. The ability to maintain suitable employment, the level of skill, salary, and general ratings of job performance can be measured. Likewise, improvements in educational and vocational skills can also be assessed. The incidence of drinking, gambling, and related problems is more difficult to evaluate, but could be estimated from the expenditure of money for such activities, and from behavioral ratings derived from interviews with significant persons in the patient's life.

Psychological tests and related measures can also be used and are a common means of assessing therapy-related changes. While having various advantages such as relative ease in administration and scoring (inventories and more objective techniques), such measures do not necessarily relate to actual behavioral changes. Changes in test responses may indeed reflect alterations in cognitive, emotional, and attitudinal sets. They may also be suggestive and indicative of possible changes in certain aspects of behavior.

As indicated above, while the evaluation of treatment is essential to proper understanding of the value and usefulness of treatment interventions, systematic research efforts for this purpose were not possible at the clinic where the procedures described were undertaken. However, since the entire treatment process described here was generally arranged as a series of carefully graduated steps, with specific subgoals and objectives defined in terms of actual behavior, the week-to-week progress of the patient in certain areas could be determined.

Thus, the patient's response of coming to treatment, coming more promptly, being willing and able to address pressing problems, finding and retaining employment, breaking very few appointments, and other such behaviors, could be evaluated in relation to the typical response of other patients at the clinic. Likewise, in view of close contacts with and collaborative efforts through probation-parole officers, evaluative comments and related feedback were also obtained from such persons. Probation officers, by virtue of their periodic home visits, and contacts with employers and family members, were often able to provide other information about the offender's behavior in the natural environment.

On the basis of such limited evaluation, and also knowledge about the specific changes in problem behaviors of the kind described in the case illustrations, it was evident that significant changes were indeed accomplished in many cases. The comparative data for the above qualitative assessment were the therapist's own previous experience with this population, the experiences of other therapists at the clinic, and differences between the patient's initial and terminal behaviors as reported to the therapist.

It is, of course, quite obvious that even the most detailed and carefully evaluated case histories do *not* provide validation of the theory and principles underlying a particular therapeutic approach. Since the therapist's behavior is guided primarily by the treatment goals, systematic control and evaluation of therapeutic procedures and variables is neither feasible nor a major objective in clinical situations.

The program described in this chapter demonstrated that offenders were more amenable to treatment than generally believed, that they could be engaged actively in such efforts, and could be assisted in a number of areas if the therapeutic approach was more relevant and appropriate to the needs of the patients. The theoretical bases underlying behavior modification principles have been the subject of considerable research in laboratory and real life situations. Likewise, research procedures designed more specifically for the systematic evaluation of behavior modification efforts have also received much discussion in the literature (*see*, e.g., Sidman, 1960; Ullmann & Krasner, 1965; Baer *et al.*, 1968).

Future Needs and Programs

On the basis of experience in the assessment and out-patient treatment of offenders, and in view of other developments in the field, a number of critical issues are seen as requiring attention in order to develop more adequate and effective programs. The problems and needs are so many, and the issues involved so complex, that a full discussion of them is not relevant to the basic purpose of this presentation. Thus, only the more important items will be discussed in this section.

There is a very great need to carefully reevaluate the basic assumptions and concepts which underlie psychotherapeutic and related treatment programs. The basic concepts used tend to determine and influence the kinds of treatment programs employed in various mental health facilities. Traditional psychotherapeutic techniques appear to have questionable relevance and effectiveness in dealing with populations differing from those upon which approaches were initially developed. There are, in addition, the fairly evident social class and other biases which further call into question some of the basic procedures in the talking, probing, uncovering, and related therapeutic techniques.

It should be noted also that the usual diagnostic and assessment procedures typically used in mental health facilities do not seem to be relevant in terms of specifically pointing to particular treatment needs and strategies. As Hollingshead and Redlich (1958) demonstrated several years ago, social class variables were more closely related to and thus predictive of, the kinds of treatment psychiatric patients received than were variables pertaining to psychiatric diagnosis. The desirability and utility of developing assessment procedures which more clearly relate to observable behavior, which can be conceptualized in a manner closely associated with the relevant treatment procedures to be used, and which allow for more individually prescribed procedures directly related to the assessed problems, has been discussed by several writers (*see*, e.g., Staats & Staats, 1964; Kanfer & Saslow, 1965; and Ullmann & Krasner, 1965).

It seems clear that mental health and other public agencies appear to be located and administered in a manner designed primarily to meet the norms and convenience of the middle class professionals working in these settings. The initial requirements typically faced by the clients in order to obtain services often pose impressive hurdles and problems.

For example, offenders seen for treatment at many clinics generally have to adjust to the 9:00 a.m. to 5:00 p.m. hours of such facilities. However, since these are also the hours covered by most employment situations, coming to the clinic means taking time off from work, relying on various excuses to employers which cannot be used on a regular basis, or otherwise simply not coming to the clinic. The real problems faced by clients in meeting the above requirements of the facilities, in addition to questions about the need they feel for such services, may readily be conceptualized and interpreted as "resistance," "lack of anxiety and motivation," or other such inferential and ascriptive statements.

The physical location, hours of service, and other programs of mental health facilities for offenders and related populations should clearly and explicitly be adjusted to meet the needs of the clients. It is a basic rule of behavior shaping that one has to be guided by – and even controlled by – the initial and available repertoire of the client. Such facilities should, therefore, be of a regional nature and specifically be located in the neighborhoods from which the bulk of the clients will come.

There is also a glaring need to develop and train a wide range of support-professionals and nonprofessionals to assist in the numerous behavior modification and other related services needed by the client population. Such developments already have a history of several years in some of the pioneer "New Career" programs which have shown much promise. It might be noted that these developments are at times perceived as a threat by some mental health professionals and also by some correctional groups who for long have been striving to achieve "professional" status.

The increasing use of and reliance upon nonprofessional staff has previously been referred to in the discussion concerning the use of a variety of change agents. In behavior modification programs there are clear opportunities for utilizing a wide range of nonprofessional staff with appropriate training and consultation. In addition, it has already been emphasized that treatment efforts have to reach out of the clinic or office to influence significant persons in the client's social environment, as well as to attempt changes in specific aspects of the environment. Here again, indigenous and other nonprofessionals can be of much assistance. Indeed, in these areas nonprofessionals often possess skills which professionals typically lack, for example, in being able to establish and maintain close contact with the families of ghetto-dwelling delinquents and offenders.

It has been noted that the notion of clients' having to pay for certain services does not seem very appropriate when working with lower social class clients. In contrast to the difficulties encountered in getting delinquents and offenders to keep their appointments, studies have demonstrated that extrinsic reinforcers (money and other tokens) can effectively be used to establish and maintain such behaviors (Slack, 1960; Schwitzgebel & Kolb, 1964; and Schwitzgebel, 1964).

The provision of essential human services includes training to meet serious deficits in educational, vocational, and social skills. To provide such training to some client populations may well require the use of extrinsic reinforcers. Such a development is no longer radical or unrealistic. Many existing federally-supported programs, such as the Manpower Development and Training Programs and the Job Corps, already provide stipends while the clients are receiving training. The use of an educational model for provision of such services (as contrasted with the usual medical model), seems to have advantages not only in providing a better conceptual scheme, but also in the way in which clients perceive *educational* rather than *psychiatric* or *mental health* services.

Elsewhere the writer has discussed the kinds of behaviorally oriented treatment programs which can use notions similar to those utilized in physical rehabilitations (Shah, 1968). For example, since many of these clients lack essential educational and vocational skills and thus have inadequate behavioral repertoires when faced with a complex and demanding social milieu, prosthetic devices, prosthetic training, and prosthetic environments can be used to more efficiently develop such necessary repertoires.

A behavioral conceptualization and approach to treatment can be applied in a variety of situations. Such an approach can be used in various out-patient settings; it has demonstrated even greater usefulness in institutional situations where the environmental variables are more readily controlled and influenced; and such approaches offer useful guidelines and behavior change technologies for larger programs aimed at social changes in the community (*see*, e.g., Ulrich *et al.*, 1966).

Whether the programs are aimed at the treatment of particular deviant individuals, or at groups of such individuals in a prison or other such settings, or even in the case of large-scale programs of social change in a community, systematic evaluation of the program is most essential. Such careful assessment is critical to a determination of the actual effectiveness of the procedures involved. Likewise, accurate and detailed feedback concerning the results of the treatment programs is essential to the continual improvement of a behavior modification technology and knowledge about human behavior.

REFERENCES

Ayllon, T. & Michael, J. The psychiatric nurse as a behavioral engineer. *Journal of the Experimental Analysis of Behavior*, 1959, **2**, 323–334.

Baer, D. M., Wolf, M. M. & Risley, T. R. Some current dimensions of applied behavior analysis. *Journal of Applied Behavioral Analysis*, 1968, **1**, 90–97.

Burchard, J. & Tyler, V. The modification of delinquent behavior through operant conditioning. *Behaviour Research and Therapy*, 1965, **2**, 245–250.

Cohen, H. L. Educational therapy: The design of learning environments. In J. M. Shlien (Ed.), *Research in psychotherapy*. Vol. III, Washington, D. C.: American Psychological Association, 1968.

Davis, K. Mental hygiene and the class structure. In P. Mullahy (Ed.), *A study of interpersonal relations*. New York: Hermitage Press, 1949.

Davison, G. C. The training of undergraduates as social reinforcers for autistic children. In L. P. Ullmann & L. Krasner (Eds.), *Case studies in behavior modification*. New York: Holt, Rinehart & Winston, 1965.

Ferster, C. B., Nurnberger, U. E. & Levitt, E. B. The control of eating. In A. W. Staats (Ed.), *Human learning: Studies extending conditioning principles to complex behavior*. New York: Holt, Rinehart & Winston, 1964.

Ferster, C. B. & Perrott, M. C. *Behavior principles*. New York: Appleton-Century-Crofts, 1968.

Goldiamond, I. Self-control procedures in personal behavior problems. *Psychological Reports*, 1965, **17**, 851–868.

Hollingshead, A. B. & Redlich, F. C. *Social class and mental illness*. New York: Wiley, 1958.

Hunt, R. G. Social class and mental illness. *American Journal of Psychiatry*, 1960, **116**, 1065–1069.

Kanfer, F. H. & Saslow, G. Behavioral analysis: An alternative to diagnostic classification. *Archives of General Psychiatry*, 1965, **12**, 529–538.

Patterson, G. R., Jones, J. W. & Wright, M. A. A behavioral modification technique for the hyperactive child. *Behaviour Research and Therapy*, 1965, **2**, 217–226.

Phillips, E. L. & Wiener, D. N. *Short-term psychotherapy and structured behavior change.* New York: McGraw-Hill, 1966.

Schwitzgebel, R. *Street corner research.* Cambridge, Mass.: Harvard University Press, 1964.

Schwitzgebel, R. & Kolb, D. A. Inducing behavior change in adolescent delinquents. *Behaviour Research and Therapy*, 1964, **1**, 297–304.

Shah, S. A. Behavior therapy and psychotherapy with offenders. Paper presented at the meeting of the American Psychological Association, Philadelphia, September 1963.

Shah, S. A. A behavioral approach to therapy with offenders. Paper presented at the meeting of the Eastern Psychological Association, Atlantic City, April 1965.

Shah, S. A. Treatment of offenders: Some behavioral concepts, principles, and approaches. *Federal Probation*, June 1966, 29–38.

Shah, S. A. Training and utilizing a mother as the therapist for her child. Paper presented at the meeting of the Eastern Psychological Association, Boston, April 1967. Appears as a chapter in B. Guerney (Ed.), *Non-professionals as Therapeutic Aides.* New York: Holt, Rinehart & Winston, 1969.

Shah, S. A. Preparation for release and community follow-up: Conceptualization of some basic issues, specific approaches, and intervention strategies. In H. L. Cohen, I. Goldiamond, J. Filipczak & R. Pooley (Eds.), *Training professionals in procedures for the establishment of educational environments.* Silver Spring, Md.: Educational Facility Press, Institute for Behavioral Research, 1968.

Sidman, M. *Tactics of scientific research.* New York: Basic Books, 1960.

Skinner, B. F. *Science and human behavior.* New York: Macmillan, 1953.

Slack, C. W. Experimenter-subject psychotherapy. *Mental Hygiene*, 1960, **44**, 238–256.

Staats, A. W. & Staats, C. K. *Complex human behavior.* New York: Holt, Rinehart & Winston, 1964.

Thorne, G., Tharp, R. & Wetzel, R. Behavior modification techniques: New tools for probation officers. *Federal Probation*, June 1967, 21–27.

Tyler, V. O. & Brown, G. D. The use of swift, brief isolation as a group control device for institutionalized delinquents. *Behaviour Research and Therapy*, 1967, **5**, 1–9.

Ullmann, L. P. & Krasner, L. (Eds.), *Case studies in behavior modification*. New York: Holt, Rinehart & Winston, 1965.

Ulrich, R., Stachnik, R. & Mabry, J. (Eds.), *Control of human behavior*. Glenview, Ill.: Scott, Foresman, 1966.

Wolpe, J. *Psychotherapy by reciprocal inhibition*. Stanford: Stanford University Press, 1958.

CHAPTER 11

Contagion as a Principle in Behavior Change

J. Douglas Grant and Joan Grant

Some three years ago, 18 felony offenders were paroled from an NIMH-funded training program in a California state prison to work in training and job development programs for the poor. Of the 18, one is back in prison, four have returned to the kind of semi-skilled jobs they held before incarceration, and one is a college student. The remaining 12 have continued in training and job and program development work. They are employed now by state and federal agencies, universities, and private corporations, working in positions of at least middle management responsibility. Their salaries range from $10,000 to $15,000 a year. They have become quite skilled in negotiating the federal and private foundation funding systems.

The performance of the 18 men is quite unlike that of similar parolees from California prisons. In discussions of the project in which the men participated, it has frequently been argued that the study has demonstrated only that some, and possibly quite rare, staff members working with some, again possibly quite rare, clients can bring about the kind of behavior change that has occurred here. Though interesting, the argument continues, the study has very little application to the problem of bringing about change in offenders generally. These comments we feel fail to take into account a contagion phenomenon that existed in the initial study and which has now become more apparent with a follow-up of the men who were in the program. It is this phenomenon we would like to deal with here.

The Original Study

The basic study has been reported in detail elsewhere (Grant, J. D., 1968; Grant, J. & Grant, J. D., 1970). Briefly, the study was

267

undertaken as a demonstration of the potential within the offender population for contributing to the solution of crime and delinquency problems. It was intended originally to train the men for positions within correctional agencies as program development assistants. The reluctance of these agencies to have anything to do with their former clients after release, along with the initiation of a number of OEO-funded job development and community organization programs throughout the state, shifted the focus of training and the job expectations of the trainees. The program was called the New Careers Development Project and the trainees called themselves new career-ists.[1]

The men who participated in the program were not representative of the California prison population, but neither were they selected as especially good risks. Two had served prior prison terms and seven had served time in juvenile institutions. Almost all had prior arrest records and long histories of known delinquency. Several were described as hardcore delinquents by correctional staff. Half of the group was in prison on charges of armed robbery.

The project required that the men read at least at the eighth-grade level and that they score at least average (90 or above) on the prison-administered group intelligence test. Eight of the men scored within the average range and 10 at an above average level. Eleven of the trainees had finished high school (some while confined) and seven had left school before graduation. Except for four who had worked at selling jobs, all had employment records, usually sporadic ones, in unskilled or semi-skilled jobs.

The group of 12 with which this paper is concerned, those still with program development work, includes the men seen as most

---

[1]"New careers" is a concept that includes developing new kinds of human service functions through redefining job functions and professional roles; providing entry level jobs for the poor and other disadvantaged groups, with provision for upward mobility; making necessary changes in agency and civil service structure to accommodate these new roles and functions; providing support and retraining for existing staff; developing links to ongoing but appropriately modified education programs that will supplement on-the-job training of the new careerists and will lead to the accreditation necessary to move upward.

The new careers movement got its start with the publication in 1965 of *New Careers for the Poor* by Arthur Pearl and Frank Riessman and with new careers demonstrations at Howard University (Community apprentice program, 1965), Mobilization for Youth (Brager, G., 1965), Lincoln Hospital (Hallowitz, E., 1968), and the present study. New careers is now supported on the federal level by the Scheuer amendment to the Economic Opportunities Act and by numerous pieces of legislation in the fields of education, health, crime and delinquency, and vocational rehabilitation. For extended discussions of the new careers concept see (Pearl, A. & Riessman, F., 1965; Riessman, F. & Popper, H. I., 1968; Workshop on nonprofessional careers for disadvantaged youth, 1966.)

delinquent by correctional staff. It includes all of the eight minority group trainees. It includes all but one of those convicted of robbery. Compared with the remaining six, the group has a slightly smaller proportion of those scoring above average in intelligence.

The training program, which lasted four months, was not seen as a rehabilitation program. Although we expected behavior change, we were not primarily concerned with changing behavior. The project was intended to develop people who could help bring about change within correctional and other human service agencies. It focused on developing knowledge around social problems and the operation of organizations, skills in working with groups, in collecting, summarizing, and interpreting data, and in writing. It dealt with questions of values and of personal behavior only insofar as problems arose in dealing with the content of the training program or with each other.

The training principles emphasized maximum participation of the trainees in developing and carrying out the training program, and provided for self-direction and self-discovery.

Specific content was fed in through four study groups which met weekly for a 2-hour period. These dealt with ways of bringing about change within organizations, group dynamics, interviewing techniques, and research, particularly concerning the issues of hypothesis-stating and program evaluation. There was also a weekly meeting devoted to the development of writing skills, and another on current social issues.

About half the trainees' time was spent in planning and carrying out team projects, a team consisting of two or three trainees with a staff member consultant. The first group of projects was concerned with issues inside the institution—for example, reasons for dropouts from the prison education program—and carried out through interviews and study groups with prison inmates and staff. The projects required developing interview schedules, interviewing, conducting study groups, and coding the information obtained, along with writing both the project proposal and final report. Later projects took up the issue of introducing nonprofessionals into service agencies. Again using inmate and staff interviews and study groups but supplementing these with consultation from staff of other state agencies, the trainees developed job descriptions for nonprofessionals in parole, in medical services, in the treatment of alchoholics, and in the care of the mentally retarded. They began by defining the unmet needs of the clients of the agency in question, then described functions that nonprofessionals could perform. They assessed problems of training, of moving nonprofessional staff into an agency's existing structure, and of developing career ladders for nonprofessionals within the agency.

The first group of men to finish training was paroled to jobs obtained by project staff and sometimes paid out of project funds. Some of the earliest jobs involved conducting surveys of new career possibilities for the poor within state and county agencies. These so-called surveys were not simply data-gathering operations. They required "selling" the new careers idea to agency and civil service staff, working with agency personnel on questions of reorganization of job functions and with civil service personnel on the development of job descriptions and career ladders. They were the crude beginnings of the more formal technical assistance positions several of the trainees hold today. Other early jobs involved work as trainers in local community action programs which were developing community organizers from the indigenous poor.

Since then the trainees have at various times held positions in city, state, and federal government, in hospitals, in universities, and in private corporations. They have been employed as staff on special education programs for the disadvantaged. They have been hired to consult on and to develop new careers programs. They have served as research assistants, trainers, technical assistance staff, community organizers, program developers, and program evaluators. They have worked in eight states and in Washington, D.C. They have shifted jobs frequently, at first because the funding on which their jobs were based was limited, later because as they became more skilled they were in demand and opportunities for their skills expanded. Most are currently employed by private corporations on funds obtained under contract with the federal Departments of Labor and of Health, Education, and Welfare.

Contagion

The contagion phenomenon was not something which we deliberately planned to utilize. It was our intent to involve the trainees in "maximum feasible participation" in the program, an endeavor that at the outset had about the same success as it has had in larger segments of the poverty program and which, when it occurred, did so in a manner largely unplanned by us.

Training was done in three nonoverlapping phases — eight men in the first, six in the second, and four in the third. During the first phase there were three staff members, two with backgrounds in psychology and experience in both clinical and research work, and one with a background in sociology and extensive experience in therapeutic community programs with both hospital and prison populations. The staff worked full-time, actually far in excess of 40 hours a week.

During Phase 2 there were two staff members, but one of them, the Project Director, was occupied almost entirely in working with the trainees paroled from Phase 1 and in developing jobs for them and for those to be paroled in Phase 2; he met with the Phase 2 trainees most evenings, but was rarely present during the daytime program. In Phase 3 the staff was reduced to the Project Director but, as in the prior phase, his time was taken almost entirely with work that kept him outside of the institution. He met with the Phase 3 trainees at the most two evenings a week.

In Phases 2 and 3, staff roles and functions were taken on, of necessity, by the trainees themselves. This process began at the close of the first training phase when it was found that three of the men were not eligible for parole as had been expected. To occupy them, they took on the tasks of reviewing and writing up the first phase program and then of planning the second. In the course of the review and the planning, they developed a number of ideas about ways of improving training and of giving both themselves and the new trainees more structured and more responsible roles in the training program. One of these men continued in prison until the end of the third phase; he became in effect the staff person for the Phase 3 trainees, backed up by weekly visits of some of the trainees already on parole.

Although this assumption of training responsibility by the trainees was consistent with the training principles and the program intent, the form of its occurrence was unforeseen. Both the diminished number of trainees in later phases and the reduction of staff were reactions to pressures to keep the program alive and to develop sources of income for the men after they had been paroled. Like other soft money programs dealing with the real problems of marginal people and their efforts to survive, the project's energies were devoted largely to the confrontation of crises.

The important point is this: the enormous and uneconomical expenditure of staff energies and time in the first phase of this program was not necessary in the later phases to produce roughly equivalent results.[2] Five of the eight Phase 1 trainees, four of the six Phase 2 trainees, and three of the four trainees of Phase 3 are still with program development work. It seems plausible that the first phase program and the staff's activities in it created a climate and set a process in motion that allowed it to be carried on by the trainees and transmitted to other trainees who could, in turn, transmit it to others.

---

[2]We do not in fact know that staff involvement in the first phase, of the intensity and level that then obtained, was necessary or related to the behavior of the Phase 1 group; nor do we know the relative role of the training experience and the job opportunities later developed in determining the fate of the individual trainees.

This spread of effect has not stopped with the third phase group. Since their release to parole, the trainees have had an increasing impact on both people and programs. Despite the diversity of their interests and experiences, they all came out of the training program with a specific set of concepts and a commitment to promote and further the cause of new careers. The 12 still in program development work have maintained widespread influence on what can be called the new careers movement. Eight of the 12 are actively involved in organizing associations of new careerists; three of the associations are in major cities, one is statewide, and one is national. The associations are efforts to organize the lobbying and political pressure power of persons in a variety of community organization and aide jobs. The national association has received a $90,000 grant to train members of local new careers associations in leadership and program development; one of the project's former trainees will head the program. Another is on the board of the National New Careers Council, a combined professional-nonprofessional organization formed to promote new careers programming and supportive legislation and funding throughout the country.

These activities are occurring outside of their regular jobs. Within the jobs themselves, the former trainees are exerting influence in a number of directions. Three of them are the senior staff of a $1.5 million new careers program funded by the Department of Labor. In this program, now in its second year, they are working with the staffs of county and private service agencies and with civil service to help these agencies create new entry and promotional opportunities for the poor through redefining job functions and the professional role. They are working also with junior college staff to help revise and develop new educational curricula to meet the needs of new careerist job training and accreditation. They work with agency staff on problems of supervision and with new careerists on problems of adjusting to a new type of work setting. Within their own organization they have created five intern positions which they are using to train new careerists as program developers. Three psychology and sociology graduate students are working full-time on program evaluation and influence between them and senior staff has gone both ways. They have also worked out procedures with a junior college to obtain credit for their work experience which they discuss in a weekly seminar with a college instructor. Recently the senior staff, graduate student staff, and interns organized a seminar on social change through a state college for which they used their own program development experience as content. As is true with other project trainees, these men are not at all awed by existing institutions, nor do they take their procedures for granted. They are more prone to action than memo-writing as a means of getting things done and have been responsible for both agency and educational innovations.

The other trainees are also helping influence the course of new careers, some through administering new careers programs, some through providing technical assistance to agencies undertaking such programs. Both here and in their past jobs it has been an unexpected finding that many of the men have been more effective in selling the idea of new careers and in providing acceptable help on its implementation than have been the professionals with whom they sometimes worked.

A final area of influence has been political. Several of the former trainees have been in touch with legislators and congressmen to enlist their support for new careers programs and legislation on both a state and federal level. They have proposed, and in one case, helped draft state legislation.

To summarize: An initial staff investment with eight men has been parleyed into impact on 18. This investment opened the way for at least 12 of the 18 to develop and to have some influence on policy and operations in new kinds of human resources programming. Much of what the men have learned has been learned on the job after initial training was over. But the commitment to new careers, its ideology, if you will, began in the training program. The men have extended this to limits and in ways we had never anticipated and have gone far beyond anything staff themselves could have done.

Conditions for Contagion

What we are calling contagion — though this is probably not the precise word for the phenomenon — is the transmission of a set of beliefs and commitments. In assuming active roles in the training program, the older trainees were doing something more than passing on information to the newer ones, or providing "training" in a narrow sense. They were also passing on their conviction that they and other deviants in the culture could contribute to that culture's development; that change, though difficult, could be brought about and could be brought about by people like themselves; that there were no absolute truths to guide social action but only approximations to the truth which must be continually tested against experience. Outside of the training program the trainees have been most effective when they have been able to transmit this sense of conviction to others with whom they work and to use it as a motivational base to get others to change what they are doing.

There seem to be five conditions necessary for this contagion phenomenon to appear. These are: providing participatory roles; making room for autonomy of action, decision, and choice; building a group culture around a cause to which one can be committed; offering a meaningful future; and allowing natural leaders to emerge.

Participation

It is essential that there be a climate that allows active participation. The usual roles of student, trainee, or patient simply will not do. Actually behavior change of any kind seems to require participatory activity. In Mobilization for Youth's homework helper program, (Cloward, 1967) in which high school students tutored younger students who were having trouble with schoolwork, the most dramatic improvement in performance was shown by the students doing the tutoring. They had shifted from a passive learning role to a teaching role that required both activity and self-directed, self-imposed learning to make it successful.

In our own study, we began with a strong commitment to participation on the part of the trainees but found it extremely difficult to implement. There was at that stage no recognized role the trainees could see for themselves, aside from the role of therapeutic group members which they had all previously played in other prison programs, but which interfered with their accomplishing much in the present one. In Phase 2, the trainees took on much of the teaching as well as a host of administrative functions. They were now enough with the game; they had knowledge to transmit and could do so with some sense of competence. Those who stayed in the institution played a full-time teacher-consultant role, while those who were out filled it on a part-time basis, returning as outside "experts" to consult with the later groups of trainees. The Phase 2 trainees in turn could play this role with the trainees in Phase 3. Equally important, both Phase 2 and 3 trainees could see men very much like themselves, in some cases men still confined as they were, in the active role and could see this role as part of the expectations for their own development.

The trainees did not perform well as passive learners, even with their fellow trainee teachers; the trainee teachers proved inept as lecturers, as had the staff before them. At the beginning of the program the staff had emphasized learning activities that involved doing rather than listening. Thus much of the learning took place around the trainees' projects. Similarly, the content seminars had an action emphasis and relied heavily on role-playing. A weekly "program planning and evaluation" session was devoted to considering the effectiveness of each program element and to planning systematic changes that were expected to increase effectiveness.

Autonomy

It is important not only to provide for active participation, but also to leave maximum options for individual choice. Learning, we said at the outset, was most meaningful when it was the result of self-initiated activity — hence the emphasis on project-related learning; the projects were tasks selected by the trainees themselves. Though there was a definite framework of givens in terms of the kind of knowledge that needed to be included, the trainees were encouraged to be innovative in both the form and specific content of their teaching. The only stipulation was that program changes be based on a specific rationale and that the changes be systematically observed to see if they were having the desired effect.

Perhaps this amount of freedom, or looseness, is possible only in a very new program that has developed none of the "we always do it this way" attitude which time frequently brings. Our program certainly became progressively more structured from Phase 1 to Phase 3, and it is possible that choice would have been seriously curtailed had the program continued over several more phases. In any case, we feel autonomy is important for the kind of development the trainee group took in later years, and particularly for the diversity that developed within the group.

Group Culture

The importance of building a group culture is stressed in therapeutic community programs in which the actions and feelings of the participants as group members are the focus of therapeutic analysis. Once established, the group can absorb new members without threat to its integrity. The older members of the group, in terms of longevity of membership, transmit to the newer ones, either directly or more often by example, the values and behavior appropriate to group members. Cultures can also be transplanted, a nucleus of group members moving to a new setting and attempting to replicate the group experience they have had.

Our program was oriented toward the solution of tasks rather than interpersonal problems, but like the therapeutic community group, one's peers were seen as a powerful force for generating change within the person. We stressed group participation in all project activities. A "living-learning" group, modeled after the larger therapeutic community group, was a daily activity and the vehicle for dealing with intra-group tensions as well as personal problems. The peer group was seen as a source of support not only in handling interpersonal difficulties but also in dealing with the content of the training program. Equally important, each member was held accountable to the group for what he was doing in the program.

But beyond this, and unlike the therapeutic community culture, we were attempting to create a climate that created commitment to a cause apart from the maintenance of the group itself. The cause was the demonstration of the development of offender manpower, more broadly, of the manpower potential of all those classed as "outs," and the building of bridges for the "outs" into the established culture. The positive use of symptoms has been advocated in mental health programming (Heimler, 1966). We were interested in developing the potential and existing strengths from the experience gained as outs. This appeal to positive strengths, by providing the opportunity for realistic use of these strengths in bringing needed change and development in our culture proves to be a viable base for starting a cause and fostering a growing commitment to it.

A Future

The fourth necessary program element—and we discuss it as such only because of its glaring omission in so many manpower programs for the poor—is that participation carries with it some assurance about having a way to move in the future. In actuality, the program nearly floundered on this issue, for the earlier expressed interest of correctional agencies in hiring the project trainees evaporated at the point of making firm commitments, and both staff and project money were diverted from training to finding and keeping jobs for the trainees. The beginning of the federal poverty program about the time the first trainees completed the program and the availability of OEO money to state and county community action agencies created the opportunities that kept the trainees going, though the jobs were temporary and often of short duration. For at least two years the project faced continual crises around keeping the men at work and solvent—almost all were released from prison to nothing in the way of community or family support, many had trouble managing their financial lives—and efforts at job-finding continued well beyond this point, though by then the trainees themselves had taken over some of the job and program development functions. Some of them have become very adept at the job- and fund-hustling game that occupies those who work on social problems outside of established civil service positions in public agencies.

Leaders

The fifth program element is the opportunity for leaders to emerge from within the group. This seems to be related to the second discussed above, the program "looseness" that allows room for individual decision and self-directed activity and latitude for program innovation. It is these natural leaders who will take the lead in transmitting the culture of the program and who are ultimately responsible for the contagion phenomenon.

We are not at all sure by what process this leadership role develops. In the training program itself, one trainee—both by his continued presence throughout the three phases of the program and by the growing evidence of his personal strength and program skill—became, in the eyes of many, the staff surrogate and leader of the group. He has since become involved in organizing new careerists on a national basis. But other of the trainees, including those who showed no outstanding strengths during training, later became effective program innovators and community organizers.

Many leaders have emerged from the program, and few followers. Though the training itself required working together, once this pressure was relieved there was rapid movement to break away. This splintering effect appears to be quite common in programs such as ours which bring disparate people together around a training need. In many of these programs cliques develop rapidly, sometimes along class lines, sometimes on other bases (Grosser, 1968). Instead of discouraging this development, as is often done, there seems to be some advantage in allowing trainees as much initiative as possible in selecting a direction in which to move. Otherwise too much energy and growth potential is drained off into in-fighting instead of task accomplishment.

In early studies with naval and marine offenders, it was found that putting together group leaders with offenders who shared similar kinds of social perception increased the rehabilitative effectiveness of the group, while forming groups in which leaders and group members had differing perceptions markedly decreased group effectiveness (Grant, J. D. & Grant, M. Q., 1959). Although we need to know a good deal more about how leaders and cliques develop, and what impact they have on their members, there does seem to be some evidence that the emergence of cliques and of multiple leadership is not necessarily a bad thing. In our own program there has frequently been tension when jobs have required that several of the men work together; they have sometimes had trouble subordinating power issues to task issues. However, all of them have shown a remarkable ability to pull together when an immediate crisis demanded it. It may be more efficient to aim for many small and diverse groups instead of one large and unified one, bringing the small groups together in councils or loose federations to work on specific issues but otherwise allowing them to retain their identity. This also permits a broader participatory base and may thus contribute more to individual growth and effectiveness.

Other Forms of Contagion

Contagion undoubtedly occurs in other types of groups than the one discussed here. The program we have described has many similarities to certain of the self-help groups, particularly those that aim at radical alteration of their participants' lives. Such groups have certainly produced dramatic behavior change in some people — it has been likened to a "conversion" experience — and the groups have been both self-perpetuating and expanding, with older members becoming active in recruiting new ones.

These groups, as does the project described here, offer participatory roles for their members, though in self-help groups the members' roles are more fixed than was the case in ours. Such groups tend to offer less of what we have called autonomy — the program is more fixed, there is less room for deviation, the badge of membership is conformity to the group's mores and values. Persons who do not fit tend to be expelled early as not suitable for the group's task, and there is considerable concern about the kind of person who makes an appropriate group member (Volkman & Cressey, 1963).

A specific and well-defined culture develops around the goals and maintenance of the group. Unlike our own program, the self-help groups tend to be more concerned with making very clear the identity of who is "in" and who is "out," and the group's values tend to be organized around the perpetuation of the group and its boundaries, particularly through intra-group contacts. The culture we sought to build was less well-articulated and there were more degrees of freedom in the accompanying belief system. There was less emphasis on being a "good" group member than on carrying a set of working principles beyond the loose group the program had developed, into other settings. Our group thus became very quickly fragmented and the men have, to varying degrees, merged themselves and their interests with other kinds of established groups, sometimes becoming identified with them, sometimes seeking to change them from within.

As a corollary, our program offered its participants a future outside of and beyond the group itself, but one that required carrying what had been learned within the group to others outside of it. The self-help groups offer their participants a new way of life and meaningful roles within the group as long as they continue as members. However, they are generally not expected to carry on the group's mission outside of the context of specific group membership.

Similarly, when leaders develop within the self-help groups, they must, if they are to function as leaders, stay within the structure of the group and adhere to its goals and tactics. If not, the existence of the group may be threatened. When this happens a segment of the group may break away or be expelled and a new group, with differing goals or tactics, may be formed. In our program the efforts of the trainees to develop in differing directions were supported and even encouraged.

Summary

We have discussed two types of behavior change programs, each with differing goals and strategies but both involving what we have called contagion. There is a third and increasingly important kind of behavior change activity taking place today. This is occurring in groups formed around social action needs. Though the main goal of such groups is to bring about social change, they do have impact on individual participants; they provide them with often intense participatory experiences, give meaning to their lives, may create or crystallize a new set of values and a new life style, and provide opportunity for personal growth (Fishman, Walker, O'Connor & Solomon, 1965).

All three of these program types are occurring outside of professional change strategies. All three are obviously producing behavior change. All three rely on influence exerted among peers. In two, professionals play at best only a minor consulting role, and in the third the professional role and function is probably a diminishing one.

Professional approaches to behavior change on either an individual or group level are totally inadequate to today's social problems, in terms of both professional manpower and available theory and techniques. It is difficult, in fact, to change the behavior of large groups of people — to rehabilitate offenders, cure addicts, educate the disadvantaged, give job training to the poor, or even find something useful and not too troublesome for young people to do — without at the same time changing the operations of organizations and institutions. Most programs designed to do something about such problems focus on the individual and ignore the social context. They also tend to impose solutions from the top. Despite overwhelming evidence that this does not work very well, there is reluctance to involve clients in change programs because the program may then very quickly alter its character, the professional role will certainly be challenged, and professional control may well be lost. If this can be faced and lived with, professionals will find they have a tremendous source of strength as well as manpower available by taking advantage of peer influence. Larger numbers of people can be reached, and reached more effectively. Influence can be extended from one program to another. Behavior change will merge with organization change.

REFERENCES

Brager, G. The indigenous social work technician. *Social Work*, 1965, **10**, 33–40.

Cloward, R. D. Studies in tutoring. *Journal of Experimental Education*, 1967, **36**, No. 1.

Community apprentice program: disadvantaged youth in human services. Center for youth and community studies, Howard University, March 1965.

Fishman, J. R., Walker, W., O'Connor, W. & Solomon, F. Civil rights activity and reduction in crime among Negroes. *Archives of General Psychiatry*, 1965, **2**, 227–236.

Grant, J. D. The offender as a correctional manpower resource. In F. Riessman, H. I. Popper (Eds.), *Up from poverty*. New York: Harper & Row, 1968.

Grant, J. D. & Grant, M. Q. A group dynamics approach to the treatment of nonconformists in the Navy. *Annals of American Academy of Political and Social Science*, 1959, **322**, 126–135.

Grant, J. & Grant, J. D. Client participation and community change. In D. Adelson (Ed.), *Community Psychology Perspectives in Mental Health*. San Francisco: Chandler, 1970.

Grosser, C. *Helping Youth*. Office of Juvenile Delinquency and Youth Development, Department of Health, Education, and Welfare, 1968.

Hallowitz, E. The expanding role of the neighborhood service center. *American Journal of Orthopsychiatry*, 1968, **38**, 705–714.

Heimler, E. *Resistance against tyranny: A symposium*. New York: Praeger, 1966.

New careers development project: Final report. Sacramento: Institute for the Study of Crime and Delinquency, 1967.

Pearl, A. & Riessman, F. *New careers for the poor*. New York: Free Press, 1965.

Riessman, F. & Popper, H. I. *Up from poverty: New career ladders for nonprofessionals*. New York: Harper & Row, 1968.

Volkman, R. & Cressey, D. R. Differential association and the rehabilitation of drug addicts. *American Journal of Sociology*, 1963, **69**, 129–142.

Workshop on nonprofessional careers for disadvantaged youth. New York University: Center for the Study of Unemployed Youth, 1966.

SECTION V

Institutional Programs for the Seriously Disturbed

The behavior modification programs reported in this section were designed for severely disturbed institutionalized patients who are traditionally difficult to treat. All of these programs exist in hospitals in which other forms of treatment are concurrently practiced. The goal in each case is the highest level of rehabilitation possible in terms of individual functioning and responsibility. In contrast to traditional psychotherapy, no program aspires to the goal of personality restructuring. Rather, the goal is to strengthen the behavioral repertoire of the individual through the addition of socially desirable, coping responses. The chapter by Slavin and Daniels, "A Behavior Modification Program on an In-Patient and Out-Patient Unit," illustrates an "eclectic behaviorism" in that they adopt a variety of behavior modification techniques including systematic desensitization and operant oriented procedures. Case studies are used to illustrate these procedures. The use of token economy management as a rehabilitation procedure is gaining increasingly wide acceptance in neuropsychiatric hospitals. The chapter by Krasner and Atthowe presents an excellent example of a token economy in action. The chapter by Peyman, "Responsibility Therapy," presents an illustration of how behavior therapy techniques can be used to advantage within the framework of a more traditional program. Of special interest is Peyman's presentation of a didactic approach to patient acquisition of adaptive social responding and personal responsibility. Attitude therapy (Taulbee and Wright) is a direct approach to the treatment of seriously disturbed patients which carries with it the advantage of quickly mobilizing the efforts of staff members throughout the hospital, especially nursing assistants, to consistent ways of responding to the patients. In some ways attitude therapy departs from the basic tenets of the other behavior modification programs described; there is less emphasis upon identifying specific behaviors and more emphasis upon working with general patterns of behavior. Furthermore, the concept of attitude therapy is reported to be based upon psychoanalytic theory. The program is included, however, because in practice the approach is quite direct and the *operations* of the program, in general, meet the criteria proposed in the introductory chapter.

Hamilton, "Environmental Control and Retardate Behavior," describes a behavior modification program in an institutional setting for moderately-to-severely retarded children, most of whom exhibit problems in management and control. The program is presented as an example of the numerous behavior modification programs presently in operation in institutions for retardates. Hamilton's chapter presents a good blending of experimental work, clinical example, and generalizations drawn therefrom.

CHAPTER 12

A Behavior Modification Program on an In-Patient and Out-Patient Unit

Douglas R. Slavin and Aubrey C. Daniels

This chapter is devoted to a description of a treatment program in a milieu setting in which the whole range of behavior modification techniques is used. Though the program uses many different techniques, from "token economy" therapy to aversive conditioning, all the approaches are derived from and theoretically related to theories of learning. Consequently, the Behavior Modification Program (the BMP) has been strongly influenced theoretically by the work of Skinner (1953) and Kanfer (1961) and has been shaped by the tradition of Lindsley (1956, 1964), Wolpe (1958), Ayllon and Michael (1959), Ullmann and Krasner (1965), and Atthowe and Krasner (1968).

The BMP rests on a model variously called a psychological model, a behavioral model, a learning theory model, or an educational model — all in contrast to traditional treatment conceptualizations which are based on the medical or disease model. The differences between the two approaches lead to a number of major issues and differences in procedures (Ullmann & Krasner, 1965) which need not be detailed here. Suffice it to say that the learning theory model results in the following assumptions. Maladaptive behaviors do not constitute a disease entity but are rather learned responses the development and maintenance of which follow the same hypotheses, rules, and laws of learning as do adaptive or normal behaviors. This view would hold that abnormal behavior is diagnosed and defined socially rather than medically. Consequently, as societies' attitudes, values, and structures change so do the nomenclature and definition of abnormality. Also, the model holds that since the maladaptive behavior is a learned response, it may be unlearned or extinguished and new adaptive behavior learned and strengthened using knowledge of the learning process derived from learning theory and experimental psychology. These assumptions result in the BMP's emphasizing changing present behavior, defined operationally, by manipulating situational variables and changing the consequences of the specified behaviors rather than emphasizing the understanding by the patient of his past behavior or experiences. The learning model approach

> does not rely on assumptions or speculations as to the ultimate or original causes of the maladaptive behavior. Such causes are as difficult to determine with any assurance as they are to manipulate effectively. Rather than attributing behavior to some unknown or underlying cause or to a diagnostic category, the major attempt has been to secure effective control of the variables which are actually maintaining the behavior. (Goldiamond, 1965, p. 851)

Because of the above orientation the BMP emphasizes behavioral definitions of a person's difficulties rather than psychodynamic explanations of patients' reported affective states. As a result the program's initial concern is defining, measuring, and recording a person's behavioral difficulties. Next a treatment program is designed to change those behaviors in the direction of increasing or decreasing the frequency of their occurrence. The treatment program is monitored closely and changes are made on the basis of the behavioral data. Treatment approaches are thus dealt with scientifically in the sense that a systematic attempt is made to measure the effects of the treatment procedure. From the above vantage point, the BMP sees no difference between the researcher and the clinician.

Setting

The Georgia Mental Health Institute is a state-owned mental health training and research facility. The physical plant is basically composed of eight in-patient and out-patient adult cottages and a child in-patient-out-patient cottage. Each adult cottage can accommodate 29 inpatients.

Since each unit has staff and trainees from all major mental health disciplines, there are many theoretical approaches to treatment within the same unit. However, the nursing staff basically operates the in-patient ward as a milieu treatment setting.

The cottage is an open ward and no patients have been committed. Male and female patients live in the same cottage. The age range of the patients is approximately 15 to 70. The mean age is approximately 23 years.

There is a relatively wide range of change worthy behavior exhibited in the cottage at any given time; however, combative patients and patients where the elopement risk is high are usually not found on the unit due mainly to the shortage of staff. Chronic regressed patients are generally not accepted because the training requirements demand a more rapid turnover of the patient population. Aside from these exceptions there is usually a representative cross sample of undesirable behavior on the cottage ranging from mildly neurotic to overtly psychotic.

Assessment and Evaluation

Patients are referred to the BMP from throughout the Georgia Mental Health Institute by various evaluation teams on the basis that the patient is "a good behavior therapy case." It is not exactly clear what criteria are used for the referral but it appears that people who have specified phobic or behavioral difficulties, such as obesity, homosexuality, etc., or who may be management problems are most frequently referred. Also, it appears that when all other approaches have failed, the BMP is tried as a last resort regardless of diagnosis. Once referred, two problems become imminent. The first problem is to define behaviorally the difficulties the patient has and the second is to design ways to measure the behavior reliably. The BMP utilizes a number of assessment procedures to aid in the behavioral definition of a person's difficulties, and to aid in planning a modification program. All candidates are administered the Reinforcement Survey Schedule (RSS) (Cautela & Kastenbaum, 1967), and the Revised Fear Survey Schedule (RFSS) which is a modification of Wolpe and Lang's (1964) original Fear Survey Schedule. The RSS is a questionnaire in which things or experiences which may be reinforcing such as watching television, eating candy, etc. are listed. The person indicates those items that he would find most rewarding. This information is used in designing token economy therapy programs and variations of the operant paradigm. The RFSS is a list of 87 things or experiences that may elicit anxiety, fear, or avoidance behavior. The list includes such commonly feared situations as flying in an airplane, speaking in public, being at a dentist's, as well as more peculiar situations, such as witnessing surgical operations. The individual indicates on a 5-point scale the degree to which these situations or things elicit fear in him. This information is used to pinpoint the situations that are conditioned stimuli for avoidance behavior. The results of the RFSS are also used to design desensitization heirarchies, as reciprocal inhibition therapy (Wolpe, 1958) is one of the frequently used techniques in the BMP.

In addition to the above questionnaires, the individual is asked to "make a list of things about yourself that you would like to change. Include everything even if you feel it is trivial (e.g., nail-biting)." In some instances of out-patient marital counseling, or in family treatment, the people are asked to make lists of behaviors they would like to see changed in other family members.

In situations where the person can be easily observed over a long period of time such as an in-patient unit, systematic observations of the patient are carried out using a time-sampling technique. A mimeographed record form is supplied to the nursing staff and every 15 or 30 minutes, the behavior the patient is engaging in is recorded. Based on this information the patient's behavior is classified into desirable behavior such as talking with others or undesirable behavior such as staying in his bedroom. Thus not only are the behavioral problems of the individual pinpointed but a measure of the frequency of the behavior is also obtained. Rarely, of course, does the individual behave in only one maladaptive fashion and rarely are his problems presented behaviorally. For example, a recent referral describes the patient as "having difficulty with dependency needs, and exhibits a depreciated self-concept and confused sexual identity." To begin to define this statement behaviorally the staff of the BMP reduced the concepts to their behavioral components. The criterion is to define the problem into countable behavior. In this case dependency needs, behaviorally, were a high rate of avoidance of decision making and verbal requests that some other person make the decision; the depreciated self-concept was a high rate of self-referred negative verbalizations and avoidance of people, and the confused sexual identity was a conditioned avoidance response to certain sexual stimuli. In many instances it becomes quite difficult to define the difficulties of people behaviorally. What, for example, are the behavioral components for a feeling of alienation, a sense of unreality, feeling anxious and depressed? What is it that one is referring to when he describes a person as "lacking impulse control," "being irresponsible," "needing nurturance," "ambivalent over expression of hostility," or, as is frequently heard, "has low self-esteem"?

Part of the difficulty, of course, stems from a history in which diffuse, vaguely defined concepts have been used to explain problems people have experienced. Initially these concepts may have had specific behavioral correlates but over time they have been corrupted into jargon, applied indiscriminately, and have lost their usefulness. It has been our experience that searching for the behavior that underlies the jargon reduces the problem to more workable terms. For example, in a group of mentally retarded adolescents, it became apparent upon observation that the label "irresponsible" resulted from the youths' being late in getting back to work after a mid-morning break.

Once the individual's problems have been defined behaviorally it becomes necessary to measure the base rate of the behavior. The base rate is the frequency of behavior per unit of time before any attempt is made to modify it directly. One of the main tenets of the BMP is that no treatment plan can begin until some attempt has been made to measure and record the behavior to be changed. It is felt that subjective assessments of behavior change are unreliable and err not only on the side of perceiving change when there is none but also err on the side of perceiving no change when in fact there is some. By having a specific record, measuring the behavior undergoing change, even very small increments in new behavior can be observed. The validation, reliability, and generality of any treatment technique must ultimately rest on systematic measurement procedures.

The obtaining of base rate data on inpatients is relatively easy if one has the cooperation of the nursing personnel. At the Georgia Mental Health Institute we have been fortunate in having a group of nursing staff personnel who have been most helpful in recording the necessary behavior. Ultimately of course this is rewarding for them as it leads to a clearer understanding of how to deal with the inpatient. However, nursing staff time is scarce and consequently self-recording techniques are also used. Most inpatients are quite able to keep a relatively reliable record of several behaviors simultaneously. In the BMP, patients are supplied with wrist golf-counters that they can use to count various behaviors. In some instances, where the time a behavior occurs is also being investigated, the patients are given mimeographed "operant record" sheets that have columns for the date, time duration, and category of behavior. The reliability of these records are initially checked against a simultaneous recording by another staff and in some instances other patients. With outpatients the reliability remains more open to question except in some instances where other family members also record the behavior.

The collected base rate data are usually plotted as a cumulative curve. The base rates and the record of the behaviors being altered are kept in the individual's chart and it is these data that are presented at staff meetings and used to assess the effect of the treatment plan. Aside from a brief lecture on plotting a graph and how to read a cumulative curve, most staff readily became proficient in using the data to discuss the patient's progress.

From the individual's chief complaint, the assessment procedures, the collection of base rate data, brief interviews with the individual, and nursing staff impressions, behavioral definitions of the problems are constructed and a modification program outlined. It is difficult to specify how a particular modification program is arrived at, as it depends on the nature of the behaviors to be changed, the techniques available to the staff, as well as the staff's ingenuity. Discussed below are the major approaches the program has used with some case illustrations.

Operant Approaches

Token plans. Historically, the BMP grew out of the work reported by Ayllon and Azrin (1968) using token economy programs at Anna State Hospital. However, since the setting is quite different both in terms of type of patients and nature of the physical and administrative organization, the token systems designed for use in the BMP are different in a number of respects. The main difference is that each token plan is individualized. As stated earlier, the unit does not operate as a token economy ward. There are a number of disciplines on the unit and consequently different theoretical approaches. Each patient has a different treatment plan, most of which are psychodynamically oriented. A patient whose therapist is a Freudian may room with a patient whose total treatment plan is a token plan. Each token plan is designed for the specific problem areas of a patient and the reinforcers are tailored to the individual.

Also, there is a wider range of pathology, motivation, and intelligence than is usually found in token economy wards. Although the first BMP patient was diagnosed as schizophrenic, the program has also treated phobics, depressives, homosexuals, problem adolescents, as well as borderline psychotics and mixed neurotics. Intelligence has varied roughly from IQ's ranging between 80 and 120. Plans have been effective with patients who had no desire to leave the unit and with those who did not want to stay.

In addition, the contingencies used are broader than those traditionally used in large token programs. The ways that patients earn tokens are as varied as is the range of problems and patients. Although tangible rewards are used when appropriate, the emphasis is on shifting toward nontangibles such as social approval as a reward. Some outpatients will work vigorously to spend a day in the unit and some inpatients will work just as vigorously to be an outpatient. Some patients work for time with a therapist or a staff member; others work for special grounds or unit privileges. Patients may work to stay in the hospital as a patient or work to get out. Variations of use of time in or out of the unit has been an effective reward in a number of cases. A given patient may earn tokens for smiling, or making positive statements about himself or appropriate compliments to others. The administration of tokens is, of course, always paired with verbal praise so that verbal rewards will become reinforcing in themselves.

Another difference is that a token plan can be the total treatment program or it may be used in conjunction with more traditional approaches to treatment or other behavior modification approaches. For most patients who are on token plans it is the total treatment program. Individual psychotherapy sessions may or may not be included in the plan. However, a token plan may be devised for a specific problem which amounts to only a small part of the treatment program. For example, one patient had a token plan designed to facilitate weight loss while she was in traditional psychotherapy to work on a marital problem as well as her obesity. Many patients on token plans are taught relaxation techniques as an alternative inhibiting response to anxiety and some are also taught assertive responses as well as being desensitized to mild phobic stimuli.

Historically most of the work reported in the literature on token plans has been with inpatients, but this approach has been an effective form of out-patient treatment as well. The problems are obviously different mainly in having control of only a few reinforcers but also in not being able to give immediate reinforcement. However, most outpatients can delay reinforcement so that this is not a serious problem. Reinforcements that have been potent are extra therapy appointments, visits back on the unit if the patient had been previously hospitalized, or the amount of time spent with the therapist. Also token plans for use with families on an out-patient basis have been designed. In one family, for example, there was a great deal of disorganization at meal time accompanied by arguments and unpleasantness. Part of the total treatment approach to the family involved rewarding tokens to all family members when they could have their meals together without arguments or disruptions. The tokens bought individually tailored rewards for each family member such as a movie for the children, a golf game for the father, and a visit to relatives for the mother. If the family was not able to meet the criterion of a "pleasant meal" then no one received anything. The designing of token plans for families is complex because rewards are usually applied on a group contingency rather than individually. In some instances, out-patient families have been worked with in which only one member of the family is on tokens. For example, a delinquent boy earned tokens for attending school, good grades, coming home on time, and washing the car. He used his tokens to buy from his family driving lessons, telephone privileges, a weekly allowance, and extra time out on weekends. The experience of the BMP with innovating different applications of the token economy or operant approach demonstrates that the approach has applicability and flexibility and can be used in most treatment settings whether a private clinic, a ward in a general hospital, a community mental health center, or even private practice.

Designing a token plan. A token plan is a behavior economy system in which tokens are earned for certain behaviors, usually designated by the staff, and those tokens can be exchanged for specified things that the patient wants. In developing a token plan for an individual or group, the first task is to define the behaviors that are to be changed and break them down into clearly definable and measurable (or countable) units of behavior. Then a plan is developed based on the base rate observations and other information about strong positive reinforcers for the patient. For example, if during the base rate period an obese patient was continuously asking when she could go to recreational activities, then going to those activities might be contingent on weight loss. She would earn tokens by losing weight and would have to pay tokens for recreational activities appointments.

For each patient there would be several ways in which they could earn and spend tokens. Token plans are generally revised at least monthly and some behaviors that earned tokens in the initial phase may be dropped out and others added, or a more complex behavior may be required. For example, if an agoraphobic patient initially earned tokens for walking alone from the Unit to the Occupational Therapy building, the second phase may no longer give her tokens for this; the rewarded activity might be changed to going shopping alone. The initial behaviors rewarded may be rather simple, for example, sitting in the day area, but in the later phases it may be that tokens are given only for patient-initiated verbal behavior in a group. This shaping of behavior is quite important in any token plan. Failures of the token plans usually are a result of asking for too much too soon.

One of the most difficult problems in setting up a token plan is balancing the system in such a way that the desired behavior will have to occur before the patient can earn certain privileges. Since there are usually multiple ways in which a patient can earn tokens, if the system is not balanced properly, a patient may be able to earn enough tokens to do what he wants by engaging in only one of the specified behaviors. A well-balanced plan is typified by the remark of an obese patient on a token plan who said, "There is no way I can do what I want to do without losing weight." Balance of a token economy can be obtained by anticipating the maximum amount of tokens earnable and then setting the total cost of all rewards slightly below this figure.

Another necessary aspect is to develop a true economy. Things must be included that the patient will work for but on the other hand they must neither be too hard nor too easy to earn as economic inflation and depression can occur. Patients are generally asked what they would like to work for and what behaviors they should practice in order to earn these privileges, ensuring that items are included that the patient is motivated to obtain. In addition this helps the patient feel he participated in designing the token plan and usually ensures his cooperation.

It cannot be overemphasized that a plan must be specific. How tokens can be earned and spent must be clearly understood by all involved with the patient. When a plan is developed copies are made for staff and the patient involved, and it is explained thoroughly to both. The initial reaction of many patients when told they were to be put on a token plan was negative, but without exception, once the plan was put into effect the response was positive. Initially the only patients put on tokens were patients for whom no other treatment worked. Although some patients are referred for whom a token plan is the treatment of last resort, an increasing number of patients are placed on tokens as the initial choice of treatment.

The case described below demonstrates more concretely the development, operation, and effect of a token plan.

Case A

The first patient on the BMP was a 25-year-old male who had been hospitalized for 9 months and who was getting progressively worse. At the time he was referred to the BMP he was withdrawing and remaining in bed for extended periods of time, not attending scheduled activities, expressing concern about "something pressing on my brain," about "electricity in my body," and about "heart trouble." He was also expressing suicidal ideation and ruminating about death.

The first problem was to determine what this patient valued and what he would work for and what were the problem behaviors of immediate concern. As it turned out, what he wanted most was to remain on the unit as a patient. The nursing staff was mainly concerned with the amount of time he remained in bed and his consequent failure to attend scheduled activities. Attendance at these activities then became the initial target behaviors to change. The patient, Mr. C., went through seven treatment phases. Each phase had a different set of contingencies for earning tokens. Tables 1 through 3 illustrate some of these different phases.

In Phase I, the patient earned tokens for being out of bed and attending scheduled activities. The tokens earned allowed him to purchase additional time in the hospital as an inpatient. In later phases these behaviors were de-emphasized and

TABLE 1

Token Plans for Mr. C.

Phase I

TO: All Staff—Unit I
RE: Mr. C.

As of Monday, March 13, 1967, Mr. C. will begin a new form of treatment. This approach, called operant conditioning, reinforces or rewards specific behaviors as they occur. Reinforcement consists of paper tokens in the form of a check. After a period of three weeks these tokens may be used by Mr. C. to buy additional time in the Institute to work on his problems. If at that time he has not accumulated enough tokens to stay, he will be discharged.

Reinforced Behaviors

Being Out of Bed

This behavior will be reinforced on an arithmetic progression resulting in an increasing reward the longer he is out of bed continuously. Note that there are no fractional reinforcements. For example, if Mr. C. were up seven hours, he earns six tokens, not ten tokens.

Reinforcements

up 2 hours	1 token
up 4 hours	3 tokens
up 6 hours	6 tokens
up 8 hours	10 tokens
up 12 hours	15 tokens
up 14 hours	21 tokens
up 15 hours	25 tokens

Cumulative reinforcement is dependent on Mr. C.'s being up continuously. If he gets up for 4 hours and then goes back to bed, the sequence starts over again when he gets up. He would receive three tokens for the four hours he was up but would start over again at two hours equal one token when he got up. This system is in effect from 7:00 a.m. to 10:00 p.m. He may be up earlier or later but he does not receive tokens for this time.

Rest hour from 1:00 to 2:00 p.m. is considered part of the sequence and is counted as if he were up. However, if he stays in bed past 2 o'clock the sequence starts over.

In order to negatively reinforce Mr. C.'s staying in bed, it is suggested that the staff not interact with him while he is in bed or sitting on his bed. Interaction should only take place outside his bedroom.

In order to facilitate bookkeeping Mr. C. will check in at the nursing station when he gets up and when he is going back to bed. Indications of deliberate deception, that is, not checking in when he goes back to bed, results in a loss of 25 tokens.

Attending Unit Activities

This behavior will be reinforced only if he stays the entire time of the activity.

Reinforcements

Patient Meeting (M, W, F)	10 tokens each
Community Meeting (W)	10 tokens
Psychodrama (W) (OT)	15 tokens
Occupational Therapy (OT) (T, Th.)	10 tokens each
Recreational Therapy (RT)	
(Monday bowling)	20 tokens
Music Therapy (TAT)	10 tokens
Film group (when scheduled)	10 tokens
Religious group (Th)	10 tokens
Other spontaneous unit activities	
(e.g., Movies, Parties, etc.)	10 tokens

Vocational Rehabilitation (VR)

Attending VR five days a week for the full schedule time.

Reinforcement

1 hour at VR

Bonus Credits

OT, MT, RT, and VR staff at their discretion may reinforce Mr. C's behavior in their activities by issuing bonus tokens varying in value from 1 to 15 tokens. In addition VR may reinforce Mr. C.'s staying longer at VR by reinforcing each additional half hour with 10 tokens.

Administration

The person assigned to Mr. C. on each shift is responsible for listing the behavior and the reinforcements given out during their shift. These notes should be recorded in the nurses note section of his chart.

Staff should continue to relate to Mr. C. as they have in the past except that they should not be interacting with him when he is in bed, or when he should be at some activity.

D. R. Slavin, Ph.D.

TABLE 2
Token Plans for Mr. C.

Phase III

TO: All Staff—Unit I
RE: Mr. C.
Token Therapy—Phase III

As of April 25, 1967, Mr. C. begins the third phase of operant conditioning therapy. During this third phase, behavior which results in his being out of the Institute or behavior which is appropriately socialized will be reinforced with tokens. Behaviors which tend to strengthen his dependency on the hospital, such as on-unit activities, will not be reinforced. However, Mr. C. will be allowed to make use of on-unit activities as he chooses. This seeming paradox (Why not cancel all on-unit activities?), is not really paradoxical as the exercise of an independent choice is considered appropriate behavior and thus opportunities to exercise that choice should be made available.

Staff should continue to pay tokens as soon after the desired behavior as is possible. Also, Mr. C. should be reassured that he is doing well and that he will be able to function outside of the Institute.

During this phase, as in previous phases, little attention should be paid to pathological behavior, such as hypochondrical preoccupations and complaints of hopelessness. As of April 25, 1967, Mr. C. had earned 2790 tokens which buys him 31 days (90 tokens per day) in the Institute. Date of termination of phase is May 25, 1967 at 10:00 p.m.

Reinforced Behaviors

Being Out of Bed

Out of bed continuously for at least 14 hours, with exception of rest hour from 1:00 to 2:0 p.m. earns 20 tokens. Any time in bed during the 14 hours cancels the earning of tokens for being up that day.

V.R. Work Adjustment

Being at VR work on time for the full two hours each day earns 60 tokens per day.

Being Out of the Institute

Being at home or on off-grounds visits earn reinforcements as follows:

Reinforcements

May return briefly for no longer than 30 minutes.

1st 5 hours	20 tokens
2nd 5 hours	30 tokens
3rd 5 hours	50 tokens
4th 5 hours	80 tokens
5th 5 hours	120 tokens

6th 5 hours	170 tokens
7th 5 hours	200 tokens
8th 5 hours	200 tokens
9th 5 hours	200 tokens
10th 5 hours	200 tokens

There is no partial credit except if Mr. C.'s return is prompted by a realistic situation, which would be that it would not make good sense for him to stay out longer. If he returns for most any reason other than that he was getting anxious, or that was all he could take, he can receive partial credit at the rate of 30 tokens per hour or portion thereof. Note that his partial credit applies only after Mr. C. has been out of the Institute at least 25 hours.

Off-grounds pass such as going to the show, shopping, etc., earn tokens at rate of 40 tokens per hour up to 120 tokens. Partial credit may be earned.

In order for Mr. C. to continue in the program he must earn at least 2100 tokens by May 25, 1967 at 12:00 p.m. Cost for time in the Institute after May 25, 1967 is 300 tokens per day.

D. R. Slavin, Ph.D.

TABLE 3
Token Plans for Mr. C.

Phase VI

TO: All Staff— Unit I
RE: Mr. C.
Token Therapy — Phase VI

As of July 5, 1967, Mr. C. earned 34 days in the hospital. In addition he found a job, and went to work each day. During Phase VI, Mr. C. will receive tokens for going to work (250 tokens per day) and for being out of the Institute (20 tokens per hour exclusive of working). Credit is obtained for being out of the Institute by rounding to the nearest whole hour (see Phase V).

During Phase VI, Mr. C. will try a week out from the Institute during which he will continue to earn tokens. He may return any time during this trial.

Again, staff should spend little time with Mr. C. when he dwells on pathological material about dying. He should be kept focused on reality problems of working and plans for the future.

D. R. Slavin, Ph.D.

---

others were emphasized. For example, in Phase II, token value for being out of bed remained the same but the token value for attending the Vocational Rehabilitation (VR) work adjustment program was doubled and "being off the Unit" was added. In Phase III, the token value for being out of bed was decreased, VR again went up in value, and "being off the Unit" was increased. In Phase IV, the emphasis was on job-seeking; Phase V emphasis was placed on obtaining a job and working; and Phase VI was working while living away from the Institute. He obtained a job during the token plan and was employed for a period of 10 weeks. At the end of 10 weeks he quit his job because, he said, "my anxiety got the best of me." He returned to the hospital for a short stay and was discharged to outpatient. Since that time he has been working on a farm raising his own cows and chickens and making a relatively independent living. Work behaviors on the farm were reinforced by tokens which could be used by Mr. C. to buy visits with staff and friends at the Institute. He was maintained on tokens for about a year and when tokens were discontinued Mr. C. maintained his level of functioning. His delusional thoughts have disappeared as well as his suicidal ideation and ruminations about death. These were dealt with simply by ignoring them and talking with him only when he engaged in appropriate conversation.

In designing token programs, the most difficult decision is deciding at what level to begin reinforcing the behavior. Though it is important to begin at a level at which the patient can succeed, it has been our experience that therapists consistently underestimate the level of functioning of the patient. A program can be designed so that the patient can earn tokens at his own rate and at higher levels of functioning if he is able to.

Case B

An example of this more flexible program is illustrated with an 18-year-old boy who was essentially mute except for a brief "yes," "no," or "I don't know" response. Mr. John Parrino, a psychology ·intern in the Behavior Modification Program, was the primary therapist. The patient was withdrawn and spent most of his time isolated in his room at home. History indicated he had been reared by a psychotic mother and that he had been previously hospitalized in another state. During the base rate period it was established that he enjoyed coming to the Institute as a day patient, that he was quite bright, and enjoyed classical music and books. This information was used to decide on the rewards that could be bought with his tokens. The target behavior selected to work on was "talking with people." Shaping procedures beginning with reading material to his therapist through to spontaneous discussion with other patients were designed into a token plan. In the token plan, initial behaviors such as just being with people were rewarded; however, if more advanced behaviors such as talking with people occurred before they were required bonus tokens could be earned. For example, Mr. H., the patient, could receive an extra 50 token bonus if he spontaneously spoke to someone during the first week of the program, whereas, the following week spontaneous speech was a formal part of the program and received only 25 tokens.

Designing programs like the above obviates the error of setting behavioral goals too low and allows the patient to progress at his own rate. In addition alternative rates are made available to him if he wants to accelerate or decelerate his rate of change. In fact the patient, Mr. H., was able to begin at higher levels than were initially set. After the 6 week token program he was interacting verbally quite spontaneously though he was still somewhat reticent. He remained on the unit as a day patient without being on a token plan program and his verbal level did not drop to base rate level. He obtained a job as a stock clerk in a drug store and he was discharged shortly afterward. He has been out of the Institute for over a year since being discharged and appears to be functioning adequately.

Operant approaches without tokens. In many instances, where one very particular behavior is being modified, it is possible to manipulate the consequences of the behavior without the need of a complex token plan. One patient who was very tangential in her thinking, behaviorally defined as "changing the topic of conversation," had all conversations with nurses terminated as soon as she changed topics. She could continue to talk with the nurses, something she greatly enjoyed, only if she could stay on the same topic. Theoretically, "time on topic" should accelerate as it is being followed by a desirable consequence and "changes topic" should decelerate as it is being followed by an undesirable consequence. Similarly, changes in the content of talk of this patient were obtained with the same procedures. Talk about present problems, jobs, and day-to-day living tasks increased as it was arranged that this would lead to nurse attention, whereas talk about guilt over sexual behavior, sexual delusions, and being upset led to termination of the conversation. Similar procedures were used with a 24-year-old female patient whose only available behavioral repertoire toward men consisted of highly flirtatious and sexually seductive responses such as wetting her lips with the tip of her tongue, talking about sexual behavior, and making subtle suggestive body movements. It was arranged that this patient would meet daily for half an hour with one of the male psychology technicians for "social talk" which was defined as relatively superficial talk about movies, books, current events, television, etc. The patient was taught how to use this material in talking with a male. Any sexually seductive behavior with the psychology technician terminated the session whereas appropriate behavior maintained the discussion and resulted in the patients' being able to meet with her therapist to deal with other problems.

It should be noted that in all instances the procedures that are to be used and the reason for using them are explained in detail to the patient. The general reason given is that the target behavior is a problem for them and the operant procedures will help extinguish the behavior.

Respondent Approaches

Another major treatment approach used in the BMP follows from Wolpe's (1958) reciprocal inhibition or desensitization methods. Wolpe suggests that if a response which is antagonistic to anxiety, such as relaxation, can be made to occur in the presence of anxiety-arousing stimuli, then the bond between the stimuli and anxiety arousal is reduced. The BMP conceptualizes much maladaptive behavior as avoidance or escape behavior which is strongly maintained because it serves to reduce anxiety. People in the BMP are instructed in relaxation techniques (Wolpe, 1958) as well as when to use these techniques. For example, they are instructed when they find themselves in a situation to become as relaxed as they possibly can, even if the new state represents only a minor decrease in anxiety. Since leaving or avoiding such situations has incrementally less anxiety-reducing effects, escape becomes less probable as an anxiety-reducing behavior.

Another variation of the use of relaxation is to condition a state of relaxation to verbally conditioned stimuli such as "calm, just relax." This is accomplished using a variation of Siprelle's (1967) anxiety-induction techniques in which patients are seen individually or in a group for training sessions. They are instructed to tense their muscles, to let themselves become tense, to imagine a situation which is fearful or anxiety-arousing for them. They maintain this state for several minutes and are then instructed that on the verbal command "calm, just relax" they are to immediately, using the previously taught relaxation techniques, become as relaxed as possible. These conditioning trials in which verbal cues are paired with anxiety reduction and relaxation are repeated several times a session. The more pairings the stronger the conditioning and the higher the probability that the verbal cues will act as conditioned stimuli for relaxation. Patients are encouraged to practice these trials several times a day. A variation of this technique in which termination of a 6 milliamp shock is contingent on saying the words "calm, relax" into a voice activated microphone was investigated by Kushner at Coral Gables, Florida.[1] In addition to these self-treatment methods, patients are taught Wolpe's method to desensitize anxiety-arousing stimuli. In Wolpe's method of desensitization, the range, intensity, and circumstance of a patient's fear is ascertained and graduated hierarchical scenes are paired with a state of relaxation; thus, the patient becomes gradually habituated to the imagined stimulus. Usually one or two hierarchies are habituated by the therapist and then the patient is encouraged to become his own therapist by constructing his own hierarchies and doing his own desensitization. Patients are instructed to set aside "home work" time for this activity. Also they are encouraged to use this approach for any behavior which they must engage in but about which they are apprehensive, such as seeking jobs or taking an exam. All the above approaches are used in conjunction with other behavior modification techniques such as individualized token economy plans. A patient may, for example, receive tokens for each session of conditioned relaxation training.

Measuring the effects of the above approaches is accomplished by using a unit of tension called the Subjective Unit of Discomfort (SUD) (Wolpe & Lazarus, 1966). A SUD of zero represents complete comfort, lack of tension and calmness; a SUD of 100 represents severe tension, anxiety, or, as one patient termed it, "complete panic." Patients recorded the frequency duration and SUD level of their anxious moments and these data are plotted to measure change. The data on one patient, for example, indicated that a decrease in reported intensity of anxiety was associated with a decrease in the frequency of attacks. The patient was an acutely anxious female with a diagnosis of schizophrenic reaction, paranoid type. Much of her anxiety was triggered by the feeling that people could read her mind and would think she was homosexual. These feelings did not always occur each time she was anxious, but they had an average base rate of five episodes a day. Because of these feelings, she avoided people and would not leave her house. This patient was on a multi-behavior treatment approach in which tokens (see Table 4) and desensitization were used. She is now at home and has been out of the hospital for over a year. She still has marked avoidance behavior; for example, she will not remain in a crowd of people, but she is able to care for her husband, child, and herself, and can spend more time outside her home with friends than she did in the past. This patient had been hospitalized and under treatment about a year prior to entering the BMP. During that time she

---

[1] M. Kushner, personal communication, December 1968.

TABLE 4
Token Plan for Out-patient Mrs. T.

Tokens may be earned in the following fashion:

(1) *Visiting:*
    (a) mother (at least two hours)   50 tokens[a]
    (b) others (at least one hour)   50 tokens
         each additional hour earns   50 tokens

(2) *Company:*
    (a) others at least 15 minutes   10 tokens
    (b) additional 15 minutes   10 tokens

(3) *Schedule:*
    (a) sticking to schedule of
         housework and activities   25 tokens

(4) *School:*
    (a) taking son to school   150 tokens

(5) *Drive-In:*
    (a) at least one showing   75 tokens
    (b) at least two showings   150 tokens

(6) *Grocery:*
    (a) going alone   100 tokens
    (b) going with husband   50 tokens

(7) *Outdoors with Neighbors:*
    (a) each "out" earns   15 tokens per 5
                               minutes, 20 tokens per
                               extra 5 minutes

[a]600 tokens = 1 day. They may be used to buy days in the hospital. (Note: nights excluded.) A day is defined as any 16 consecutive hours or less, up to but not past 11:00 p.m.

could not function outside of the hospital and had difficulty being with other patients on the unit.

A problem commonly reported by many patients is difficulty with sleeping. A variation of relaxation techniques is used in the BMP to help condition sleeping behavior. The first step is to develop a ritualized series of behaviors in which the last behavior is always the same. These behavior series come to act as discriminative stimuli (SD) for sleep when they are followed by or are contiguous with a state of relaxation and sleep. Once the form of the SD's is agreed upon the person is instructed to practice relaxation in bed immediately following the last SD in the series which is usually turning out the light. Coincident with relaxation they can only think about some situation or fantasy that is pleasant and appealing. They must always think about the same situation every time they are trying to sleep. This fantasy is a cognitive SD for sleep. They continue to become progressively more relaxed until sleeping.

Case C

A 27-year-old woman came for help with insomnia. She had been taking several meprobromate tablets trying to get to sleep and the evening before coming for help took eight tablets. She reported that she had chronic insomnia that began shortly after she was married and moved to Georgia. A stimulus analysis of her sleeping behavior indicated that there had been major changes in the stimulus patterns or discriminative stimuli (SD) that initially controlled sleep. Previously she slept alone, and now she sleeps with her husband in the same bed; previously her bedroom had been several floors above street level and now it was at street level; previously her bedroom had been at the front of the building and the street had been busy with night traffic noises, and now her bedroom was at the back of the building, far from any noise.

The present SD's were changed to match as close as possible the old SD's. She moved her bedroom to the front of the building where there was more night traffic noise, and she slept alone on a chaise lounge. A prescribed series of sleep preparing rituals was designed. No drugs were allowed and turning on a small night light would serve as the final external SD of the series. The patient was taught relaxation techniques; her self-selected SD was thinking about being adrift in a canoe wrapped up warmly in blankets. The first night she had some difficulty in maintaining the cognitive SD. She slipped into anxiety-arousing thoughts about work and took one pill to induce sleep. With continued treatment, however, she reported no further difficulty. She moved back into her old bedroom with her husband and was able to go to sleep easily using the cognitive SD of being adrift in a canoe as a stimulus for sleep. There has been only mild and intermittant return of her insomnia since she moved back into her bedroom.

Another technique which is used in the BMP is covert sensitization (Cautela, 1967). In this approach aversive imagery is paired with approach behavior such as eating, stealing, etc., in order that the approach behavior acquire aversive properties.

Case D

An obese 28-year-old woman came for help. Her favorite pastime was nibbling at candy all day long. She was instructed to keep a record of food she ate and particularly of the amount of candy she consumed. Imagery of herself approaching, handling, and consuming candy was paired with imagery of vomiting on the candy, becoming nauseous as she approached the candy, and imagery of the candy as being full of worms. She was instructed to practice these pairings in her imagination at home. Since treatment she has not eaten any candy and along with other diet control has lost 16 lbs. in three months. Other problems such as anxiety and fear of interpersonal interactions with men have been handled by other techniques, such as reciprocal inhibition, but her weight loss has so enhanced her self-esteem that these other problems are more easily dealt with.

Case E

A variation of Cautela's approach was used with a 32-year-old male homosexual who was being seen privately by the first author. A stimulus analysis of the cues that elicited arousal indicated that male lips and genitalia were conditioned stimuli associated with kissing and fellatio. During every session with the therapist the patient was instructed to fantasize a seduction scene. When the cues leading to arousal were clearly visualized the patient was instructed to indicate this by pressing a switch which operated a projector. The slides that were immediately projected on a large screen in front of the patient consisted of male genitalia and male lips in various states of syphilitic deterioration in which syphilitic sores and lesions were prominent. The slides, in color, were obtained from the Federal Communicable Disease Center in Atlanta.

The above procedure was designed to extinguish approach responses and arousal responses to men. To strengthen approach and arousal responses to females the patient was encouraged to use, while masturbating, stimuli involving females, such as pictures of female breasts and genitalia, or fantasies about women. Also, he was instructed to write out in detail a description of a woman toward whom he could feel some arousal. Included in the description was what she would look like, how she would behave toward him, and what kind of personality she would have. He was encouraged to use this kind of female in sexual fantasy during masturbation. Also he was instructed in flirting and was encouraged to try flirting with some of the women at work who reminded him of the ideal woman. The theory underlying these approaches is to condition stimuli associated with women that would lead to arousal by pairing the stimuli with the arousal and tension reduction accompanying masturbation. In addition an approach toward women that was gratifying and rewarding— flirting with women at work—should strengthen the approach response to females and increase the probability of arousal to female stimuli.

One problem that occurred early in the treatment of this patient was the inability of any female stimuli to elicit arousal. Consequently, it was decided that during masturbation the patient would begin with male stimuli and then slowly replace parts of the fantasy with female stimuli. For example, the patient may begin with imagery involving his having anal intercourse with another male (active), then move to anal intercourse with a female and then imagery of vaginal intercourse with a female. At present this patient is still in treatment, but he reports an increase of frequencies of arousal to females from zero per day to an average of four or five times per day. Also, he has no difficulty in visualizing female stimuli during masturbation. He has dated a woman from work twice. He still engages in homosexual activity but reports that it is less pleasurable and the frequency of contacts has dropped about 50 percent.

All of the respondent approaches discussed here thus require two major prerequisites to be successfully employed: first, that the patient is capable of using imagery and learning relaxation, and second, that he is cooperative and willing to engage in the treatment techniques. Where these prerequisites are not obtained, real stimuli such as slides, film, or actual events (e.g., riding in elevator for elevator phobia) are used. Cooperation has been shaped by using tokens for the number of trials accomplished. Generally the respondent methods have failed when the patient was unable to learn the proper relaxation techniques, or was deficient in using imagery.

Results and Problems

By the gross criterion of recidivism rates, the BMP has been quite successful. Only one of the patients returned to base rate levels of behavior and it appeared that she would probably need to be re-hospitalized. The patient was a 36-year-old white woman whose major behavioral difficulty was a fear of being alone. She was treated initially by the standard Wolpian technique of desensitization with only mild success. Part of the difficulty stemmed from the fact that when she had a home visit, her husband reinforced her avoidance behavior of being alone by elaborate arrangements to have someone with her at all times. Frequently, he would come home from work in the middle of the day if another person could not be obtained. On the unit an operant program was begun in which the patient earned tokens for being alone for longer and longer periods of time and for being further and further away from people by walking about the spacious grounds of the Institute. This program was markedly successful as the tokens bought more time for her in the BMP and she was able to reach criterion at a rate much more rapidly than had been expected. Unfortunately at that point her husband was transferred to another state and the later phases of the token program could not be initiated. A letter was received from the patient about a month after discharge indicating that her old behavior had returned to its previous level and she was thinking of applying for admission at a local treatment facility near her city.

The failure of the case highlights two problems. The first is a major one in any treatment approach—the role other family members play in maintaining and reinforcing the patient's maladaptive behavior. It is not necessary to postulate complex need states on the part of family members, such as needs to keep the patient sick in order to prevent the family members' own breakdowns. It is only necessary to teach the family members new behaviors which are low in their heirarchy but which, when emitted, can reinforce more appropriate behavior in the patient. Family members frequently act from ignorance rather than from complex dynamic interactions. Once they are informed how to behave and are reinforced for that new behavior by the therapist and by changes in the patient they begin to change quite rapidly.

Case F

A good example of the above is the role a husband played in maintaining his wife's delusional symptom. She believed that any food she touched was instantly contaminated and therefore could not be eaten. This behavior generalized to food prepared by others except food prepared by her husband. Consequently her husband who was very sympathetic and understanding of her anxiety and her difficulties would prepare most of the meals for the family. Frequently the patient would begin to suspect that this food also was somehow contaminated and consequently the family would go out to eat. They would try several restaurants with much oscillating on the part of the patient as to its being contaminated or not. The husband of the patient was instructed in the operant dimensions of his wife's behavior and it was pointed out to him how his responses were maintaining the behavior. A program was designed for shaping the wife's behavior by changing the contingencies. Only one meal would be prepared by the husband and if the wife did not want to eat it she did not have to but the family would go ahead and eat. If the wife could prepare just a part of a meal such as dessert or coffee the family could go out to eat the next day, something which the wife actually liked to do. One restaurant would be tried and again the family members would eat their food and the wife could do as she wanted. If she did not eat, there would be no other food until the next meal. The husband was instructed to pay little attention to his wife's eating behavior and attend to her with affection and approval when she would prepare meals and/or when she would eat the food she prepared or the food prepared for her in the restaurant. Within a 6-week period of time the wife was preparing and eating all the meals at home. Her feeling that the food was contaminated had disappeared except for infrequent and mild recurrences. The husband was encouraged and reinforced for reinforcing his wife and the new behavior on both their parts has not returned to base rate level.

Another problem that leads to failure with operant approaches is economic inflation. If there is nothing available to buy with the tokens, the tokens rapidly lose their value and the rate of emission of new behavior drops to zero. In one instance with a group of acting-up adolescents almost all the reinforcing events that could be bought with tokens became unobtainable. Escorted walks to a nearby shopping plaza had to be discontinued because of staff shortages, and movies were discontinued for several months because of budget cuts in the recreational therapy department. Consequently the adolescents had more tokens than they could spend and so acting up continued.

A final problem which determines the success or failure of the operant token plans is the question of when to discontinue the tokens. Theoretically, it is argued, the new behaviors that are being learned are inherently self-reinforcing and have a greater probability of eliciting social reinforcement in the environment. The difficulty is to decide when the behaviors are being maintained by self-reinforcement and/or by verbal and social reinforcers. The two ways the BMP has found relatively successful are first to discontinue the tokens and measure the changes in the frequency of the target behavior. If the rate begins to slow down or begins to return to base rate level, the tokens are still needed; if the behavior does not change in its frequency of occurrence, it is time to discontinue the tokens. Some prediction of the length of time still needed in a token program can be made by the rate of return to base rate levels when the tokens are withheld. If the slope is steep, a longer time on the tokens will be required than if the slope is very gradual. Both decelerations indicate, however, that tokens are still needed. A second method is to ask the patient if he thinks he can get along without the tokens and would he like to try to keep the new behavior occurring without tokens. Usually patients are fairly accurate and honest in their reactions though it is suggested that behavioral data still be collected and the token plans reinstituted if indicated.

The Future

Aside from the above difficulties and failures the BMP continues to grow and plans are being made for a more extensive follow-up program on discharged patients as well as a more complete assessment of patients who have already been discharged since the inception of the program.

Also, the use of behavior modification groups or behavior education groups is being investigated (Parrino *et al.*, 1968). The use of subprofessionals as well as lay people such as volunteers and parents is being explored and discussions with local university psychology departments concerning training programs for such groups is already under way. And finally the use of behavior modification in the community mental health movement is being investigated and small consultative programs have begun with a half-way house program for mentally retarded adults and with a county home for delinquent and foster children.

REFERENCES

Atthowe, J. M. & Krasner, L. A preliminary report of the application of contingent reinforcement procedures (token economy) on a "chronic" psychiatric ward. *Journal of Abnormal Psychology,* 1968, **73**, 37.

Ayllon, T. & Azrin, N. *The token economy: A motivation system for therapy and rehabilitation.* New York: Appleton-Century-Crofts, 1968.

Ayllon, T. & Michael, J. The psychiatric nurse as a behavioral engineer. *Journal of Experimental Analysis of Behavior,* 1959, **2**, 323–334.

Cautela, J. R. Covert Sensitization. *Psychological Reports,* 1967, **20**, 459–468.

Cautela, J. R. & Kastenbaum, M. A reinforcement survey schedule for use in therapy, training and research. *Psychological Reports,* 1967, **20**, 1115–1130.

Goldiamond, I. Self-control procedures in personal behavior problems. *Psychological Reports,* 1965, **17**, 851–868.

Kanfer, F. H. Comments on learning in psychotherapy. *Psychological Reports,* 1961, **9**, 681–699.

Lindsley, O. R. Operant conditioning methods applied to research in chronic schizophrenia. *Psychiatric Research Reports,* 1956, **5**, 118–139.

Lindsley, O. R. Direct measurement and prosthesis of retarded behavior. *Journal of Education,* 1964, **147**, 62–81.

Parrino, J., Slavin, D., Miller, J. & Lyons, T. The use of behavior education groups and behavior modification techniques with psychiatric In-patients. Unpublished mimeograph, Georgia Mental Health Institute, Atlanta, Georgia, 1968.

Skinner, B. F. *Science and human behavior.* New York: Macmillan, 1953.

Siprelle, C. Induced anxiety. *Psychotherapy: Theory, research and practice,* 1967, **4**, 36–40.

Ullmann, L. & Krasner, L. (Eds.), *Case studies in behavior modification.* New York: Holt, Rinehart & Winston, 1965.

Wolpe, J. *Psychotherapy by reciprocal inhibition.* Stanford: Stanford University Press, 1958.

Wolpe, J. & Lang, P. J. A fear survey scheduled for use in behavior therapy. *Behaviour research and therapy*, 1964, **2**, 27.

Wolpe, J. & Lazarus, A. A. *Behavior therapy techniques: A guide to the treatment of neuroses*. New York: Pergamon Press, 1966.

CHAPTER 13

The Token Economy as a Rehabilitative Procedure in a Mental Hospital Setting[1]

Leonard Krasner and John M. Atthowe, Jr.

One of the more recent developments in rehabilitation procedures in mental hospital settings has been the establishment of token economy programs. As other chapters in this book describe token programs in settings other than mental hospitals, this chapter will focus on token programs as they developed in mental hospitals, the techniques involved in setting up such programs, the results of such programs, and implications for future programs.

The token economy is a highly complex program involving the behavior of all of the individuals in the ward setting, including both staff and patients. It is not a mechanical program but rather a humanistic one which focuses on treatment of the individual patient as a human being who can determine his own fate. It basically involves the development of techniques of training the staff so that they can react to patients in such a way as to maximize the likelihood of the patients receiving positive reinforcement from others.

A major thesis of this chapter is that token economy programs are illustrative of the more general approach of behavior modification or behavior therapy. Thus we must start with a delineation of what behavior modification is. This is not easy because it is clear that there are considerably different and sometimes incompatible views on this subject, and it would take more than a few sentences to adequately conceptualize the parameters of behavior modification or therapy.

However, at this point, behavior therapy can be conceptualized as a behavior influence procedure which utilizes the findings of experimental, especially learning, and social psychology in directly

[1]Support for research described in this paper came, in part, from USPHS Research Grant No. 11938 from the National Institute of Mental Health.

modifying the behavior of individuals who have been labeled in some manner as being socially deviant. Within this rubric, a behavior modification program would involve such behavior influencing procedures as contingency management, positive and negative reinforcement, extinction of undesirable behavior, shaping of alternative desirable behavior, desensitization to aversive stimuli, modeling or vicarious reinforcement, self-reinforcement, shaping self-control, the maximization of expectancy of help in both the giver and the recipient of reinforcement, and emphasizing the importance of training in order to shape staff, patient, and community behavior. As we shall see, token programs contain all of these elements and as such are clearly prototypical behavior therapy.

Specifically, a token economy program may be defined in terms of the operations involved in planning for it, setting it up, and carrying it out. This involves at least five procedures. *First*, there is systematic observation of the patient's behavior and its consequences in the ward environment. *Second*, there is the designation of certain specific behaviors as desirable, hence reinforceable. These may include behaviors such as dressing, shaving, talking, working, writing, or any other behavior that is socially useful and of initial low frequency. This designation may be made by the staff, by the patients, or by a combination of both. The *third* element is the determination of what environmental events may serve as reinforcers for the individual; that is, what are the good things in life or what is a person willing to work for? This may include food, a bed, a smile, a chance to sit in a chair, an opportunity to see a therapist, a pass, or even discharge from the hospital. Anything a patient frequently does on his own can serve as a reinforcer for less frequent behavior (Premack, 1965). For example, we found that sitting in over-stuffed chairs on the ward was not only all that some patients did, but it was also their prime reinforcer. The *fourth* element is a medium of exchange, the token, which connects elements two and three. The token stands for the back-up reinforcer (it can act as a discriminative or a reinforcing stimulus or both) and as such may be a real tangible object such as a plastic card or a green stamp that one can handle, or it may be a mark on a piece of paper or a point scored which the individual knows is there but to which he has no access. The *fifth* element relates to the economic or supply and demand aspects of the program. For example, what value (how many tokens) should you receive for shaving yourself in relation to how many tokens are necessary to purchase a desirable reinforcer such as a package of cigarettes? At this point we begin to enter a very complex relationship which is clearly analagous to what occurs in our everyday life. There is one notable difference however. In the world outside the hospital, man's wants are generally unlimited and their satisfaction limited. In the hospital, patients' wants are generally limited; consequently positive reinforcers are hard to find.

Historical Background

Before describing our own experiences with token programs, it is important to place these programs within a historical context. The most direct origin of these programs is in the work of Ayllon (Ayllon & Azrin, 1965). Ayllon's program, to be described briefly later, was formulated in the context of the application of *operant conditioning* techniques to molar behavior in a psychiatric ward. Thus the token approach is traceable to Skinner's (1938) formulation of the differences between operant and respondent behavior and its application to the control of the behavior of organisms starting with the rat and the pigeon. Previous works (Krasner & Ullmann, 1965; Ullmann & Krasner, 1965) have traced the development of operant procedures to individuals with the social label of psychosis, neurosis, behavior problem, or mental retardation.

A second, and related, historical context into which the development of token economies can be fit is the growth and development of behavior therapy and behavior modification procedures in general. The behavior modification approach emphasizes changing behavior *directly* and clearly disavows a disease model of causation. The token economy program represents an extension of the procedures used in earlier "one-to-one" applications of operant procedures to emotionally disturbed individuals. The verbal conditioning studies (Krasner, 1958, 1965a) illustrated how the effects of verbal behavior could be systematically manipulated by the contingent responses of the experimenter. Out of these various studies emerged strong evidence that certain behaviors or physical objects could serve as reinforcing events when they were used systematically to follow specified verbal and motor behaviors.

There have also been a number of investigations which have demonstrated that many of the disturbing programs and behaviors of hospitalized patients had been maintained by intermittent reinforcement or reinforcement of undesirable behavior by the hospital staff within a hospital setting (Gelfand et al., 1967). Ayllon and Michael (1959) demonstrated this point with a series of studies showing how such behaviors as psychotic talk, withdrawal, hoarding, and refusal to eat, are actually maintained rather than discouraged by social reinforcement.

In addition the token economy is historically related to the use of procedures which involve the control, to varying degrees, of the hospital environment to attain a specific objective with patients. This line of development goes back to at least the moral treatment program developed by Pinel, Rush, and other hospital superintendents of the early 1800's. The general approach of the moral treatment group was to view the patient as a responsible individual; in many ways not very different from the therapist himself. "There but for the grace of God go I," expressed the attitude of the therapist. With this in mind his approach to the patient involved creating an atmosphere in the hospital which made certain demands upon the patient such as working, taking certain forms of recreation, and being generally alert to the world about him while being encouraged to do these things. In effect the therapists were saying that this is "the kind of treatment program I would expect if I were to be hospitalized" which could certainly happen since what is involved is a difficulty in problems of daily living and not physical disease. Bockoven (1963) and Dain (1964) have presented excellent reviews of the historical growth and the eventual destruction of moral treatment. Its failure was primarily that of neglect in the training of new therapists, in not systematizing the techniques, and in the ascendance of the medical model in psychiatry.

Another predecessor to the token program is the movement initiated in the mid-1950's called therapeutic community or milieu control (Jones, 1953). The aim of these programs was to control the patient's environment in such a way that "good" behavior would be likely to occur. In many ways the theoretical rationale of the thera-puetic community was very different from that of a token economy. However, in their desire to affect the attitudes of the staff and to foster democratic decision making on the part of patients, the therapeutic community advocates laid the basis for the token programs. It is very meaningful in explaining token programs to staff to emphasize the continuity of token programs with the familiar, late, and perhaps, unlamented, therapeutic community program.

Instituting Token Programs

It is true of any research program that it is unwise to undertake it unless there is full support from the institutional management. This is especially so with token economy programs. Support in this instance does not necessarily mean financial in the sense of funds for staff over and above usual coverage. Token programs do not require augmented staff. However, support is absolutely necessary on a subtler level. Staff, such as aides and nurses, will be required to do things differently. The basic prescription of noncontingent TLC (tender loving care) is changed to contingent TLC, and the TLC is mediated via tokens. In every institutional setting there is strong resistance to change. A way of life is being tampered with. "We have *always* done things this way." The fact that a new method may be more efficient and actually more enjoyable to the staff is never accepted at face value.

Management support in effect means that the key power people in the institution are giving their sanction for doing something differently, but this should never be forced down the throats of the staff. Management may not be clear as to what is involved in the program, but it must indicate that it is taking the responsibility for bringing about *change*. This support may be communicated directly by memorandum or more effectively through the subtle unofficial grapevine which exists in every institution. This latter route is far more effective. The attitudes of the staff, however, should be favorably modified before the research or treatment aspect of the program is instituted if covert resistance is to be eliminated.

The first step in planning the program is the designation of the goals of the program. This would be determined by observation of the patients selected, their age, and their problems. For example, what is a reasonable goal for a particular individual? Could he return to his family? Will he be placed in a foster home? Could he be living by himself or with a group of other ex-patients?

It is the setting of goals (or target behaviors), which is not only the first task but is also the major task. More often than not it is the *failure* to set the goals which undermines any treatment program. Once there can be agreement on the goals, the means to achieve them are far less difficult. The fact that the delineation of goals is the first step in any behavior therapy program should not mean that such programs are inflexible. Goals or specified desirable behaviors are constantly changing. For example, the behavior such as shaving oneself which pays off this week with one token may be incorporated into a more complex behavior such as that of "appearing neat" the following week.

However, the initial step of setting goals is still quite limited. A broader issue is at stake, one that most investigators find difficult to verbalize; namely, what is the social goal or overall purpose of doing a particular investigation? Do you want to do a research project that will compare the effectiveness of a token program with some other kind of procedure or a particular kind of control procedure? Does the investigator wish to set up a demonstration program that will have some dramatic effects in the institution? Does he wish to set up a program for the ordinary "way of life" on the ward that will result in a more exciting life for the individual patient and the staff? Or is the goal to return the patient to the community and to keep him there? Whatever this broad goal may be, it will determine the procedures the investigator will use in setting up his training program for the staff and those he will use to influence the management of the institution as to the feasibility and desirability of the program.

Staff Selection and Training

In setting up a token program, the training of the staff is a key element. Basically a token program requires that the ward staff has been trained to react in a specific and contingent manner to the patients. There are several points that must be considered. There is the initial selection of the staff, the training of the staff, and the setting up of the record-keeping procedures so that the staff tasks are minimal and self-monitoring.

The selection of staff could involve working with those people who are already on the ward, training a new staff of nurses and attendants, staffing a token ward with a new breed of staff, the psychological technician, or some combination of the above. Seeking volunteers from the various services is effective if chronic malcontents can be screened out.

As in any program involving the effects of staff behavior upon patients, the selection of staff for a token economy program is crucial. The essence of a token program are the contingencies administered by the staff. A token program is not an automatic one in which staff act as robots but rather a program in which, to some extent, thoughful decisions must be made continuously by the staff. Not only is training in new behaviors involved, but a considerable amount of unlearning of previous attitudes. Because of the general training in noncontingent TLC, the hospital staff is likely to reinforce and maintain many undesirable behaviors. As an extreme illustration of this, Ayllon and Michael (1959) observed a nurse who nods her head and looks as if she is raptly interested as the patient describes her delusional thoughts while the nurse, in reality, is not listening. Yet the verbalization of the delusional material is being maintained by the behavior of being listened to. A happy balance must be established between selecting individuals who are completely untrained in hospital procedures and those who are so well-trained that they cannot change.

A discussion of staff selection implies starting a token program from scratch, which is the usual procedure. However, it is far more likely that a token program would be initiated on an ongoing ward with much the same staff already there. This means that the plans for a token program have to be presented in such a way that they will not increase the staff's anxiety which is always felt whenever a new program is introduced on a ward. The presentation must not only allay any imagined threat to the status of staff members but, at the same time, it must engender the staff's enthusiasm which is as much a prerequisite for the success of a token program as it is for any treatment program. In larger programs, the communication difficulty can be bypassed by creating a policy committee, a research, training and treatment committee, from among the number of *all* the participating hospital services. Let the main dissenters help solve the problems.

It is strongly suggested that the individual planning the token program, whether he be a psychologist, psychiatrist, social worker, or nurse, be the one who initially presents the idea of a token program to the staff. Frequent contact and discussion with the staff must be considered an integral part of the program and cannot be left to technicians. The specifics of the presentation will, of course, vary according to the details of particular programs. However, the presentation should include at least the following elements: the presentation should continue over the life of the program; the staff should not be "talked down to"; the continuity with what people do routinely should be stressed; the key role of the nursing staff in carrying out or sabotaging the program should be emphasized; the importance of record-keeping, "to see how well we are doing," must be pointed out but not to the point of making it look like a burden; that there will be considerable prestige involved in being connected with a new and innovative program should be implied; and staff participation in solving problems and developing contingencies should be fostered. Staff members frequently have their own pet ward problems that they would like resolved.

A major ingredient of a token economy program, therefore, is the training program set up by the investigators to train the staff. The staff is trained by the token handling itself in what to observe: the behavior of patients, the consequences of such behavior in terms of the reactions of others, and how to control their own behavior so as to react appropriately to the patients. The point is repeatedly made (e.g., Ayllon & Azrin, 1968) that the staff in a mental hospital should always use a reward or incentive system and minimize the use of punishment. However, as Ayllon and Azrin point out, as much as rewards are desirable and effective, "in practice rewards are usually intuitive, incidental, infrequent, often trivial, unstandardized, and given with little regard to their relationship to the rewarded performance" (p. 10). Thus the starting point in a training program, after the initial selection of the staff, is demonstration to the staff that the new program represents nothing radically new. This is important because anything that is considered radically new is frightening and uncomfortable to a hospital staff. The major change between what they had been doing in the past and what would be required of them now is greater systematization, a more specific contingency reward system, and continual feedback as to the effectiveness of their treatment methods.

Each of the programs set up thus far has developed its own training procedures. A written manual outlining the psychological principles is very useful. Mertens and Fuller (1964), for example, had developed one for use with staff and patients. The manual by Schaefer and Martin (1969) is particularly useful in that it includes many useful suggestions on record-keeping and other specific behaviors expected of staff. The use of standardized films, such as the film Reinforcement Therapy distributed by Smith, Kline, and French (1966) which includes a description of the token economy program at Patton State Hospital and the use of tokens with retarded children are helpful.

In the planning and training phase, discussions, group meetings, and role-taking, are all useful training techniques. The period of staff training should last at least several weeks. After the selection and initial training of staff, patients must be taught the potential value of tokens and how to use them. With patients who are in relatively good contact this can be done by group meetings, explanations, films, manuals, and making a few frequently utilized reinforcers (such as food or going to the "mess hall," tobacco products, money, etc.) contingent upon the receipt of tokens. Patients can also be useful in making suggestions both as to target behavior and the rewards for which tokens may be utilized. With patients who are severely regressed, it may be necessary to shape token responsivity in small, specific steps. For example, a patient may be handed a token and told to hand it right back in order to get a cigarette. If he doesn't respond, the aide may have to do everything at first, including handing the token to the patient and then taking it out of his hand and replacing it with a cigarette, or modeling the actual behavior involved. These kinds of training procedures should last until the staff feels most patients are familiar with the program. This should probably take two to four weeks. It is better if all of the contingencies are not imposed initially. Receiving something extra should be stressed rather than the avoidance of unpleasant activities. Very costly "incentives," such as getting drunk, assault, AWOL, etc, should be introduced after the program is established.

An Illustrative Token Economy

Ayllon and Azrin (1965) reported the results of the first use of a token economy program in a psychiatric hospital ward. In a later book (1968) the authors go into great detail about their program and its results. The behaviors selected for reinforcement by Ayllon and Azrin included such things as serving meals, cleaning floors, sorting laundry, washing dishes, and self-grooming. Reinforcement, in many cases, was the opportunity to continue to engage in these activities. Thus the reinforcers selected were *part of the normal hospital environment.*

Ayllon and Azrin (1965) made no *a priori* decisions about what might be an effective reinforcer, but observed the patients' behavior to discover what they actually did, the first step in any token or behavior modification program. The reinforcers included such items as: rooms available for rent; selection of people to dine with; passes; a chance to speak to the ward physician, chaplain, or psychologist; opportunities for viewing television; candy; cigarettes; and other amenities of life. Tokens serve to bridge the gap between behavior and an ultimate reinforcement. These investigators placed particular emphasis on the objective definition, the quantification of the responses and reinforcers, and upon programming and recording procedures, all of which are basic aspects of behavior therapy.

Ayllon and Azrin (1965) reported a series of six experiments in each of which they demonstrated that target behavior changed systematically as a function of the token reinforcement. One experiment is typical of the procedures they developed. The behavior in which they were interested consisted of work assignments on the ward. A patient selected the job he most preferred from a list of available jobs for which he could receive tokens. After 10 days he was told that he could continue working on this job but would be given no tokens for it. Of the eight patients observed, seven selected another job immediately, and the eighth patient switched a few days later. In the third phase of the experiment, the contingencies were reversed (a procedure frequently employed in operant field research) and the jobs that had been preferred originally again earned tokens. All eight patients immediately switched back to their original jobs.

The results of six experiments described by Ayllon and Azrin demonstrated that the reinforcement procedure was effective in maintaining the desired performance. In each experiment the performance fell to near zero when the established response-reinforcement relation was discontinued. On the other hand, reintroduction of the reinforcement procedure restored performance almost immediately and maintained it at a high level.

The Ayllon and Azrin token economy was used on a ward for long-stay female patients in a midwestern state hospital. Another token economy program (Krasner, 1965b, 1966; Atthowe, 1966; Atthowe & Krasner, 1968) was set up in a Veterans Administration Hospital in California.

An 86-bed closed ward in the custodial section of the hospital was selected. The median age of the patients was 57 years and more than one-third were over 65. The overall length of their hospitalization varied from 3 to 48 years, with a median length of hospitalization of 22 years. Most of the patients had previously been labeled as chronic schizophrenics; the remainder were classified as having some organic involvement.

The patients fell into three general performance classes. The largest group, approximately 60 percent of the ward, required constant supervision. Whenever they left the ward, an aide had to accompany them. The second group, about 25 percent, had ground privileges and were able to leave the ward unescorted. The third group, 15 percent of the patients, required only minimal supervision.

In order to insure a stable research sample, 60 patients were selected to remain on the ward for the duration of the study. The patients selected were older and had, for the most part, obvious and annoying behavioral deficits. This "core" sample served as the experimental population in studying the long-term effectiveness of the research program, the token economy.

Based on the work of Ayllon and his associates and the principle of reinforcement as espoused by Skinner (1938, 1953), every important phase of ward and hospital life was incorporated within a systematic contingency program. The attainment of the "good things in life" was made contingent upon the patient's performance.

If a patient adequately cared for his personal needs, attended his scheduled activities, helped on the ward, interacted with other patients, or showed increased responsibility in any way, he was rewarded. The problem was to find rewards that were valued by everyone. Consequently, tokens, which in turn could be exchanged for the things a patient regards as important or necessary, were introduced.

Cigarettes, money, passes, watching television, etc., were examples of the more obvious reinforcers but some of the most effective reinforcers, such as sitting on the ward or feeding kittens, were idiosyncratic.

In general, each patient was reinforced immediately after the completion of some "therapeutic" activity but those patients who attended scheduled activities by themselves were paid their tokens only once a week on a regularly scheduled pay day. Consequently, the more independent and responsible patient had to learn "to punch a time card" and receive his "pay" at a specified future date. He then had to "budget" his tokens so they covered his wants for the next seven days.

In addition, a small group of 12 patients was in a position of receiving what might be considered the ultimate in reinforcement. They were allowed to become independent of the token system. These patients carried a "carte blanche" which entitled them to all the privileges within the token economy plus a few added privileges and a greater status. For this special status, the patient had to work 25 hours per week in special vocational assignments and assume more responsibility in the operation of the ward. In order to become a member of the "elite group," patients had to accumulate 120 tokens which entailed long-term planning and a considerable delay in gratification.

The general outline of the investigation involved a 6 month baseline period, a 3-month shaping period, and an 11-month experimental period. During the baseline period, the frequency of particular behaviors was recorded daily, and ratings were carried out periodically. The shaping period was largely devoted to those patients requiring continual supervision. These latter patients were very apathetic and withdrawn. They seemed to have no wants and would do nothing without staff intervention. At first, the availability of canteen booklets, which served as money in the hospital canteen, was made contingent upon the amount of scheduled activities a patient attended. It soon became clear that almost one-half of the patients were not interested in money or canteen books. They did not know how to use the booklets, and they never bought things for themselves. Consequently, for six weeks patients were taken to the canteen and urged or "cajoled" into buying items which seemed to interest them (e.g., coffee, ice cream, pencils, handkerchiefs, etc.). Then all contingencies were temporarily abandoned, and patients were further encouraged to utilize the canteen books. All the while every idiosyncratic act of each patient was noted and recorded. Next, tokens were introduced but on a noncontingent basis. No one was allowed to purchase items in the ward canteen without first presenting tokens. Patients were instructed to pick up tokens from an office directly across the hall from the ward canteen and exchange them for the items they desired. After two weeks the tokens were made *contingent* upon performance and the experimental phase of the study began.

Other than an automatic timer for the television set, the only major piece of equipment was the tokens. After a considerable search, a durable and physically safe token was constructed. This token was a $1\frac{3}{4} \times 3\frac{1}{2}$ inch plastic, nonlaminated, file card which came in eight colors varying from a bright red to a light tan. Different exchange values were assigned to the different colors. The token had the appearance of the usual credit card so prevalent in our society.

Whenever possible, the giving of the tokens was accompanied by some expression of social approval such as smiling, "good," "fine job," and a verbal description of the contingencies involved. For example,

"Here's a token because of the good job of shaving you did this morning."

At the completion of the experimental period, there was a significant increase in all target behaviors. An example is the frequency of attendance at group activities. During the baseline period, the average hourly rate of attendance per week was 5.85 hours per patient. With the introduction of tokens, this rate increased to 8.4 the first month and averaged 8.5 during the experimental period, except for a period of 3 months when the reinforcing value of the tokens was increased from one to two tokens per hour of attendance. Increasing the reinforcing value of the tokens increased the contingent behavior accordingly. With an increase in the amount of reinforcement, activity increased from 8.4 hours per week in the month before to 9.2 the first month under the new schedule. This gain was maintained throughout the period of greater reinforcement and for 1 month thereafter.

A widening of interest and a lessening of apathy were shown by a marked increase in the number of patients going on passes, drawing weekly cash, and utilizing the ward canteen. Of the core sample of 60 patients, 80 percent had never been off the hospital grounds on their own for a period of eight hours since their hospitalization. During the experimental period, 19 percent went on overnight or longer passes, 17 percent went on day passes, and 12 percent went out on accompanied passes for the first time. In other words, approximately a half of those who had been too apathetic to leave the hospital grounds increased their interest and commitment in the world outside. Furthermore, 13 percent of the core sample left on one or more trial visits of at least 30 days during the token program. Of those who left the hospital four out of every 10 remained out of the hospital.

For the entire ward, the lessening of apathy was dramatic. The number of patients going on passes and drawing weekly cash tripled. Twenty-four patients were discharged and 8 were transferred to more active and discharge-oriented ward programs as compared to 11 discharges and no such transfers in the preceding 11-month period. Of the 24 patients released, 11 returned to the hospital within nine months. Discharges were not stressed nor programmed in this study. A discharge meant that the patient's performance had improved to the point that it would have been "poor treatment" to keep him hospitalized. The high rate of return in this and most other programs points to the necessity of further shaping to maintain the ex-patient in the community.

Independence and greater self-sufficiency were shown by an increase in the number of patients receiving tokens for shaving and appearing neatly dressed. Fewer patients missed their showers, and bed-wetting markedly diminished.

At the beginning of the study, there were 12 bed-wetters, 4 of whom were classified as "frequent" wetters and 2 were classified as "infrequent." All bed-wetters were awakened and taken to the bathroom at 11:00, 12:30 p.m., 2:00, and 4:00 a.m. regularly. As the program progressed, patients who did not wet during the night were paid tokens the following morning. In addition, they were only awakened at 11:00 p.m. the next night. After a week of no bed-wetting, patients were taken off the schedule altogether. At the end of the experimental period, no one had wet for the preceding four weeks. For all practical purposes, there were no bed-wetters on the ward. The aversive schedule of being awakened during the night together with social pressure from other patients whose sleep had been disturbed plus the receiving of tokens for a successful non-bed-wetting night seemed to instigate getting up on one's own and going to the bathroom, even in markedly deteriorated and lobotomized patients.

Another ward problem which had required extra aide coverage in the mornings was the lack of "cooperativeness" in getting out of bed, making one's bed, and leaving the bed area by a specified time. Just before the system of specific contingency tokens were introduced, the number of infractions in each of these areas was recorded for three weeks. This three week baseline period yielded an average of 75 "infractions" per week for the entire ward, varying from 71 to 77. A token given daily was then made contingent upon not having a recorded infraction in any of the three areas above. This token was given as the patients lined up to go to breakfast each morning. In the week following the establishment of the contingency, the frequency of infractions dropped to 30 and then to 18 by the end of the second week. The next week the number of infractions rose to 39 but then declined steadily to 5 per week by the end of nine weeks. During the last six months, the frequency of infractions varied between 6 and 13, averaging 9 per week.

These few illustrations are cited as evidence for the effectiveness of the tokens in shaping socially desirable, responsive, and active behaviors. As such, they are consistent with the earlier reports of Ayllon and Azrin and the subsequent investigators of token economy (e.g., Schaefer & Martin, 1966).

Economic Variables

We have offered this description of our experiences with a token program primarily to illustrate a number of important points in setting up and running token economy programs. In planning a token program one must consider the economic realities of life. For example, what is the relationship between token intake and expenditure, and wages and prices? Winkler (1968a,b) has used a token economy similar to the ones we have described on a mental ward in a hospital in Australia to ingeniously investigate hospital economics.

Our own program involved elementary economic systems, such as the discount system (tokens remaining at the end of a month were then discounted at 75 percent for the following month so that patients would be more active) and the banking system (so that people could save for long-term objectives such as a trial visit, moving into the "elite" group, etc.). It is, however, the Winkler studies which raise many exciting research opportunities for testing economic theory within token programs and vice versa.

Winkler (1968a) reports the results of a token economy program which has many of the same features as those of the earlier programs but with some additional novel features added. This program was established in a closed female ward with patients averaging 49 years of age and 12 years of hospitalization in Gladesville Hospital, New South Wales, Australia. The patients' behavior was characterized by an excessive amount of violence and screaming as well as apathy and general lack of response to the ward environment. Winkler gave particular emphasis to economic factors. For example, prices and wages were initially arranged so that the patients' average daily income tended to exceed their average daily expenditure. This basic economic fact of life, that income must equal or exceed output, is necessary for a viable economy. However, the economic aspects of a token economy may be in dispute just as a Keynesian approach in our broader society may differ from a more standard conservative approach.

Winkler reports that without exception, every type of behavior that was reinforced improved. In addition, behaviors not specifically in the program, such as making loud noises, decreased. Winkler also reported a significant improvement in staff morale as indicated by a drop in absenteeism. Absenteeism in the four months after the program began was 24 percent below the absenteeism for the months before the program, while in a comparable ward, absenteeism over the same periods dropped only 3 percent. In almost every token study, staff morale has noticeably improved.

In the next phase of his program Winkler (1968b) was concerned with the effect on behavior of the relationships between the number of tokens in the patients' possession (savings), the system's economic balance, and amount of reinforcement (wages). At any one time, a token system can be regarded as having a certain economic balance which may be regarded as the discrepancy between total patient income (the total number of tokens given to the patients) and total patient expenditure (the total number of tokens spent). Under normal circumstances the economic *balance* determines the speed with which patients accumulate tokens, and hence is involved in determining the number of tokens in the patient's possession at any one time (his *savings*). If income consistently exceeds expenditure over a period of time, savings will automatically increase, and, if expenditure exceeds income, savings will decrease. Both economic balance and savings are affected by many different factors in a token system, but they are perhaps most strongly affected by changes in wages and changes in prices.

Studies were designed to separate savings from economic balance in order to examine whether savings did affect token earning behavior. Savings were manipulated by abruptly changing the currency used in the system. For three weeks a new token was made the only legitimate currency, and the old tokens were useless until the three weeks ended. In effect, savings were abruptly reduced to zero for all patients. Simultaneously all prices were dropped to one token; wages remained unchanged. Expenditure was therefore lowered and economic dis-equilibrium occurred. Under the usual token system, when balance is religiously maintained such a disequilibrium would not occur without high savings. But, with the introduction of the new token, the equi-librium coincided with low savings. If savings and not the economic balance between income and expenditure were affecting performance, token-earning behavior would improve rather than deteriorate as savings increased over the 3-week period.

In six of the seven token-earning behaviors which were investi-gated, the mean daily performance in the first week of the experiment was higher than the baseline performance. The percentage improve-ments ranged from 2 percent to 52 percent, indicating that despite a higher income, the drop in savings coincided with improved perfor-mance. Tidy appearance was the only behavior not to improve. In six of the seven token-earning behaviors, mean daily performance in the first week of the experimental period was superior to the mean daily performance in the third week of the experiment when savings were high. In the third week, six of the seven behaviors had deteriorated 16 percent to 44 percent below the initial baseline. Getting up was the only behavior that did not noticeably deteriorate.

This experiment then indicated a close relationship between savings and token-earning behavior or performance. Performance under low savings was better than performance under high savings; a reduction in savings improved performance. The experiment suggests that economic balance does not affect behavior directly, but rather indirectly through the way in which it affects savings. However, the initial impact of eliminating patients' savings and decreasing prices while holding income constant was not controlled. In many instances abrupt change alone will produce an initial spurt in patients' performance. Nevertheless, Winkler's systematic observations substantiate our unsystematic observations at Palo Alto that a substantial increase in savings (tokens in the bank) will generally reduce token-earning behavior. Too many tokens on hand can result in the "wealthy" patient readily paying for nontherapeutic excesses (getting drunk, going AWOL, etc.) and not working. The most notable exception to this generalization is the "chronic hoarder" who now collects tokens rather than broken glass. We have also found that if a patient owes too many tokens, his performance will also deteriorate. That is why fines or penalties should be minimized or eliminated altogether. We would like to see Winkler's study replicated with prices exceeding income as well as income exceeding expenditure.

Winkler concludes that the process by which savings control behavior involves more than a simple fluctuation in primary deprivation level. Further analysis of the relationship between token deprivation and primary deprivation should clarify these issues. Winkler's approach, described here in some detail, represents a method of studying the natural process of reinforcement.

Extension into the Community

It was observed that most of the patients who earned their way into the "elite" group on the ward (Atthowe & Krasner, 1968) not only left the hospital but also secured a job. Progression through the token program plus working 30 to 40 hours per week in a sheltered workshop seemed to have been major contributing factors. All too often work activity or activity therapy in the mental hospital is unrelated to what the patient will do when he leaves the hospital. Therefore, we developed a series of graduated work situations within and outside the hospital.

The vehicle for this development was a nonprofit corporation, the Veterans Workshop, Inc., established both in the hospital and in the community (McDonough, 1969). Patients through the use of tokens were shaped to work their way into the workshop's on-the-grounds activity where they received a small hourly wage. In a gradual shaping process, patients were then weaned off tokens and onto greater amounts of money. In addition, patients could graduate from low-paying and simple tasks such as bundling papers for immediate reinforcement to salvaging and reconditioning telephones to soldering and wire harnessing. These latter tasks were both more demanding and higher paying. The highest paying and more prestigious tasks, however, were in the community. Three service stations are run completely by patients and ex-patients aided by a single staff member. Other off-station activities include house renovation, painting, and gardening.

Patients are being shaped in successive steps from an institutional existence, to sheltered work, and hopefully to independent work within the community. But work does not account for all of the ex-patient's day. He must live in a society of many different people with differing beliefs and values. He must be responsible for his own health and finances, and he must provide entertainment for himself when he is not working. Consequently, patients are being shaped in gradual steps to assume more and more responsibility for their own health and welfare within the hospital so that they may move into sheltered living arrangements in the community (one-quarter and half-way houses) and on to independence (*see*, Atthowe & McDonough, 1969). Tokens and positive reinforcement, whether the reinforcers be money, social recognition, or heighten status, provide an important basis for movement off the back wards and out into the community. The establishment of contingencies, the shaping of relevant behavior, and the "fading out" of tokens are necessary features in such a program.

Another interesting extension of token programs into the community is the "Spruce House" program in Philadelphia (Henderson, 1969). Instead of dealing with patients on the way out, Spruce House treats patients on the way in. Patients who have been diagnosed as requiring hospitalization at the State Hospital are admitted to Spruce House and thereby remain in the community. As a residential treatment program, Spruce House is oriented toward the development of social and vocational skills within a context of everyday living. The token program retains the economic structure of the larger community; residents are paid for socially or vocationally adaptive behavior and are charged for food, rent, cigarettes, etc. Spruce House functions both as a day and as a night hospital. In either case it provides a sheltered environment outside the confines of the hospital.

The next step in the extension of operant techniques into the community is the shaping of hospital personnel to follow their discharged patients and to maintain the ex-patient within the community (Atthowe, 1969b). Staff members could receive tokens or points for the number of patients discharged, the length of time a patient spends in the community, the time the ex-patient spends working, etc., and these tokens in turn could be exchanged for "hours-off," merit raises, etc.

The Hospital as a Social Institution

There is one other aspect of token programs which has to be emphasized if future programs are to be successful. In order to understand the evolution and present status of token programs, it is necessary to take a broad view of the hospital as a social system with its own system of reinforcers. The token programs, as other research programs, face many obstacles which are independent of the details of the research design. The following sets of variables must be considered in setting up research programs such as token programs in a mental hospital (Atthowe, 1969a):

1. The hospital is a self-perpetuating social system with predetermined roles and statuses, with reinforcers and contingencies, assigned to the groups and individuals comprising the system. The social system may comprise a ward staff, the hospital personnel, the patients, the local community, or any combination of these groupings.
2. Parts of the social system, such as the ward and hospital staffs, represent the experimenter variable as well as often being the experimental variable. As experimenters, the staff must be trained in the research procedures and plans.
3. The experimental subjects, the patients, consist of nonvolunteers for the most part who live and die and carry on the activities of daily living during the duration of the research in the experimental setting.
4. Hospital research is best seen as experimental social innovation, rather than research, *per se*. As such, experimental social innovation necessitates long-term and often continuous experimentation. To be effective, innovative programs must produce a relatively enduring change in the social system in which the patients find themselves; the experimental manipulation involves the creation and the persistence of an atmosphere in which communication and cooperation among staff members is a necessity. Shaping the entire social system is as much a part of the research design as the shaping of patients.

Institutional research or experimental social innovation usually takes the form of a field experiment. Its objectives are to test the effectiveness of certain conditions (e.g., treatments) which we intentionally manipulate. In so doing, we not only must test for the effectiveness of the experimental conditions, *per se*, but also their effects on the entire social system in order to insure the adoption of positive results within the system and the continuance of the program as a service function. In order that future research may again be undertaken at the same institution, the researchers must not merely pull out and write their papers. They must establish the program within the system with reinforcers to maintain its continuance. Each research program creates the atmosphere for the next one. The major objective of innovative programs is to improve or to show positive gains in the status of the patients *and* to insure the perpetuation of the gains, or, in other words, to demonstrate (behaviorally) some positive gain in a manner that can be understood by all the members of the social system. The more immediate and frequent the feedback, the easier it will be to advance the program.

In viewing the hospital as a self-perpetuating social system, it is then not surprising that token programs have elicited both enthusiasm and concern. The enthusiasm is manifested by the growth of token programs not only in mental hospitals but on into other insitutions such as those working with retardates, delinquents, and disruptive children in the classroom (Krasner, 1968; Krasner & Atthowe, 1969). The concern is manifested by the growth of administrative difficulties these programs are encountering in some mental hospital settings. It is not within the scope of this paper to discuss this in detail. However, we would like to point out several paradoxes in the current situation in regard to token economy programs in mental hospitals. These paradoxes give us a clearer understanding of these programs. Paradoxically, concern about the program increases as they appear to be effective rather than the greater acceptance that one would expect for successful programs. Some hospital staff such as nurses, attendants, psychiatrists, or psychologists oppose token programs; yet almost all reports of token programs point up that one of the major effects of these programs is the improvement of staff morale (e.g., Baldwin, 1967). In some instances, hospital administrators are reluctant to proceed with these programs yet such programs would appear to be the answer to an administrator's prayer in that they help the patients, make life more tolerable for staff, and are dramatic showpieces of a hospital treatment program at no extra cost.

Speculation as to how to explain these paradoxes leads us to the conclusion that the token programs may indeed be threatening to the social structure of current mental hospitals. Setting up a token program may be compared with the procedures used in the kinds of social planning involved in setting up utopian societies. Skinner (1948) foresaw the social implications of his operant work earlier than anyone else by setting up a token economy in a novel called *Walden Two*.

In setting up a token program, the planners are forced to ask some very basic questions, such as: What is good or desirable behavior?

What are the real reinforcers in life? What are the goals of life? These are not only difficult questions, they are also very disturbing ones. In a haphazard, unsystematic, and unplanned way, they are being approached all the time in the hospital and outside. But, for the token program, they must be approached systematically. The essence of the token program is planning so that everyone knows what he is doing. In effect the token programs are threatening to everyone concerned. The psychiatrist or psychologist is no longer the exclusive therapist. The real treatment power is avowedly in the hands of the nurses, aides, and patients, where it should be. The nurses and aides feel threatened because this may appear to make more work demands and because it apparently contradicts the accustomed medical model and traditional practice of "mental health," namely, giving tender loving care, non-contingently.

Tokens programs are a terrible threat to everyone involved because the programs *do what* they are supposed to. In effect these token economy programs are *correctly* interpreted and reacted to as a threat to the mental illness model game that we have all been playing for so long. They are a threat to the existing denigrating social role of "mental patient" and his ostracism from the community. They are a threat to the existing social roles in institutions of psychiatrists, psychologists, nurses, aides, and possibly even administrators. Token programs then may be far more revolutionary as an approach to deviant behavior than we realize at this point. Token programs in isolated back wards are tolerated and even encouraged, but unit or hospital programs are reacted to as threats to the self-perpetuating social system we call mental health.

Token programs can be used to change not only individual behavior, but social systems and institutions as well. The token economy then is one of the techniques of social change which may be the behavioral scientist's partial equivalent of the student revolution. In either case, the establishment may not be ready for change.

REFERENCES

Atthowe, J. M., Jr. The token economy: Its utility and limitations. Paper presented to Western Psychological Association, Long Beach, California, April, 1966.

Atthowe, J. M., Jr. Experimental social innovation: Shaping the social system. *Newsletter for Research in Psychology*, 1969, **11**, No. 2, 39–41. (a)

Atthowe, J. M., Jr. Experimental social innovation: Shaping the social system. Paper presented to American Psychological Association, Washington, D.C., August, 1969. (b)

Atthowe, J. M., Jr. & Krasner, L. A preliminary report on the application of contingent reinforcement procedures (Token economy on a "chronic" psychiatric ward). *Journal of Abnormal Psychology*, 1968, **73**, 37–43.

Atthowe, J. M., Jr. & McDonough, J. M. *Operations Re-entry*. 30 minute film, 1969, available from Social and Rehabilitation Services (HEW), Washington, D.C.

Ayllon, T. & Azrin, N. H. The measurement and reinforcement of behavior of psychotics. *Journal of the Experimental Analysis of Behavior*, 1965, **8**, 357–383.

Ayllon, T. & Azrin, N. H. *The token economy*. New York: Appleton-Century-Crofts, 1968.

Ayllon, T. & Michael, J. The psychiatric nurse as a behavioral engineer. *Journal of the Experimental Analysis of Behavior*, 1959, **2**, 323–334.

Baldwin, V. L. Development of social skills in retardates as a function of three types of reinforcement programs. *Dissertation abstracts*, University of Oregon, 1967, **27** (9-A), 2865.

Bockoven, J. S. *Moral treatment in American psychiatry*. New York: Springer, 1963.

Dain, N. *Concepts of insanity in the United States*, 1789–1865. New Brunswick, N.J.: Rutgers University Press, 1964.

Gelfand, D. M., Gelfand, S. & Dobson, W. R. Unprogrammed reinforcement of patients' behaviour in a mental hospital. *Behavior Research and Therapy*, 1967, **5**, 201–207.

Henderson, J. D. *Spruce House*. 30 minute film, 1969, available from Social and Rehabilitation Services (HEW), Washington, D.C.

Jones, M. *The therapeutic community*. New York: Basic Books, 1953.

Krasner, L. Studies of the conditioning of verbal behavior. *Psychological Bulletin*, 1958, **55**, 148–170.

Krasner, L. Verbal conditioning and psychotherapy. In L. Krasner and L. P. Ullmann (Eds.), *Research in behavior modification*. New York: Holt, Rinehart & Winston, 1965, 211–288. (a)

Krasner, L. Operant conditioning techniques with adults from the laboratory to "real life" behavior modification. Paper presented to American Psychological Association Sept., 1965. (b)

Krasner, L. The translation of operant conditioning procedures from the experimental laboratory to the psychotherapeutic interaction. Paper presented to the American Psychological Association. New York, Sept., 1966.

Krasner, L. Assessment of token economy programmes in psychiatric hospitals. In R. Porter (Ed.), *The role of learning in psychotherapy*. London: Churchill, 1968, 155–174.

Krasner, L. & Atthowe, J. M., Jr. Token economy bibliography. State University of New York, Stony Brook, New York, 1969.

Krasner, L. & Ullmann, L. P. (Eds.), *Research in behavior modification*. New York: Holt, Rinehart & Winston, 1965.

McDonough, J. M., The Veterans Administration and community mental health: New approaches in psychiatric rehabilitation. *Community Mental Health Journal*, 1969, **5**, 275–279.

Mertens, G. C. & Fuller, G. B. *The manual for the alcoholic*. Minnesota: Wilmar State Hospital, 1964.

Premack, D. Reinforcement theory. In D. Levine, (Ed.), *Nebraska symposium on motivation*. Lincoln: University of Nebraska Press, 1965.

Reinforcement Therapy. 45 minute film, 1966, available from Smith, Kline, and French Laboratories, 1500 Spring Garden St., Philadelphia, Pa.

Schaefer, H. H. & Martin, P. L. Behavioral therapy for "apathy" of hospitalized schizophrenics. *Psychological Reports*, 1966, **19**, 1147–1158.

Schaefer, H. H. & Martin, P. L. *Behavioral therapy*. New York: McGraw-Hill, 1969.

Skinner, B. F. *The behavior of organisms*. New York: Appleton-Century-Crofts, 1938.

Skinner, B. F. *Walden two*. New York: Macmillan, 1948.

Skinner, B. F. *Science and human behavior*. New York: Macmillan, 1953.

Ullmann, L. P. & Krasner, L. (Eds.), *Case Studies in behavior modi-fication.* New York: Holt, Rinehart & Winston, 1965.

Ullmann, L. P. & Krasner, L. *A psychological approach to abnormal behavior.* Englewood Cliffs, N.J.: Prentice-Hall, 1969.

Winkler, R. Ward management of chronic psychiatric patients by a token reinforcement system. *Australian Psychologist*, 1968, **3** (abstract). (a)

Winkler, R. Healthy and unhealthy economies. *Australian Psychologist*, 1968, **3** (abstract). (b)

Winkler, R. The conceptual analysis of token systems. *Australian Psychologist*, 1969, **4** (abstract).

CHAPTER 14

Attitude Therapy: A Behavior Modification Program in a Psychiatric Hospital

Earl S. Taulbee[1] and H. Wilkes Wright[1]

Around the turn of the 19th century the emergence of a concept of a special therapeutic environment, faith in the potential recovery of most mentally disturbed patients, and the introduction of a treatment philosophy recognizing that man's behavior is changed by a system of rewards and punishments, marked the beginning of the humane treatment of the mentally disturbed. The change in public attitude which occasioned this was not the recognition that the individual was sick rather than inhabited by evil spirits, but the recognition of the similarity between the behavior of the emotionally disturbed person and that of the "ill-behaved" child.

With the acceptance of this more humanitarian concept, treatment was undertaken by those called moral therapists,[2] whose treatment concepts and approaches were logical, humanistic, and applicable to a variety of behavior patterns. They acknowledged the human dignity of the patient, advocated that he be given as much freedom and responsibility as he was capable of assuming, and opposed in principle and spirit the system of restraint treatment.

---

[1]Now at the VA Center, Bay Pines, Florida. The hospital program described in this chapter would not have existed except for the creativity, leadership, and organizing skills of L. B. Lamm, M. D., Hospital Director at the time of initiation of this program, and the Chief of Staff, J. C. Folsom, M. D., who succeeded Dr. Lamm as Director. That such an innovative approach to treatment could be so successfully implemented testifies to the high level of dedication, skill, and enthusiasm of the entire hospital staff. Despite the authors' indebtedness to the administrative, professional, and subprofessional personnel of the hospital, the opinions expressed in this chapter are those of the authors and in no way represent the views of the Veterans Administration.

[2]As Bockoven (1956) has pointed out, early psychiatrists used "moral" as the equivalent of "emotional" or "psychological." Stresses of a psychological nature were referred to as *moral causes*. Treatment was called *moral treatment*, which meant that the patient was made comfortable, his interest aroused, his friendship invited, and discussion of his troubles encouraged. His time was managed and filled with purposeful activity.

Later, around mid-19th century, the attitude towards the emotion-ally disturbed shifted again, with the psychological conceptualization of treatment as practiced by the moral therapists being replaced by a medical concept. This shift followed the rapid gains in knowledge in the fields of neurology, anatomy, and physiology and resulted in the construction of large, centralized psychiatric hospitals. Individuals manifesting psychiatric symptoms were considered "sick" in the medical sense, and it was generally accepted that it was just a matter of time before a physiochemical basis of mental illness would be found. In the meantime, even though these "sick" individuals were not held responsible for their behavior, the public needed to be protected from them. Consequently, as asylums were built, the custodial asylum director replaced the moral therapist. With the adoption of the medical conceptual model, the increased number of big, centralized asylums or hospitals, and the decrease in number of admitted patients dis-charged as "cured," the hospitals quickly became overcrowded and had no choice but to provide little more than custodial care. Laqueur (1962) has pointed out that by 1917, most hospital care for the sufferer from psychosis and disabling psychoneurosis was strictly custodial. Shelter, food, clothing, and moderately kind supervision contributed the major part of the treatment.

The belief that the emotionally disturbed are manifesting an illness of as yet undiscovered etiology persisted largely unchallenged until quite recently. Even the tremendous influence of the psychoanalysts did not change this, despite the emphasis they placed on psychological factors in mental illnesses. Insulin and electroshock, chemotherapy, psychosurgery, restraints, and custodial care continued as the principle treatment modalities in the majority of psychiatric hospitals. There is, however, a rising tide of protest. The adequacy of the treatment of mental patients is being openly and vigorously challenged. The current writings of the eminent psychiatrist Thomas Szasz (1969) have a familiar ring and might well have been those of the moral therapists around the beginning of the 1800's. He says, "In my opinion, mental illness is a myth. People we label 'mentally ill' are not sick, and involuntary mental hospitalization is not treatment. It is punishment . . . it is necessary to distinguish between *disease* as a *biological condition* and the *sick role* as a *social status . . . illness* is a biological (physio-chemical) abnormality of the body or its functioning. A person is sick if he has diabetes, a stroke, or cancer. The *sick role*, on the other hand, refers to the social status of claiming illness or assuming the role of patient. Like husband, father, or citizen, the *sick role* denotes a certain relationship to others in the society (p. 55)."

The newer behavior therapies have not altered hospital treatment programs greatly, although they do offer many advantages over the more "dynamic" therapy—such as shorter length of treatment, availability for a larger number of patients, less verbal skill required, and other purported advantages. The question still remains as to what is to be done with the thousands of geriatric, nonmotivated, alcoholic, character disordered, and brain-damaged patients who aren't considered to be particularly responsive to either psychoanalytic or conditioning procedures. Behavior therapists have been concerned primarily with the removal of particular symptoms of individual patients, although there have been recent attempts to deal with large groups of institutionalized persons manifesting maladaptive behavior by the use of "token reinforcement" programs. There is an increasing conviction that a special therapeutic life-like environment must be established in which older behavior patterns can be modified or extinguished and new ones acquired through the application of learning principles.

One attempt to create such a special therapeutic environment for dealing with large populations of institutionalized persons, is the *Attitude Therapy* program to be described in this chapter, which was developed at the Veterans Administration Hospital, Tuscaloosa, Alabama. Underlying this treatment model and philosophy is the assumption that maladaptive behavior has been learned and results largely from the individual's distorted perceptions of himself and others. Further, it is assumed that there are maladaptive or troublesome behavioral patterns for a particular patient which can be identified and modified in order to effect better adjustment, providing the proper therapeutic situation is established. The goal then is to identify such a *behavior pattern*,[3] not an isolated symptom, note how it works, and then create an interpersonal situation in which the patient is rewarded for changing this maladaptive pattern of behaving.

Treatment Framework

Prior to the latter part of 1962, the treatment program at the Veterans Administration Hospital in Tuscaloosa, Alabama (TVAH), was quite traditional. The treatment philosophy and some of the treatment techniques of that program, like treatment programs in many psychiatric hospitals today, were no more progressive than the *Moral Therapy* programs developed during the first half of the 19th century. About a half of the patients at the TVAH had been hospitalized

---

[3]The term behavior pattern is used to represent a class or type of behavior as contrasted to specific, isolated behavioral acts.

continuously for five years or more. The majority of the hospital's 964 beds were assigned to chronic patients. Seventy-five percent or more of all patients were on locked wards. The treatment attitudes and philosophy of many of the professional and subprofessional personnel caring for the patients could be described more accurately as custodial rather than therapeutic. As only a small number of patients was discharged monthly, the waiting list was long and the reward for waiting, subsequent custodial care.

With the assignment of a new Hospital Director and a new Chief of Staff—both of whom were young, experienced, enthusiastic, and progressive—the changes that were effected in initiating an open hospital program are reminiscent of Pinel's removal of the chains from patients in the Bicetre in 1793, which initiated the program of scientific, humane treatment of patients with mental disorders. One of the most important of these changes was the adoption of a treatment philosophy holding that: (1) there is no such thing as a hopelessly ill mental patient, (2) that regardless of age, intelligence, chronicity, diagnosis (functional or organic), level of anxiety, etc., there are maladaptive behavior patterns for a particular patient that have been learned, and which can be identified and modified providing the proper therapeutic situation is established, and (3) that such a therapeutic situation can be established by the prescription of certain interpersonal *attitudes* in a manner consistent with learning theory principles of reward and punishment.

This treatment philosophy reminds one of William Tuke's conviction that mental illness resulted from stresses which could be psychological as well as physical and his advocacy that the patient be given as much freedom and responsibility as he was capable of assuming; of Pinel's faith in at least the potential recovery of his patients and his advocacy of a system of rewards and punishments adapted to the patient's behavior; of Vering's emphasis on the need for an individually prescribed treatment environment for a particular pattern of maladaptive behavior; and of the many others who stressed the similarity of the behavior of a "lunatic" and an obstinate, ill-mannered, and unruly child, and recommended shaping the conduct of both by studying the precepts and skills used by educators. Even our current awareness of the need for a more scientific approach to treatment was recognized by men in that era. One can hardly review these facts without having serious doubt as to whether many of today's psychiatric hospital treatment programs really are progressive. This doubt is reflected in another of Szasz's statements, "The Bedlams of old have been replaced by state mental hospitals and community mental health centers. But the social reality remains the same: commitment is still punishment without trial, imprisonment without time limit, and stigmatization without hope of redress (p. 57)."

The most recent historical antecedent for Attitude Therapy was a program developed at the Menninger Clinic in the 1930's. This program was well described in the writing of W. Menninger (1936) in which he outlined a hospital environment which could be used to meet the emotional needs of the patient. The psychiatrist treating the patient would prescribe the attitude to be taken by staff personnel in their contacts with the patient. The great importance of consistency in the treatment of patients was stressed. The clinic staff was assisted by the psychiatrist to find ways of: (1) providing a suitable outlet for a patient's aggressions, (2) encouraging advantageous identifications, (3) providing channels for the atonement of guilt, (4) affording a means of obtaining love, (5) encouraging the acting out of fantasies, and (6) providing an opportunity to create.

Although one who studies the Menninger article and this chapter will see similarities between the programs described, there are many very significant differences. Some of these differences stem from the comparative size of hospitals and the staff-patient ratios. A program possible in the small, well-staffed in-patient clinic rarely has applicability without modification in a very large patient population which is staffed, numerically, quite poorly. As will be seen in the following paragraph, the modifications needed to apply Attitude Therapy in the TVAH have resulted in some of the most dramatic, and potentially most significant, insights into the treatment of the psychiatric patient.

At Menninger's, the psychoanalytically-oriented person-to-person psychotherapy was viewed as the core of treatment, with an individualized hospital environment prescribed by the psychiatrist to meet the particular patient's needs. At Tuscaloosa, the individually prescribed, flexible, treatment situation carries the major therapeutic impact. The responsibility for treatment is largely on the nonprofessional staff, with the professionally trained acting as consultants or simply becoming a part of the entire treatment situation.

Adams (1948), and Carson, Margolis, Daniels, and Heine (1962), have attested to the very difficult communication problems to be resolved when implementing the Menninger program. Not only must the psychiatrist continuously keep all personnel informed as to how he wants the patient treated, but he must be sure that all personnel interpret the prescription in a uniform, consistent pattern. These writers noted that subprofessional groups tend to interpret statements in terms of their professional orientation and training.

Although a high level of effective communication is essential in creating a consistent therapeutic environment, neither Adams nor

Carson *et al.*, perceived that problems in communication are a consequence of the status hierarchy of the treatment team. The communication problem at Tuscaloosa has not been of particular significance.
The treatment teams there are team-centered, rather than leader-
centered. The treatment prescription is not passed down from leader to
team but is arrived at in a democratic way by group consensus with
equal weight being given in most instances to the vote of each team
member.

Another very significant difference exists between the Menninger
and Tuscaloosa programs, a difference which makes Attitude Therapy
a suitable subject for this volume. At Menninger's, the focus was
upon the resolution of psychodynamic conflicts of the patients. At
Tuscaloosa, the focus is on behavior. Psychodynamics are by no means
ignored, but the goal of treatment is to identify maladaptive behavior
patterns and establish a therapeutic situation which rewards more
adaptive ways of behaving. Little importance is attached to whether
or not the patient develops insight during the treatment process. What
the treatment team hopes to achieve is the development of new
behavior patterns which will permit the patient to relate and communicate in more effective ways than he could before.

To implement an Attitude Therapy program, the hospital's new
Director and new Chief of Staff immediately effected changes in the
administrative procedures, treatment philosophy, and hospital
organization. An initial step was the introduction of the treatment
philosophy described above, predominately through an active educational program for the personnel interacting directly with the patients,
and for adjunct personnel as well. The second major step was the
division of the hospital into smaller, independent treatment units. At
first only two psychiatric units and one psychiatric medically infirm
unit were organized, with one of the psychiatric units assigned approximately 500 patients. While more units would have been desirable,
the necessary professional staff was not available. Each unit was
delegated complete treatment responsibility for all patients assigned
to it.

It was recognized that although everyone in the treatment situation
would have significance to the patient, those with the greatest contact
would have, potentially, the greatest therapeutic impact. It was
believed that the nursing assistants could be trained to deal with
patients in a highly therapeutic fashion, and that they would enjoy
such a role. Therefore, the major portion of the direct therapeutic
responsibilities of the hospital was delegated to ward personnel, of
whom there were relatively many, and taken from the professional
staff, of whom there were few. Psychologists were assigned as
treatment team leaders.

The treatment team, in a real functional sense, is the very foundation of the treatment program. The team leaders have the responsibility for coordinating the activities of all unit personnel toward structuring an environment in which the effectiveness of the reinforcement process can be maximized to produce the desired behavioral changes. Team members include physicians, psychologists, social workers, nurses, nursing assistants, physical medicine and rehabilitation personnel. Members of the family who can be encouraged to become actively and directly involved in the patient's treatment, as well as administrative and service personnel in the hospital who socially interact with the patient in the special treatment situation that is structured for him, are also on the team.

It is the team leader's responsibility to see that things get done and decisions are made. He is the spokesman for the treatment team and integrates the functioning of the unit into the functioning of the hospital as a whole. It is the leader's responsibility to protect the democratic character of the decision making process. He may do this by insuring that the report, for example, of a nursing assistant who believes there is a need for a change in the Attitude prescribed for a particular patient, is carefully and thoughtfully considered by the group. However, it is recognized that the strict medical decisions are the province of the physician, and he has responsibility for them. In making these decisions the physician is alert to the psychological factors involved, and his decision may be made on the basis of these unless there are medical contraindications. Members of the patient's family are encouraged to attend the treatment planning conferences and patient progress staffs — in essence, to become members of the treatment team. At these meetings the maladaptive interacting behavior is pointed out, plans for changing it are discussed, and the cooperation of the family is solicited. It is believed that the treatment program is most effective when family members become involved. All important decisions made concerning the patient (e.g., privileges, leaves, trial visits, discharges, changes in treatment Attitude) are made by the treatment team.

In general, both patients and relatives have reacted very positively to this team approach to treatment. Many letters from family members have been received containing such statements as: "I feel it was a privilege to meet with the staff and discuss his case"; "We don't have to wait to see one particular doctor now; we can talk with anyone available"; and "It is a good feeling to know that everyone is interested in my husband." Patients themselves have commented, "I have the same people with me all the time," and "I feel I am part of a group and treated as an individual."

Progressive treatment and an open hospital invariably introduce more tension and involve running more risks than maintaining a closed custodial institution. A treatment team in which all members share equally in making decisions is likely to be less conservative than one individual alone accepting responsibility for therapeutic decisions. At the same time, the treatment team seems more able to withstand the pressure from community sources, which are concerned with keeping the patient hospitalized, than would be true of a single individual making the treatment decisions.

Behavior Modification

As seen above, it is a basic belief at the TVAH that there are learned maladaptive or troublesome behavior patterns for a particular patient which can be modified, at least to some extent, in order to effect a better adjustment, providing the proper therapeutic situation is established. The first step in doing this is to identify such a behavior pattern, not an isolated symptom, note how it works, and then create an interpersonal situation in which the patient is rewarded for changing his maladaptive pattern of behavior. This is accomplished by pre-scribing the appropriate treatment Attitude which is then applied consistently around the clock by all personnel having contact with the patient. The Attitudes prescribed, which will be discussed in detail later, are: Active Friendliness (AF), Passive Friendliness (PF), Matter-of-Fact (MOF), No Demand (ND), and Kind Firmness (KF). It is at the Treatment Planning Conference (TPC) that the patient is told how the team members are going to treat him, in essence what Attitude is being prescribed, and what they in turn expect of him. This rather direct and structured approach gives the patient the feeling that the team knows what it is doing, and that he can and will be helped.

It is important to emphasize that all personnel coming in contact with the patient *must* behave in a consistent fashion. The effectiveness of a treatment situation would be reduced sharply if the patient were treated consistently with one Attitude on the ward, but treated differ-ently in the dining room by dietetic workers, or on the hospital grounds by engineering personnel. While it is a somewhat imposing task to orient and train administrative and service personnel in a hospital to assume therapeutic responsibility for the individual patient, doing so provides unexpected dividends. The hospital is no longer divided into those who treat patients and those who do not. Everyone is involved in the treatment process, and every treatment gain or success is to be shared equally. Providing the program is at all successful, the ingre-dients necessary for high total staff morale are present.

It is possible to structure a *Patient Treatment Situation* (PTS), which is similar to the *Therapeutic Community* Maxwell Jones (1953) described, in which the effectiveness of a reinforcement process can be maximized to produce desired changes in the patient's total life field. Traditionally, the therapeutic situation is narrowly defined and primarily concerned with the interaction of two individuals—the patient and a therapist. In the PTS there are many more participants, a greater emphasis on interpersonal aspects, a wider range of responses being reinforced or extinguished, and greater use of social reinforcement.

One of the major difficulties in applying operant methods is getting new responses initiated so they can be reinforced. In Attitude Therapy, this problem is minimized. The PTS is not one in which the treatment team passively waits for the individual to make adaptive responses and then reinforces them. Instead, a special situation is created in which the patient has little choice but to give the desired response. In the Skinnerian sense, the team not only provides the bar but sees that it is pressed. This is particularly apparent in the operation of the Anti-Depressive program to be described at a later point. In this program a depressed patient must respond with the desired response—externalized anger—if he is to be reinforced by the avoidance of the aversive situation and by receiving more positive social reinforcement. Very frequently, as will be seen, this treatment technique departs radically from what is generally considered to be *tender loving care*. With the geriatric patient this departure takes the form of refusing to do for him what he might reasonably be expected to do for himself. While many such patients would prefer to be waited on, it is the patient's ability to function independently which will largely determine whether he can exist outside a hospital environment. While "talking" therapy may be a part of the PTS, less emphasis is placed on verbal behavior in the usual sense, and more on feelings, attitudes, and motor behavior.

The PTS does not depend on any one individual for its effectiveness, but on many, all reinforcing the patient in a consistent and systematic manner. This reinforcement is of a social nature and is applied primarily through the use of prescribed Attitudes. The PTS is fairly rigidly defined and the patient's role, the role of the members of the staff, and frequently that of the key members of the family are rather well-structured. For example, at one TPC, a manipulative, alcoholic patient had a MOF Attitude prescribed, was told that he had made a mess out of his life, and that he had been able to succeed in getting his mother and wife to help make and keep him sick by the way they had treated him. He was told further that if he got drunk while on pass or leave from the hospital and was placed in jail, neither the treatment team nor his family would come to get him out. He was told that he would have to serve his sentence and then he could return to the hospital for additional treatment. At a patient progress staff meeting a dominating, oversolicitous mother was politely told to be quiet and let her dependent, reticent, dominated son talk for himself. It becomes obvious why it is highly desirable, if not essential, for key members of the family to become an active part of the PTS.

Expectation plays a major role in the PTS—expectations on the part of both staff and patient. The rather definite structure which is provided enhances the patient's expectations of health and conveys to him, to put it in the words of the Hospital Director, "that we know what we are doing, that he can be helped, and that we are going to help him." Consensus is reached between staff and patient as to what each expects of the other. The patient comes to realize that getting help is a complex matter involving many psychological and sociological factors. For example, in a therapy interview, a demanding, manipulative patient, who was on a MOF Attitude, asked a rhetorical question, "When the nurses and nursing assistants on the ward won't let me have my way and do as I want to, that's part of my treatment?" The patient had begun to learn that throughout his life he had been able to manipulate, in a maladjusted way, his parents and others around him in order to gratify his own desires and needs; further, he had been trying desperately to do the same thing to the staff. Through excellent communication on the part of all the members of the treatment team, including his parents, and their consistent refusal to respond in the way he desired, he had begun to change and to become aware of the change in himself.

The first step in establishing the type of treatment environment described is to obtain information pertinent to the following questions: (1) What personality characteristics, behavior traits, or patterns are most likely to affect the treatment situation and outcome? (2) What behaviors need to be reinforced, extinguished, modified, or learned? and (3) How can this best be done?

Valuable information can be obtained which will help in deciding whether, for example, the patient is depressed and should be on KF and the Anti-Depressive program; he is an acting-out, demanding, manipulative person who needs a MOF Attitude; he is a fearful, socially withdrawn individual with whom an AF approach should be used; or, whether he is a very angry, resentful, striking out individual who should be put on a ND Attitude. In most instances this necessary information can be obtained by brief intake psychological assessment. Seldom is there concern with obtaining a diagnostic label for the patient, but instead there is an interest in obtaining a dynamic and behavioral picture of him.

Once the behavioral pattern to be modified or extinguished has been identified, the PTS necessary for effecting this change is established by prescribing the appropriate treatment Attitude. The five basic Attitudes, or combination of these, prescribed according to a patient's intrapsychic and interpersonal problems will be described briefly. The reader is referred to earlier papers for further description of the Attitudes and examples of their application (The Treatment Team, 1965; Folsom, 1966; Folsom & Taulbee, 1967).

Active Friendliness (AF)

This Attitude is prescribed for the patient manifesting a behavior pattern characterized by apathy, shyness, regression, failure proneness, and social withdrawal. The basic principle underlying this Attitude is providing the patient the attention, reassurance, and support he needs before he is able or willing to request it. Such an individual usually has a long history of failure and emotional rejection and has learned to handle the resulting anxiety by avoiding close interpersonal relationships. The purpose of prescribing this Attitude is to provide him with a treatment situation characterized by friendliness and acceptance, and one in which he is rewarded, socially, for any accomplishments, no matter how minute. Terms that have been used by others in describing this or similar approaches are "TLC" (tender loving care), and "giving love unsolicited." Personnel working with patients who have AF prescribed may accompany them on walks, take them to the canteen, attend activity therapy assignments with them or interact with them in other such ways. The following case illustrates the effectiveness of AF with a long-term chronic patient.

Case

At the time *Attitude Therapy* was instituted, 72-year-old *Mr. A.* was on a closed geriatric ward. He had been transferred to TVAH 21 years previously, diagnosed as Mental Deficiency, Severe, with Psychotic Reaction. Although he made some rapid improvement after admission, his condition soon stabilized, but discharge never seemed likely. In 1961 he began to deteriorate and regress. He became a feeding problem, lost interest in his surroundings, and ceased communicating except when he could not avoid it. He became disoriented and confused and was placed on a locked ward. The treatment team recognized that he needed to be treated on the Geriatric Reality Orientation (GRO) Program (to be described later) but he was too regressed and withdrawn for that prescription to be practical. Instead, AF was prescribed and he was assigned to Mrs. T., Nursing Supervisor, who had organized the GRO program. She began working with the patient on a one-to-one basis, giving him warm attention and taking him with her wherever she went. As soon as the patient responded, he was placed on an open ward during Mrs. T.'s tour of duty and everyone having contact with him practiced AF. This worked well until Mrs. T. was assigned to a different shift which resulted in the patient's immediate regression and retreat to the closed section. Since his response to AF had been positive, the team assigned him to Mrs. T. for reality orientation and special attention. Initially he refused this prescribed program but eventually capitulated. For the first two weeks on GRO he was totally uncooperative and verbally abusive to Mrs. T. for having deserted him and for now wasting his time. Quite suddenly, he changed dramatically. He stated he was ready for GRO. He began working hard and following directions well. Within seven months he had completed both phases of the GRO program, had "graduated," and was fully privileged and relating to others pleasantly. Following an additional year, during which time he regained self-confidence and contact with the community, he was discharged to a nursing home where he continues to do very well.

Passive Friendliness (PF)

This Attitude is quite similar to AF except that the staff waits for the patient to take the initiative in relating to them rather than their reaching out to him. This is necessary in view of the fact that the type of individual for whom this Attitude usually is prescribed has developed a cynical, bitter, and distrustful approach in his interpersonal relationships. For him, this manner of creating emotional distance has been found to be the most effective one for alleviating or preventing anxiety. However, this is not without its price as this manner of behaving generally provokes rejection by others and results in further frustration of his basic need for more positive interactions. The important elements in this PTS are that no relationships are forced upon him; he is permitted to maintain his spatial and emotional distance between himself and others until he is able to make "reaching out" responses; opportunities are provided for him to emit these desired responses, and when they do occur they receive immediate social reinforcement. PF is prescribed for the suspicious, distrustful, paranoid individual who is prone to project his unacceptable hostile and sexual impulses onto others, and for those individuals whose emotional problems would likely be intensified by a team member's being actively friendly.

The following case illustrates the use of PF.

Case

Mr. B. was a 34-year-old, frightened, preoccupied, dependent, suspicious, ex-marine. Upon admission, his affect was inappropriate and he said that he had had "a religious problem about sex which has been torturing my soul and body for 25 years." He was experiencing delusions and visual hallucinations of male and female sex organs. Mr. B. was uncomfortable around everyone but particularly around women because he thought they hated him. He was extremely preoccupied with thoughts of women, marriage, and sexual relations — a defense against his strong homosexual impulses (he reported several homosexual experiences about which he felt very guilty). During the first few days of hospitalization a ND Attitude was prescribed as it was believed that he might become very combative and strike out against others. This was soon changed to PF and he was given a full assignment of activities. Every time he passed the nursing office he would duck his head but peer inside. Except for a greeting or smile, personnel left him to his own devices. One day he came up to a nurse and asked why medicine was given to "everybody but me." The psychiatrist on the team promptly prescribed a small dose of tranquilizers three times a day. The patient gradually began to converse more and more freely with the nurse at these times of contact. He soon began seeking out both male and female employees and patients to interact with and to joke about the "pretty girls," referring to the student nurses. After approximately 10 weeks of hospitalization the patient went on a 15-day leave of absence with his parents. He adjusted well during this time and was subsequently discharged.

Matter-of-Fact (MOF)

Of the five primary Attitudes prescribed, MOF is by far the most commonly used. It is prescribed for the narcissistic, manipulative, acting-out sociopath; the complaining, somatically preoccupied, hysterical, and hypochondriacal neurotic; the patient suffering from alcohol or drug addiction; and for other patients (such as the organic) who are in need of a reality oriented, well-structured environment. When these individuals manifest such behavior as complaining about hospital routine and somatic ailments in order to gain sympathy or attention, attempt to get out of activity assignments, to play one team member against the other, they are dealt with in a very matter of fact way and their behavior pointed out to them.

Case

Mr. C. was a young, married, suspicious, jealous, attention-seeking, ex-serviceman. He was given a diagnosis of paranoid schizophrenia and transferred from a Naval Hospital where he had been admitted because of his threats to shoot the President and a senator (this was soon after President Kennedy's assassination). He stated in his admission psychological evaluation, "I am writing you to let you know I am a calm, well-adjusted person. I was ordered into the hospital due in part to a letter I wrote so I could get some attention and be near my wife. I ended up here after a Board. I need to go home and support my wife." A MOF Attitude was prescribed. It was pointed out to him that he was mentally ill and in need of help, and that he would be given a full schedule of activities. He soon began to accept the fact that he did have problems and was started in intensive individual and group psychotherapy, which became a part of his well-structured PTS. Progress was fairly rapid and marked, and he remained in the hospital only about two months. His adjustment to the birth of his first child which occurred during this time was very good. The wife and daughter moved to Tuscaloosa in order that he could continue out-patient treatment. Mr. C. enrolled in a trade school in an electronics course and upon completing it accepted a training position with a major national computer firm. Now, approximately four years later, the patient is doing well outside of the hospital and has not had to seek further psychological treatment.

No Demand (ND)

This Attitude means just what the words say—"no demand." Except for four rules which the individual is told he must obey, no demands whatsoever are placed upon him. The four rules which he must follow are: (1) he may not leave the treatment program without permission of the team, (2) he may not hurt himself, (3) he may not hurt anyone else, and (4) he must take his medication if it is prescribed. The ND Attitude is prescribed for those individuals who have learned that overtly hostile, aggressive, belligerent behaviors are for them the most effective ways of adjusting and reducing their anxiety levels. In emotionally loaded situations, especially those that have a greater "pull" for warm, tender feelings, such individuals are made very anxious and feel more comfortable when they are acting rough and tough. Their ever-ready temper outburst or aggressive attack frequently is effective in controlling others. The ND Attitude gives the person little to strike out against and no authority to attack. Their rage behavior, which generally is maintained by the secondary reinforcement it brings (e.g., counteraggression, attention, getting his way), is quite readily extinguished. Consequently, this Attitude is used relatively infrequently and for brief periods.

Case

Mr. D., an emaciated, agitated, hostile, and demanding person, was brought to the hospital by the deputy sheriff. His clothes and person were dirty and malodorous and he was verbally abusive, profane, and obscene. Being placed on a closed ward immediately triggered an explosive torrent of hostility and anger. A ND attitude and medication were prescribed. He was informed of the four rules, and although he threatened to whip everyone on the ward, he was careful not to physically touch anyone. His behavior remained much the same through the following day. He refused to bathe, wash, shave, or take off his clothes at night. His meals were set before him with "Mr. D., here is your breakfast." He refused the food, stating that it was "swill fit for hogs." No effort was made to encourage him to eat, but he began to eat on the morning of the second day following admission, hesitantly at first but soon with enthusiasm. He began to seek out staff to talk with and it was then possible to suggest bathing, shaving, and clean clothes. He seemed to expect the staff to somehow take advantage of his initial compliances. Treatment personnel were quick to comment on his improved appearance, but careful not to say anything that the patient could interpret as criticism for earlier behavior. Within 10 days he was fully privileged and his behavior revealed how starved he was for friendly interpersonal contacts. Had he been forced to comply to rules of conduct when he first came to the ward, his resistive and angry behavior would have been reinforced rather than extinguished.

Kind Firmness (KF)

This treatment Attitude is basic to the treatment program for depression and is prescribed for patients whose major pattern of behavior is characterized by depression, guilt, feelings of inadequacy and worthlessness, reflecting an internalization of their hostility and conflicts. When the KF Attitude is prescribed it means that all personnel working with the patient are to deal with him in a kind but firm, determined, and resolute manner. They are to see that he carries out all assigned menial, monotonous tasks, and they are not to give him any positive reinforcement. Since KF is prescribed for all patients placed on the Anti-Depressive program, it will be discussed in greater detail later in connection with that program.

Special Treatment Programs

While the major treatment emphasis at the TVAH is on providing an individualized PTS for each patient through the prescription of certain Attitudes, there are two particular programs operating within this framework which are worthy of special attention. These are the Anti-Depressive (AD) program and the Geriatric Reality Orientation (GRO) program.

Anti-Depressive Program

The purpose of this program is to provide a well-structured, consistent, kind but firm PTS for the patient who usually attempts to ward off anxiety and to adjust by behaving in a self-punitive, self-depreciating, and guilt-ridden manner. The manifested behavior of patients placed in the program is characterized by depression, immobilization, guilt, self-doubt, and self-derogation, irrespective of psychiatric diagnosis. Since depression is the most common symptom in all mentally disturbed individuals, and the one most likely to result in the most dire consequence — suicide — the importance of its early detection and treatment cannot be overemphasized.

The physical environment consists of a small, windowless, dull room, containing a few chairs and a table. The patient spends all of his waking hours in the room performing menial, monotonous, non-gratifying tasks under the close scrutiny of nursing assistants who constantly criticize the way he does the job. Tasks assigned include such things as sanding small blocks of wood with a fine grain sand-paper (hence, the room was called the "sanding room" by the patients), bouncing a ball within a 6-inch square on the floor, counting tiny sea-shells into a cigar box, and having to start over whenever he is distracted and loses count. The KF Attitude prescribed indicates to the personnel that they are to deal with the patient in a firm, convincing manner, but with kindness. They are not to grant any of his wishes, such as to go away and leave him "alone to die" or suffer, nor are they to give him any positive reinforcement. Although the patient is treated impersonally and is criticized about the quality of his performance, he is never belittled nor ridiculed. He can hardly continue his behavioral pattern of ruminating, self-doubting, and worrying about "right and wrong" while carrying out the activities prescribed. The purpose of this program is to provide the opportunity and reason for an overt expression of the patient's resentment and hostility. He needs to learn that there are situations in which aggressive responses are not only appropriate but are encouraged and rewarded. In this PTS, such responses are met with social approval, and aversive stimulation is terminated—reactions which are in contrast to the psychological and/or physical punishment the individual has been conditioned to expect.

Case

When *Mr. E.* was 12 years of age his mother abandoned the home leaving him with his father who remarried two years later. Apparently, the early intrafamilial relationships gave rise to a psychodynamically complex, recurring behavior pattern involving attempts to interject himself between the significant male and female in his environment. Occupationally, he had been very successful, rising to a position of department chief in a financial organization. There was an attractive woman in the organization who held a position of equal responsibility and in whom the president of the organization confided. Mr. E. made efforts to dislodge the woman from her position. When he failed, his own productivity dropped and he became increasingly upset. He had a mild heart attack which resulted in an enforced leave of several weeks. Immediately upon his return to work he made a final desperate effort to establish himself as the president's only confidant. When this failed he made a direct appeal to the Chairman of the Board to whom he verbalized some paranoid ideation. The consequences were that he was fired, became depressed, and suicidally preoccupied. A psychiatrist, convinced that the veteran was a danger to himself, sent him to the hospital. At the time of admission, Mr. E. was confused, agitated, and obsessed with thoughts of death and destruction. The treatment team prescribed KF and placed him on the Anti-Depressive program. A very stern attitude was required to get him to perform assigned tasks. He wept a great deal the first day but this seemed to subside as his attention became focused more on what he was doing. The first night after being placed on the program he complained that he was unable to sleep so was taken back to the "sanding room." Five days of continually pressuring him for better or more work were required before any overt signs of hostility were detected. Initially, these were verbal and tentative — not indicative of a readiness to come off the AD program. It was not until he threw a block across the room and dared anyone to make him continue sanding that the nursing assistant terminated the AD treatment; at that point in time Mr. E. certainly was not depressed. He has experienced some interpersonal difficulties since discharge but depression has been notably absent, and he has not sought further treatment.

Geriatric Reality Orientation Program

The second special treatment program developed at Tuscaloosa was the Reality Orientation (RO) Program, more commonly referred to as the Geriatric Reality Orientation Program. This program was designed to treat those patients manifesting a moderate to severe degree of organic cerebral deficit, usually the result of arteriosclerosis. However, it is equally suited for the younger patient who is manifesting confusion and disorientation as a result of other brain trauma. The reader is referred to articles previously published for a more detailed description of the program (Taulbee & Folsom, 1966; Folsom, 1967; Taulbee, 1968).

A variety of principles and techniques based primarily on discoveries of educators and learning theorists are used. The program makes use of reality orientation classes, operant conditioning procedures, and, usually, the prescription of MOF and/or AF Attitudes. Materials used in the classroom (some of which are used occasionally in the patient's own room) include individual calendars, word-letter games, blockboard, felt board, mock-up clock, unit building blocks for coordination and color matching, plastic numbers, and large piece puzzles. Perhaps the most prominent classroom feature and the material most commonly used is the reality orientation board. Listed on the board are such items of information as the name and location of the hospital; the current year, month, and day of the week; the name of the next meal; the weather; and other information considered desirable at the time. Although there are regularly scheduled classes, the teaching process goes on continually and individually on the unit.

One of the first steps in prescribing this particular treatment program is to obtain a psychological evaluation. This is done in order to assess the degree and type of impairment as well as strengths and to get a picture of the patient's behavior which should be reinforced and that which should be extinguished. An attempt is made to correct, to whatever degree possible, any defects in vision, hearing, or speech. The patient's reeducation is started by helping him use the part of his cerebral functioning that is still intact.

For the confused, elderly individual the treatment environment should be consistent, calm, supportive, reassuring, and not overly demanding. The Attitude most frequently adopted to provide this is AF or PF. Such a PTS makes the patient feel that he is not worthless and in the way, that life has not passed him by, and that there are people who are interested in him. However, the AF or PF Attitude may be combined with one of the other Attitudes whenever indicated. For example, on occasion a MOF approach may have to be used to see that the patient does for himself the things that he should do and is capable of doing; or he may become depressed and have the AD program prescribed. The two following case examples will illustrate how the RO and operant conditioning procedures are used in this treatment program.

Case A

Mr. F. was a very successful businessman until he suffered a stroke at the age of 67 which left him confused, disoriented, and paralyzed on the right side. At the TPC the Treatment Team reported that he was very hostile, yelled and screamed when he didn't get his way, was disoriented most of the time, and seldom said anything that was relevant or coherent. When he was brought to staff he was slouched down in his wheelchair and was drooling. He did not know the year of his birth, his age, nor the current date. When he was asked if he could swallow he replied, "not very good," so he was encouraged to swallow and shown how to wipe his mouth. The patient was told, "You can get well enough to go home if you try. Every day all of us are going to remind you what day it is, that you are not to be yelling and screaming, that you are to sit up in your chair, and that you are not to be drooling. We are going to count with you and give you a calendar. We are going to expect you to remember your age, the date, your birthdate, and where your wife is. You have stayed in bed too much and we are going to get you up and back home. We are going to get pictures of your family to put by your bed. We are going to get football and baseball schedules, and watch the games on TV with you." (Social history information revealed that his two main interests had been baseball and TV.). Further aspects of the program were explained to him by the team leader and then he was asked, "How does that sound to you?" The patient replied, "It sounds good to me." The nursing supervisor remarked that she had never seen the patient as alert or lucid. The treatment plans called for the personnel to get him to walk, to watch TV with him, to remind him to stop screaming and drooling, to get him on graduated exercises, and to see that he wore his dentures. By the end of the interview the patient was quiet, had completely stopped drooling, was sitting erect in his chair, and made relevant comments about his condition and the planned treatment program. A MOF Attitude was prescribed; he was started on the GRO program, and all personnel were to follow through on this round the clock. Mr. F. began to show immediate improvement. There was a noticeable decrease in his screaming, yelling, drooling, and he began walking with assistance whereas before that he had been completely bed-ridden.

Case B

Dr. G., a severely regressed, confused, disoriented, 41-year-old physician was admitted as a transfer from a private hospital. He had attempted suicide by shooting himself in the right temple. Immediately after the incident surgery was performed in the right temporal region and left hemiplegia resulted. Dr. G. had been hospitalized for excessive drinking and use of narcotics prior to the suicide attempt. From the time of his admission until about two years later the patient remained confused, disoriented, hostile, profane, and totally uncooperative. He was extremely demanding of personnel and was considered to be hopeless. After this period of time he was presented at a TPC for review and placement on a more effective treatment program. During the conference he was

loud, profane, verbally abusive, and threatened the interviewer. A MOF Attitude was used in dealing with him. It
was pointed out to him that he had shot himself, that he was
mentally ill, and in a mental hospital. His anger was reflected
to him and his demands and attempts to prescribe his treatment
were met by the reply that although he was a physician, he was
now a patient and the team would decide his treatment. The
patient was allowed to express his rage but the team stead-
fastly refused to reject him and informed him that he couldn't
frighten them away by his threats. During the following months
he was seen once a week by the team and his progress reviewed. At times he appeared confused but at other times he
was quite lucid. The team felt that he was capable of doing
much more for himself than he had been willing to do previously.

This problem was handled in a matter-of-fact manner. He
was given an electric razor and told that he not only could,
but would be expected to start shaving himself. He was told
that he should push his own wheelchair from the day room to
his bed instead of expecting the nursing assistant to do it for
him. This at first took one hour but during the next few weeks
was reduced to 15 minutes. He was assigned to manual arts
therapy where he was encouraged and expected to work on
toys for retarded children. For the first time since his injury
he read medical journals. His successes were pointed out to
him in order to cut through his protests of inability to perform.
Attention and approval were given to him by the team for his
achievements. Outbursts of anger decreased in frequency. On
occasion, his anger was useful in motivating him to achieve.
For example, at one point he became so angry at a nursing
assistant that he waved his paralyzed hand over his head.
He had never been known to move this hand to such an extent
before. This was pointed out to him. As he progressed, it was
arranged for him to make brief visits to the home of a friend
who had maintained contact with him. His family visited him
on one of these occasions and pictures of the patient and the
group were made. When shown to him later in the hospital,
he denied having made the visit but talked about the good food
he had eaten there. The ultimate goal is to return this patient
to live with his family. There is much work yet to be done with
him but the entire treatment team has been gratified by his
progress. The reader who is interested in seeing how social
reinforcement was used to modify Dr. G.'s locomotive be-

havior is referred to an article by Milby, Stenmark, and Horner (1967).

During the period of time this program has been in effect, many patients have improved to the point where they have left the hospital, some after as many as 20 years, to return home, or go into nursing homes or foster homes. These patients have suffered from acute and chronic brain syndromes, CNS syphilis, and neurological disorders of various kinds. Whether their poor memory, regression, confusion, or disturbed adjustment was a result of emotional factors, brain damage, or both, they learned, their behavior was modified, and they now live again outside of the hospital.

Program Evaluation

The goal of a psychiatric hospital, like that of any hospital, is to treat efficiently and expeditiously. Thus, length of stay in the hospital (release rate), adequacy of posthospital adjustment, increase in the number of patients served without an increase in the number of beds, and discharge of long-term hospitalized individuals are often viewed as the best available criteria for evaluating the effectiveness of a hospital treatment program. Although the measure of rapid release must include a minimum period of time in the community before it can be considered an adequate criterion, there are, nevertheless, some social gains. These gains include preventing the patient's developing "hospitalitis," the estrangement from his family and friends, and his acquiring institutional values and attitudes which are nonconducive to optimum functioning outside of the hospital. Adjustment to the nonhospital community is very complex and difficult to evaluate. Therefore, it is nearly impossible to predict a patient's posthospital adjustment, based on his condition at the time of discharge. The patient, responding to the reinforcing contingencies in the hospital, may produce marked changes in his behavior, but upon discharge he almost always returns to the same environment that made the symptoms necessary in the first place.

Since a rapid turnover rate can result in a "revolving door" policy for the more recently admitted patient and custodial care for the long-term patient, an evaluation of effectiveness of a treatment program should take into consideration the average length of hospitalization for the patient population. It is well known that the probability of release is a function of several factors with one of the most important being the length of time spent in the hospital. Using the criteria mentioned above for evaluating the effectiveness of a treatment program, the TVAH hospital records for the past several years reveal very significant changes. The current discharge rate is 425 percent higher than it was in 1962. This increase was accomplished without a detectable increase in the rate of readmissions. As concerns the greater utilization of beds, it is projected that the hospital will serve 800 more veterans during Fiscal Year 1969 than it did in Fiscal Year 1962 — without an increase in space or personnel. The staff numbers less than 700, a slight decrease from what it was in 1962. At the time the treatment program was introduced, 46 percent of all patients had been hospitalized continuously for five years or more, and 22 percent had been hospitalized less than one year. Today, these figures are reversed, reflecting much greater treatment efficiency, and they are not inflated figures resulting from a revolving-door policy. Reliance on drugs has steadily decreased to a point where the drug cost per patient is as low as or lower than any comparable VA hospital. The hospital has accomodated a steady flow of visitors, now numbering in the hundreds, each spending from one to five days observing and learning the treatment techniques. As a consequence, several other hospitals have instituted similar programs with a relatively high degree of success, at least initially.

The major research undertaking of the TVAH staff to this point has been an attempt to assess the effectiveness of the Anti-Depressive treatment program.[4] The design of the study was relatively simple. During a specified period of time every patient admitted to the hospital who was considered to be in need of treatment for depression, who could complete a battery of psychological tests, and for whom there was no serious contraindication for not being on medication, was used as a subject. This selection procedure yielded a total of 68 patients from the two psychiatric units, 34 treated with KF and 34 treated with AF. Each patient was randomly assigned to one of six groups: KF only, KF and placebo, KF with anti-depressive medication, AF only, AF with placebo, and AF with anti-depressive medication. Subjects were treated as indicated until it appeared that the depression had been alleviated, at which time a different Attitude (usually MOF) was prescribed. Hospital treatment from this point followed the usual pattern. A battery of psychological tests consisting of the Minnesota Multiphasic Personality Inventory (MMPI), the Tennessee Self Concept Scale (TSCS), and Leary's Interpersonal Check List (ICl), was administered at four points; before treatment was started, and two weeks, six weeks, and six months after the initiation of treatment. Study of the demographic data failed to disclose any significant

---

[4]Investigators for the study were J. C. Folsom, M. D.; R. F. Horner, Ph. D.; W. E. Patterson, Jr., Ph.D.; and the authors.

differences between the main experimental groups. Forty-one percent of each group had carried schizophrenic diagnoses, usually of long standing. Both groups contained two patients diagnosed as chronic brain syndrome with depression. The remaining patients were largely diagnosed as anxiety reaction with severe depression.

There was marked consistency of results across tests. Significant test findings suggest the following conclusions. Both KF and AF resulted in significantly more "normal" appearing profiles through the third testing. On the fourth testing, while those treated with KF had continued to make significant gains since the previous testing, those treated with AF had regressed significantly and their test scores were elevated almost to the pretreatment levels. The most clearly established gains were made by patients treated by Attitudes alone (KF and AF — without drugs or placebos). The addition of medication appeared to dilute the effectiveness of the treatment Attitudes, and for these groups no significant changes of any kind could be found. However, the differences among the subgroups must be considered highly tentative because of the small number of subjects.

The findings are interpreted to indicate that the warm and supportive treatment environment of AF does serve to alleviate the feelings of unworthiness, guilt, and depression but these feelings return when this support is withdrawn. The individual enters treatment aware of vast differences between what he is and what he would like to be, and these differences are never recoinciled though he is more comfortable when surrounded by warm, supporting people who bolster his ego.

KF, in requiring that the individual externalize his hostility and take an aggressive stand in support of his own value and worthwhileness, a stand which is rewarded, teaches the patient a lesson that he greatly needs to learn. Apparently this is what happens, as the patient continues to improve after leaving the hospital. Differences between self and ideal self in the KF groups had disappeared to a significant degree by the final testing.

There were some interesting additional observations. At the time of the fourth and final testing, six of the 68 subjects still remained in the hospital. All six had been treated with AF. Of the patients discharged from the hospital prior to the fourth testing, those treated with KF averaged 14 fewer days of hospitalization than those treated with AF. Five patients were dropped from research upon medical advice. In each case the individual had increasingly lost control to a point where he constituted a clear danger to himself and/or others. All five of these patients were on AF. Immediately upon being dropped as research subjects they were placed on the AD program and treated with KF. All responded well and made uneventful recoveries.

Summary

For a brief period early in the 19th century, between the primitive era when the emotionally disturbed were considered demon-possessed, and the emergence of the conviction that disturbed people were suffering from an organic illness, the treatment of psychiatric patients was undertaken by those called moral therapists. These therapists viewed disturbed behavior as a consequence of emotional and character underdevelopment. They treated by reeducation, using reward and punishment, and environmental manipulation to effect behavior modification, with a surprisingly high degree of reported success.

Although for the past 100 years the sickness concept has persisted, it has contributed little to a rationale for understanding or treating psychiatric patients. During the last half of this period the learning process has become increasingly well understood. The more recent contributions of scientific psychology have clarified how behavior patterns are acquired and modified. The reward and punishment contingencies, the psychosocial environment with its unique interpersonal expectancies, and the influence of psychodynamic factors are all revealed as having great importance. These advances in knowledge, far from challenging the views of the moral therapists, serve as an endorsement but provide a much more sophisticated basis upon which to formulate treatment techniques and programs.

The staff at the Tuscaloosa VA Hospital have adopted the basic beliefs and philosophy of the moral therapists: that the mentally ill have acquired patterns of "misbehavior," that these are changed not by medicine but by rewards that bring pleasure and punishments that bring displeasure, that the patient should assume as much responsibility for his behavior as he is capable of assuming, and that those working with patients should have faith in at least the potential recovery of most of them.

Treatment programs at the TVAH expose the patient to a psychosocial environment where the expectations, and reward and punishment contingencies are so consistently present that new behaviors emerge and if rewarded, persist. For aggressive, striking-out behavior, the PTS contains no counteraggression, thus making the patient's behavior pointless and purposeless. For the withdrawn, emotionally distanced individual the PTS surrounds him with loving, solicitous people who are ready to respond to his slightest move in their direction. For the patient who has internalized his resentment and hostility, the PTS is such as almost to force an overt expression of these feelings, such action being rewarded. For the overly sensitive, distrustful, and suspicious person who might panic if threatened by any close interpersonal relationship, the PTS permits the individual to temporarily maintain spatial and emotional distance. For the manipulative, acting-out, and demanding person who refuses to accept the reality and consequences of his behavior, the PTS no longer rewards such be- havior and forces the individual to look more realistically at what he is doing.

Applying the usual criteria for measuring hospital treatment effec- tiveness, and considering the results of one small research project completed to date, it is suggested that the psychological treatment model herein described constitutes a significant and promising step forward.

REFERENCES

Adams, E. C. Problems in attitude therapy in a mental hospital. *American Journal of Psychiatry,* 1948, **105**, 456–461.

Bockoven, J. S. Moral treatment in American psychiatry. *The Journal of Nervous and Mental Disease,* 1956, **124**(2), 167–194.

Carson, R. C., Margolis, P. M., Daniels, R. S. & Heine, R. W. Milieu homogeneity in the treatment of psychiatric inpatients. *Psychiatry,* 1962, **25**, 285–289.

Folsom, J. C. Attitude therapy has marked effect. *U.S. Medicine,* 1966, **2**(7), 1–6.

Folsom, J. C. Intensive hospital therapy of geriatric patients. In J. Masserman (Ed.), *Current psychiatric therapies.* Vol. VII. New York: Grune & Stratton, 1967. Pp. 209–215.

Folsom, J. C. & Taulbee, E. S. Attitude therapy. *Journal of the Fort Logan Mental Health Center,* 1967, **4**(2), 47–57.

Jones, M. *The therapeutic community.* New York: Basic Books, 1953.

Laqueur, H. P. Epilogue. In E. Kraepelin (Ed.), *One hundred years of psychiatry.* New York: Philosophical Library, 1962. Pp. 157–160.

Menninger, W. C. Psychiatric hospital therapy designed to meet unconscious needs. *American Journal of Psychiatry,* 1936, **93**, 347–360.

Milby, J. B., Jr., Stenmark, D. E. & Horner, R. F. Modification of locomotive behavior in a severely disturbed psychotic. *Perceptual & Motor Skills,* 1967, **25**, 359–360.

Szasz, T. The crime of commitment. *Psychology Today,* 1969, **2**(10), 55–57.

Taulbee, L. R. Rx: Nursing intervention for confusion of the elderly. *The Alabama Nurse,* 1968, **22**, 1–3.

Taulbee, L. R. & Folsom, J. C. Reality orientation for geriatric patients. *Hospital & Community Psychiatry,* May 1966. Pp. 133–135.

(The) Treatment Team, VA Hospital, Tuscaloosa, Alabama. Attitude therapy and the team approach. *Mental Hospitals,* 1965. Pp. 307–323.

CHAPTER 15

Responsibility Therapy

D. A. R. Peyman

The basic goal of the Alabama State Hospital Therapy program is to enable patients to leave the hospital as soon as possible and, more importantly, to decrease the probability of their return. To achieve this goal, we believe it is what the patient does for himself more than what the therapist does that helps. Therapists may guide patients to consider alternative courses of action and to utilize helpful coping behaviors, but it is only the patient who can make the changes in himself essential to more effective living.

Therapy programs often seem to emphasize the process of therapy or the techniques of the *therapist* as the essential ingredients for successful therapy. Although we do not deny that such variables play important roles our emphasis is on the individual and what he does with what he learns in the therapeutic situation. We try to assist him but the responsibility for attaining a better adjustment is his. If he is to leave the hospital and live effectively in the outer community, it is he *and only he* who can make the changes necessary in himself to accomplish this.

Most persons hospitalized for emotional problems have engaged in behavior considered sufficiently deviant by either the patient, himself, or someone else to warrant hospitalization. We assume that his behavior is learned and, although it may include a lifetime of faulty habit patterns, we believe it can be modified or unlearned. We believe that most individuals who come to the hospital possess the necessary qualifications for altering themselves. They are capable of changing behavior patterns that have hindered their adjustment, and can learn more effective or desirable coping techniques. We believe that they can make sufficient changes in themselves so that the need for hospitalization or professional care is minimized. The changes that the patient makes in himself help him to become more responsible, and it is the attainment of a more responsible position that helps the individual to shorten his stay and remain out of the hospital.

We postulate a continuum of responsibility ranging from a near zero extreme, requiring complete care, to some optimum level where an individual is more or less autonomous and self-directing. Since our goal is to increase responsibility in a person, we use a reference point, the degree of responsibility the person actually takes, and try to increase it. If the person, for any reason, is unable or unwilling to assume significant amounts of responsibility, our program will probably take the form of behavior shaping until he demonstrates increased self-direction. When this begins to occur, additional freedom for self-responsibility is given. For those who seem least able to take responsibility, we may utilize manipulative techniques, but we advocate that ultimately such manipulation must end and the individual must take the initiative for his own development and self-direction.

Our entire program, in its various forms, is directed toward helping individuals make the necessary changes to achieve a more responsible and, therefore, more effective life. The emphasis of our program is not on the therapist who stimulates those changes in the patient but on the patient himself, who is, after all, the only person able to effect change in himself and to continue this necessary process throughout life.

The program to achieve this is in the process of evolving from a diverse ancestry. The approach has grown from work mostly with hospitalized psychotic patients. It was developed because of dissatisfaction with previously used techniques, including nondirective, psychoanalytic, and eclectic. Individual and group psychotherapy sessions were held with a variety of patients, and although a fair percentage of the patients left the institution and did not return, there seemed to be a lack of conviction among the therapists that they were making significant contributions to any changes in the patients. Also, there was a notable absence of feedback from patients as to the value of the psychotherapy sessions. The psychotherapy sessions were held for two or three hours per week, and these were the only occasions during which the patients seemed to contribute thought or activity to modify themselves. The patients were dissatisfied with even this minimal activity; it seemed that many of them expected the mere passage of time to solve their problems, or that an extended rest was all they required. Some perceived their stay as equivalent to a prison term and thought that it would pay for past errors so they could begin a new life free from tension. Most patients appeared to want changes made *for* them rather than by them. The hospital housed a large number of patients, more of whom arrived daily. Some went home and some remained to add to a backlog of chronic patients who lingered more or less indefinitely in the hospital. Long-term therapy was undesirable from the point of view of both the patients and the hospital.

A short-term approach was needed, one that could reach patients to whom a variety of psychiatric labels were applied: psychoses, alcoholism, psychoneuroses, and personality disorders. Further, the responsibility of the patient for his own welfare had to be stressed. The approach developed by the hospital staff in working with such people was markedly influenced by the work of Ellis (1962) with his rational-emotive therapy and by Phillips (1956) with his stress on interference therapy.

Our starting point was to assume that most behavior is learned. We stressed that the behavior which caused the patient to be hospitalized was, for the most part, learned, and that new and more effective behavior patterns could be learned and substituted for the old. We further hypothesized that we were not dealing with a simple S-R relation, but that the individual himself played an important role in determining the behavior he exhibited. We held that the conceptual frame of reference the individual maintains at the time of action is significant in determining his perceptions and his resulting behavior. The assumption of a phenomenological frame of reference is important because part of our therapy is aimed at assisting the patient to modify his underlying frame of reference, including the beliefs, attitudes, ideas, and thought processes that we believe lead to his self-defeating behavior. Our stress, on the learning of new behavior is, thus, not limited to extinguishing some previous response, but includes the modification of the underlying frame of reference. We assume that man is an active as well as a reactive organism. He is not the passive product of environmental forces but is capable of profiting from past experiences, evaluating possible consequences of different actions, estimating crude probability values of desirable or undesirable outcomes, increasing his repertory of responses to situations, modifying his frame of reference, and so on. In this sense, he is an active organism and can take the responsibility for modifying himself and becoming more self-directing than he has been in the past. To stress this, we have labeled our therapeutic approach "Responsibility Therapy." This label identifies the goal or end of therapy whereas most other labels identify the means. Thus, nondirective, psychoanalytic, supportive, etc., refer to the techniques used or the theoretical foundations involved. Our term, responsibility therapy, allows for almost any variety of procedures or of theoretical orientations if they can be pragmatically justified to result in increased self-responsibility.

We view the approach as "emotional problem solving." By this we mean to exclude from consideration many problems that an individual may have, i.e., economic, physical deformities, and so on, not with the belief that these are of no consequence but, rather, that they do not come under the purview of our particular discipline. We refer individuals with such problems to appropriate specialists, and we deal with his emotional reactions to such problems. We are concerned with the degree of intensity of these reactions — whether they are too intense or too mild — although concern is primarily expressed about the too intense emotions. When one's emotional response to a perceived stimulus is intense, some behavior, usually overt, follows as if to reduce the intensity of the emotion. A judgment is then made by the individual, or by others, that some of the behavior is indeed deviant or inappropriate. The individual then may be hospitalized, imprisoned, referred for treatment, and so on; thus, there are consequences of the behavior. We conceptualize the following chain: (1) a stimulus (internal or external), (2) perception of the stimulus by the person, (3) response with an emotional reaction, (4) behavior, in response to the emotion, and (5) certain consequences of that behavior. Any of the steps, (2), (3), or (4), might be interpreted to be an "emotional problem." Our emphasis is on solving emotional problems.

The above is probably the simplest arrangement of the steps. Various other possibilities may occur, notably that the consequences could influence both (2) and (4). Our therapy program stresses an attack on two parts of the paradigm, (2) and (4), the perception of the stimulus by the person and the behavior. In general, because the individual is hospitalized as a consequence of some undesirable behavior, the behavior should be altered to avoid a repetition of the hospitalization. A case in point is the individual who is hospitalized for excessive drinking. It seems clear that the excessive drinking behavior must be either curtailed or eliminated. However, the example of excessive drinking also illustrates the importance of the modification of (2), the perceptual basis, which we look upon as the source of the emotional reaction which in turn has led to excessive drinking as a way of reducing the experienced stress. In order for the individual to learn to live effectively without relying upon alcohol, he must find some means of eliminating his experienced stress or else learn to endure moderate amounts of stress without the use of alcohol. It would be even more desirable for him to learn to prevent or at least reduce the frequency of the arousal of experienced stress. The sources of the difficulty seems to be in the frame of reference of the individual and his self-defeating behavior. Much of our therapy is concerned with assisting the person in the modification of the self-defeating aspects of both his frame of reference and his behavior.

Another example is to be found in the depressed individual who may discover the social undesirability of a depressed appearance and learns to modify his behavior so as to *appear* cheerful. The resulting behavior is termed a "smiling depression." From our point of view the source of the depression must be dealt with. We look upon this source, in general, as lying in the individual's frame of reference which must be the target of modification.

In order to encourage patients to deal with their problems, a start is made by providing introductory information about emotional difficulties. A few days after a patient enters the hospital, he attends a series of didactic lectures in which the basic principles of the therapy program are outlined. These lectures clearly stress that the responsibility for change lies with the patient.

The didactic lectures are completed in four consecutive days and are titled: (1) "Learning to be Responsible," (2) "Learning to Live with Feelings and Thoughts," (3) "Learning to Think," (4) "Learning to See," and (5) "Learning by Doing." Our stress on the concept of learning is no accident since we are emphasizing that the individual's future and his ways of dealing with problems are, indeed, his responsibility. Furthermore, it is stressed that he must learn to deal more effectively with his problems than he has in the past, or he will continue to reap unpleasant consequences, such as hospitalization. The theme of the first lecture is self-responsibility and emphasizes that the individual is responsible for himself in the sense that his perceptions, his attitudes, and his beliefs lead to certain emotional reactions to which he will, in turn, react and which play a most significant part in his life. He is responsible for maintaining his beliefs, his attitudes, and, in general, his point of view. We are not usually concerned with the origin of these beliefs, or ideas, and are not arguing that the person is responsible for acquiring them, but that he is responsible for continuing to hold them. If, in the past, his frame of reference has led to adjustmental difficulties, he can do something about modifying these attitudes, beliefs, and thoughts. He is the only one who can modify them. If his behavior in dealing with his emotions has been unacceptable from various points of view, then it is his responsibility to modify that behavior or else continue to take the consequences for it. If he chooses to maintain some socially undesirable, self-defeating behavior, then he has chosen to take the consequences of this behavior and this, too, is his responsibility. Throughout our contacts with the patients, our stress is on the responsibility of the individual. This is in contrast to what many of these people have earlier experienced where the responsibility for their care was taken by staff members, and where the patient was looked upon as someone, who was "mentally ill," and needed rest or the attention of the staff members. In such cases, the patient seemed quite willing to toss the responsibility to those who were willing to take it and this, of course, rarely led to significant changes on the patient's part. It is suggested that there was a strong tendency to encourage a dependent, passive attitude in the patients, which tended to perpetuate the patient role, sometimes permanently.

An important point is that the total process of therapy, as we envision it, need not be completed while the patient is in the hospital. What seems important is that significant steps are taken by the individual to modify his behavior and his frame of reference, and this process can be continued by the patient, often without professional assistance, when he leaves the institution. This point is often in contrast with the expectation of a patient's family who send him to a hospital "to get well." As we view it, the individual in therapy starts a process of modifying his behavior and his perceptual frame of reference, and this process may continue into the indefinite future.

The general content of the lectures has been incorporated in a series of five booklets, "Learning to Live Effectively," that were prepared for the patients by staff members in the Psychology Department of the hospital (Dorman, Mahan, Paul, Peyman, Reynolds, and Webb, 1965). These booklets have the same titles as the lectures listed earlier. These booklets are made available to all patients, who are encouraged to read them on the wards. The preparation of the booklets was encouraged by the patients, many of whom indicated they believed they would learn more effectively with written materials than with audited information. Also, the books serve to keep the information in front of the patient during his leisure hours.

The material in these booklets is written in a simple manner, pitched at an elementary school achievement level. The first book is, more or less, a composite of the more detailed contents in the other four books.

In Part I, "Learning to be Responsible," the first two pages read:

> If a man were driving along in his car and the car started to run poorly, he would probably stop, take a look under the hood, and ask himself (perhaps somewhat impatiently), 'What is wrong?' Clearly there is some problem in the way the car is running, and the man is attempting to deal with the problem by finding out what the trouble is. He asks, 'What is wrong?' so that he can do something about it.
>
> Problems in people are, of course, very different from problems in cars. Cars have mechanical problems, whereas problems in people who come to a mental hospital are what we call *emotional problems*. When an individual has come to this kind of hospital, we may suppose that he, like the car, has not been running too well and that he therefore has emotional problems.
>
> When a car has a mechanical problem, it can be fixed by a mechanic. When people have physical ills and go to a regular hospital, they can be treated by a medical doctor. But with people who come

to a mental hospital, the problems are not mechanical *or* physical, but rather, emotional. While mechanics can fix cars and doctors can treat physical ills, with emotional problems we have to be our own mechanics; we have to do our own work on the problems.

When a car works poorly we are quick to ask, 'What is the problem? What is wrong?' But when we human beings have emotional trouble, we seem to have great difficulty in looking for the problem. What we seem to do is look for someone to blame instead of looking inside of ourselves for the source of the difficulty.

Now you have come to the hospital because you wanted some help, or because someone you know felt you needed some help. Perhaps you understand only too well that you have problems; but, whether you do or not, *someone* was concerned about you and felt you needed help. The first suggestion we have for you is that you fully understand you are *here* because you *do* have problems.

And *you have the problem*! Not your brother, your sister, your family, or the whole world, but you!

Most of your problems have to do with the way you get along with other people, how you feel about the folks you know, and how you feel about yourself. If you are feeling blue or depressed (as many people here are), you are certainly aware of a problem in you. This is an emotional problem. If you can understand that this is a problem in you, then you can start asking, 'What is wrong?' and you can start figuring out *why* you feel blue or depressed.

The next few pages explain how human beings look for someone or something to blame for their problems. Then, the easy reasons for coming to the hospital are enumerated, such as: "I am sick," "I need a rest," "I'm having a nervous breakdown," or "They brought me here to get rid of me."

These reasons are explored and questioned; for example, in dealing with the often-cited phrase "nervous breakdown" it is written:

> If you are saying this, a good question to ask yourself is 'Just what is a nervous breakdown?' Does it, in fact, mean that your nerves are broken? This is very unlikely. The term 'nervous breakdown' is a pat label which keeps you from looking for the real problems. It could mean a million things.
>
> Does it, for you, mean being frightened much of the time? Does it mean you are an anxious person? Do you feel, perhaps, that you are going to lose your mind at any minute, or that you are going to die very suddenly? Are you often tense? Is this what you mean by a nervous breakdown? Is it possible that you are depressed and sit around moping and stewing about the past, telling yourself you are no good and how nobody cares anything about you? Is this what you mean by a nervous breakdown? Until you find out what you do mean, it will be pretty difficult to work on the problem.

"Finding the Problem" is the next subject:

> What do you suppose *has* brought you here? How can you understand what your problems are? For many, one problem is that

they don't know what the problem *is*! It is necessary to figure this out, because until we understand 'what's wrong,' there is little that can be done to change it. When we say your problems are *in you*, what do we mean by that? Are your problems in your left foot or your right finger? This is certainly not what we mean. We mean that your problems are in two very important parts of you—those parts which make you a human being and guide your every action. Those two parts are your *thinking* and your *feelings*. Everyone knows that if a human being could not think or could not feel there would be nothing to him but an empty shell. If he could not think and could not feel, he would be powerless to move.

It's to see how important thinking and feeling is to an individual's very being. You deal with your problems by the way you think and by the way you handle your feelings. By thinking and feelings, you either work out your problems or make more problems for yourself. So, when we say your problems are in you what we really mean is that your problems are in the way you think, the way you manage your feelings, and the way you act as a result.

"Feelings Make Problems" is one of the many problems cited.

When you start figuring out what your problems are, a good place to look is in your feelings. You can begin to name some of your problems if you start identifying some of your feelings. Many of the problems we talk about are *problems* of *feeling*. Learning to live with our feelings is extremely important and will be talked about in Part Two.

But at this point, it is important to make clear to you that your feelings have a great deal to do with your being here. Many of us seldom take a good look at our feelings. We often have vague or sometimes intense feelings of hurt but do not try to put into words just what the hurt is. It is important to *name* your feelings for yourself, to identify them, to get them into words. Only then can you really begin to understand your problems. *What* is the hurt? *What* are the feelings? Are they anger, jealousy, fear, guilt, sexual feelings, worthlessness, or despair? How do you feel now? How did you feel before you came to the hospital? By finding words for your feelings, you can begin to do something about handling them better in the future.

After dealing with the identification of problems the discussion turns to learning to cope with problems. We can learn to change our attitudes, habits, and ways of thinking, behaving, and dealing with our feelings so we can live a more effective life. At the conclusion of Book I the theme of responsibility is summarized:

A person accepting responsibility for his own life and his problems makes certain acknowledgments to himself: 'First, I do indeed have problems, and these problems are in myself, in my own thinking, the way I get along with others, and the way I look at life. Second, since I do have problems and do not like the way I feel much of the time or the way my life has been going, I must begin to make some changes. These changes do not involve changing the world, but rather changing some things in me. Third, I recognize that I cannot make changes overnight, that it will be difficult, and that it will require a lot of effort and time in order to change. *But I am willing to make this effort.*'

If a person approaches his emotional problems in this manner, he is well on the way to getting himself straightened out. He will be able to feel more comfortable and at peace with himself, and he has a better chance of staying out of the hospital. This is our hope for you here at the hospital, and this is why we work in this direction. It is not easy to make changes in yourself. At times it requires a great deal of effort and sometimes hurtful soul-searching. It takes lots of practice and much trying out of new things. But you do have a choice, and you can change if you want to. You can change yourself and change your life. Life doesn't have to run you; *you* can run your life.

We hope by now you have some idea of what your problems may be. Your responsibility involves recognizing that your problems are in you, and that you must do something about them. The link between understanding they are in you and making the necessary changes lies in an awareness of what they are. We have talked of areas which you may consider: problems of feeling, problems in thinking and attitudes, and problems in behavior—problems of depression, problems of dependency, and problems of limit testing. The rest of this book is concerned with helping you to understand more fully how these problems work in you and what you can do about them. As for right now, you have moved forward a big step if you have accepted your responsibility. If you do not feel responsible, you are moving further and further away from any solution to your problems, which are bound to become more and more serious in the future.

Above all, we do not want you merely *to say* to us, 'Yes, I'm responsible for myself, my problems, and for doing something about them.' It's not a matter of learning words. It is a matter of actually *doing* something about your life. Don't just say you are responsible. Be *responsible*!

At the end of the didactic series the patients are placed in discussion groups, which meet two or three times per week on the ward, if suitable space is available, or in appropriate space elsewhere. Some of the group leaders prefer holding the groups elsewhere because they find a greater degree of attention and interest when the patients are off the ward. The primary purpose of these discussion groups is to clarify, in detail, the principles outlined during the didactic series and to encourage the patient to apply, in a concrete fashion, the abstract principles to himself and to other patients in the group. Thus, they are encouraged to give voice to specific examples of applying these principles, and to understand how problems develop and what steps they might take to overcome or deal more effectively with them. The influence of group pressures on a patient to modify his faulty thinking and perceptions or to alter his socially questionable behavior is pronounced, and often appears considerably more effective than the influence of any staff member. Patients are given specific assignments to work on, such as what they can do to modify their attitudes and what specific steps they can take to alter their overt behavior while they are in the hospital. Assignments may be made to carry out certain steps after the therapy sessions, to encourage attention and effort to working on specific problems while the patients are not engaged in some organized therapeutic activity.

There is considerable variability in the conducting of these large therapy groups, depending upon the experiences, inventiveness, and individuality of the therapists. Some of the group leaders have had some limited formal class work in psychology. Others have come from diverse educational backgrounds and received all their experiences in working with patients while employees of the hospital Psychology Department. In any case, originality and inventiveness are encouraged, and within the reasonable limits of good taste, any promising techniques are tried. A promising innovation is a technique of "critiquing," in which other staff members attend the large group sessions to formulate impressions, constructive criticisms, and suggestions which are communicated to the group leader immediately afterwards. The intention is to offer suggestions which hopefully lead to greater effectiveness of the leader and to overall program improvement. This technique serves not only to give feedback to the individual conducting the group but also as a means of developing and communicating new approaches, ideas, and techniques. The "critiquing" groups are open to any staff members who wish to attend.

Although the general content of the large therapy groups, and for that matter, of the overall program, is essentially that presented in the didactic lectures, the techniques are varied. It would be impractical to make a definitive list of all the techniques used but a few may be mentioned for illustration. Candy, cigarettes, coffee, and expressed approval, have been used to reinforce individuals who make contributions in the group. Two different techniques are involved. There is an increasing tendency to identify problem behavior patterns or deficits and to make a concerted effort to reinforce desired behavior and not to reinforce undesired behavior. These decisions are made in an interdisciplinary diagnostic and treatment clinic held for each patient. Recommendations are made as soon as possible after admission and at irregular intervals during his stay in the hospital. If some increased social activity is recommended for a patient and if behavior appears in the group, such as spontaneous interaction with a new arrival, reinforcement is administered. For another patient, the recommendation might be to exhibit less social aggression and to be more attentive to others. If such a person listens with apparent attention while another patient speaks, he would be reinforced. A second procedure is to allow the group leader to exercise discretion in determining whether a response should be reinforced.

The use of such extrinsic reinforcers has led to striking results. For example, leaders report a marked increase in verbal contributions. Nevertheless, as extrinsic reinforcers are administered, we encourage the individuals to reinforce *themselves* for their own contributions. We encourage them to set up their own programs for self-reinforcement within the group interaction, to define some desired immediate goal for themselves and then reinforce themselves when they attain it.

Guides for leading the discussion of key concepts have been developed for the group leaders. A few of the topics for which guides have been prepared are: "Feelings and Emotions," "Stimulus Value," "Guilt," "Problems in Thinking," and many others. These topics, which have emerged from the experiences of group leaders, have been supplemented and revised with the experiences of new personnel and are always in a state of change. As new editions are developed, they are communicated to group leaders for guidance in setting up their own program. It is to be stressed that these guides are not developed to function as agenda to be followed scrupulously by the group discussion leaders, but are to be viewed as potentially valuable distillates of the experiences of others who have led such groups.

Role-playing in various forms is encouraged. Typically, the patients become involved only with coercion, whether or not the therapist participates. Sometimes, particularly early in a program, patients are brought from other wards to play roles. Chronic patients who have developed attitudes of pessimism are often remarkably responsive to patients who have successfully coped with their problems. Almost any content may be acted out. Among the most common situations are those involving hospital staff, patient, and family interactions. It has been desirable to begin by introducing relatively nonthreatening, nonemotional examples, and gradually, over several sessions, introduce more emotionally loaded problem situations. Role-playing serves primarily to elicit feelings and emotional reactions which usually come to the surface much more readily than when the individual is indulging merely in a verbal account of his behavior. Concern is often expressed about returning to life outside, either in social contacts or in employment or school situations in which the individual anticipates numerous interactional problems. Many of these fears concern other people's attitudes toward ex-patients, "crazy people," expecting them to be violent, murderous, and in general, to manifest the traditional stereotypes. Often the patients are reluctant, at first, to verbalize such concerns, but many of these concerns can be verbalized and simulated in role-playing situations.

Action groups in contrast to verbal groups are encouraged, particularly with patients who do not appear to obtain optimum profit from purely verbal techniques. These action groups include participation in various types of constructive behavior. If the individual is reluctant to speak in groups he is encouraged to engage in such behavior. Confrontation of feared situations or events is encouraged and the individual is constantly encouraged to develop new methods or techniques to deal with problem situations. Stress is placed upon overt behavioral attempts to deal directly with problems.

Relaxation through techniques in progressive relaxation (Jacobson, 1938) is encouraged, and self-instructional programmed information is made available for the acquisition of such techniques. There are also programmed materials on emotions available to the patient so that self-instruction is made possible. The use of films for instructional or discussion purposes is also encouraged, as is the use of slides, poetry, narratives, or for that matter any other stimulus material that elicits constructive behavior. The emphasis is on a pragmatic approach; any modality (within reasonable limits) that proves effective is appropriate.

In general there is encouragement of interference with maladaptive or self-defeating behavior, modification of faulty attitudes, and the extinction of unacceptable behavior. There is an emphasis in the groups on altering behavior and a further emphasis on modifying underlying self-defeating attitudes. A widely used device is the formula "I.C.C.R.," with the letters standing for "Identify," "Challenge," "Contradict," and "Repeat." The person is to "Identify" the self-defeating attitude, belief, or thought that he holds and then demand evidence of himself for holding this belief. This is the "Challenge" part of the formula. If the individual is unable to support his belief, he can "Contradict" it. He is to "Repeat" this procedure each time he experiences the unpleasant emotion which in turn indicates the presence of some self-defeating attitude. The procedure sounds deceptively simple; actually it is a rather arduous and time-consuming procedure. The first step, "Identify," requires considerable effort for many. The person must recognize his emotional reaction (obvious to some, but not to others) and the perception that has led to it. He must be acquainted with the relation between such a belief as "I am worthless" and unpleasant feelings. Some of the most important self-defeating beliefs are listed by Ellis (1962).

The next step is to challenge the irrational idea, so that the individual has to defend his maintaining it. He challenges the validity of the idea or his judgment that it is "awful" to hold such ideas. He is encouraged to search diligently for evidence to support his position. This procedure is in marked contrast to the commonsense procedure of denying such beliefs or combating them with counterevidence. The method is often difficult to communicate because at first, it sounds strange and peculiar. To some, "It is consistent with the rest of the ideas of those crazy psychologists." The person is directed to dwell on the matter and consider and examine every shred of evidence he adduces. If he can offer any significant earthbound evidence to support his beliefs, he may, with our blessings, continue to hold them, but if he cannot, then he might do well to modify them. For many patients, particularly depressed ones, a major difficulty lies in their condemnation of their feelings or in their condemnation of themselves for having such feelings. Such a person is persuaded to challenge his belief that "It is wrong (awful, terrible, wicked, etc.) to feel this way." He is to demand of himself some evidence — any evidence — that having such experiences actually hurts anyone, including himself, in any way. His most usual response is that he might act in that fashion. Here, of course, another issue enters. We are not defending an amorality of actions but only of feelings and thoughts. The person had better exercise some controls over his actions if he is to live in reasonable harmony in our society, and we suggest he will be better able to exercise such controls if he can accept his feelings and thoughts without condemning them. The person is required to spend much time on this matter because he is the one who has to be satisfied that there is no substantial foundation for continuing to hold such self-defeating beliefs.

When he does find that he cannot support them, he is able to contradict them. It is to be noted that a contradiction is not an opposite. If he contradicts the belief, "It is terrible for me to feel this way," he concludes, "It is not terrible to feel this way." This is a far cry from the opposite, "It is wonderful to feel this way."

The final step, "Repeat," is an important one to stress. The person will have to repeat the procedure every time the unpleasant emotion occurs, even though this occurs numerous times each day. This procedure is widely used by the patients, and many of them just drop the mnemonic device we have supplied and call the process "I.C.C.R.-ing." A point that must be stressed is that the individual who applies it will probably not receive marked tension reduction the first time he uses it. It is not a magic formula that, once uttered, solves the difficulty. He must realize that he will have to apply it repeatedly over a period of time before any significant results are obtained. Thus, he should not be led to expect immediate returns, but he should be encouraged to repeat it frequently. Too many patients expect a miraculous change in themselves once they apply this formula, and when they quickly find that such a miracle does not occur, they become disenchanted. However, those who apply this procedure over a period of time usually report significantly effective results.

As patients show progress and demonstrate that they are expending effort in working on their problems, they may be moved to small groups where considerably more emphasis is placed upon each individual's problems and the development of more effective solutions to these problems. These groups meet on the average of three times per week and consist of between 8 and 12 patients.

In addition to these small groups there are patient-led groups which meet on the wards, usually in the late evening, after regular staff hours. These groups are relatively unstructured and function more or less autonomously, with staff members of the Psychology Department acting as consultants when needed. These groups have proven particularly valuable in thrashing out issues that, for one reason or another, are difficult to deal with in other groups. These patient-led groups may function, at times, as specific problem solving groups in which problems immediately affecting the members can be effectively dealt with on the spot.

In addition to these groups, a continuing series of didactic lectures is conducted for relatives and friends of patients. The content of these lectures consists of the same principles communicated to the patients. The therapy procedures are described to provide an indication of what might be expected from the patient when he returns and what contributions individuals in the home environment can make in the patient's rehabilitation. The content is realistic and emphasizes the "emotional problem solving" approach that is the central theme of our therapy program.

Another segment of the total program is a direct approach to the treatment of alcoholic patients. At present, admission to this program is restricted to volunteers. Patients may have been involuntarily hospitalized but must voluntarily agree to participate in this program and not be under duress or threat to be in it. Voluntary admission to the program is stressed because of the general emphasis on individual responsibility. It is argued that no reasonable method known can force an individual to refrain from consuming alcohol, but rather the individual must be willing to find some way to abstain. The restriction of admission to voluntary patients theoretically restricts participation in the program to individuals who, at least, give lip service to a desire to abstain from drinking and to take some measures to accomplish this goal. The program is based on the premise that individuals consume alcohol because they have found it to be an effective substance in reducing tension, and on the basis of previous learning, continue to consume alcohol when they are in situations they perceive as stressful or when they experience stress. The general order of events is: drinking followed by a reinforcing or rewarding experience of tension reduction and, usually, at a considerably later time, a negatively reinforcing experience such as a hangover, loss of job, or threatened family relations. Such a sequence of events increases the probability of excessive drinking behavior. Our program plays a role in assisting the individual to interfere with this chain of events in two ways: by assisting the individual to modify the action part of the paradigm and to attack the point of view part, to avoid tension before it is developed.

The core of the program is the use of mild electric shock applied when the individual imbibes alcohol. He is presented with small one-ounce paper cups filled, respectively, with dilute portions of blended whiskey, vodka, wine, beer, water, and a nonalcoholic soft drink. He is asked to consume each of these in turn. When he imbibes the alcohol he is given a direct current applied to the arm for 30 seconds duration; voltage 40 volts and amperage 5–8 milliamps. The equipment used to present the electric shock is a stimulator used in earlier times for electroconvulsive therapy with patients. When the patient drinks the nonalcoholic beverages he is not given the shock. On the first treatment session the individual is required to drink all the beverages. During the following sessions the patient is given the opportunity to choose among the beverages presented and is allowed to leave off one or more of the beverages of his choice. Each time he chooses a beverage containing alcohol, he is given 30 seconds of shock treatment. This procedure is repeated on a half-dozen occasions for the next 10 days at the end of which the patient is released from the hospital.

It is stressed to the patients that the purpose of this procedure is not to prevent them from consuming alcohol, because the patient, himself, is really the only person who can keep himself from drinking, but that the purpose is to create an anxiety response to the presence of alcohol. There is a paradox involved: on one hand we argue that alcohol is a way of reducing tension and on the other that we are deliberately associating anxiety with alcohol. We reason that tension in the presence of alcohol, when recognized by the individual, will serve as a signal to him that he is in a situation that may lead to drinking, and that he has an opportunity to engage in some alternate form of behavior. The analogy is drawn to the signal lights on the dashboard of a car which serve to indicate that a danger is at hand, or that a problem may develop. Another analogy is to a cautionary traffic light that alerts the individual to exercise vigilance. The stress throughout the program is on the individual's responsibility to find more desirable ways of dealing with stress than drinking. To assist him in achieving this goal various devices are used, for example: the entire group of patients involved in the treatment program are present while a shock is being administered, in order to see the effects of it on others and, perhaps, share vicariously the experience. Initially, each patient was given the shock in private, but upon the recommendation of the patients, the entire group now acts as observers. A large mirror is placed in front of the patient while he is receiving the shock, so he may observe himself. A polaroid photograph is taken of the patient while undergoing the treatment, and he is permitted to take the photo with him upon discharge. He is encouraged to refer to the photo when he is outside the institution and is tempted to drink. One ex-patient who had been through the program took a rather improbable job as bartender and reported that he placed the picture of himself receiving the treatment above the cash register and observed it each time he rang up a sale.

In stressing the individual's responsibility to cease drinking, the purposes that alcohol serves for the patient are emphasized, particularly its tension-reducing qualities. The identification of just what tensions the alcohol is reducing for the individual is stressed so that he becomes aware of what positive function alcohol is serving for him. The patient is then urged to develop reasons convincing to himself that he should give up alcohol and learn to live without it. This is no small task. Too many individuals point out that relatives disapprove or that the long-term consequences are undesirable from the point of view of other people. These reasons are rarely of sufficient importance to the person to lead to alternative behavior because the alcohol has been too effective in reducing his immediate and intense misery. He is encouraged, also, to list reasons that are convincing to him to refrain from drinking and to record these on cards he can carry and refer to when he leaves the hospital.

While in the hospital, attendance is required at weekly Alcoholics Anonymous meetings. The patients are also encouraged to affiliate with A.A. groups when they leave the hospital, and with the patient's permission, a letter is written to an appropriate A.A. chapter. Thus, both the patient and the A.A. chapter are alerted to follow-up service following discharge.

The patient is encouraged to explore a variety of forms of behavior other than those he has used in the past to assist him in tension reduction. These may include the development of job training, further education, instruction in progressive relaxation, development of hobbies, and development of techniques for accomplishing rapid stress reduction. As in other aspects of the therapy program, emphasis is placed upon the point of view in our basic adjustmental paradigm. It is important to discover how the individual is perceiving situations and, in essence, his evaluations of events, his judgments about them, his self-defeating beliefs, attitudes, etc. Much of the treatment time expended is directed toward assisting the patient to modify his self-defeating attitudes.

After 10 days in the program the patient is released from the hospital with instructions to return at the end of one month, and then six months later, for further exposure to the conditioning procedure. He is asked to remain overnight on each occasion, receiving one treatment the afternoon he arrives, and another the following morning.

This program, in the relatively short time it has been developed, has indicated its effectiveness in various ways. There is an increasing number of referrals of new patients to the program from patients who have gone through it, returned home, and recommended to their friends who drink excessively that they, too, should attend the program. This is in marked contrast to previous treatment programs for alcoholism in this institution. Many participants have been treated by other agencies prior to taking part in this program and report that the results are markedly different and more successful than they have been in previous treatments. It is difficult to obtain firm data to demonstrate the effectiveness of the program because of difficulties involved in the follow-up of patients after they leave the hospital. One striking piece of information is the relatively low recidivism rate found in patients who have gone through this program; that is, the number of individuals who have completed the program and who have returned to the hospital for treatment of alcoholism. It is currently 10 percent. This figure has held approximately constant over a period of about two years. This is not to imply that the success rate is 90 percent but that only 10 percent are known to return for treatment. This is in marked contrast to a figure considerably higher before the advent of this program when the recidivism rate was roughly 80 percent. All in all the alcohol treatment program shows marked promise and is expected to be expanded and developed in the future.

Another growing part of the hospital program, mentioned earlier, is the development of token programs for individuals and for entire wards. When patients are unable or unwilling to respond to the verbal and action types of treatment, they are often involved in token economies. Much assistance for administering these programs is given by patients. While wards are involved and, with few exceptions, such wards house the more chronic patients. In general, the procedures reward and encourage constructive, desirable, and socially acceptable behavior with desirable objects, materials, or privileges. Socially undesirable behavior is dealt with by extinction procedures. As the patients progress in self-determination and socially responsible behavior, they are moved to wards where increasing self-management is stressed, and the individual can take ever-increasing responsibilities.

Individual token programs are set up with token procedures designed to shape specific acceptable behavior patterns. Here, as is the case with ward programs, the individual is encouraged to become self-directing and to set up programs for self-reinforcement so that he can organize his own reinforcement program, and in essence, become self-directing. Our general approach is to encourage self-responsibility and autonomy because this is primarily what is expected of the person when he leaves the hospital. We might say that our purpose in starting people on a token program is to get them off the token program; that is, to be sufficiently self-directing to no longer require the use of such concrete devices. Our stress throughout the program is on developing the potentialities of the person as an "active" being in contrast to being a "reactive" being. Tendencies toward self-responsibility are encouraged. In the absence of evidence of any significant degree of self-responsibility, behavior shaping is conducted until the person shows evidence of self-direction. At this point, he is encouraged to pursue the procedure on his own.

In evaluating our program, the most striking evidence lies in the verbalized attitudes of patients. Staff members, who were here prior to the inauguration of our present program, are impressed by the obvious changes of patients whose attitudes have altered from one of dependency to one of self-assertive responsibility. Also, the reports of patients who have elsewhere experienced unsuccessful treatment often consist of remarks to the effect that, "This is the first time I have known there was anything I could do about myself," or "I wish I had known about this 10 years ago."

We have made some efforts to measure changes in achievement before and after exposure to didactic groups. It is not difficult to demonstrate that people can alter their responses to questions after being exposed to instruction. Thus the changes in achievement scores to tests of the content of the didactic series is to be expected if the patients are attentive and if the class leader is communicating. Such changes may only reflect patients' reinforcing the class leader, an attempt to avoid further exposure to the lectures if they do not answer correctly, or perhaps a rather passive effort to earn an early release from the hospital by responding in the way they think they are supposed to answer. Changes in achievement test scores, then, do not necessarily reflect changes in attitudes or beliefs. It is often difficult to interpret such test scores. Bernard, Kinzie, Tollman, and

Webb (1965) studied the effects on psychiatric patients of a series of five lectures on the psychology of adjustment. The MMPI and the Personal Health Inventory were administered before and after exposure to the lectures. Significant changes occurred in the group attending the lectures as compared to the control group.

Our hope for future program development is basically in the direction of prevention. It is hoped that the principles that we believe to be effective in modifying or correcting behavior can be used to prevent ineffective behavior, and materials for such use are being composed. We hope that such information can be included in school programs. We also are in the process of developing our techniques to work more effectively with low literacy individuals and with those in lower socioeconomic groups so that our techniques and concepts can be more effectively communicated and applied to them.

The program is ever-changing; as more skills and techniques are being developed by group members, they are being communicated to other members, tried, and evaluated. Staff members are encouraged to question their procedures and to continue searching for more effective ways of assisting patients. The program is always in transition and, hopefully, will lead to major changes in developing self-direction attitudes and behavior in the most important members of the groups — the patients.

In the foregoing, others who participate in the total therapy program have not been stressed, since in Responsibility Therapy the patient is the most important member. The idea of the staff doing something *to* the patient is discredited. However, no matter what therapy is used, consistency is important and facilitates the learning process in the patients. A nursing colleague who is an advocate of the team approach illuminated this point when she said, "I have been teaching attitude therapy for many years to nursing personnel, but it did not work until all who were involved with patients used the same approach." This is our goal now and for the future: that patient, physicians, nursing personnel, psychologists, social workers, maintenance staff, patient activity workers, diet kitchen workers, and all other individuals who work closely with the patient will be part of the therapy team and will be called upon to contribute their own expertise to Responsibility Therapy.

REFERENCES

Bernard, J. L., Kinzie, W. B., Tollman, G. A. & Webb, R. A. Some effects of a brief course in the psychology of adjustment on a psychiatric admission ward. *Journal of Clinical Psychology*, 1965, **21**, 322–326.

Dorman, L. B., Mahan, M., Paul, W. C., Peyman, D. A. R., Reynolds, R. D. & Webb, R. A. Part one: Learning to be responsible. In *Learning to live effectively*. Alabama State Hospitals, 1965. (Mimeo).

Ellis, A. *Reason and emotion in psychotherapy*. New York: Lyle Stuart, 1962.

Jacobson, E. *Progressive relaxation*. Chicago: University of Chicago Press, 1938.

Phillips, E. L. *Psychotherapy: A modern theory and practice*. Englewood Cliffs, N. J.: Prentice-Hall, 1956.

CHAPTER 16

Environmental Control and Retardate Behavior[1]

John Hamilton

Gracewood State School and Hospital is a typical state institution for the retarded. Its residential population, males and females of all ages, approximates 2000, as does its waiting list. The residents are housed in separate buildings called cottages which hold about 60 each. Despite improvements over the years, overcrowding and understaffing continue to exist. Residents attend a variety of recreational, educational, and work activities which take them to other areas, but the cottages remain home base. The more severely retarded the resident, the more time he spends in the cottage; therefore, the more influential is that environment on him.

Recognizing the importance of these living environments, a program has been conducted during the past four years aimed at developing more effective procedures at the cottage level. The operational framework has been the application of reinforcement principles to the analysis and control of behavior (e.g., Keller & Schoenfield, 1950; Skinner, 1953; and Holland & Skinner, 1961). There have been numerous applications of operant conditioning methods to the modification of specific behaviors (Harris, Wolf & Baer, 1964; Wolf, Risley & Mees, 1964; Patterson & Ebner, 1965; Ullmann & Krasner, 1965; Wahler et al., 1965; and Ferster & Simons, 1966; to name a few), and the applied research in this area has continued to multiply

[1]This program was aided by Hospital Improvement Project Grant MH-01722-02 from the National Institute of Health. Specific acknowledgements are difficult to make since so many played significant roles in planning and implementing the goals of this program. The following deserve special mention for their contributions to and assistance with this report: Pat Allen, Emilie Davall, Billie Farris, Don Gannon, Susan Hunt, Nancy Martin, Richardean Martin, Lynn Stephens, and D. W. Tyler. The superintendent, Norman B. Pursley, provided active and continued support without which this program could not have been implemented. In addition to his readiness to experiment with new ideas and encourage changes within the program, he was instrumental in generalizing procedures and results to other areas of the institution.

productively. Applications through systematic environmental control in psychiatric institutional settings have been clearly demonstrated in the work of Ayllon and his co-workers (Ayllon & Michael, 1959; Ayllon & Haughton, 1962, 1964; Ayllon, 1963; and Ayllon & Azrin, 1968). During the past few years, there has been an enhanced interest in the application of such programming procedures in institutions for the retarded (e.g., Girardeau & Spradlin, 1964; Bensberg, 1965; Bensberg, Colwell & Cassel, 1965; Edwards & Lilly, 1966; Whitney & Barnard, 1966; Birnbrauer, 1967; Burchard, 1967; Lent, LeBlanc & Spradlin, 1967; and Watson, 1967).

The site selected for this experimental program was a unit containing five cottages in which more than 300 retarded females resided. The age, intelligence, and diagnostic distributions were representative of the total institution, so that, except for the female bias, the findings would be applicable to the general institutional population. The five cottages were interconnected under one roof, each with a fenced-in outdoor play area. Included in the unit was a central kitchen and large dining room. The unit was originally staffed by 40 attendants and consultative and supporting staff from psychology, social work, cottage supervision, resident training, nursing, secretarial, housekeeping, supply, maintenance, and food service.

The basic problem which initially prevailed was the lack of opportunity for change in the organization, either at the resident or staff level. The residents were provided minimal opportunities for new learning since their existing levels of performance were interpreted as their optimal levels of performance. The cottage personnel seemed very isolated from the higher level staff members who were in position to implement changes.

The initial changes were in the physical environment (Pursley & Hamilton, 1965). There was a regrouping of the cottages (previously grouped on a random basis) which resulted in the distributions listed in Table 1.

TABLE 1
Resident Statistics by Cottages Following Regrouping

Cottage	N	IQ Range	Average IQ	Age Range	Average Age
I	54	below 20	below 20	10–33	19
II	57	10–46	26	12–48	21
III	59	20–77	44	10–21	16
IV	61	20–65	36	17–44	25
V	87	23–83	48	18–61	38

The immediate result of the regrouping was that two of the four cottages that were previously locked became open cottages. The more homogeneous groupings also made it easier to design programs to meet the needs of the populations within each of the cottages. Other physical changes included providing individual clothes lockers in the open cottages; introducing normal living room furniture such as tables, chairs, and couches; converting all beds to double bunks which halved the previously required dormitory space; and installing toilet, shower, and bedroom dividers to provide more personal privacy.

Altering, modifying, and refining the physical environment continued to be important throughout the project. However, the real foundation for improvement in resident care resulted from the development of changes in management and treatment philosophies and practices.

Organizational Effectiveness

The following conversation between a supervisor and an attendant occurred on a winter evening in a badly overheated cottage:

S. It sure is hot in here!
A. Yes, it sure is.
S. How long has it been this way?
A. Since I came on duty several hours ago.
S. Why didn't you open some windows or turn down the radiators?
A. Nobody told me to.

During the past few decades, increasingly important contributions have been made in the areas of organization and management. The most significant pioneering work was done by Elton Mayo in his enlightening series of experiments at the Hawthorne works of the Western Electric Company in Chicago between 1927 and 1932 (Gellerman, 1963). Since then, helpful extensions and contributions have been made by such people as Whyte (1955), White (1959), McGregor (1960), Gellerman (1963), Argyris (1964), Herzberg (1966), and Likert (1967). One finding has been that many of the traditional concepts of organization inhibit productivity. Organizational philosophies today still vary widely. At one end of the continuum the emphasis is on productivity in which management relies on the authoritarian approach in making all decisions regarding goals and methods of implementation, using the employees in an exploitative sense to fulfill these ambitions. At the other end of the continuum is the employee-centered approach which emphasizes individual and group participation in organizational goals and methods of implementation. Research has shown that the more that an organization moves toward the employee-centered approach, the more productive it becomes. The reason for this seeming paradox is that individuals have a wide variety of abilities, skills, and resources which tend to be suppressed in an authoritarian structure. Under the authoritarian structure, the good employee is the one who does as he is told. In such systems the individuals have little or no control over their own work environment and, in general, are in the dehumanized position of being used by the organization. Consequently, morale tends to be low, turnover and absenteeism high, self-esteem and individual initiative low, and productivity at a minimally acceptable level. As organizations move toward the employee-centered approach, the individuals gain more responsibility and control over their own work environment; they participate more in organizational decisions, they feel more freedom in expressing their own personal feelings and suggestions, they have the opportunity to raise their own levels of competence, and they have less need for such combative tactics as work restriction and absenteeism.

Most of this research has been done in industrial organizations which produce a tangible product. However, the analogy to other types of organizations seems quite clear. In institutions for the retarded the care, development, training, and education of the residents are analogous to the product of the industrial organization. In the typical institution it is the attendant who is at the bottom of the authoritarian pyramid but *it is the attendant who most directly controls the care and the development of the residents*. The extent to which the organizational structure is employee-centered may well be the most significant factor in determining the quality of treatment given to the residents.

In the organizational unit described in this report, the goal has been to shift from the authoritarian toward the employee-centered approach. It is difficult to objectively evaluate the extent of this shift or its effectiveness on resident programming. However, it was our impression that as progress was made, morale at all levels was increased, tension was reduced, individual self-expression was enhanced, and resident care, treatment, and programming were facilitated.

The attendants in each cottage were administratively responsible to one supervisor. Each of the five cottage supervisors was administratively responsible to the unit director. Various supportive services such as psychology, social service, nursing, and speech therapy were available as needed. However, they were not administratively responsible to the cottage supervisor nor were the cottage supervisors administratively responsible to them. Each cottage was staffed by a team of regular and supportive personnel. Once a week a meeting was held in each cottage which was attended by the unit director, cottage supervisor, as many attendants from all shifts as possible, and as many members from the supportive services as possible. The meetings were informal and stressed group participation. Their purpose was to discuss resident problems and programs. For example, if a child was presenting problems a behavior modification plan was discussed. Once a group decision was reached, the program was put into effect. The more honest and direct the group participation, the more realistic, creative, and consistent were the programs.

In addition to increased participation in resident programming, cottage personnel were given more direct responsibility for such things as their own job assignments, time scheduling, and reports of performance. The idea that most attendants want to avoid responsibility, work only because they have to, and want to do as little as possible is a gross miscalculation which leaves the authoritarian approach as the only alternative. We found that cottage attendants under the appropriate conditions were not only eager for more active participation and responsibility, but had a great deal to offer.

Controlling Problem Behaviors

There is a tendency in the overcrowded, understaffed cottage setting to define behavior problems as only those behaviors which are disruptive such as violent, noisy, and destructive behaviors. The withdrawn, unresponsive resident is not generally considered a problem. There is also a tendency to consider problem behaviors as being irrational, abnormal, deviant, and pathological, and not as consequences of environmental conditions.

In working with behavior problems we accepted the basic tenet that behavioral development follows lawful learning processes (Eysenck, 1947; Dollard & Miller, 1950; and Skinner, 1953). Within this framework it is not meaningful to categorize behaviors as deviant, abnormal, or pathological since they are logical consequences of their developmental histories. Sidman (1960) spoke directly to this point in a series of animal experiments which illustrated the normality of the processes underlying behaviors which initially seemed bizarre and nonadaptive. Ayllon, Haughton, and Hughes (1965) produced and eliminated a bizarre behavior pattern (compulsive broom-carrying) in an institutionalized patient through standard reinforcement and extinction procedures.

Our procedure in dealing with a behavior problem was first to specify the behavior as clearly as possible and then to attempt to determime its reinforcing consequences. When these could be clearly specified, behavior modification programming was used to alter the consequences.

Most of the residents exhibiting serious disruptive-type behaviors were grouped together in Cottage II. The frequency of behavior problems was so high that the cottage staff was spending most of its time attending to them. The environment was conducive to the development and maintenance of undesirable behaviors because they were such effective attention-getters. Consequently, there were high rates of behaviors such as fighting, destroying property, tearing clothes, breaking windows, self-abuse, and violent temper tantrums. These behaviors were reduced by using a procedure which altered their reinforcing consequences. The method was confinement to an area for a period of time, usually 30 minutes, immediately following the un-desired behavior. In this area[2] there was a row of chairs, bolted to the floor, with locked restraining belts. For each chair, a bell-ringing timer was provided to ensure accuracy of the time-out durations. No one interacted with residents during periods of confinement. In this way a large number and wide variety of behavior problems were controlled (Hamilton, Stephens & Allen, 1967).

When the reinforcing consequences of a particular behavior problem occurred only in the cottage setting, the problem was usually corrected if all occurrences of the undesirable behavior were unre-warded. To be effective all significant persons in that environment needed to be consistent in the behavior modification procedures that were adopted. However, in the relatively restrictive environment of the cottage there were numerous sources of variability and inconsistency. For example, there were differences in interpretation and implementa-tion of programs, uncontrolled behavior of cottage visitors, and uncontrolled behavior of other residents. By working together these sources of variability were gradually minimized, but environmental control remained the biggest problem. The following case illustrated one of the effects of personnel turnover on one behavior modification program.

Case

Betty Jean, a moderately retarded 20-year-old girl, occa-sionally experienced grand mal epileptic seizures. In addition

---

[2]This area was referred to as a time-out area because there the resident was removed from the usual reinforcing consequences of the undesirable behavior. Time-out from positive reinforcement has been considered to be a punishing stimulus (Azrin & Holz, 1966). Other aversive consequences of the procedure such as the discomfort of con-finement and restraint were also part of the punishing situation. The procedure may most appropriately be described as punishment in operational terms since it is a consequence of a behavior that reduces the future probability of that behavior (Azrin & Holz, 1966).

she developed the technique of faking seizures which she frequently used as a means of having her wishes fulfilled. The
fact that these seizures were under her control was evidenced
by the convenience of their occurrences and their immediate
termination when positive alternatives were offered. For
example, if while lying on the floor in this "seizure" activity
she were told she could go to the store, she would immediately
jump up and race from the cottage. There were also directly
observable differences between real and fake seizures. In
order to alter their reinforcing consequences, she was restrain-
ed to her bed whenever fake seizures occurred and left there
until they ceased. Restraint to the bed was used instead of
ignoring the seizure since she usually cut, scrapped, and bruis-
ed herself on the floor, which was perhaps the reason that it
was such an effective manipulative technique. Although observed during this time, she was given no social reinforcement.
The results of this program are presented in Figure 1 in a
cumulative record of frequency of seizures over a 270-day
period.

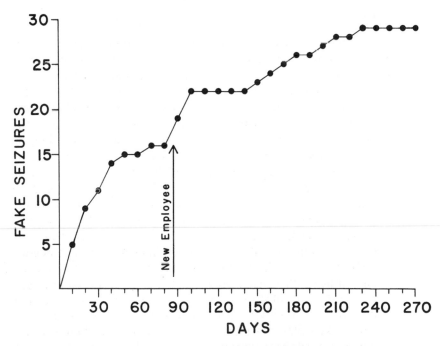

Fig. 1. Cumulative record of the number of fake seizures occurring over a 270-day period.
The arrow indicates the point at which a new employee started to work.

In the absence of the usual reinforcing consequences, the fake seizures were brought under control quite rapidly and by the end of 60 days occurred rarely. When a new employee came to work, they returned to the frequency at the onset of the program. The increase in the rate in the presence of the new employee indicated that although Betty had learned that with the standard people in her environment these seizures were no longer useful, she still needed to test out the new person. As the new employee learned to follow the program consistently, the accelerated recurrence of symptoms was temporary with no recurrences for the next 120 days. This type of phenomenon is not unusual, but unfortunately in the typical cottage setting the pertinent variables are not usually so clearly specifiable. For example, from days 140 to 230 there were seven recurrences before the rate was again reduced to zero level, but the contributing factors were not determined.

Some undesirable behaviors have reinforcing consequences which occur outside the cottage environment and create additional problems of control.

Case

One such case was a severely retarded 21-year-old girl named *Lillian* who controlled the cottage personnel by breaking windows with her hands when her demands were not met. Cottage programming reduced the average frequency of this behavior from one a day to one a week. One remaining consequence of window-breaking was an occasional trip to the hospital for treatment of more serious lacerations. During these visits she was played with, joked with, given presents such as empty plastic bottles, and in general was positively reinforced by the hospital staff. This was a consequence outside the cottage for a behavior which was occurring in the cottage. Since there were so many different physicians and nurses attending to the residents, program control was established in the following manner. Whenever Lillian needed to be treated at the hospital one of the cottage staff accompanied her with a sign saying, "Lillian is on a special program, please do not talk to her, give her anything, or show her any unnecessary attention. When you have finished treating her, I will take her back with me." As the hospital staff cooperated, window-breaking occurred less frequently and was eventually controlled with only occasional recurrences spaced many months apart.[3]

Some undesirable behaviors persist which have no apparent reinforcing consequences in the present environment. For example, mildly self-abusive behaviors may be completely ignored and yet they continue. This does not mean that they were always ignored and during their developmental stages may have been actively reinforced until well established. Behaviors which were reinforced in the past may have reinforcing consequences in the present, but in the less obvious form of conditioned reinforcers (Staats & Staats, 1963. pp. 95–98). The following is an example of a case of stereotyped behavior which had no apparent reinforcing consequences in the cottage environment.

Case

Janice, a moderately retarded 21-year-old, would sit and bump her back against the cement wall of the cottage. Time samples and frequency counts taken prior to programming indicated that she spent about one-third of her waking hours engaged in this stereotyped behavior. In the past, periods of encouraging her to stop and periods of completely ignoring the behavior had been equally ineffective.

The program consisted of adding an aversive consequence by placing Janice in the time-out area for a period of 30 minutes following each occurrence of wall-bumping behavior. As a result, wall-bumping occurred only on 11 more occasions and was eliminated by the ninth day. The behavior recurred on only three subsequent occasions. Three months later she went home for a short vacation. The stereotyped behavior recurred once prior to and once after returning from this vacation. In each case the time-out procedure suppressed the behavior. Home vacations for Janice have always been upsetting events which were followed by temporary regressions in general behavior.

---

[3]Case reports like this are presented as descriptive techniques rather than as experimental verifications. Therefore, they need to be interpreted cautiously in regard to specifying the pertinent variables. In this case, for example, it would appear that the addition of the hospital program was the primary influential variable in controlling the window-breaking behavior. In the absence of more verifiable indices such as reversal or multiple baseline procedures, all that may be said is that the hospital program in combination with the continuing cottage program seemed to be an important addition.

The third recurrence was several months later as a result of participation in an experimental program. The program consisted of a lever pulling task for 20 minutes a day, during which she received candy rewards under various schedules of reinforcement. Regardless of the scheduling, she invariably earned a handful of rewards following each 20-minute session. The problem started when the first extinction series was begun, during which Janice received no rewards regardless of how many times she pulled the lever. After one or two sessions she became very upset and the stereotyped rocking recurred not only during the sessions but in the cottage. Previously she had been bringing rewards back to the cottage before eating them which suggested that they were used as evidence to the staff and other residents that she had done a good job. Therefore, she was given a handful of noncontingent rewards prior to the onset of the sessions, which she also brought to the cottage and which resulted in the abrupt termination of the crying and rocking responses.

In some cases the disciplinary procedures themselves seemed to be perpetuating and maintaining the very behaviors they were intended to control. For example, with more capable residents the standard procedure for inappropriate behavior was deprivation of privileges (dances, parties, movies, canteen, etc.) for as long as two weeks. A number of residents were on almost continuous restriction, because new misbehaviors occurred before old restrictions were terminated which resulted in an accumulation of consecutive restrictions. Ironically, the new misbehaviors often were consequences of the old restrictions. For example, on Monday one resident was restricted from all activities for a week because of a violent temper tantrum. On Thursday she became upset because she had to miss a dance party, had another temper outburst, and had another week's restriction added, which created a continuing cycle of frustrations and violent reactions. A different approach was adopted, placing the consequences of the residents' behavior under their own control. Restriction was limited to 24 hours from the time of the last punishable incident. If, having been restricted at 12:00 noon on one day, a resident had a tantrum at 1:00 p.m., the restriction was extended until 1:00 p.m. the following day. To get off restriction, one had to behave for a 24-hour period. This procedure was very effective in quickly controlling residents who had been chronic behavior problems.

As behavior problems were minimized, more time was available for the development and strengthening of appropriate behaviors. The shortsightedness in programming suppressive techniques for behavior problems without also programming positive reinforcement procedures for appropriate behaviors became apparent. One possible reason for this lag was that suppressive techniques were easier to apply following inappropriate behaviors than were positive reinforcements during periods of appropriate responding. However, the positive reinforcement methods appeared to have more far-reaching consequences. By directly strengthening appropriate behaviors, new response patterns tended to replace less appropriate response patterns, and regressions were not likely to occur. On the other hand, when punishing consequences were removed, there was a tendency for undesirable behaviors to return if they had not been replaced by other behaviors.

The suggestion that inappropriate behaviors are operants that compete with other operants (Lindsley, 1956; Ferster & DeMyer, 1961; Sidman, 1962; and Staats & Staats, 1963) implies that inappropriate responses would be weakened in a setting which concentrated on reinforcing only appropriate behaviors. In fact, it would be possible to consider the frequency of behavior problems as a measure of program inadequacy. Consequently, more time was spent engaging the residents in activities throughout the day which provided more opportunities for the reinforcement of appropriate behaviors. With this change in program emphasis, suppressive techniques such as isolation, restraint, and confinement to the time-out area were reserved for behaviors which were physically aggressive or destructive.

Developmental Skills

Toilet Training

Since the publication of Ellis' article (1963) on a stimulus-response reinforcement analysis of toilet training, operant conditioning procedures have been applied to toilet training in institutions for the retarded (Ball, 1966; Dayan, 1964; Baumeister & Klosowski, 1965; Bensberg, Colwell & Cassel, 1965; Gorton & Hollis, 1965; Hundziak, Maurer & Watson, 1965; Giles & Wolf, 1966; Miron, 1966; Comtois & Holland, 1967; Kimbrell, Luckey, Barbuto & Love, 1967; and Rosenberg, 1967). In these programs the usual procedure has been to set up a training schedule, based on the times when most accidents occurred, and then to reinforce appropriate toileting behavior. The general finding has been that with consistent programming, successes on the toilet increase and accidents in the cottage decrease.

In a review article of toilet training programs, Watson (1967) commented that from many reports it was difficult to determine the effectiveness of the training procedures after the programs were discontinued. His experience at Columbus State School indicated that residents tended to regress when they were no longer in a rigidly controlled program. He attributed such regression to the following: (1) a breakdown in stimulus control when a project was ended; (2) a loss of stimulus control when the environmental conditions were changed, such as transferring a resident back to his home cottage or introducing new personnel into the training cottage; and (3) a failure to bring the cues related to toileting behavior under control of the retardate's own physiological bladder and bowel stimuli.

Our initial attempt at toilet training was with 10 profoundly retarded girls who were moved to a separate section of Cottage I. Progress was rapid and within two months accidents were occurring infrequently. To test the adequacy of training, the program was discontinued. The residents continued to use the toilets with very few accidents. It appeared that toilet training had been achieved but at that point different staff were brought to the area. Toilet proficiency regressed to its original level; the residents were no longer using the toilets independently. When the original staff members returned to the area, the residents once again appeared to be toilet trained. Through observation, it was found that the training staff had been inadvertently cueing the residents to the toilet area. They had become so familiar with the residents that they were anticipating their needs and providing prompts. For example, when one girl began to fidget, which was a sign that she needed to void, the trainer began glancing from her to the toilet area adding a slight nod of the head. The most crucial and difficult step in toilet training had not been accomplished: cues relating to toileting behavior were not under the retardate's own control. The cottage staff had been well-trained in anticipating the toileting needs of the residents, but the residents had not learned to anticipate their own needs.

The next attempt was with 12 different profoundly retarded females who had IQ's below 20, could not talk, and were being provided total care in feeding, toileting, bathing, and dressing. They were assigned to a small area containing six double bunks, dayroom space, and toilet chairs. Concurrent with toilet training they were coached in dressing and feeding. All showed marked improvement in a short period of time and eventually, in most cases, mastered these skills. The toilet training procedure was as follows:

Command training (7 days). The purpose of this phase was to teach the residents to follow verbal commands. They were given daily individual training sessions during which they received consumable and social rewards for learning to follow commands such as "come here," "sit down," "stand up," "go to the water fountain," and "go to the toilet." By the end of this period, they had each learned an average of 16 out of the 18 commands.

Phase I (11 days). Prior to training, each resident was checked every two hours on a 24-hour basis for wetting and soiling accidents. During this period the daily totals ranged from 91 to 125, with a daily average of 103 accidents. The first phase of the standard graph in Figure 2 illustrates these frequencies.

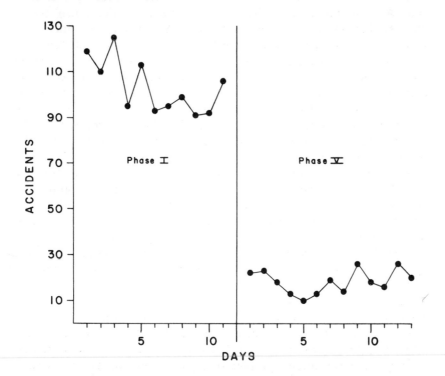

Fig. 2. Total number of accidents per day for 12 girls before and after toilet training.

Phase II (19 days). At nine scheduled times daily, which were determined from base rate data in Phase I, each resident was placed on the toilet chair according to the following step-by-step procedure: (1) called to the toilet, (2) told to pull down pants, (3) told to sit on the toilet, (4) allowed to sit for five minutes or until voiding, and (5) told to pull up pants. A potato chip was given for each of the steps successfully completed and an extra candy reward was given immediately when voiding occurred. (In all subsequent programming no distinctions were made between wetting and soiling as accidents or successes.) Accident and success records were maintained on a 24-hour basis. The effect of the scheduling was a reduction of accidents to an average of 11 per day for all 12 girls as compared to 103 per day during the base rate period. Successes on the toilet increased rapidly during the first few days of training and remained at about 60 per day for all 12 girls. These results indicate that effective scheduling can be a quick and easy way to reduce accidents.

Phase III (28 days). The toilet chairs were placed in the open cottage and some of the residents began to use them on their own during unscheduled times. This was the ultimate aim of the program, but it was difficult to keep adequate records and to give appropriate rewards. Therefore, the toilet area was enclosed with a locked gate. A doorbell buzzer was installed on the gate. The girls were still scheduled at the previously specified times but the attendant now stood at the door of the area and called the girls individually to come to the toilet. By rewarding successive approximations each girl was taught to press the buzzer. After pressing the buzzer, each girl was admitted and the previous reward procedure for toilet training was continued. At any time during the day a resident could use the toilet by simply pressing the buzzer, after which she was admitted and given appropriate reinforcements for voiding. The buzzer system, which provided a cue for immediate reinforcement from the staff, was important in bridging the gap from scheduled placements to teaching the residents to go as needed. During this period the accident rate remained about the same, but the success rate increased from approximately 60 to 75 per day for the total group.

Phase IV (19 days). During this phase the verbal prompting from the staff at scheduled times was discontinued and it became the responsibility of each girl to respond to her own bowel and bladder stimuli. Each girl was rewarded with potato chips for sounding the buzzer and with candy for producing on the toilet. Successes dropped from 75 to an average of 40 per day indicating that the scheduling and prompting were related to the high success rates of previous phases. The accident rate during Phase IV increased from an average of 11 to an average of 18 per day for the group. Accident and success rates were to a large degree independent of each other; the success rate during this phase was reduced by a daily average of 35, whereas, the daily average accident rate only rose by 7.

Phase V (13 days). This phase was designed to determine what effect, if any, the previous training had on accident rates when residents received no prompting, no scheduling, and no reinforcements for successes on the toilet. The door was removed from the toilet area and the residents were free to enter and use the toilets at any time. Each resident was checked every hour in order to record accidents. The average daily accident rate during this period was 18 compared to 103 during the pretraining period as illustrated in the Phase V section of Figure 2. No trends indicating increases or decreases in accidents were observed during this period. These data indicate that some phase or phases of the toilet training procedure were effective in reducing accidents and building appropriate toilet behavior.

At this point, four of the 12 residents were completely toilet trained, four were having no accidents during waking hours but were wetting the bed at night, and the remaining four were still having some accidents during the day and night.

Phase VI (29 weeks). During this 29-week period all 12 residents had free access to the toilet area without any formal scheduling. A buzzer, which was activated each time the door opened, was installed to alert the staff who gave consumable rewards for successes. The purpose of this extended program was to further improve those residents who were still having some accidents and to strengthen the newly acquired toileting behavior. By the end of this period the total number of accidents for all 12 residents for a 24-hour period averaged about five, which were primarily attributable to a few residents who had accidents at night. In most instances, the residents took care of their own toilet needs including the use of toilet tissue without assistance. These residents were then transferred to a different section of the cottage under different personnel where they maintained this level of toilet training proficiency without the continuation of programming.

Subsequent work with toilet training included both larger and smaller groups. In general the effectiveness of the procedure increased as the group size decreased. The reason seemed to be that in small groups more individual attention was possible and there was more flexibility in adjusting the programs to the needs of the individuals. The larger group programs tended to become routine and stereotyped with less attention to individual differences. For example, subsequent programs which were conducted with individuals were successful in each case in relatively short periods; whereas, one conducted with 20 residents only reduced accidents by about a third over a period of one year.

From the work done with toilet training some observations were made which may serve as guidelines for future toilet training programs: (1) Toilet scheduling, planned on an individual basis at those times when most accidents occurred, with or without reinforcing contingencies, sharply reduced accidents. Scheduling, however, was only an initial step in the toilet training process and by itself was not a sufficient condition for teaching independent performance on the toilet. (2) Programs for large groups which did not take into account individual differences were not very effective. Best results were obtained when individual data were maintained and programs were designed to fit the needs, deficits, and progress of each individual. (3) Time alone was not a sufficient condition for new learning. If a newly initiated program did not begin to show changes in behavior within a few days or at most a few weeks, the program needed reevaluation and possible revision. Also, when changes in toileting behavior reached a plateau, they tended to remain there until the program was altered. (4) A contrast effect was found which may be a clue to a useful training procedure. For a 2-week period, night wetters were given extra fluid before retiring which resulted in a sizable increase in the frequency of wetting accidents at night. When this condition was terminated, accidents were reduced and remained below previous levels. The extra intake condition seemed to have resulted in an increased retentive capacity when returned to normal intake conditions. (5) Residents were easily taught to void more frequently at scheduled times by giving rewards for producing on the toilet, but such increases were not always accompanied by equivalent reductions in accidents. The relationship between successes on the toilet and accidents is an obscure one and the two are by no means reciprocal. A decrease in success rates was usually reflected in an increase in accident rates, but an increase in success rates did not always result in a decrease in accident rates as sometimes both remained high. Increasing the frequency of scheduling was not in itself a useful method of reducing accidents. In fact, excessive scheduling tended to have the undesirable effect of more frequent accidents which may have been due to reduced retentive capacity (just the opposite effect of the previously discussed increased retentive capacity following a period of increased fluid intake).

In the toilet training projects reported here, insufficient emphasis was given to teaching the residents to respond appropriately to the internal physiological stimuli which precede voiding. The response that needs to be reinforced is the act of going to the toilet when necessary, not just the act of voiding on the toilet. This might be accomplished by gradually fading out the verbal prompting and the physical assistance given at scheduled times until each resident could *initiate* and proceed through the entire sequence of responses without assistance.

Self-Dressing

The technique of dressing is another self-help skill which has been developed, refined, and extended in institutional settings for the retarded (Ball, 1966; Bensberg, Colwell & Cassel, 1965; Bensberg & Slominski, 1965; Breland, 1965; Gorton & Hollis, 1965; Roos, 1965; Comtois & Holland, 1967; Karen & Maxwell, 1967; Kimbrell, Luckey, Barbuto & Love, 1967; and Minge & Ball, 1967). The development of this skill results in a saving of time and energy for the staff, which can assist in movement from custodial care to more diversified developmental training.

Our initial programs for dressing training were guided by the work of Cecil Colwell who had developed a successful self-dressing program at Pinecrest State School in Louisiana. Colwell, a consultant to Gracewood, demonstrated a reinforcement shaping procedure that has become the standard method used to teach the skill of dressing (discussed in detail by Breland, 1965). The resident is reinforced for performing the last step in the dressing sequence and successively larger units of the sequence are added in a backward manner until the complete task is accomplished. For example, in teaching a resident to put on socks the first response to be reinforced may be pulling on the sock after it has been placed over his foot. When this has been learned, the next increment may be pulling the sock over the heel and up. The trainer continues in this backward manner until the total response has been mastered. The following sections describe some of the dressing programs used with different levels of retarded residents.

Cottage I. These profoundly retarded residents were being completely dressed and undressed with no emphasis on training. The initial program included four profoundly retarded residents selected from the 12 in the Cottage I toilet training program. Each received training sessions twice a day with bits of cookies as rewards. The standard items of clothing used were pullover shirts, short pants with elastic waistbands, underpants, socks, and tennis shoes. These four progressed at different rates and one mastered the entire process including putting on socks and shoes, except for tying. This success encouraged the inclusion of dressing training as a part of the daily routine for the 12 residents. Instead of simply being dressed in the morning and undressed at night, they were put through the appropriate reinforced steps which were individualized to the different levels of achievement.

Over several months all showed significant improvements in dressing ability with some becoming relatively independent. It may not be necessary to set aside special times during the day for training sessions; instead it would be ideal to use every instance in which custodial care is provided as an opportunity for self-care training.

Cottage II. Fourteen girls from Cottage II, who presented the most difficult dressing problems, met together at the regular dressing time every morning in a room isolated from the rest of the cottage. These residents ranged in ages from 12 to 31 with an average age of 21; IQ scores, except for two who had scores of 32, were all below 20. The dressing sequence consisted of removing the night wear, panties and gowns, and afterwards, putting on various items of clothing including shirts, shorts, dresses, bras, socks, shoes, and fastening zippers, hooks, buttons, and snaps. For each item the trainer rated each girl every day on the degree of independence exhibited with each item of clothing by checking one of four categories: (1) no assistance or directioh required, (2) verbal urging necessary, (3) physical assistance necessary, or (4) total help required. The trainer announced that it was dressing time, gave each girl her clothes, and left her to her own resources. The trainer provided minimal assistance as indicated by each individual's performance. For example, if after a few minutes a resident was making no attempts to put on her dress, the trainer would tell her to put on her dress. If she did not adequately perform this function after a reasonable length of time, she was given some physical assistance such as holding the dress up for her or helping her pull it down. Finally, if no progress was indicated, the dress was put on for her. Verbal praise was given as frequently as possible following efforts, approximations, and successful performances.

The results of this program which was conducted for 78 days are presented in the standard graph in Figure 3. Depending upon the items of clothing to be used each day, each girl received a percentage score. The data points for each week represent the average percentages for the 14 girls for: (1) items done alone, (2) items done with verbal urging, (3) items done with physical help, and (4) items not done. During the first week of the program, the level of completely independent dressing achievement rose to approximately 35 percent. By the seventh week it had nearly doubled and remained at that level for the duration of the program. As dressing skills improved, less verbal urging and physical assistance were required as indicated by the gradual drop in these functions. The most stable function was the one indicating items not done which showed only a minor decline throughout the program. This indicates that the major improvements in performance were

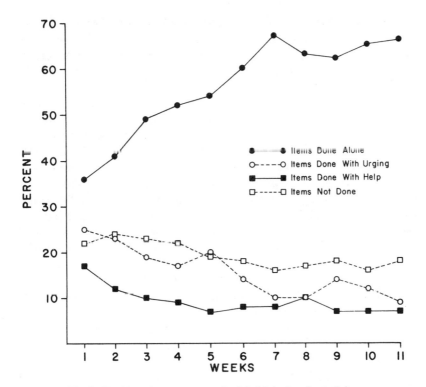

Fig. 3. Weekly percentage socres for 14 girls in dressing training.

attributed to learning to do independently those things that could be done previously with either verbal or physical assistance. Only a few of the items that required total assistance at the outset were learned. For example, only one resident learned to tie her shoes. The various dressing items listed in order of increasing difficulty were: shirt, shorts, placing on shoes, socks, zippers, buttons, dresses, snaps, bras, and tying shoes.

Cottage III. In Cottage III there were 10 girls who required daily assistance in order to dress properly. They ranged in ages from 10 to 20 with an average age of 14½; IQ scores ranged from 20 to 50 with an average score of 36. Every morning these girls were given dressing training in a room isolated from the rest of the dormitory. The following visual cues were used to aid them in positioning their clothes more easily: green tape on the front of the panties; blue tape on the front of the slips; gray tape on the front of the bras; and red tape on the right shoe with a corresponding piece on the right leg. On the day that the cues were introduced the girls were instructed on the purpose and use of each cue. They were then asked to put on one specific item of clothing at a time. Each girl who performed this properly was given individual praise, whereas, each who did not perform the task correctly was given assistance but no verbal reinforcement. One by one the cues were discontinued as the girls appeared not to require them.

Prior to the training program, about 30 percent of the clothing items were put on correctly without assistance. On the first day with the aid of the visual cues dressing performance improved to an achievement level of greater than 70 percent. The cues were then phased out one at a time (in this order: slips, shoes, bras, and pants) over a 30-day period with no significant decrement in the level of achievement. During the last few days with no visual cues, 80 percent of the items of clothing for all girls were put on correctly and independently. The next step was to promote generalization to the cottage environment; therefore, the program was moved into an area of the dormitory in which they dressed by themselves every morning. After dressing, each girl approached the instructor who evaluated her performance and gave either praise or assistance. Their proficiency was maintained and continued to improve over the next few weeks, resulting in an achievement level of greater than 95 percent.

After several weeks the formal program was discontinued and the girls dressed in their regular living areas with the other residents. Records were continued during the next eight days in order to evaluate generalization. Ratings were unobtrusive as all residents in the cottage were formally checked every morning before breakfast and all inappropriate dress was corrected. The average level of achievement for this period was better than 90 percent.

Self-Feeding

Self-feeding is a convenient skill to teach, because the positive reinforcer is a natural part of the performance situation; appropriate behavior is rewarded with food. The method is a behavior shaping procedure which rewards approximations to the goal of independent feeding (Colwell, 1965; Gorton & Hollis, 1965; Comtois & Holland, 1967; Watson, 1967; and Zeiler & Jervey, 1968). As in dressing, the final step of the act is taught first with gradual increments until the total sequence is performed without assistance. For example, the first step may be to hold a filled spoon a few inches from the child's mouth and guide his hand until it touches the spoon before feeding him, gradually fading the guidance until he touches the spoon without help. The next step may be to shape the response of grasping the spoon before the reward of eating. Next, the distance he has to reach for the filled spoon may be gradually increased until he is lifting the spoon from the plate. The rate of advancement is determined by each individual's progress, but should be sufficiently gradual so that errors and failures are minimal. Eating too fast, grabbing with hands, throwing utensils, and other such inappropriate behaviors can be controlled by withdrawing and withholding food for a brief period immediately following the undesirable behaviors.

Success was achieved in self-feeding training with the profoundly retarded whenever it was possible to provide unhurried, individualized training over an extended period of time. The 12 residents who were isolated from the total cottage in the separate toilet training project also ate in a separate area. Through this training method they attained feeding skills in a few weeks. The problem encountered in conducting self-feeding programs with larger numbers is that individualized training is difficult to arrange in the typically understaffed dining room setting. There is a way in which the necessary individualized training may be provided: more capable residents may be recruited on a volunteer basis, using incentive payments or privileges as motivators, and assigned to each resident who needs training in self-feeding. Under supervision these trainers can perform outlined steps of the self-feeding sequence. The supervisor determines when a resident is ready for the next step in the sequence and teaches it to the trainer. Our initial experience with this approach indicated that the trainers (some quite severely retarded themselves) could be taught to follow consistently the steps in the sequence as they were needed, but the supervisor had to determine when to move to the next step in the sequence.

Inappropriate dining room behavior sometimes becomes a problem. The dining room is a crowded, active place and it can be a pleasant time for relaxed dining and visiting, providing the noise level and disruptive behaviors are not excessive. Probably the most effective method of controlling inappropriate behaviors such as line-breaking, food-throwing, food-stealing, fighting, and temper tantrums is to send misbehaving residents from the dining room and to deny them the remainder of their meal (Hamilton & Allen, 1967). Since allowing the one who misbehaves to continue eating might reinforce the inappropriate behavior, this may be the most justifiable use of missing meals as a corrective measure. In this program the procedure of sending those who misbehaved to their cottage immediately following occurrences resulted in a rapid and continued reduction in inappropriate dining room behavior. Such programming reduced the need for supervision in the dining room and allowed more training opportunities.

Sheltered Workshop Program

Most of the residents in Cottage IV were lethargic, complacent, inactive, and dependent, exemplifying patterns of behavior which tend to be characteristic of moderately to severely retarded residents who have been institutionalized for a long period of time. They were totally reliant on the adults in their environment for decisions as what to wear, when to eat, when to brush their teeth, when to go to bed, when to get up, and how to occupy their time. Only a few assisted in such cottage routines as cleaning, bed-making, and sorting of laundry and even fewer had regular job assignments in other areas of the institution. Residents who had comparable intellectual abilities upon admission but who had been in the institution for shorter periods of time, had generally progressed more.

This length-of-institutionalization factor may be better understood by considering the course of institutional development over the years. Due to the increase in staff and annual budgets, the severely retarded resident who is institutionalized today receives more opportunities for training and development than he did 10 years ago. Consequently, many of these long-term residents either continued to function at the same level as when admitted or in many instances regressed. Higher level residents on the other hand had more opportunities for advancement since they could perform better initially and, therefore, were given more individual responsibility.

Having fallen into the pattern of dependency, the residents in Cottage IV seemed very limited in their capabilities and motivation to improve themselves. In order to evaluate work motivation some structured tasks were devised in which a few residents working together engaged in activities such as folding, sealing, and stamping leaflets. Records were maintained so that progress could be evaluated and it was found that the residents could be motivated to work and to work productively. This initial success encouraged the staff to develop a sheltered workshop for the cottage.

Two major sources of production resulted. The first was in collaboration with the local Dymo Tape Company and consisted of screening scrap sections of Dymo tape, cutting out the defects, and cutting them into one foot test sections. The other major project, bow-making, used both hand operated and electrically operated machines. These projects included a variety of tasks which were broken down into assembly line steps. For example, bow-making comprised: loading the machine, turning the handle, cutting the ribbon, sorting the colors, punching holes in cards, mounting bows on cards, inserting bows in plastic bags, sealing the bags, adding labels, and packing in shipping boxes. The profits from the contracts and sales were used by the cottage for supplies, equipment, and recreational activities. The results of the program have been twofold. First, the residents continued to show high motivation and improved productivity during working hours. Second and perhaps more important, their general state of alertness and activity generalized to the dormitory setting where they showed increased interest in learning to do things for themselves. They became more responsive to each other and to the outside activities that were available to them. They began to assist more in the routine cottage activities and many were eventually able to acquire and maintain regular job assignments in other areas of the institution.

Parents

Parents were encouraged to visit and talk with staff members; however, for the most part they did not feel a welcome part of those areas of the institution in which their children lived. It seemed important to design programs aimed at promoting greater involvement with families; consequently, an experimental open house was held in one of the cottages. All families of that cottage were invited and more than 100 relatives attended. During the open house, the families ate with their children in the dining room, became acquainted with the cottage staff, the other children, and the other families, and were given a detailed presentation of the goals, procedures, and activities of the cottage. The day was climaxed by a discussion session during which questions and complaints were aired. As the families became better acquainted with the programs, cottage routines, goals, and the staff, the customary concern over lost clothes and other trivia was replaced by a better understanding and more enthusiastic support for the overall program. The open house procedure was repeated successfully in this and another cottage.

This approach seems to be promising in establishing a more constructive relationship with parents. The parents felt more comfortable visiting in the cottages as the prevailing feeling of mystery was overcome by providing them with information. Another outcome was that the staff became more relaxed with the parents, and a group feeling appeared to emerge in which all were interested in attaining the same goal—improved care for the children. It seems apparent that a greater involvement of the parents, who have typically been neglected, is needed in planning a productive program for the residents.

Social Reinforcement

Attention from adults may serve as effective reinforcers for modifying behavior in children (Harris, Johnston, Kelley & Wolf, 1964; Harris, Wolf & Baer, 1964; and Patterson, 1965). The more impoverished the social reinforcement history the greater the effect that praise or approval may have in modifying behavior (Bandura & Walters, 1963; Gewirtz & Baer, 1958; and Zigler, 1963). Our observations with institutionalized retardates (who were characterized by a history of social deprivation) indicated that the adult social attention factor may have been the most influential reinforcer in all behavior modification programming, although its influence with some profoundly retarded residents was not so evident. The examples given in the following sections are not intended as experimental verifications but as supportive evidence of this social reinforcement hypothesis.

In Cottage III, the automated teaching of reading skills was initiated. In a small room adjoining the cottage, a panel with plexiglass windows was mounted on one wall. In the next room, containing the programming and recording equipment, assortments of words and pictures were projected on these windows. One picture and five words were simultaneously presented to the subject, who selected the appropriate word by pressing a window. An incorrect response was followed by a buzzer and it was necessary for the subject to make a correct response before the next slide was presented. A correct response was reinforced by a chime, and delivery of a small candy pellet, and a slide change. The residents in the program were free to use the teaching machine whenever they wished. Each of the non-readers selected for the program was given a key which turned the machine on and off and coded the performance records for identification purposes. In addition to high work motivation and rapid progress under this system, an interesting pattern of behavior occurred regarding the candy reinforcers. Instead of eating the rewards as they were earned, all of the girls saved their rewards and took them back to the cottage to show to all staff members before eating them. The number of rewards appeared to signify the quantity and quality of their performance. The staff naturally gave words of encouragement, praise, and pats on the back at these times. It was interesting that these retarded girls were able to delay what was previously considered to be more primary needs so that they might receive social attention. This pattern of behavior emerged in practically all cases in which consumable rewards were used.

Another example of the power of social reinforcers was demonstrated in the workshop program in Cottage IV. As reported previously, this was an active program resulting in high levels of motivation over extended periods of time. Initially the use of a reward procedure, broadly based on productivity, was planned under the assumption that the novelty would eventually wear off and motivation would decline. It was unnecessary to implement such a program as the level of motivation remained high and, if anything, continued to increase. Productivity provided a continuous measure of achievement for the residents as well as a stimulus for attention and praise from the staff and visitors to the area. It is natural for an adult to say "you have done a good job" when a tangible product is available for observation.

In Cottage II a token program was in effect for several months in which English halfpennies were awarded for the successful performance of behaviors such as toothbrushing, dressing, and following instructions. The tokens, awarded throughout the day, were stored by the girls in banks mounted on the walls. The tokens were visible through a plexiglass panel and each girl's bank was identified by her picture. At various times during the day, the banks were opened and the residents were allowed to spend their tokens. In the token room were several coin operated machines including a coke machine, a candy dispenser, a juke box, and a teaching machine which dispensed pieces of candy for correct responding. Although these severely retarded girls liked what the tokens could buy, the delay in reinforcement was long and variable and their value as conditioned reinforcers was questionable. The token system may have served more as a structuring device for the staff than as a reinforcing system for the residents. Invariably more was given to the residents at reinforcement times than tokens. Additional comments as "here you are," "good girl," "you did a good job" were a natural part of the token dispensing process. It seemed that the most important aspect of the token system was the positive, social attention from the staff which was given with the tokens following appropriate responses.

Programming social reinforcement is a complex process. For example, routinely saying "good girl" following a specific behavior loses its effectiveness unless the behavior itself is in the process of change and continual improvement. The problem may be twofold in that a certain amount of satiation occurs and that the adults who dispense social reinforcers may need to experience the feeling that the resident has done a good job in order to honestly and enthusiastically give attention and praise. The following case illustrates the effectiveness of social reinforcement along with some of the problems in its programming.

Case

Carol, a 14-year-old severely retarded girl who habitually tore her clothes without any apparent provocation, required frequent changes of her dress every day. For over a year an effort was made to suppress the behavior by programming consequences such as confinement to the time-out area, short-term isolation, being placed in a sleeve jacket, and completely ignoring the behavior. Not one of these programs had any substantial effect. One of the attendants pointed out that only punishment procedures had been used and suggested that a positive approach be tried. Following this suggestion, Carol was given social reinforcement at the end of every hour during which she did not tear her clothes. A timer was set to ring every hour at which time one of the cottage staff found Carol and checked her clothes. If they were torn she was ignored and the timer was reset; however, if they were not torn she was given a great deal of attention with such comments as "good girl, you didn't tear your clothes, I'm very proud of you."

There was a gradual reduction in clothes tearing through the 24th day of the program at which time there were no occurrences for a period of several weeks. This was the longest absence of clothes tearing that had occurred in over a year. Following this respite she began to tear her clothes again: the programmed social reinforcement over such an extended period of time seemed to have lost its effectiveness. Initially, the praise, following periods when no clothes were torn, was genuine because the staff was pleased with Carol's progress. However, with time it appeared as if the staff lost enthusiasm for praising this behavior and that Carol became satiated with this type of programmed attention. Although social reinforcement is a very powerful technique, care must be taken to avoid monotonous, routine programming. In reconsidering Carol's case, as the tearing behavior was controlled, social attention should have been used to strengthen other alternative behaviors which were incompatible with clothes tearing.

Institutionalized retardates appear to be good candidates for social reinforcement techniques as most have already experienced extensive social deprivation when they arrive at the institution. With the enhanced deprivation of institutionalization they remain receptive to social attention from the adults in their environment. The competition for this attention is so fierce that in an uncontrolled environment many of the behaviors that develop are undesirable. The primary challenge for the institutional worker is to use this need for adult attention advantageously by giving social reinforcement to only the appropriate classes of behavior.

Conclusion

Highlights of a program whose purpose was to develop more effective training and management procedures with institutionalized retardates have been presented. This experimental project gave further support to the finding that basic reinforcement principles can be applied productively to institutional settings; therefore, these results may serve their best purpose by encouraging more widespread applications. The challenge now is for a greater emphasis on the identification of specific factors from the complex of variables which exist in the application of behavior modification programs to institutional settings. The best example of this type of emphasis presently available is in the carefully planned and detailed work of Ayllon and Azrin (1968) in their development of a motivational system with psychiatric patients at Anna State Hospital.

REFERENCES

Argyris, C. *Integrating the individual and the organization.* New York: Wiley, 1964.

Ayllon, T. Intensive treatment of psychotic behavior by stimulus satiation and food reinforcement. *Behaviour Research and Therapy*, 1963, **1**, 53–61.

Ayllon, T. & Azrin, N. *The token economy: A motivational system for therapy and rehabilitation.* New York: Appleton-Century-Crofts, 1968.

Ayllon, T. & Haughton, E. Control of the behavior of schizophrenic patients by food. *Journal of Experimental Analysis of Behavior*, 1962, **5**, 343–352.

Ayllon, T. & Haughton, E. Modification of symptomatic verbal behavior of mental patients. *Behaviour Research and Therapy*, 1964, **2**, 87–97.

Ayllon, T., Haughton, E. & Hughes, H. B. Interpretation of symptoms: Fact or fiction? *Behaviour Research and Therapy*, 1965, **3**, 1–7.

Ayllon, T. & Michael, J. The psychiatric nurse as a behavioral engineer. *Journal of Experimental Analysis of Behavior*, 1959, **2**, 323–334.

Azrin, N. H. & Holz, W. C. Punishment. In W. K. Honig (Ed.), *Operant behavior: Areas of research and application.* New York: Appleton-Century-Crofts, 1966. Pp. 380–447.

Ball, T. S. Behavior shaping of self-help skills in the severely retarded child. In J. Fisher & R. E. Harris (Eds.), Reinforcement theory in psychological treatment: A symposium. *California Mental Health Research Monography*, No. 8, 1966, 15–24.

Bandura, A. & Walters, R. H. *Social learning and personality development.* New York: Holt, Rinehart & Winston, 1963.

Baumeister, A. & Klosowski, R. An attempt to group toilet train severely retarded patients. *Mental Retardation*, 1965, **3**, 24–26.

Bensberg, G. J. *Teaching the mentally retarded.* Atlanta: Southern Regional Education Board, 1965.

Bensberg, G. J., Colwell, C. N. & Cassel, R. H. Teaching the profoundly retarded self-help activities by behavior shaping techniques. *American Journal of Mental Deficiency*, 1965, **69**, 674–679.

Bensberg, G. J. & Slominski, A. Helping the retarded learn self-care. In G. J. Bensberg (Ed.), *Teaching the mentally retarded.* Atlanta: Southern Regional Education Board, 1965. Pp.51–97.

Birnbrauer, J. S. Project at Murdoch Center, N. C., personal communication, 1967.

Breland, M. Application of method. In G. J. Bensberg, (Ed.), *Teaching the mentally retarded.* Atlanta: Southern Regional Education Board, 1965. Pp. 143–158.

Burchard, J. D. Systematic socialization: A programmed environment for the habilitation of antisocial retardates. Unpublished manuscript from Murdoch Center, N. C., 1967.

Colwell, C. Teaching in the cottage setting. In G. J. Bensberg (Ed.), *Teaching the mentally retarded.* Atlanta: Southern Regional Education Board, 1965. Pp. 159–163.

Comtois, D. R. & Holland, H. O. Operant conditioning: One year's experience with habit training the severely and profoundly retarded. Mimeographed paper, Mount Pleasant State Home and Training School, Michigan, 1967.

Dayan, M. Toilet training retarded children in a state residential institution. *Mental Retardation*, 1964, **2**, 116–117.

Dollard, J. & Miller, N. *Personality and psychotherapy.* New York: McGraw-Hill, 1950.

Edwards, M. & Lilly, R. T. Operant conditioning: An application to behavioral problems in groups. *Mental Retardation*, 1966, **4**, 18–20.

Ellis, N. R. Toilet training the severely defective patient: An S-R reinforcement analysis. *American Journal of Mental Deficiency*, 1963, **68**, 98–103.

Eysenck, H. J. *Dimensions of personality.* London: Routledge, 1947.

Ferster, C. B. & DeMyer, M. K. The development of performances in autistic children in an automatically controlled environment. *Journal of Chronic Diseases*, 1961, **13**, 312–345.

Ferster, C. B. & Simons, J. Behavior therapy with children. *Psychological Record*, 1966, **16**, 65–71.

Gellerman, S. W. *Motivation and productivity.* American Management Association, 1963.

Gewirtz, J. L. & Baer, D. M. Deprivation and satiation of social reinforcers as drive conditions. *Journal of Abnormal and Social Psychology*, 1958, **57**, 165–172.

Giles, D. K. & Wolf, M. M. Toilet training institutionalized, severe retardates: An application of operant behavior modification techniques. *American Journal of Mental Deficiency*, 1966, **70**, 766–780.

Girardeau, F. L. & Spradlin, J. E. Token rewards in a cottage program. *Mental Retardation*, 1964, **2**, 345–351.

Gorton, C. E. & Hollis, J. H. Redesigning a cottage unit for better programming and research for the severely retarded. *Mental Retardation*, 1965, **3**, 16–21.

Hamilton, J. & Allen, P. Ward programming for severely retarded institutionalized residents. *Mental Retardation*, 1967, **5**, 22–24.

Hamilton, J., Stephens, L. & Allen, P. Controlling aggressive and destructive behavior in severely retarded institutionalized residents. *American Journal of Mental Deficiency*, 1967, **71**, 852–856.

Harris, F. R., Johnston, M. K., Kelley, C. S. & Wolf, M. M. The effects of positive social reinforcement on regressed crawling of a nursery school child. *Journal of Educational Psychology*, 1964, **55**, 35–41.

Harris, F. R., Wolf, M. M. & Baer, D. M. Effects of adult social reinforcement on child behavior. *Young Children*, 1964, **20**, 8–17.

Herzberg, F. *Work and the nature of man*. Cleveland: World, 1966.

Holland, J. G. & Skinner, B. F. *The analysis of behavior*. New York: McGraw-Hill, 1961.

Hundziak, M., Maurer, R. A. & Watson, L. S. Operant conditioning in toilet training of severely mentally retarded boys. *American Journal of Mental Deficiency*, 1965, **70**, 120–124.

Karen, R. L. & Maxwell, S. J. Strengthening self-help behavior in the retardate. *American Journal of Mental Deficiency*, 1967, **71**, 546–550.

Keller, F. S. & Shoenfield, W. N. *Principles of psychology*. New York: Appleton-Century-Crofts, 1950.

Kimbrell, D. L., Luckey, R. R., Barbuto, P. F. P. & Love, J. G. Operation dry pants: An intensive habit-training program for severely and profoundly retarded. *Mental Retardation*, 1967, **5**, 32–36.

Lent, J., LeBlanc, J. & Spradlin, J. A demonstration program for intensive training of institutionalized mentally retarded girls. *Project News of the Parsons State Hospital and Training Center*, 1967, **3**, 1–18.

Likert, R. *The human organization*. New York: McGraw-Hill, 1967.

Lindsley, O. R. Operant conditioning methods applied to research in chronic schizophrenia. *Psychiatric Research Reports*, 1956, **5**, 140–153.

McGregor, D. *The human side of enterprise.* New York: McGraw-Hill, 1960.

Minge, M. R. & Ball, T. S. Teaching of self-help skills to profoundly retarded patients. *American Journal of Mental Deficiency*, 1967, **71**, 864–868.

Miron, N. B. Behavior shaping and group nursing with severely retarded patients. In J. Fisher & R. E. Harris (Eds.), Reinforcement theory in psychological treatment: A symposium. *California Mental Health Research Monography*, No. 8, 1966, 1–14.

Patterson, G. R. Responsiveness to social stimuli. In L. Krasner & L. Ullmann (Eds.), *Research in behavior modification.* New York: Holt, Rinehart & Winston, 1965, Pp. 157–178.

Patterson, G. R. & Ebner, M. J. Application of learning principles to the treatment of children. Paper presented at the meeting of the American Psychological Association, 1965.

Pursley, N. & Hamilton, J. The development of a comprehensive cottage-life program. *Mental Retardation*, 1965, **4**, 26–29.

Roos, P. Development of an intensive habit-training unit at Austin State School. *Mental Retardation*, 1965, **3**, 12–15.

Rosenberg, J. An investigation into the effects of prompting-attention in an operant conditioning control of nocturnal enuresis. Unpublished dissertation, Florida State University, 1967.

Sidman, M. Normal sources of pathological behavior. *Science*, 1960, **132**, 61–68.

Sidman, M. Operant techniques. In A. J. Bachrach (Ed.), *Experimental foundations of clinical psychology.* New York: Basic Books, 1962. Pp. 170–210.

Skinner, B. F. *Science and human behavior.* New York: Macmillan, 1953.

Staats, A. W. & Staats, C. K. *Complex human behavior.* Holt, Rinehart & Winston, New York, 1963.

Ullmann, L. P. & Krasner, L. *Case studies in behavior modification.* New York: Holt, Rinehart & Winston, 1965.

Wahler, R. G., Winkel, G. H., Peterson, R. F. & Morrison, D. C. Mothers as behavior therapists for their own children. *Behaviour Research and Therapy.* 1965, **3**, 113–124.

Watson, L. Application of operant conditioning techniques to institutionalized severely and profoundly retarded children. *Mental Retardation Abstracts*, 1967, **4**, 1–18.

White, R. W. Motivation reconsidered: The concept of competence. *Psychological Review*, 1959, **66**, 297–333.

Whitney, L. R. & Barnard, K. E. Implications of operant learning theory for nursing care of the retarded child. *Mental Retardation*, 1966, **4**, 26–29.

Whyte, W. F. *Money and motivation*. New York: Harper & Row, 1955.

Wolf, M., Risley, T. & Mees, H. Application of operant conditioning procedures to the behavior problems of an autistic child. *Behaviour Research and Therapy*, 1964, **1**, 305–312.

Zeiler, M. D. & Jervey, S. S. Development of behavior: Self-feeding. *Journal of Consulting and Clinical Psychology*, 1968, **32**, 164–168.

Zigler, E. Social reinforcement, environment and the child. *American Journal of Orthopsychiatry*, 1963, **23**, 614–623.

Comments

Perhaps the most important summary comment concerns the existence of commonalities across programs. There is an obvious emphasis upon adaptive, environmental functioning as the criterion of change. There are no intrapsychic subgoals such as "improved self concept" or "freedom from repressed impulses." The criterion tends to be an overt, observable, measurable environmental response. Thus, for example, Kennedy is interested in returning school children to the classroom, Madsen *et al.*, are interested in decreasing the frequency of certain specific disruptive patterns of classroom behavior, and Lewis wishes to reduce a complex of environmental behaviors to a manageable level so that the child may again function in his home environment.

It must be noted also that modest attainments are accepted as progress — the goals are not all encompassing. While it has become popular to think in terms of working with the "total organism" the position taken in this volume is quite contrary to that view. It is assumed that strengthening an individual's response repertoire in a circumscribed area can have positive, long-lasting results, primarily through reinforcing environmental feedback. This point is particularly apparent in the chapter by Lewis in which he discussed the Re-ED program as a vehicle to help the child regain equilibrium with his environment.

The important agents of change are nonprofessional mental health workers, particularly nursing assistants and counselors. Parents and teachers have been incorporated effectively in a number of the programs as the most important agents of change. Obviously, the ability to use nonprofessionals and paraprofessionals in this role reflects, in part, the goals and philosophy of the behavior modification orientation. The traditional intrapsychic, language-oriented approaches to psychotherapy have placed demands upon the therapist which can be met only through extensive training and indoctrination. Although a good behavior modification program presents a most difficult problem in human engineering, the basic principles involved are relatively simple to understand and communicate; furthermore, the operations of behavior modification programs are observable, measurable, and subject to revision through feedback. The chapter by Haring presents a good example of continuous corrective feedback. From another point of view the influence of operant methodology is pervasive. In some instances the operant approach is clearly apparent in the program's operations (e.g., Haring). In other programs operant methodology is viewed as a conceptual guide, a goal to be approached rather than a reality of the present (e.g., Rickard & Dinoff).

The programs possess marked differences too, which make the commonalities even more impressive. *Population* differences are extreme, ranging from mildly to severely behaviorally disturbed children, juveniles, young and adult legal offenders, outpatient and inpatient psychiatric cases, and retardates. The *nonprofessional agents of change* (albeit with professional support, program planning, and consultation) constitute a diverse group: parents, teachers, college corpsmen, prison guards, hospital aides, and patients and offenders themselves. While all of the program directors are mental health specialists, they were trained at different educational institutions and exposed to divergent theoretical and applied notions concerning psychotherapy and behavior control. It seems only fair to state that all of the contributors do not adhere with equal rigor to the behavioristic framework emphasized in this volume, but all report programs wherein the "hallmarks" of behavior modification are readily identifiable.

Problems associated with adequate program research have been noted by most of the contributors. In general, the more global the criteria and encompassing the program the less adequate the efforts at evaluation, at least to this point. Most of the programs have systematically evaluated at least some aspect of their program. It is obvious that programs such as these are rather far removed from the experimental laboratory, and most of the research efforts to date must be described as tentative. Behavior modification programs already in existence should be encouraged to accelerate their research efforts and new programs under development should incorporate a research design from the outset.

Author Index